FROM READING TO REVISION

FROM

READING

TO

REVISION

SCOTT RICE

San Jose State University

WADSWORTH PUBLISHING COMPANY

I(T)P® *An International Thomson Publishing Company*

Belmont • Albany • Bonn • Boston • Cincinnati • Detroit • London • Madrid
Melbourne • Mexico City • New York • Paris • San Francisco • Singapore • Tokyo • Toronto • Washington

English Editor	ANGELA GANTNER WRAHTZ
Editorial Assistant	ROYDEN TONOMURA
Production	ROBIN LOCKWOOD
Print Buyer	BARBARA BRITTON
Permissions Editor	ROBERT KAUSER
Interior and Cover Designer	CLOYCE WALL
Copy Editor	TOM BRIGGS
Compositor	PATRICIA BONN
Printer	QUEBECOR PRINTING/FAIRFIELD

*This book is printed on
acid-free recycled paper.*

Library of Congress Cataloging-in-Publication Data
Rice, Scott.
  From reading to revision / Scott Rice.
    p. cm.
  Includes bibliographical references.
  ISBN: 0-534-21996-9
  1. College readers. 2. English language—Rhetoric—Problems,
exercises, etc. 3. Editing—Problems, exercises, etc. I. Title.
PE1417.R497   1996
808'.042—dc20   95-43067

For more information, contact Wadsworth Publishing Company:

Wadsworth Publishing Company
10 Davis Drive
Belmont, California 94002, USA

International Thomson Publishing Europe
Berkshire House 168-173
High Holborn
London, WC1V 7AA, England

Thomas Nelson Australia
102 Dodds Street
South Melbourne 3205
Victoria, Australia

Nelson Canada
1120 Birchmount Road
Scarborough, Ontario
Canada M1K 5G4

International Thomson Editores
Campos Eliseos 385, Piso 7
Col. Polanco
11560 México D.F. México

International Thomson Publishing GmbH
Königswinterer Strasse 418
53227 Bonn, Germany

International Thomson Publishing Asia
221 Henderson Road
#05-10 Henderson Building
Singapore 0315

International Thomson Publishing Japan
Hirakawacho Kyowa Building, 3F
2-2-1 Hirakawacho
Chiyoda-ku, Tokyo 102, Japan

Contents

INTRODUCTION   1

Reading to Write   1
   Reading to Remember and to Criticize   5,   Reading Like Writers   8

Reading to Revise   13
   The Revising Process   15

Revising for Unity, Coherence, and Emphasis   16

Reading and Revising: One Example   22

George Orwell, *Shooting an Elephant*   23

"And afterward I was very glad the coolie had been killed; it put me legally in the right and it gave me sufficient pretext for shooting the elephant. I often wondered whether any of the others grasped that I had done it solely to avoid looking like a fool."

   *Profile   27,   Exercise   28,   First-Person Narration   29,   Indirect Quotation   29,
   The Generic The   29,   Conjunctive Openers   30,   Revision Strategies   30,
   Student Revisions   31,   Revision 1: Michael Stamps   31,   Revision 2: Roopa Belur   33,
   Revision Assignments   35,   Writing Assignments   36*

ESSAYS

Edward Abbey, *Even the Bad Guys Wear White Hats*   37

"Our public lands have been overgrazed for a century. The BLM knows it; the Forest Service knows it. The Government Accounting Office knows it. And overgrazing means eventual ruin, just like stripmining or clear cutting or the damming of rivers. Much of the Southwest already looks like . . . a cowburnt wasteland."

   *Profile   42,   The Uses of the Personal   43,   Using Fragments   43,
   Revision Strategies   44,   Student Revision: Jodi A. Edwards   45,
   Revision Assignments   49,   Writing Assignments   50*

Virginia Woolf, *The Death of the Moth* 314

"Yet, because he was so small, and so simple a form of the energy that was rolling in at the open window and driving its way through so many narrow and intricate corridors in my own brain and in those of other beings, there was something marvelous as well as pathetic about him."

Tristram Wyatt, *Submarine Beetles* 321

"One summer evening, I watched the tide as it flowed gently up the creek like a river in reverse, creeping slowly over the salt-marsh shore in Norfolk, England. Out of the corner of my eye I saw a flash of red. A small, shiny black-and-red beetle had run in and out of its burrow . . ."

SHORT STORY

Guy de Maupassant, *The Bell* 328

"He had known better days, in spite of this misery and infirmity. At the age of fifteen, he had had both legs cut off by a carriage on the highway near Varville. Since that time he had begged, dragging himself along the roads, across farmyards, balanced upon his crutches which brought his shoulders to the height of his ears. His head seemed sunk between two mountains."

Contents of Topics

Preface

This reader is based on the following assumptions:

1. If our students are to improve their powers of expression, the primary subject of our writing classes must be language.

2. Every writing course must also be a reading course (and vice-versa).

3. All of us, teachers and students, must commit ourselves to the lifelong project of becoming better readers.

4. Even in a "student-centered" writing class there must be room for demanding and stimulating reading.

5. In composition classes alone are students likely to confront their reading as writing, as specific instances of language well used (and therefore as something applicable to their own writing).

6. Writing is improved in the revision stage, and from properly attentive reading (modeled and practiced in the classroom) students can develop the criteria to guide their revisions.

7. Grammatical and mechanical issues are also rhetorical issues, and as such are best studied in specific contexts.

8. In a composition course, classroom time can be used most profitably in attentive reading and in group revision (whether of professional or student writing).

With these assumptions in mind, the following collection presents thirty-four essays and articles and one short story (whose presence is explained in the Introduction). I have attempted to strike a balance between established chestnuts ("The Death of the Moth," "Shooting an Elephant," "Once More to the Lake"), more recent classics ("The Way to Rainy Mountain," "Marrying Absurd," "Tucson Zoo"), and contemporary pieces that either have not yet appeared or are just beginning to appear in composition readers ("Shoe and Tell," "Fancydancer," "Father Stories"). In addition to familiar and argumentative essays, I have also included informational writing ("In Virgin Forest," "Submarine Beetles," "Maya Art for the Record") so that students can appreciate the connections between "literacy" and "real world" writing.

It is difficult in one academic term to change the reading and writing habits of a lifetime, but one term is long enough to begin acquiring habits and attitudes from which one can benefit for years to come.

I gratefully acknowledge the valuable contributions of the following reviewers: Gail Garloch, Oklahoma City University; Patricia Jackson, Rensselaer Polytechnic Institute; and Barbara C. Mallonee, Loyola College (Maryland).

Introduction

> ... My study periods I spent in the school library and one day happened to pick up a book by Guy de Maupassant. I had no idea who he was. I opened the book and read a story named in English "The Bell." It was the only story in the book I read.
>
> It was the first story I really read, for to read is also to write, and as I read this story I wrote it, and I liked what I wrote.
>
> —William Saroyan, *Bicycle Rider in Beverly Hills*

Reading to Write

William Saroyan did not have a mystical encounter in the school library. Instead, he had his first conscious experience of reading like a writer. That is, he found himself reading so closely, with such absorption, that he seemed to understand and approve every creative choice of the author. So attuned was he to the narrative logic of the story, he seemed to enter into de Maupassant's mind and share in the telling, share in decisions about detail and dialogue and incident. No others would seem to do. "The Bell" seemed to emerge from Saroyan's own imagination.

With persistence, we can have the same experience as William Saroyan, an Armenian-American teenager sitting in a Fresno schoolhouse reading a translation of a nineteenth-century French writer. With patience and application, we can have the same experience. We can have it because, as ordinary readers, we are already partway there, partway toward "writing" what we read. What Saroyan describes is different only in degree from the collaborative act we call reading.

For reading, as Saroyan discovered even before his revelation in the library, is teamwork. It requires not only our passive cooperation but our active assistance. To make sense out of what we read, we must indeed *make* sense, not simply find it. We must not only recognize vocabulary and understand sentence structure but also heed cues, create pictures, connect, construe, and infer. We must remember and anticipate. Reading a novel, then, is not simply a matter of running a film through the VCR in our mind. It is to receive a script, and then to cast, direct, and produce a movie. It is to be in charge of scenery, costuming, and special effects (helped along, of course, by authorial suggestions). And all reading demands a similar effort. To read is not simply to record another's message; it is to process it. It is to interpret and convert and transform. To this extent, any kind of reading is already, to some degree, "writing."

Now, assume for a moment that we have gone beyond the least demanding kind of reading, reading simply for entertainment. Assume that we have gone beyond casually skimming books for vicarious adventure and romance, beyond word-surfing texts for the occasional insight or the odd bit of information (did you know that the average automobile tire contains two-and-a-half gallons of recoverable petroleum?). Assume that we have gone beyond the kind of active reading that adds to our store of ideas and information, the kind that requires us to attend closely and remember. Assume that we have even learned to read critically, not only following sequences of information and lines of reasoning but confronting and evaluating and testing them. Having gone this far, we have already accomplished a great deal. Active reading, whether for retention or evaluation, does not merely entertain; it leaves us more informed, more aware, more sensitive. How much more could we ask from our reading?

For one thing, as Saroyan testifies, to "really" read, to read until we "write," is its own reward ("as I read this story I wrote it, and I liked what I wrote"). There is a pleasure to be found in contemplating anything well made, a pleasure in grasping its internal logic and appreciating the role of its components, in seeing how one part complements another or how it performs two or three functions at once. This awareness is what Saroyan meant by "writing" de Maupassant's short story; simply put, he could see what was being done and why, and he shared in the creative satisfaction.

More than giving us another source of enjoyment, though, and increasing our comprehension, reading like writers offers an even greater benefit: it improves our own writing. We learn in two principal ways, by watching others and by trial and error. To read like writers, as we shall see, involves both. To begin with, such reading encourages attention to craft and to the potential that craft finds and realizes in the subject. It encourages an appreciation of how the writer has done justice to the material, has given it the care and treatment it deserves. But, in concrete terms, what does all this mean?

It means being conscious of the choices that the writer has made in arranging and presenting the material, from global choices to local, from choices about organization and development and voice to choices about phraseology and punctuation. Particularly, it means thinking habitually in terms of alternatives, of other ways of doing, and—inevitably—of their consequences. Initially, such a reader may consider options briefly in his or her mind, the way one must evaluate possible moves during a chess game. When studying instructive games, though, serious chess students set up a board and play out the alternatives, testing plausible options or "candidate moves," even trying to outthink the masters. By doing so, they elevate their abilities, from affirming someone else's decisions to originating their own.

Whether evaluating a position in our own game or someone else's, we exercise the same powers of calculation.

But how does an apprentice writer "get out the board" and test options? How does one combine informed observation with trial and error? By revision—by treating published work not as "the final word" but as one more draft, as something dynamic and changeable and subject to one's own authority. In a sense, we cut in on a George Orwell or a Gretel Ehrlich, on a staff writer for *The New York Times* or a contributor to *Scientific American* or *Natural History*. We cut in and take control of their work, beginning with a thorough reading and rereading until we have a comfortable sense of its nature and purpose. Having such a sense (however imperfect at first), we address what we judge to be its most crucial and defining elements. Perhaps it is the basic architecture of the piece, the way the writer has chosen to introduce and arrange the material—such as beginning with an anecdote before moving to an explanation, or starting with a generalization before moving to specific support. Perhaps it is the writer's involvement or detachment, or it is the tone as created by emotional or neutral language, or the level of detail, or the choice of verb tense, and so on.

Having identified the crucial elements, our next step is to test alternatives, to follow some paths not taken. We revise. We change a key element, then, for consistency, make adjustments to related elements, observing the rhetorical ripple effects. And then we evaluate the results, first judging our revision in its own right, then comparing it to the original. Each will comment on the other. And there are few risks in the process. An ineffective choice, understood, can reveal as much as an effective one. We can learn as much from "bad" writing as from "good," as much from our failures as from our successes.

For practical purposes, will these revisions be actual improvements on the originals? Are we likely to outdo respected professionals? Very likely not, but in the process of testing their decisions, of reconfiguring their work, we will arrive at a better appreciation of what they have done. By making changes, by trying out alternatives and weighing their effects, we will sharpen our own writing instincts and add to our stock of writing experience. And having sharpened our judgments by active involvement in the work of master prose writers, we can turn to our own writing with more maturity, more confidence.

For a brief illustration, let us consider the opening paragraph to George Orwell's much-read "Shooting an Elephant":

> In Moulmein, in lower Burma, I was hated by large numbers of people—the only time in my life I have been important enough for this to happen to me. I was sub-divisional police officer of the town, and in an aimless petty kind of way, anti-European feeling was bitter. No one had the guts to raise a riot, but if a European woman went through the bazaars alone somebody would probably spit betel juice over her dress. As a police officer I was an obvious target and was baited whenever it seemed safe to do so. When a nimble Burman tripped me up on the football field and the referee (another Burman) looked the other way, the crowd yelled with hideous laughter. This happened more than once. In the end

the sneering yellow faces of young men that met me everywhere, the insults hooted after me when I was a safe distance, got badly on my nerves. The young Buddhist priests were the worst of all. There were several thousands of them in the town and none of them seemed to have anything to do except stand on street corners and jeer at Europeans.

Suppose we start with a global decision to present the story in the first-person singular (*I*). What happens if we replace the first person with the third (*he/she*)? Instead of Orwell telling about something that happened to himself, he represents the episode as happening to someone else:

> In Moulmein, in lower Burma, he was hated by large numbers of people— the only time in his life he had been important enough for this to happen to him.

Now we no longer have the self-mocking tone of the original. Instead of a self-critical narrator, we have someone taking what will strike many as a superior tone with his subject. There is still a measure of detachment, but it is not that of time, of the older person looking back on his younger self, but that of someone writing from outside the experience. We are hearing not from the source but from an external narrator passing judgments on someone else (someone in whose moccasins he has perhaps not walked). The rest of the story—arrangement, details, language—all must be adjusted to fit this external narrator. And the impact of the story will be substantially different. The story will be about something else.

Or suppose we test some local choices, such as Orwell's wording in several of his sentences, especially his use of the *passive voice*. Instead of

> I was hated by large numbers of people . . .

we have,

> In Moulmein, in lower Burma, large numbers of people hated me—the only time in my life I have been important enough to stimulate such feeling.

And later, instead of the hapless official, the focus is on the hostile, aggressive throng:

> Because I was a police officer, they made me an obvious target and *baited me* whenever it seemed safe to do so.

By removing the passive voice, we dilute the narrator's portrayal of his own helplessness. In passive voice constructions, the subject is indeed *passive* (submissive, being acted upon: "I was hated"). In active constructions, the subject is an *agent,* is in some kind of control. Because Orwell wants to stress his powerlessness (despite being a power-wielding colonial administrator), he chooses the passive voice. As he states several times in the paragraph, things were *happening* to him; he was not making them happen.

And so on. Applying a consistent strategy, we can make almost endless changes in Orwell's essay, each suggesting related changes, each altering the impact of the story. *Granted, the effect will usually be to weaken the original* (if another way would have worked better, Orwell would probably have chosen it himself), but the object is not to improve on Orwell. The object is to grasp his writer's logic and the propriety of his strategic and tactical decisions. What better way is there to appreciate the aptness of a choice than to try another?

So how does such intervention in the work of others improve our own writing? By exercising the same judgment. By requiring us to manipulate the same elements. By involving us in the same problems that drive every writing task—problems posed by subject and audience and occasion and purpose. Such intervention engages and extends the same know-how demanded by our own writing, including—to some extent—even that of discovering subject matter. As one authority has observed, "Attention to *how to say* helps writers find *what to say*." By reading like writers, by immersing ourselves in form as well as content, we discover how the one suggests the other.

Reading to Remember and to Criticize

To understand reading like writers, let us begin by illustrating the other two kinds of intensive reading, *reading to remember* and *reading to criticize*. For our subject, we will use the opening to an essay on canine overpopulation by David Quammen, first published in *Outside* magazine. Read the passage carefully, with the intention to remember. There will be a quiz.

> Let's begin slowly, with a relatively safe statement: Not all dogs are bad.
>
> [1]We Americans live today amid a plague of domestic dogs, a ridiculous and outrageous proliferation of the species, true, but not every one of those animals is damnable beyond redemption. [2]Not every one has had its soul twisted by misery and neglect, spending long days chained or fenced within a tiny yard and taking its revenge by barking at the neighbors. [3]Not every one is ill-trained, intermittently hysterical, half insane from sensory deprivation. [4]Not every one is indulged to prowl free, defecating on other folks' lawns and reorganizing other folks' garbage, playfully snapping the necks of other folks' cats. [5]A few dogs, worthy beasts, help blind people to cross streets. [6]Several reportedly perform ranch chores. [7]Dozens of canines in the U.S. alone fulfill a useful service as the quiet, well-behaved pets of old people and shut-ins. [8]The rest, unfortunately, are as we know them. [9]But dogs are a sensitive subject; some dog owners, like some tobacco smokers and most members of the Ku Klux Klan, tend to be passionately defensive about what they are pleased to think of as their own rights. [10]Consequently, you find two diametrically opposed and quite equally extremist points of view: on the one hand that all dogs are irredeemably noxious and should be banished, at least from our cities and suburbs, by enlightened legislation; and on the other hand, that some dogs are okay, at least some of the time. [11]My own view is a moderate one that falls about halfway between these two.
>
> Brothers and sisters, as the Lord is my witness: We got too many dogs.

To test your ability to read actively and attentively, answer the following:

1. How much of the passage can you recall without looking back and rereading it? To confirm your memory, write out a summary of the passage.

2. Examine your summary. Does it contain the beginning "safe statement"? Does it reflect the organization of Quammen's passage, the "not

every one" section (sentences 1–4), the begrudging admission of canine usefulness (sentences 5–7), the final statement about the canine controversy and the three positions?

3. How would you describe the tone of the passage? How does the choice of language contribute to this tone?

4. In your own language, what is Quammen's actual position?

To test your ability to read *critically*—that is, to read for response and even rebuttal—answer the following (you may read and reread the passage, even underlining and making notes in the margin, paraphrasing ideas in more comfortable or more direct language):

1. What tone does Quammen establish by stating his proposition in negative instead of positive terms ("Not all dogs are bad" rather than "Most dogs are bad")?

2. What does he accomplish by using words like *plague, ridiculous, outrageous, damnable, redemption*?

3. In his zeal to push his argument, how consistent is he being? Do most dogs spend their time chained or fenced in small yards (sentence 2), or are most dogs permitted to prowl free (sentence 4)? (By stating the propositions in negative terms, Quammen disguises this inconsistency.)

4. How does Quammen implicate the reader when he states, "The rest, unfortunately, are as we know them"?

5. What does Quammen accomplish by equating dog owners with tobacco smokers and the Ku Klux Klan? In fact, what does he accomplish by equating smokers with Klan members?

6. What are we to make of his characterization of "the two diametrically and quite equally extremist points of view," and the characterization of his own viewpoint as a moderate one?

7. From studying Quammen's statement, what do you learn about the advantages and disadvantages of argumentative exaggeration, of irony and humor?

Instructions: Reading to Remember   A lucky few have "flypaper" memories. With little effort, they can retain much or most of what they read. The rest of us, however, have to make do with memories that are more like wax paper. If we want to retain and, more important, *assimilate* what we have read (digest it, connect it with our existing store of knowledge and ideas), we have to make a deliberate effort. Otherwise, we read haphazardly, accidentally and unsystematically picking up random bits. An essay or chapter we have read is like an apple from which we have taken a bite or two, then discarded.

And our schooling has not always alerted us fully to the challenges of reading. For one thing, we are taught the basic distinction between literacy and illiteracy, but then left to assume that all literacy is equal. The fallacy here is that, having developed our "reading skills" to the twelfth-grade level, we have presumably mastered most of what there is to know about reading.

In truth, we are just beginning, for reading—like writing—is an "open" activity, one we can never totally master, one we can spend the rest of our lives trying to perfect.

For another thing, to worsen the problem, college courses often require too much reading, so much reading that we can often do little more than skim—much like watching videos on fast forward. We get the message that quantity outweighs quality—that it is better to fly through five books at warp speed, even if we later struggle simply to remember their titles, than to read one book carefully and be able to explain and discuss it. Intentionally or unintentionally, schools encourage us to speed-read, and speed-reading has much in common with speed-eating: both hinder enjoyment and both hamper digestion. Recognizing this, one teacher has even proposed that schools offer courses in *slow*-reading.

The following routine can help you retain more of what you read:

Step 1: Skim the piece (the essay, article, chapter, section) to get an overview of its content and organization.

Step 2: Read to remember, following the line of thought, the sequence of information, the pattern or stages of development. If the material is difficult, stop periodically and review what you have read to that point. Don't hurry. Be patient.

Step 3: When you have finished, do not rush to your next project. Wait. Reflect on what you have just read; give it a chance to soak in. Try to remember as much as you can. It may help to write out a summary *from memory* (this practice will also help you retain more of your future reading).

Step 4: Write a brief commentary—a response, an evaluation, an interpretation—making an effort to connect your reading with other reading and, even more important, with your own experience and opinions.

Step 5: Finally, as a last resort, if the reading is extremely difficult, select a key passage and *paraphrase* it; that is, reword it, sentence by sentence, clause by clause, into your own language, consulting a dictionary for important words, even familiar ones (one of the best uses of a dictionary is to look up words you already know).

Again: (1) skim, (2) read, (3) reflect, (4) summarize, and (in special cases) (5) paraphrase.

Note: Underlining and highlighting can help, but not as procrastination techniques ("I will underline now, and remember later").

Instructions: Critical Reading *Critical* comes from a word meaning "to separate, judge." In turn, to judge is "to form an opinion or estimation after careful consideration" (*American Heritage Dictionary of the English Language*, Third Edition). Only by reading and rereading can we consider carefully and arrive at useful and defensible opinions. Thus, we begin as if we were reading to remember.

Step 1: We skim.

Step 2: We read carefully with the intention to remember.

Step 3: We review.

Then,

Step 4: We reread, underlining in the text, *restating ideas in our own language,* writing comments in the margins (or elsewhere if we are not working with a photocopy or our own book). Having understood the writer's argument, we are now examining its soundness, looking for strengths and weaknesses.

Step 5: We write an outline-summary of the work.

Step 6: We use this outline-summary to analyze the logical integrity of the work (What are its underlying assumptions? Is the method of demonstration valid? Are there any inconsistencies? What are the strong and weak points of the argument? And so on).

Reading Like Writers

Now, to take our reading even one step farther and see how we might read like writers, we will look again at the opener to David Quammen's essay on the canine explosion, "The Descent of the Dog."

> Let's begin slowly, with a relatively safe statement: Not all dogs are bad.
> [1]We Americans live today amid a plague of domestic dogs, a ridiculous and outrageous proliferation of the species, true, but not every one of those animals is damnable beyond redemption. [2]Not every one has had its soul twisted by misery and neglect, spending long days chained or fenced within a tiny yard and taking its revenge by barking at the neighbors. [3]Not every one is ill-trained, intermittently hysterical, half insane from sensory deprivation. [4]Not every one is indulged to prowl free, defecating on other folks' lawns and reorganizing other folks' garbage, playfully snapping the necks of other folks' cats. [5]A few dogs, worthy beasts, help blind people to cross streets. [6]Several reportedly perform ranch chores. [7]Dozens of canines in the U.S. alone fulfill a useful service as the quiet, well-behaved pets of old people and shut-ins. [8]The rest, unfortunately, are as we know them. [9]But dogs are a sensitive subject; some dog owners, like some tobacco smokers and most members of the Ku Klux Klan, tend to be passionately defensive about what they are pleased to think of as their own rights. [10]Consequently you find two diametrically opposed and equally extremist points of view: on the one hand, that all dogs are irredeemably noxious and should be banished, at least from our cities and suburbs, by enlightened legislation; and on the other hand, that some dogs are okay, at least some of the time. [11]My own view is a moderate one that falls halfway between these two.
> Brothers and sisters, as the Lord is my witness: We got too many dogs.

Instruction for Reading Like Writers   The following routine can help you:

Step 1: Identify the basic thesis of the work.

Step 2: Make a thumbnail outline (one that identifies any subdivisions or parts).

Step 3: Identify the crucial rhetorical elements that give the work its character: the principle of organization, the presence of the author, the tone, and so on.

Step 4: Test revisions: Restructure the piece; make the author more or less visible; address a different audience; be more or less formal; change the tone; and so on.

Step 5: Evaluate the consequences, and compare the revision with the original.

Let us apply the process to Quammen's opening paragraph.

Step 1   What is Quammen's basic thesis? Obviously, that most dogs are bad (expressed negatively: "Not all dogs are bad"). Adjusting for irony, Quammen is arguing that we have too many dogs in the city, particularly when their owners do not give them the necessary training and attention.

Step 2   We might outline the passage like this:

P1 *Opening statement:* Not all dogs are bad.

P2 America has too many dogs but not all are unredeemable.
Not all dogs misbehave (implying most do).
Some dogs are useful.
Dog owners are stubborn.
The two "extremist" positions: All dogs should be banished; a few
    dogs can be saved.
The "moderate" writer is somewhere in between.

P3 *Address to readers:* We have too many dogs.

Note: The outline of an entire essay need not be this detailed. A sentence or two on each paragraph may do the job.

Step 3   What is the most conspicuous rhetorical feature of Quammen's opener? Most readers would probably identify its irony, established at once in his perverse opening sentence: "Let's begin slowly, with a relatively safe statement: Not all dogs are bad."

A statement is *ironical* when it expresses something different from its literal meaning. Quammen is being ironical first by pretending that his statement is "relatively safe" and then by pretending that he is denying an established truth, that most dogs are bad. By expressing the highly debatable idea as a given, he suggests that it does not have to be defended, that the burden of proof is on those who want to deny the badness of most dogs. Without irony, he would have expressed his proposition as a positive, "Most dogs are bad," but then he would also have had a fight on his hands.

Most readers will see the joke. Even as he begins his attack on dogs (which is actually an attack on dog owners and breeders), he masquerades as their defender. The rest of the opener continues in the same spirit: additional ironic statements compounded by exaggerated, even biblical language ("a *plague* of domestic dogs," "a *ridiculous and outrageous proliferation* of the species," "*damnable beyond redemption*").

Step 4   Here is *one way* we might revise the passage, sentence by sentence, to eliminate the irony while remaining true to the theme of the original, the point Quammen is trying to make behind all the exaggeration. Again, he opens:

P1 Let's begin slowly, with a relatively safe statement: Not all dogs are bad.

Take away the tongue-in-cheek pretense of beginning slowly and safely, leaving the reader off guard and unprepared for the "relatively safe statement." As the rest of the essay supports, Quammen is saying that, in the city, most dogs are "bad"—in part because of their owners' neglect and abuse, but also because selective breeding has exaggerated a trait that makes them especially unsuited for city living—barking. A more straightforward opening, and one that does not use the abrupt address to the audience ("Let's" = Let us), is:

> **Americans must face a disturbing reality: With a few exceptions, dogs do not belong in the city.**

S1: We Americans live today amid a plague of domestic dogs, a ridiculous and outrageous proliferation of the species, true, but not every one of these animals is damnable beyond redemption

To change the general tone, we express the main idea directly and without repetition, removing the exaggerated language ("plague," "outrageous proliferation," "damnable," "redemption"). The result is a controversial but defensible opinion:

> **American cities today are overpopulated with domestic dogs, few of whom can ever be useful companions or pets.**

S2: Not every one has had its soul twisted by misery and neglect, spending long days chained or fenced within a tiny yard and taking its revenge by barking at the neighbors.

We remove the ironic negative ("not every one") and the exaggeration expressed by "soul" and the questionable notion that the dogs are deliberately seeking revenge:

> **Most have been twisted by misery and neglect, spending long hours chained or fenced in tiny yards and taking out their frustrations by barking at the neighbors.**

S3: Not every one is ill-trained, intermittently hysterical, half insane from sensory deprivation.

Again, we express the idea affirmatively, and we remove the exaggeration of "sensory deprivation" (literally, an artificial experiment in which a subject is sealed in an unlit and soundproof chamber for psychological observation). Also, we place the standard *and* before the last item in the series:

> **Most are ill-trained and often frenzied from being denied the freedom and exercise they need.**

S4: Not every one is indulged to prowl free, defecating on other folks' lawns and reorganizing other folks' garbage, playfully snapping the necks of other folks' cats.

We lessen the formality, something Quammen used in keeping with his exaggerated posture ("indulged to prowl free," "defecating"). We also remove the examples of indirectness and the emphatic repetition of "other folks'," a phrase revealing one principal grievance, that the neighbors of dog owners are the primary victims of canine misbehavior.

> **Many are allowed to run free, leaving their droppings on other people's lawns, overturning garbage cans, and killing cats.**

S5: A few dogs, worthy beasts, help blind people to cross streets.

"Worthy beasts" is an extreme concession to offset the depiction of most dogs.

> **Granted, a few dogs are useful, like those serving as guide dogs for the blind.**

S6: Several reportedly perform ranch chores.

"Reportedly" is of course sarcastic, and "several" exaggerates the rarity of working farm and ranch animals. Quammen also wants to remind readers that most dogs were originally bred for practical purposes, not to be pets or ornaments or status symbols.

> **In the country some dogs actually do the work for which they were originally bred.**

S7: Dozens of canines in the U.S. alone fulfill a useful service as the quiet, well-behaved pets of old people and shut-ins.

Quammen again exaggerates the rarity of dogs who are actually useful. His essay is about dog problems in America, so "in the U.S. alone" is a further swipe at the entire species:

> **Other dogs serve as the quiet, well-behaved pets for old people and shut-ins.**

S8: The rest, unfortunately, are as we know them.

By indirection, Quammen repeats the mythical truism with which he began: Most people know that the majority of dogs are useless and troublesome:

> **Most dogs, though, create the problems many of us know only too well.**

S9: But dogs are a sensitive subject; some dog owners, like some tobacco smokers and most members of the Ku Klux Klan, tend to be passionately defensive about what they are pleased to think of as their own rights.

More comic exaggeration: comparing dog owners to smokers and the Ku Klux Klan (a double stroke because, of course, most would not demote smokers to the moral plane of the Ku Klux Klan). "Tend to be" is an understatement; he means they are fanatical in defense of their alleged rights (the weaker one's position, the more energetically one must defend it). "Pleased to think of" is an expression often used to identify wrong-headed assumptions.

> **But dogs are a sensitive subject; most dog owners cling stubbornly to their rights to have the animals.**

S10: Consequently you find two diametrically opposed and equally extremist points of view: on the one hand, that all dogs are irredeemably noxious and should be banished, at least from our cities and suburbs, by lightened legislation; and on the other hand, that some dogs are okay, at least some of the time.

"Diametrically opposed" and "extremist" exaggerate the conflicting views. The joke, of course, is in pretending that one of the positions—the occasional toleration of some dogs—is an extremist one. Most readers would find the extremism in posing such an opposition. The tone is further enhanced by "irredeemably noxious," "banished," and "enlightened legislation." At this point, many will see that Quammen is winking at his readers, acknowledging that he is having some fun. By claiming dogs "should be banished, at least from our cities and suburbs, by enlightened legislation," he is not even pretending to be neutral or even-handed:

> **As a result, there are two conflicting opinions on the subject: that dogs can never adjust to city life and should be banned, and that people should, within reason, have unrestricted rights to dog ownership.**

S11: My own view is a moderate one that falls halfway between these two.

Further irony: He is a moderate, he who has been arguing that most dogs are bad.

> **My opinion falls somewhere between the two.**

P3 Brothers and sisters, as the Lord is my witness: We got too many dogs.

A melodramatic finale. He addresses his readers (as "brothers and sisters," pulpit language), invokes God, and then—after all this formality—changes the tone and states his thesis colloquially (not, "We *have* too many dogs").

> **Fellow Americans, we have to do something about all these dogs.**

Now, to put it all together:

[P1]Americans must face a disturbing reality: With a few exceptions, dogs do not belong in the city.

[P2] [1]America today is overpopulated with domestic dogs, few of whom can ever be useful companions or pets. [2]Most have been twisted by suffering and neglect, spending long hours chained or fenced in tiny yards and taking out their frustrations by barking at the neighbors. [3]Most are ill-trained and often frenzied from being denied the freedom and exercise they need. [4]Many are allowed to run free, leaving their droppings on other people's lawns, overturning garbage cans, and killing cats. [5]Granted, a few dogs are useful, like those serving as guide dogs for the blind. [6]In the country some dogs actually do the work for which they were originally bred. [7]Other dogs serve as quiet, well-behaved pets for old people and shut-ins. [8]Most dogs, though, create the problems many of us know only too well. [9]But dogs are a sensitive subject; most dog owners are stubbornly devoted to their rights to have the animals. [10]As a result, there are two conflicting opinions on the subject: that dogs can never adjust to city living and should be banned, and that people should, within reason, have unrestricted rights to dog ownership. [11]My opinion falls somewhere between the two.

[P3]Fellow Americans, we have to do something about all these dogs.

Step 5 What do we learn from this one revision? To begin with, by comparing what the author chose with some possibilities he rejected (consciously or unconsciously), we can better appreciate his argumentative strategy. Anyone writing for an American publication inherits a large audience of dog lovers. As someone has observed, in America the dog is a sacred cow. How, then, does Quammen raise an idea most readers will find unthinkable? He does it by using irony and humor, beginning with the impertinence of representing his attack as a defense. Humor dilutes anger, suggesting goodwill.

Once we confront his basic argumentative strategy, sentence by sentence, phrase by phrase, we can then observe how many further decisions it drives, from phraseology (expressing a positive as a negative), to word choice (the exaggerated, sometimes theological language), to self-portrayal (a fanatic unsuccessfully masquerading as a moderate). And the aptness of his choices are thrown into stark relief by comparison with the relatively lifeless revision. Among numerous failings, the bland revision lacks the urgency of the original, its sense of the problem's gravity. The more serious and direct revision seems only to state the obvious, pointing out what many already know but also do not lose sleep over (unless the neighbor's dog is keeping them awake). It raises a familiar problem: Dogs are an annoyance of urban living that we have learned to accept; why get so worked up about it now? Quammen's treatment, then, gives the dog problem the status of a fresh crisis. It is a device of *emphasis*.

Quammen's opening strategy is lively and humorous, but it is only an introductory strategy. The remainder of his essay is more serious, discussing dogs from a somewhat more scientific and historical perspective, with only occasional lapses into the barbed hyperbole of the opening sentences.

Reading to Revise

"What are you looking for?" Kennedy asked. "Besides tracks?"

"Nothing in particular," Leaphorn said. You're not really looking for anything in particular. If you do that, you don't see things you're not looking for."

—Tony Hillerman, *Talking God*

A fictional lieutenant in the Navajo Tribal Police, Joe Leaphorn is sifting for clues at a crime scene on the sagebrush flats of northern New Mexico. Writers (and other seekers) can learn from what Lt. Leaphorn is *not* doing. He is not working from a checklist: "75 Things to Look for at a Crime Site." Nor is he searching with tunnel vision, on the lookout for any one or two things. He is simply looking, with an impartial eye, for whatever might be useful.

As Leaphorn knows, each crime scene (each problem) poses its own set of challenges. It has its own integrity and asks to be looked at afresh, on its own merits. If Leaphorn assumes that his experience is exhaustive, that he has seen it all, or if he thinks too generically, he may distort the present scene to fit a preconception, an existing model. Instead, Leaphorn approaches each case as a novelty, as an unprecedented combination of challenges. Past solutions may or may not apply. They are but candidate explanations, having no special status. Leaphorn will not permit bias or laziness to transform his experience into a liability.

Using Joe Leaphorn as our inspiration, how should we read a text, whether our own or someone else's, and then set out to revise it? *With an open mind.* Except in the most general terms, we should not start with any preconceived notion of where to make changes. Read closely, a piece of writing will tell us what it is and what it needs or can accept. It will have its own character, its own personality—determined, of course, by its mission, by its subject and audience and occasion and purpose. Except in the most flexible terms, it should not be judged by what something else is, not even by some category into which it may fall (say, the argumentative or comparison-and-contrast essay). Each new member of a class extends and upgrades and challenges our notion of the class, its limits and powers. A basketball coach, for example, might cherish a profile of the ideal player, but then along comes a Dennis Rodman or a Charles Barkley.

In revising a published work, as in reading it, we should accept it on its own terms. We should read it carefully and then look for the source of its character, trying to appreciate how *this* writer has written on *this* object for *this* occasion. Taking our cue from Wallace Stegner ("No writer ever learned anything from a generalization"), we should look for its uniqueness, not its generic character. In particular, we try to identify major decisions about arrangement and presentation, about tone or level of formality or degree of concreteness. Then we revise the work with one or more of these major decisions in mind. In the process, we also address the structure of individual paragraphs and sentences, changing whatever is dictated by our revision strategy. We may even reword some passages simply because we think we can improve on the original.

In revising our own work, we are less likely to make sweeping changes for their own sake. After all, we are trying to complete a practical task, not experiment for the sake of instruction. At first, knowing our usual weaknesses, we may be tempted to look for something "in particular" (to use Leaphorn's phrase), but we should be scouting for anything improvable, looking at *what we have written*, not at *what we were trying to write*. Common sense, of course, dictates that we work from the top down. Why spend fifteen minutes polishing a sentence from a paragraph that we may later discard?

Generally, in top-down revision, we get an overview, reading the essay quickly for a sense of its totality, its shape and proportion. If the introduction or opening is too long, we look for ways to condense it (perhaps we can even eliminate the first paragraph or two). If some of our developing material seems emaciated, we flesh it out. If something seems misplaced, we relocate it. If, in developing one part, we render another part unnecessary, we cut it. If some of the transitions seem choppy, we smooth them over. And so on. Later, we work our way down to the parts and repeat the process, but always with an eye to their contribution to the whole. The essay, the section, the paragraph, the sentence—all have a wholeness to consider and parts to be harmonized.

The Revising Process

How does one go about revising a piece of writing? The same way one goes about improving any large and complex production (even a brief essay involves thousands of decisions, conscious and unconscious, large and small). There are more ways and combinations of ways than one can count. Still, despite the endless possibilities, each having its own set of consequences, revisions fall into four categories. Whether our revisions are global or local, drastic or minor, we can make only the following changes (changes, as we shall see, that are often interrelated or overlapping): *addition, subtraction, substitution*, and *rearrangement*. That is:

1. We can introduce new material—new information, ideas, incidents.

2. We can condense and cut.

3. We can remove some material or structures to make room for other material or structures.

4. We can change the sequence of information, ideas, or words.

In the following essays, we will explore these possibilities at greater length. In the meantime, we can illustrate the principles as they apply to a single sentence, the concluding sentence to Jared Diamond's essay, "What Are Men Good For?":

> That's why the question "What are men good for?" continues to be debated within our societies, as well as among anthropologists.

Consider the following revision:

> **That is why we continue to debate the question: "What are men good for?"**

The revision *adds* the part of the word left out in the original contraction ("that's why" = "that *is* why"). It also adds an introductory colon to further emphasize the point of contention. It *subtracts* "within our societies, as well as among anthropologists"—something already stated earlier in the essay, to make room for the *substitution* "we." Then it *rearranges* the wording so that the passive voice ("continues to be debated") can be *substituted* with the active voice ("continue to debate"). What is the effect of the revision? The final sentence is more compact, more abrupt, more emphatic. By streamlining and rearranging the wording, we postpone for the climactic final position the question that is also the title of the article: "What are men good for?"

Some editors contend that we do not begin to write until we have a draft. Ninety percent of writing is revision, they insist. And revision demands that we alternate between stepping back and diving in, between taking a long view and addressing particulars, applying what we know from reading and from our own practice. In weighing options and testing effects, we sharpen our judgments, for this and for later writing. In other words, each writing project is not only an end in itself but practice for the next one, so even a "failure" may be immensely instructive. A great chess master once observed that to become a good player one must lose a lot of games. One of life's compensations is that we usually learn more from our failures than from our successes.

Revising for Unity, Coherence, and Emphasis

In revising for clarity and effectiveness, there are three related and overlapping qualities to strive for: *unity, coherence,* and *emphasis.* These qualities are forever assuming new forms, never taking the same one in any two paragraphs or pieces of writing, not even by the same writer. No discussion, then, can do them justice. We can only look at how these qualities operate in particular instances. We can only look at individual cases and ask what unity, coherence, and emphasis mean *there.* With this realization in mind, we will examine how they are differently realized in two quite dissimilar paragraphs, one from an argumentative essay by Paul Gruchow, the other from a personal reminiscence by E. B. White.

First, Paul Gruchow writes about the increasing uniformity of the American urban landscape:

> [1]We now perceive the homogenization of urban America as a truism. [2]The pervasive influence of the mass media and the concentration of economic power have helped to create a society in which many local, or even regional, distinctions have vanished. [3]We all watch the same television programs, read essentially the same newspapers, shop in the same national stores, live in the same houses, and subscribe, mostly, to the same middle-of-the-road politics and philosophy of life. [4]A person crossing the country from one airport or commercial strip or housing development to the next has only the local road signs and certain peculiarities of flora—if there are palm trees in the boulevards, it can't be Ohio—as reliable visual clues to place. [5]This monotony of physical detail has, perhaps, promoted social stability and a certain kind of economic efficiency. [6]But we rightly wonder what strengths of culture, what resiliency, we have sacrificed in adopting such bland uniformity.
>
> —"A Backyard Robin, Ho-Hum"

Generally speaking a paragraph has *unity* when it is "about one thing," when all its sentences serve a governing purpose, treating a common subject and developing a central theme or idea. In some cases, like Gruchow's, a topic sentence identifies that idea: "We now perceive the homogenization of urban America as a truism." Such a sentence immediately orients the reader and prepares for the sentences that follow. In this case, it states what the writer holds to be self-evident (American homogenization), preparing for the next sentence, which restates and develops the idea in cause-and-effect form: "The pervasive influence of the mass media and the concentration of economic power have helped to create a society in which many local, or even regional, distinctions, have vanished."

The next two sentences reinforce the idea. Sentence 3 affirms the relative sameness of American life: "We all watch the same television programs, read essentially the same newspapers, shop in the same national stores, live in the same houses, and subscribe, mostly, to the same middle-of-the-road politics and philosophy of life." As a result, sentence 4 remarks, a traveler finds little to distinguish one locale from another: "A person crossing the country from one airport or commercial strip or housing development to the next has only the local road signs and certain peculiarities of flora—if there are palm trees in the boulevards, it can't be Ohio—as reliable visual clues to place." Urban America is truly *homogeneous* (from a word meaning "same kind").

Sentences 5 and 6 remark on the trade-offs of such homogeneity: "This monotony of physical detail has, perhaps, promoted social stability and a certain kind of economic efficiency. But we rightly wonder what strengths of culture, what resiliency, we have sacrificed in adopting such bland uniformity."

From the first to the last sentence, then Gruchow's paragraph displays unity of subject and theme. It is "about one thing"—American homogeneity—and it never digresses. It enforces unity of subject by the repetition of key words, synonyms, and related terms *(homogenization, pervasive influence, concentration, all, same, monotony, bland uniformity)*. And it achieves unity of theme by a logical sequence of statements developing the central idea.

But to be economically and effectively unified, a paragraph must be more than a sequence of sentences on the same subject. The sentences must show *coherence* or "stick together," and they stick together when each successive sentence relates clearly to previous ones. More important, coherent sentences look both forward and backward: even as they develop an idea, moving forward, they also build on preceding sentences. Momentum (moving forward) depends on memory (looking back). Each successive remark, in other words, makes sense in light of the previous statement while preparing for the next.

Gruchow's sentences *cohere*, being a sequence of logically related statements. His opener introduces the theme (the fact of America's homogenization). His second sentence restates this idea, first by identifying the causes (mass media and the concentration of economic power), then by summarizing the effects: "many local, or even regional, distinctions have vanished." Sentences 3 and 4 continue the cause-effect pattern, Sentence 3 attests to the sameness of our experience: "We all watch the same television programs, and read essentially the same newspapers, shop in the same national stores, live in the same houses, and subscribe, mostly, to the same middle-of-the-road politics and philosophy of life." And as a result of such common behavior, sentence 4 explains, someone traveling from one part of the country to the next will see virtually the same urban sights (testifying to the disappearance of local and regional distinctions). Because of this monotony, sentence 5 concedes, we may be more socially stable and economically efficient, but at the price identified in sentence 6: the loss of cultural assets like resiliency, the strength and resourcefulness developed by adjusting to new environments.

Aside from connecting his sentences logically, Gruchow achieves coherence through the repetition of words like "we." In sentence 3 it refers back to "urban America" in sentence 1, and to "a society" in sentence 2: we live in *that* America, *that* society. (Elsewhere, "we" identifies the readers with whom Gruchow wishes to connect.) Gruchow also sticks his sentences together by using terms relating to those in previous statements ("television programs" in sentence 3 exemplifies "mass media" in sentence 2, for example). And finally, Gruchow strengthens coherence by using demonstrative words referring to previously mentioned terms and ideas. Thus, in sentence 5 he mentions "*This* monotony" and in sentence 6 "*such* bland uniformity."

Finally, to be effective, to be convincing and memorable, a unified and coherent paragraph must also have *emphasis* (from a word meaning "to show"). If our readers had photographic memories, if they accepted on faith everything we had to say, and if they did not need to understand the basis for our beliefs, we would not have to *show* (prove, demonstrate) anything. We could get away with simply "telling," presenting unsupported, undeveloped thesis statements. And writers would publish only outlines, not entire essays and books.

But readers must be convinced of the truth and value of what we have to say, and they must linger over the subject long enough for it to "take." Writing does not convince simply because it presents certain conclusions, however clearly. It convinces because it provides readers with a significant mental experience. It describes a scene or narrates an action vividly enough for the reader to feel like a witness; it gives enough information for the reader to exercise personal judgment; it provides enough support for our arguments that the reader will understand, if not share, our point of view.

In the process of establishing unity and coherence, how does Gruchow achieve emphasis? He achieves it first by fully developing his governing idea—restating, illustrating, explaining, and concluding. He begins with his thesis statement: the truism of American homogenization. If it is a self-evident truth, why go on? But Gruchow amplifies his remark. Sentence 2 not only identifies the cause (mass media and the concentration of economic power) but restates the idea in more detail: "many local, or even regional, distinctions have vanished." Now we know what he means by "homogenization." The first sentence would have left some readers wondering, thus inviting an explanatory comment.

Sentence 3 continues to drum on the idea, using repetition of a theme word to underscore the point: "We all watch the *same* television programs, read essentially the *same* newspapers, shop in the *same* national stores, live in the *same* houses, and subscribe, mostly, to the *same* middle-of-the-road politics and philosophy of life." As a result, sentence 4 testifies, someone crossing the country finds little evidence of local or regional distinction. And to conclude development of his point, the one expressed so simply in his opening sentence, Gruchow reflects on the consequences of so much national uniformity: We may be more stable and efficient, but we have lost the powers that we develop by learning to adjust.

Emphasis, then, not only amplifies, repeating and expanding a message so that the reader gets the point. It also signals the importance of our subject, its urgency and value: America's loss of regional diversity warrants more than our brief acknowledgement. It warrants our sustained attention as we explore its causes and ponder its consequences.

Reminiscing about childhood vacations at a Maine lake, E. B. White finds another recipe for unity, coherence, and emphasis:

¹It seemed to me, as I kept remembering all this, that those times and those summers had been infinitely precious and worth saving. ²There had been jollity and peace and goodness. ³The arriving (at the beginning of August) had been so big a business in itself, at the railway station the farm wagon drawn up, the first smell of the pine-laden air, the first glimpse of the smiling farmer, and the great importance of the trunks and your father's enormous authority in such matters, and the feel of the wagon under you for a long ten-mile haul, and at the top of the last long hill catching the first view of the lake after eleven months of not seeing this cherished body of water. ⁴The shouts and cries of the other campers when they saw you, and the trunks to be unpacked, to give up their rich burden. ⁵(Arriving was less exciting nowadays, when you sneaked up in your car and parked it under a tree near the camp and took out the bags and in five minutes it was all over, no fuss, no loud wonderful fuss about trunks.)

—"Once More to the Lake"

Gruchow's first sentence could well have opened his essay ("We now perceive the homogenization of urban America as a truism"). As it is, it opens a sub-section. White's opener, however, alludes to something said earlier, cohering with the previous paragraph: "It seemed to me, as I kept remembering all *this*, that *those* times and *those* summers had been infinitely precious and worth saving." At the same time, however, it announces the unifying idea of his paragraph: the preciousness of his memories. In broad, abstract terms, sentence 2 explains why the remembered times were so valuable, so worthy of preservation: "There had been jollity and peace and goodness." Then, in concrete terms, sentence 3 begins an enumeration of those memories so jolly, peaceful, and good. First, it opens with a generalization—"The arriving . . . had been so big a business"—then follows with a cataloging of this big business: "at the railway station the farm wagon drawn up, the first smell of the pine-laden air, the first glimpse of the smiling farmer, and the great importance of the trunks and your father's enormous authority in such matters," and so on. Sentence 4 concludes the big business of arriving: "The shouts and cries of the other campers when they saw you, and the trunks to be unpacked, to give up their rich burden."

The concluding sentence is a parenthetical remark, a relevant digression—("Arriving was less exciting nowadays, when you sneaked up in your car . . . no fuss, no loud wonderful fuss about trunks"). This "digression" not only contrasts the excitement of his family's arrival, it confirms the truth of the opening remark—why "those times and those summers had been infinitely precious and worth saving." While they spare us so much effort, modern conveniences like the automobile also deprive us of the "wonderful fuss."

Even as White's first sentence announces his central idea, it contains demonstrative words that signal its coherence with previous paragraphs: "It seemed to me, as I kept remembering all *this*, that *those* times and *those* summers had been infinitely precious and worth saving." This topic statement introduces the justification in the next sentence: "There had been jollity and peace and goodness." But this is an abstract assertion, so sentence 3 illustrates, first with a generalization, then with a list of supporting details: "The arriving (at the beginning of August) had been so big a business in itself, *at the railway station the farm wagon drawn up, the first smell of the pine-laden air, the first glimpse of the smiling farmer . . . and at the top of the last long hill catching the first view of the lake after eleven months of not seeing this cherished body of water."* Sentence 4 continues "the business" of the previous sentence by completing the list: "The shouts and cries of the other campers when they saw you, and the trunks to be unpacked, to give up their rich burden." ("Shouts and cries," of course, illustrates "jollity" in sentence 2.)

Sentence 5 completes the logical progression by making an aside: today's arriving entails much less suspense and ceremony. The fun has been stolen by the automobile, further emphasizing the value of those bygone summers "infinitely previous and worth saving." The direct allusion, of course, is to sentence 3, which sentence 5 parallels in structure: Both begin with a generalization and conclude with a detailed illustration. The repetition of "arriving" further underscores the connection. Thematically and structurally, then, White's parenthetical remark is an integral part of the paragraph.

White's paragraph coheres, constituting a sequence of related statements flowing easily into and out of one another, in the process developing a unifying idea. A chain of pronouns reinforces the clear logical connections, opening with the first person ("I," "me"), identifying the speaker, then in sentence 3 turning to the indefinite *you* (inviting identification with the reader): "*your* father's enormous authority in such matters . . . the feel of the wagon under *you* . . . shouts and cries of the other campers when they saw *you* . . . when *you* sneaked up in *your* car."

But what about emphasis? United, coherent, but relatively unemphatic, White's paragraph would read something like this:

> [1]It seems to me, as I kept remembering all this, that those times had been precious. [2]There had been jollity, peace, and goodness. [3]The arrival at the beginning of August had been a big business. [4]Arrivals today were much less exciting.

To see how White achieved emphasis, let us make a sentence-by-sentence comparison with an unemphatic revision.

> It seems to me, as I kept remembering all this, that those times and those summers had been infinitely precious and worth saving.

> It seems to me, as I kept remembering all this, that those times had been precious.

First of all, White dwells on "those times" by multiplying the phrase into "those times and those summers," an intentional redundancy called *pleonasm* (repeating the same idea in different words, like "safe and sound," "hale and hearty"). Those times he is remembering, after all, were those summers. And those times and those summers were not just "very precious," the most commonplace way to express the idea, but "*infinitely* precious." And by implication, whatever is precious is worth saving, but for emphasis White makes the implicit explicit: "infinitely precious *and* worth saving."

> There had been jollity and peace and goodness.

There had been jollity, peace, and goodness.

To extend his listing and invite the reader to linger over each item, White repeats the conjunction *and*, a device called *polysyndeton* ("many connectors"). He might also have said "joy," but the more antique-sounding "jollity" suggests merriment and celebration, like the welcoming shouts and cries of the other campers.

> The arriving (at the beginning of August) had been so big a business in itself, at the railway station the farm wagon drawn up, the first smell of the pine-laden air, the first glimpse of the smiling farmer, and the great importance of the trunks and your father's enormous authority in such matters, and the feel of the wagon under you for a long ten-mile haul, and at the top of the last long hill catching the first view of the lake after eleven months of not seeing this cherished body of water.

> The arrival (at the beginning of August) had been a big business.

Instead of simply summarizing or *telling* us about the arrival, White then depicts the scene. But he does not use "arrival," a simple static noun. Instead, he uses "arriving," so the *-ing* can call attention to the duration of the event, which he will then prolong with rich detail, from the scene at the railway station to the arrival at the lake. But arriving had not simply been a big business, but "a big business *in itself*"—a further underscoring that signals his intention to develop the idea.

Having called attention to the spectacle of arriving, White then details its stages. To further unify and emphasize the listing, White introduces each item in his list with the generic *the*: "*the* farm wagon drawn up . . . *the* first glimpse of *the* smiling farmer . . . *the* great importance of *the* trunks . . . *the* feel of *the* wagon under you . . . at *the* top of *the* last long hill catching *the* first view . . ." The repeated *the* underscores the repeated, timeless nature of the event. And in addition to this emphatic repetition, there is the use of *first*: "the *first* smell of the pine-laden air, the *first* glimpse of the smiling farmer . . . the *first* view of the lake."

> The shouts and cries of the other campers when they saw you, and trunks had to be unpacked, to give up their rich burden.

This "sentence" completes White's portrayal of the big business of arriving. Grammatically, it is a fragment, an incomplete sentence. Within the structure of the paragraph, though, it coheres with the previous sentence by continuing the emphatic listing, the final stage in the elaborate ceremony of arrival. It further coheres with the previous sentence by again mentioning (and dwelling on) the trunks. And like sentence 2, it also contains some intentional redundancy or pleonasm: within the context of the scene, "shouts" and "cries" refer to the same noisy greetings.

> (Arriving was less exciting nowadays, when you sneaked up in your car and parked it under a tree near the camp and took out the bags and in five minutes it was all over, no fuss, no loud wonderful fuss about trunks.)

> (Arrivals today were much less exciting.)

This parenthetical remark further expresses White's central idea, but by contrast: Today's experiences help him appreciate the infinite preciousness of yesterday's. In addition the second use of "arriving" stresses the idea of duration, except now there is no climactic, intensifying build-up. Today the business is over in five minutes. And to further emphasize this idea, White again uses repetition: "no *fuss*, no loud wonderful *fuss* about trunks."

White has indeed *remembered* his childhood adventures at the lake, has recalled them in vivid, lingering detail for the reader to experience with him. Good remembering requires immersion, sustained imaginative presence in the past—emphasis.

For certain terms to be useful (for example, to allow us to make certain crucial distinctions), they must have precise definitions, drawing razor-sharp boundaries between themselves and related terms. But for others to be useful, they must be inexact—elastic, inclusive, open-ended, ever susceptible to fresh interpretation. Otherwise, they contain and limit rather than broaden our understandings. Thus, every time writers, especially talented ones, address or readdress a subject, they expand, explore, and redefine unity, coherence, and emphasis. And every time sensitive readers sit down to read, they do so unburdened by rigid preconceptions, open to whatever means the writers have discovered.

For practical purposes, then, unity, coherence, and emphasis exist only in the concrete, in individual passages where they are uniquely but also only partially realized, as in the Gruchow and White examples. We can recognize these qualities in the work of others, and discover them as we attempt our own writing, and we can spend a lifetime increasing our understanding of them, but we can never exhaust them, no matter how much we read and write.

Reading and Revising: One Example

The following is one of the most frequently read essays in the English language, George's Orwell's "Shooting an Elephant." To illustrate how a writer might approach the work more instructively, using it to experiment with techniques of arrangement and presentation, the essay is accompanied by discussions of its more conspicuous rhetorical and stylistic features, then by two sample student revisions. In the revisions, the writers test the consequences of presenting Orwell's experience from different times and points of view. The results reveal as much about "Shooting an Elephant" in particular as about personal-experience writing in general.

Shooting an Elephant

GEORGE ORWELL

In Moulmein, in lower Burma, I was hated by large numbers of people—the   1
only time in my life that I have been important enough for this to happen to
me. I was sub-divisional police officer of the town, and in an aimless, petty
kind of way anti-European feeling was very bitter. No one had the guts to
raise a riot, but if a European woman went through the bazaars alone somebody would probably spit betel juice over her dress. As a police officer I was
an obvious target and was baited whenever it seemed safe to do so. When a
nimble Burman tripped me up on the football field and the referee (another
Burman) looked the other way, the crowd yelled with hideous laughter. This
happened more than once. In the end the sneering yellow faces of young
men that met me everywhere, the insults hooted after me when I was at a
safe distance, got badly on my nerves. The young Buddhist priests were the
worst of all. There were several thousands of them in the town and none of
them seemed to have anything to do except stand on street corners and jeer
at Europeans.

All this was perplexing and upsetting. For at that time I had already made   2
up my mind that imperialism was an evil thing and the sooner I chucked up
my job and got out of it the better. Theoretically—and secretly, of course—I
was all for the Burmese and all against their oppressors, the British. As for the
job I was doing, I hated it more bitterly than I can perhaps make clear. In a
job like that you see the dirty work of Empire at close quarters. The
wretched prisoners huddling in the stinking cages of the lock-ups, the gray,
cowed faces of the long-term convicts, the scarred buttocks of the men who
had been flogged with bamboos—all these oppressed me with an intolerable
sense of guilt. But I could get nothing into perspective. I was young and ill
educated and I had to think out my problems in the utter silence that is imposed on every Englishman in the East. I did not even know that the British
Empire is dying, still less did I know that it is a great deal better than the
younger empires that are going to supplant it. All I knew was that I was stuck
between my hatred of the empire I served and my rage against the evil-spir-
ited little beasts who tried to make my job impossible. With one part of my
mind I thought of the British Raj as an unbreakable tyranny, as something
clamped down, in *saecula saeculorum*,[1] upon the will of prostrate peoples; with
another part I thought that the greatest joy in the world would be to drive a
bayonet into a Buddhist priest's guts. Feelings like these are the normal by-
products of imperialism; ask any Anglo-Indian official, if you can catch him
off duty.

One day something happened which in a roundabout way was enlighten-   3
ing. It was a tiny incident in itself; but it gave me a better glimpse than I had
before of the real nature of imperialism—the real motives for which despotic
governments act. Early one morning the sub-inspector at a police station the

[1] "Forever and ever"—phrase from Latin prayers.

other end of town rang me up on the 'phone and said that an elephant was ravaging the bazaar. Would I please come and do something about it? I did not know what I could do, but I wanted to see what was happening and I got on to a pony and started out. I took my rifle, an old .44 Winchester and much too small to kill an elephant, but I thought the noise might be useful *in terrorem*. Various Burmans stopped me on the way and told me about the elephant's doings. It was not, of course, a wild elephant, but a tame one which had gone "must." It had been chained up, as tame elephants always are when their attack of "must" is due, but on the previous night it had broken its chain and escaped. Its mahout, the only person who could manage it when it was in that state, had set out in pursuit, but had taken the wrong direction and was not twelve hours' journey away, and in the morning the elephant had suddenly reappeared in the town. The Burmese population had no weapons and were quite helpless against it. It had already destroyed somebody's bamboo hut, killed a cow and raided some fruit-stalls and devoured the stock; also it had met the municipal rubbish van and, when the driver jumped out and took to his heels, had turned the van over and inflicted violences upon it.

The Burmese sub-inspector and some Indian constables were waiting for   4
me in the quarter where the elephant had been seen. It was a very poor quarter, a labyrinth of squalid bamboo huts, thatched with palm-leaf, winding all over a steep hillside. I remember that it was a cloudy, stuffy morning at the beginning of the rains. We began questioning the people as to where the elephant had gone and, as usual, failed to get any definite information. That is invariably the case in the East; a story always sounds clear enough at a distance, but the nearer you get to the scene of events the vaguer it becomes. Some of the people said that the elephant had gone in one direction, some said that it had gone in another, some professed not even to have heard of any elephant. I had almost made up my mind that the whole story was a pack of lies, when we heard yells a little distance away. There was a loud, scandalized cry of "Go away, child! Go away this instant!" and an old woman with a switch in her hand came round the corner of the hut, violently shooing away a crowd of naked children. Some more women followed, clicking their tongues and exclaiming; evidently there was something the children ought not to have seen. I rounded the hut and saw a man's dead body sprawling in the mud. He was an Indian, a black Dravidian coolie, almost naked, and he could not have been dead many minutes. The people said that the elephant had come suddenly upon him round the corner of the hut, caught him with its trunk, put its foot on his back and ground him into the earth. This was the rainy season and the ground was soft, and his face had scored a trench a foot deep and a couple of yards long. He was lying on his belly with his arms crucified and head sharply twisted to one side. His face was coated with mud, the eyes wide open, the teeth bared and grinning with an expression of unendurable agony. (Never tell me, by the way, that the dead look peaceful. Most of the corpses I have seen looked devilish.) The friction of the great beast's foot had stripped the skin from his back as neatly as one skins a rabbit. As soon as I saw the dead man I sent an orderly to a friend's house nearby to borrow an elephant rifle. I had already sent back the pony, not wanting it to go mad with fright and throw me if it smelt the elephant.

5

The orderly came back in a few minutes with a rifle and five cartridges, and meanwhile some Burmans had arrived and told us that the elephant was in the paddy fields below, only a few hundred yards away. As I started forward practically the whole population of the quarter flocked out of the houses and followed me. They had seen the rifle and were all shouting excitedly that I was going to shoot the elephant. They had not shown much interest in the elephant when he was merely ravaging their homes, but it was different now that he was going to be shot. It was a bit of fun to them, and it would be to an English crowd; besides they wanted the meat. It made me vaguely uneasy. I had no intention of shooting the elephant—I had merely sent for the rifle to defend myself if necessary—and it is always unnerving to have a crowd following you. I marched down the hill, looking and feeling a fool, with the rifle over my shoulder and an ever-growing army of people jostling at my heels. At the bottom, when you got away from the huts, there was a metalled road[2] and beyond that a miry waste of paddy fields a thousand yards across, not yet ploughed but soggy from the first rains and dotted with coarse grass. The elephant was standing eight yards from the road, his left side toward us. He took not the slightest notice of the crowd's approach. He was tearing up bunches of grass, beating them against his knees to clean them, and stuffing them into his mouth.

But at that moment I glanced round at the crowd that had followed me. It was an immense crowd, two thousand at the least and growing every minute. It blocked the road for a long distance on either side. I looked at the sea of yellow faces above the garish clothes—faces all happy and excited over this bit of fun, all certain that the elephant was going to be shot. They were watching me as they would watch a conjurer about to perform a trick. They did not like me, but with the magical rifle in my hands I was momentarily worth watching. And suddenly I realized that I should have to shoot the elephant after all. The people expected it of me and I had got to do it; I could feel their two thousand wills pressing me forward, irresistibly. And it was at this moment, as I stood there with the rifle in my hands, that I first grasped the hollowness, the futility of the white man's dominion in the East. Here was I, the white man with his gun, standing in front of the unarmed native crowd—seemingly the leading actor of the piece; but in reality I was only an absurd puppet pushed to and fro by the will of those yellow faces behind. I perceived in this moment that when the white man turns tyrant it is his own freedom that he destroys. He becomes a sort of hollow, posing dummy, the conventionalized figure of a sahib. For it is the condition of his rule that he shall spend his life in trying to impress the "natives," and so in every crisis he has got to do what the "natives" expect of him. He wears a mask, and his face grows to fit it. I had got to shoot the elephant. I had committed myself to doing it when I sent for the rifle. A sahib has got to act like a sahib; he has got to appear resolute, to know his own mind and do definite things. To come all that way, rifle in hand, with two thousand people marching at my heels, and then to trail feebly away, having done nothing—no, that was impossible. The crowd would laugh at me. And my whole life, every white man's life in the East, was one long struggle not to be laughed at.

---

[2]Surfaced with crushed stone, a gravel road.

6

But I did not want to shoot the elephant. I watched him beating his   7
bunch of grass against his knees with that preoccupied grandmotherly air that
elephants have. It seemed to me that it would be murder to shoot him. At
that age I was not squeamish about killing animals, but I had never shot an
elephant and never wanted to. (Somehow it always seems worse to kill a *large*
animal.) Besides, there was the beast's owner to be considered. Alive, the
elephant was worth at least a hundred pounds; dead, he would only be worth
the value of his tusks, five pounds, possibly. But I had got to act quickly. I
turned to some experienced-looking Burmans who had been there when we
arrived, and asked them how the elephant had been behaving. They all said
the same thing: he took no notice of you if you left him alone, but he might
charge if you went too close to him.

It was perfectly clear to me what I ought to do. I ought to walk up to   8
within, say, twenty-five yards of the elephant and test his behavior. If he
charged, I could shoot; if he took no notice of me, it would be safe to leave
him until the mahout came back. But also I knew that I was going to do no
such thing. I was a poor shot with a rifle and the ground was soft mud into
which one would sink at every step. If the elephant charged and I missed
him, I should have about as much chance as a toad under a steam-roller. But
even then I was not thinking particularly of my own skin, only of the watch-
ful yellow faces behind. For at that moment, with the crowd watching me, I
was not afraid in the ordinary sense, as I would have been if I had been
alone. A white man mustn't be frightened in front of "natives"; and so, in
general, he isn't frightened. The sole thought in my mind was that if anything went wrong those two thousand Burmans would see me pursued,
caught, trampled on, and reduced to a grinning corpse like that Indian up the
hill. And if that happened it was quite probable that some of them would
laugh. That would never do. There was only one alternative. I shoved the
cartridges into the magazine and lay down on the road to get a better aim.

The crowd grew very still, and a deep, low, happy sigh, as of people who   9
see the theater curtain go up at last, breathed from innumerable throats.
They were going to have their bit of fun after all. The rifle was a beautiful
German thing with cross-hair sights. I did not then know that in shooting an
elephant one would shoot to cut an imaginary bar running from ear-hole to
ear-hole. I ought, therefore, as the elephant was sideways on, to have aimed
straight at his ear-hole; actually I aimed several inches in front of this, thinking the brain would be further forward.

When I pulled the trigger I did not hear the bang or feel the kick—one   10
never does when a shot goes home—but I heard the devilish roar of glee that
went up from the crowd. In that instant, in too short a time, one would have
thought, even for the bullet to get there, a mysterious, terrible change had
come over the elephant. He neither stirred, nor fell, but every line of his
body had altered. He looked suddenly stricken, shrunken, immensely old, as
though the frightful impact of the bullet had paralyzed him without knock-
ing him down. At last, after what seemed a long time—it might have been
five seconds, I dare say— he sagged flabbily to his knees. His mouth slob-
bered. An enormous senility seemed to have settled upon him. One could
have imagined him thousands of years old. I fired again into the same spot.
At the second shot he did not collapse but climbed with desperate slowness

to his feet and stood weakly upright, with legs sagging and head drooping. I fired a third time. That was the shot that did for him. You could see the agony of it jolt his whole body and knock the last remnant of strength from his legs. But in falling he seemed for a moment to rise, for as his hind legs collapsed beneath him he seemed to tower upward like a huge rock toppling, his trunk reaching skyward like a tree. He trumpeted, for the first and only time. And then down he came, his belly toward me, with a crash that seemed to shake the ground even where I lay.

I got up. The Burmans were already racing past me across the mud. It 11 was obvious that the elephant would never rise again, but he was not dead. He was breathing very rhythmically with long rattling gasps, his great mound of a side painfully rising and falling. His mouth was wide open—I could see far down into caverns of pale pink throat. I waited a long time for him to die, but his breathing did not weaken. Finally I fired my two remaining shots into the spot where I thought his heart must be. The thick blood welled out of him like red velvet, but still he did not die. His body did not even jerk when the shots hit him, the tortured breathing continued without a pause. He was dying, very slowly and in great agony, but in some world remote from where not even a bullet could damage him further. I felt that I had got to put an end to that dreadful noise. It seemed dreadful to see the great beast lying there, powerless to move and yet powerless to die, and not even to be able to finish him. I sent back for my small rifle and poured shot after shot into his heart and down his throat. They seemed to make no impression. The tortured gasps continued as steadily as the ticking of a clock.

In the end I could not stand it any longer and went away. I heard later 12 that it took him half an hour to die. Burmans were bringing dahs and baskets even before I left, and I was told they had stripped his body almost to the bones by the afternoon.

Afterward, of course, there were endless discussions about the shooting of 13 the elephant. The owner was furious, but he was only an Indian and could do nothing. Besides, legally I had done the right thing, for a mad elephant has to be killed, like a mad dog, if its owner fails to control it. Among the Europeans opinion was divided. The older men said I was right, the younger men said it was a damn shame to shoot an elephant for killing a coolie, because an elephant was worth more than any damn Coringhee coolie. And afterward I was very glad that the coolie had been killed; it put me legally in the right and it gave me a sufficient pretext for shooting the elephant. I often wondered whether any of the others grasped that I had done it solely to avoid looking a fool.

1936

Profile   In his "autobiographical" narrative[3] Orwell recounts an eye-opening experience as a British colonial administrator, an experience that taught him how much imperialism debases both the subjugator and the subjugated. The stance is that of an older, wiser person looking back on his younger, greener self, and his method is a combination of narration and exposition, of

[3]From 1922 to 1927 Eric Blair (Orwell's real name) served in the British civil service as a member of the Indian Imperial Police. There is no evidence, however, that he ever shot an elephant.

story-telling and intermittent commentary. Sometimes action and explanation appear in the same sentence: "It had been chained up, *as tame elephants always are when their attack of 'must' is due,* but on the previous night it had broken its chain and escaped." Sometimes entire paragraphs are devoted primarily to one or the other (the early paragraphs, where Orwell explains his predicament, are chiefly expository; the account of the shooting is vividly narrative).

In keeping with his purpose—to point to a clear moral—Orwell uses a *subjective first-person narrator* ("I")—that is, someone directly involved in the story who freely exercises his right to comment on significance, to assign values and pass judgment, to explain. (By contrast, *objective narrators* simply report but do not editorialize.) Thus, although the narrative and descriptive details are graphic, sometimes shockingly so, the essay focuses on the internal changes worked in the narrator, the lesson he learns. From his infection with racist sentiments, to his isolation from other Europeans, to his helplessness before the will of the mob, it is the effect of the events on the narrator, his enlightenment, that concerns the reader.

Exercise   The following is paragraph 6. Working sentence by sentence, identify subjective and objective details, and then separate exposition (explanation, commentary) from narration and description. When do any seem to be borderline or to overlap?

[1]But at that moment I glanced round at the crowd that had followed me. [2]It was an immense crowd, two thousand at the least and growing every minute. [3]It blocked the road for a long distance on either side. [4]I looked at the sea of yellow faces above the garish clothes—faces all happy and excited over this bit of fun, all certain that the elephant was going to be shot. [5]They were watching me as they would watch a conjurer about to perform a trick. [6]They did not like me, but with the magical rifle in my hands I was momentarily worth watching. [7]And suddenly, I realized that I should have to shoot the elephant after all. [8]The people expected it of me and I had got to do it; I could feel their two thousand wills pressing me forward, irresistibly. [9]And it was at this moment, as I stood there with the rifle in my hands, that I first grasped the hollowness, the futility of the white man's dominion in the East. [10]Here was I, the white man with his gun, standing in front of the unarmed native crowd—seemingly the leading actor of the piece; but in reality I was only an absurd puppet pushed to and fro by the will of those yellow faces behind. [11]I perceived in this moment that when the white man turns tyrant it is his own freedom that he destroys. [12]He becomes a sort of hollow, posing dummy, the conventionalized figure of a sahib. [13]For it is the condition of his rule that he shall spend his life in trying to impress the "natives," and so in every crisis he has got to do what the "natives" expect of him. [14]He wears a mask, and his face grows to fit it. [15]I had got to shoot the elephant. [16]I had committed myself to doing it when I sent for the rifle. [17]A sahib has got to act like a sahib; he has got to appear resolute, to know his own mind and do definite things. [18]To come all that way, rifle in hand, with two thousand people marching at my heels, and then to trail feebly away, having done nothing—no, that was impossible. [19]The crowd would laugh at me. [20]And my whole life, every white man's life in the East, was one long struggle not to be laughed at.

First-Person Narration   First-person narratives often invite us to look as critically at the narrator as at the action, as objectively at the speaker's responses as at the events. Everything we read in a first-person narration is, after all, *of* the narrator as well as *about* the subject—the language, the choice and arrangement of details, the commentary. Thus, in "Shooting an Elephant," we see Orwell characterizing himself even as he characterizes the sordidness of colonialism. When he observes that the Burmans did not "have the guts" to raise a riot, sees the crowd reacting with "hideous laughter," and speaks of "sneering yellow faces," he dramatizes his susceptibility to the very feelings he abhors, his moral collapse under the weight of enforcing an unjust colonial authority. A third-person (*he/she*) narrator might report such feelings in the young Blair, but without the immediacy and authenticity of a first-hand report.

Indirect Quotation   In paragraph 3 Orwell half quotes, half summarizes the sub-inspector's phone message: "Would I please come and do something about it?" To present a direct quote, he would have had to interrupt his narration and allow the sub-inspector to deliver his own lines: "Will you please come and do something about it?" Had he merely summarized the phone message, it would have gone something like, "[he] said that an elephant was ravaging the bazaar and asked me to come and do something about it." Instead, Orwell does something in between: He quotes indirectly, keeping some of the flavor of the original while maintaining his own narrative voice. In the final paragraph he uses indirect quotation one more time: "the younger men said it was a damn shame to shoot an elephant for killing a coolie, because an elephant was worth more than any damn Coringhee coolie."

Indirect quotation is especially appropriate in a subjective first-person narration like "Shooting an Elephant" because it allows the narrator to remain in the forefront of the story. The focus, after all, is on the impact of the events on the narrator, not on a dramatization of the events for their own sake. Thus, only one character in the essay other than the writer has her own lines, the old woman who shoos the children away from the dead coolie. But her brief exclamations cannot drown out the narrator's voice.

The Generic *The*

> *The* wretched prisoners huddling in *the* stinking cages of *the* lock-ups, *the* gray, cowed faces of *the* long-term convicts, *the* scarred buttocks of *the* men who had been flogged with bamboos—all these oppressed me with an intolerable sense of guilt.

In contrast to the indefinite articles (*a* and *an*), *the* usually serves as a simple definite article, indicating a specific person or object (*the* writer whose pen name was George Orwell; *the* essay he would entitle "Shooting an Elephant"). In paragraph 2, however, Orwell uses *the* in its less common generic sense. "*The* wretched prisoners" and "*the* gray, cowed faces" refer not to specific individuals but to those whom the young Orwell witnessed over and over, the habitual victims of colonialism. The generic *the* appears often in series, as it does here and in paragraph 1 ("*the* sneering yellow faces of young men . . . *the* insults hooted after me . . . got badly on my nerves").

Notice, though, that these cumulative, generic experiences got on his nerves, as he reports, and convinced him to resign his position. It was, however, *one very particular experience*, one related to us in minute, gruesome detail, that finally opens his eyes.

Conjunctive Openers   At the risk of offending the style police, Orwell frequently opens sentences with coordinating conjunctions (*and, but, for, or, nor, yet, so*). Technically, repunctuated, any sentence opening with *and* or *but* could become a part of the previous sentence. But like many other modern writers, Orwell uses words like *and* and *but* as coherence devices to suggest a closer relationship between some of his statements, even while he wishes to give them the force of separate assertions.

> . . . all these oppressed me with an intolerable sense of guilt. *But* I could get nothing into perspective.

> The crowd would laugh at me. *And* my whole life, every white man's life in the East, was one long struggle not to be laughed at.
> *But* I did not want to shoot the elephant.

Coherence devices point in both directions, forward and backward. At the beginning of a sentence, an *and* or a *but* suggests a close relationship with the previous sentence even while forecasting the nature of the statement to follow (it will be parallel, additional, contradictory, and so on). Paragraphs are formations of sentences, and coordinating conjunctions help readers identify the role of individual sentences in the formation.

Revision Strategies   In "Shooting an Elephant" the selection, arrangement, and presentation of details all stem from Orwell's basic narrative strategy, the decision to give a first-hand account of a personal experience from the vantage of later years. That is, he presents an insider's view from the outside, the older self looking back on the experiences and reactions of the younger self. Despite what his younger self may have grasped, it presumably took Orwell years to put the event in proper perspective, and to find the proper words. This strategy drives all of Orwell's choices—choices of detail, language, incident, commentary, and tone. Consider the opening sentences:

> In Moulmein, in lower Burma, I was hated by large numbers of people—the only time in my life that I have been important enough for this to happen to me. I was sub-divisional police officer of the town, and in an aimless, petty kind of way anti-European feeling was very bitter. No one had the guts to raise a riot . . .

"I was hated by large numbers of people—the only time in my life that I have been important enough for this to happen to me." Who but an older, somewhat self-mocking narrator could have made such a remark? Yet it identifies the subject and sets the tone for the rest of the essay: It is about a life lived amidst hatred and resentment, told by someone willing to admit that he fell prey to a syndrome common to colonial administrators ("Ask any Anglo-Indian official, if you can catch him off duty"). And would the young Blair have been able to describe the anti-European feeling as only "aimless and petty," he who admits to having been happily willing to bayonet a priest? On the other hand, would an objective narrator have spoken so dismissively of anti- European sentiment, or observed that "No one had the guts to raise a riot," in just those words? And would such a narrator have spent so much time explaining motives, or shaping narrative events to fit the explanations?

Student Revisions

The following illustrate two revision strategies. The first uses a much less subjective first-person narrator, one attempting simply to record the facts as accurately as possible and holding commentary and interpretation to a minimum. The narrator is not "Orwell"—the seasoned essayist—but the young Eric Blair, a person writing in his journal in the immediate wake of the event, years before experience and reflection will place it in perspective.

The second revision also uses the first person, but the narrator is now a Burman, someone writing from the perspective of a sensitive and observant non-European, one of those subjected to British colonialism. He cannot read the young officer's mind, but he can make some worthwhile inferences based on what he can see. Both revisions place the event in a different perspective, giving it new if related meanings. Both require significant changes in wording and presentation.

Revision 1

As set down in the field journal of sub-divisional officer Eric Blair, Moulmein, Lower Burma.

Today it was my duty to shoot an elephant. I received a call from the sub-inspector this morning. I was told that an elephant was loose in the bazaar and asked to take charge of the situation. Without hesitation, I took my Winchester, got on my pony, and headed out.

I was stopped on the way by various Burmans who informed me about the elephant's doings. As it turned out, it was not a wild elephant, but a trained one which had gone into heat. For this reason, it had been chained up. Yet, despite such precautions, it had broken loose sometime last night and escaped. Its trainer had set out in pursuit only to head in the wrong direction and was by then a twelve-hour journey away. The elephant had suddenly appeared in town this morning. By the time I had arrived, the elephant had already destroyed a hut, killed a cow, and eaten the stock of some fruit stalls. The elephant had also overturned a rubbish van.

I met up with the Burmese sub-inspector and some Indian constables who were waiting for me in the quarter where the elephant had gone, but were unsuccessful in getting any definite information. Some of the people said the elephant had gone in one direction, some said it had gone in another, others had, until my inquiry, been unaware of its presence at all.

It was then that I heard a loud cry of an old woman, who with a switch was shooing away a dispersing crowd of children. More women followed, clicking their tongues and shouting at the children. I rounded a hut and saw a dead body sprawled in the mud. The corpse was an Indian male, dark-skinned, semi-nude, and had not been dead for many minutes. I was told by the people that the elephant had unexpectedly come around the corner of the hut, surprising its victim. The elephant had caught the deceased with its trunk, put its foot on his back, forcing him to the ground. As the rains had softened the ground, the deceased's face had plowed a trench approximately one foot deep and two yards long. He was prostrate, his arms stretched to either side, head turned to the left. The weight of the elephant's foot had stripped the skin clean from his back. At that point, I sent one of the orderlies to George's house to get his elephant rifle. Then preferring to proceed on foot, I dismounted and had the pony sent back.

The orderly returned with the rifle and five cartridges. I put the shells in my pocket, resting the butt of the gun on the top of my left boot. In the meantime, some Burmans had arrived and told me that the elephant was only a few hundred yards away in the paddy fields. As I started out, the inhabitants of the quarter who had gathered now began to follow me. Once they had seen my rifle they deduced that I was going to shoot the elephant and were now announcing it throughout the quarter. I marched down the hill there, rifle over my shoulder, the people from the quarter following along. At the bottom of the hill, I saw the elephant grazing some eight yards from the metalled road, not seeming to notice either me or the crowd's presence.

I halted on the road. The elephant continued to graze. A number of people had assembled in the wake of my progression toward the elephant. A mass of approximately two thousand individuals stood behind me. With my back to the villagers, I again rested the butt of the gun on my boot while taking a shell from my pocket. The eyes of those who stood near me followed my every movement. Smiles spread across their faces as I pulled out the cartridge. The elephant remained fixed. I shifted the weight of the gun to my right foot as I inspected the cartridge. Those who stood at the front of the gathering brought themselves two steps closer to me. I looked back to the cartridge, feeling it in my hand. The other hand held the business end of the rifle. A man with a dah in one hand and a basket in the other nodded at me. The elephant was still grazing. I glanced over my shoulder. The mass of people now blocked almost sixty yards of road as well as thirty yards on either side of the road. I took out another cartridge and looked over the two of them together. I lifted up the rifle, resting it in the crook of my arm.

There would be no laughing today.

I took a few steps off the road in the direction of the elephant only to have my boot sink up to the laces into the mud. I slipped a little on the road's slight embankment but was able to keep from falling. I looked back at the crowd of people. Back on the road, I shoved the cartridges into the magazine and lay down to get a good aim.

The people now grew very still and I peered through the rifle's cross-hair sights. I aimed for the elephant's brain, setting the sight forward from what would be its earhole. I pulled the trigger, and for me the effects of the explosion were negated as the shot went home. The mass of spectators gave out a round of shouts and cries. At last, after approximately five seconds, the elephant lowered itself to its knees. I fired again into the same spot, at which he returned to his feet and stood upright, its head hanging down, its mouth slobbering. I fired a third time. The elephant trumpeted once. Effective, the shot brought it down.

I got up. The Burmans had already proceeded past me across the mud. The rifle had succeeded in bringing the elephant down, but it was not yet dead. I could see far into its throat through its wide open mouth. After waiting for five minutes for its breath to catch and fail, I fired the two remaining shots into his heart. Blood poured from its wounds, still it did not die. Its steady breathing continued without a pause. I sent an orderly back for my smaller rifle, emptying shot after shot into his heart and down his throat. The shots made no impression and the breathing continued.

In the end, having no more ammunition, I went away.
(next morning)

I heard from one fellow that it had taken the elephant almost thirty minutes finally to expire. I was also told that the Burmans had stripped its corpse by the afternoon, leaving most of the inedible pieces amongst the bones.

The elephant's owner is furious, but he won't be able to do anything about it. It's fortunate for me that the elephant killed a man, for it provided a sufficient pretext for the shooting. It put me legally in the right.

Anyhow, some men told me it was a "damn shame" to shoot an elephant.

—*Michael Stamps*

Revision 2

In 1967, a few months before he died, U Po Kyin, a Burmese public official, published his autobiography, Experiences—*his reminiscences as an orderly to sub-divisional police officer Eric Blair during the British regime in Burma. This narrative focuses on the author's moments of personal insight, the predicament of an anti-imperialistic white man in a hostile environment and the enigmatic nature of his dilemma.*

In the days of the British rule in Moulmein, Burma, sub-inspector Blair and I went on daily inspection tours. As a native I was familiar with the area and thus was often preferred to an English orderly. It was also, perhaps, Officer Blair's intention to identify with the natives, or at least to mitigate to some extent the tension that loomed between the colonial officials and the local population. In the course of our rides, we met with ample evidence to confirm the anti-British feeling of the oppressed and their determination never to forgive or forget the oppressors. It was not uncommon to see a Burman spitting betel juice on a European woman when she went through the bazaars or Buddhist monks jeering at Europeans on street corners. And as a white police officer, Blair was an obvious target. Time and time again insults and taunts were hurled at him. On one side, I comprehended the difficult situation the anti-imperialistic officer Blair was in. On the other side was the pitiful spectacle of the oppressed: the wretched prisoners huddling in the stinking cages of the lock-ups; the gray, cowed faces of the long term convicts; and the scarred buttocks of the men who had been flogged with bamboos. It was on one such day of continued observation that an incident occurred which furthered my insight into the emotions and motivations of both the oppressors and the oppressed.

It was a rain-washed morning of a dull summer day. The police room clock struck eleven. Officer Blair entered looking rather less tense than usual, perhaps essaying to treat his mundane tasks with renewed vigor and enthusiasm. Just as he was sorting some insignificant papers on his rickety desk, we heard the startling ring of the phone. It was the sub-inspector at the police station on the other end of town. The sudden twitch of Officer Blair's brow revealed that something serious had occurred. An elephant was ravaging a bazaar. Would he do something about it? This development instigated a flurry of activity in an otherwise quiet police station. Unsure of what we could do to control the situation, we got onto our ponies, and headed towards the affected area. Officer Blair had picked up his small .44 Winchester rifle, probably hoping to frighten the animal with its reports.

A small crowd had already gathered. Fervor and excitement were in the air. Various exaggerated versions of the elephant's doings were being discussed in whispers. It was not, of course, a wild elephant but a tame one which had gone "must," broken its chains, and escaped. The terrifying destruction of its rampage prompted us into a furious hunt for the animal. Our search at first proved futile. The elephant seemed nowhere to be found. Failing to receive any definite information, we were about to leave when we heard a scandalized cry, "Go away, go away, child, this moment!" Officer Blair and I rushed to the spot and found an old woman shooing away a bunch of naked children. What Officer Blair saw this particular morning was something far removed from his ordinary range of experience. The dead body of a black Dravidian coolie lay asprawl on the wet earth. He was lying on his stomach, head sharply twisted to one side, and his eyes wide open. People said that the elephant had caught him unawares, put a foot on his back, and ground him into the earth. A huge crowd had now gathered murmuring amongst themselves, some even clicking and exclaiming at the ghastly sight. Suddenly, there was an uproar and people began to run towards the paddy fields.

The elephant had been spotted. As Officer Blair and I began to move towards it, the entire population of the quarter flocked out of the houses. Finally grasping the urgency, Officer Blair sent me to borrow an elephant rifle and some ammunition from a friend who fortunately lived nearby. In a short time I was back with the weapon and five cartridges. We approached to within thirty yards or so of the animal. It seemed calm, harmless, tearing up bunches of grass and beating them against his knees before stuffing them in his mouth.

It was then that I noticed a change in Officer Blair. He appeared agitated. He pondered. He sighed. He despaired. He seemed to be torn by a dilemma. He glanced first toward the unthreatening elephant, then toward the still growing crowd of onlookers. There was an eerie silence, broken occasionally by a murmur or a wave of whispers. Officer Blair looked as if he might prefer returning to the station. He was plainly reluctant to shoot the now harmless animal, yet the crowd was expecting nothing else.

The elephant was separated from us by a small stretch of dismal looking ground. Officer Blair, still looking confused, stretched out on the ground and took aim at the animal. After a moment more of hesitation he finally pulled the trigger. A roar of shouting and cheering arose from the crowd. A mysterious transformation had come over the elephant. The huge animal looked stricken, as if shrunken and paralyzed with fear. Seconds later he sank flabbily to his knees. Another shot reverberated, this time silencing the crowd. The elephant did not immediately collapse but instead attempted to rise, although his legs sagged and his head drooped. Officer Blair fired a third shot. This time the earth seemed to engulf the massive creature. The elephant's crash shook the ground while a gleeful murmuring ran through the sea of natives. The elephant was now gasping for breath, its mouth wide open. It trembled in pain. Firing two more shots from the large rifle in a futile attempt to end the animal's agony, he took up his own small weapon and fired shot after shot down its throat. Blood welled out like lava from an erupting volcano, yet the animal continued to breath.

Looking distraught and no longer able to watch the suffering of the animal, Officer Blair finally left. The Burmans rushed to the dying animal with dahs and baskets for its flesh. We were later told that it took half an hour for the elephant to die. Did Officer Blair act out of panic, or did he succumb to the need to maintain an appearance of imperial control? Was this the cause of his shooting the elephant? Did he have to satisfy the natives in spite of his feelings? Was this the reason for his agitation? These are questions I have asked myself. They remain unanswered.

—Roopa Belur

Revision Assignments   Select one of the following strategies and revise "Shooting an Elephant." Include a brief statement explaining your choice and its effect on the arrangement and presentation of material.

1. Tell the story as the young Blair might have written about it immediately afterward in his journal (for his eyes only). Think carefully about this angle: Blair would be his own audience, able to divulge what he cannot tell other white men. Also, not writing for outsiders, there is much he would not need to explain. (Perhaps you could have several journal entries, covering the tension between himself and the Burmans and culminating with the elephant episode.) And finally, and most important, he will not have had twenty years to put the event in perspective.

2. Tell the story in the first person as Blair might have told it immediately afterward, perhaps to the other Europeans he mentions in the last paragraph. What might he dare to imply rather than state outright? (Remember "the utter silence imposed on every Englishman in the East." The young Blair would not admit openly to his feelings of disloyalty.) If you are familiar with Joseph Conrad's *The Heart of Darkness* (a novelistic treatment of European colonialism in Africa), your model might be Marlow on the deck of the *Nellie*.

3. Give an objective, third-person account of the shooting, perhaps a reasonably detailed version as it might have appeared in a contemporary Anglo-

European newspaper. (The goal is to refrain entirely from interpretive re-marks, especially those that point to the moral of Orwell's version. Never-theless, an astute reader may be able to catch some hints of the point.)

4. Retell the event for a contemporary American audience, one that does not have access to the original version (Orwell originally directed his es-say at fellow Englishmen, those who shared both guilt and knowledge of colonialism). In other words, retell Blair/Orwell's story for a modern American audience, which, of course, would know little about the details of British colonialism in India and Burma. (This approach may require some library research.)

5. Tell the story using a third-person narrator, beginning with the moment Blair is on the ground aiming the elephant gun. You will want to fill in the background information (how did he get there?), while keeping con-tact with "the present" and maintaining the sense of tension and sus-pense. In other words, use a series of flashbacks or explanatory, summary remarks. The question: Will he shoot?

6. As an exercise in illustrating and exploring the values of emphasis, use a first-person narrator to retell the elephant episode *as economically as possi-ble* while at the same time retaining what you judge to be the major de-tails of the story.

Writing Assignments

1. Write about a discovery experience of your own, an occasion that either changed or clarified your thinking on a crucial issue (it does not have to be as lofty a subject as imperialism, but a subject vital to your life or your relationships). Begin by setting the stage, by establishing the circum-stances that led to your mental breakthrough. Such breakthroughs, as the term suggests, seem to occur abruptly, yet are usually the result of a lengthy process, a period of doubt, confusion, unease. Be careful to iden-tify any conflicts or tensions that may have been involved (for Blair/Or-well there were several: between himself and the other Europeans, be-tween himself and the Burmans, between his wish not to shoot the elephant and the pressure of the crowd).

2. Orwell learns that "when the white man turns tyrant it is his own free-dom he destroys." Some would argue that this insight applies to personal as well as to political relationships. Discuss the following: When one turns tyrant and dominates another—a spouse, a lover, a child, a friend—it is one's own freedom (and much more) that one destroys.

Even the Bad Guys Wear White Hats

EDWARD ABBEY

When I first came West in 1948, a student at the University of New Mexico, I was only twenty years old and just out of the army. I thought, like most simple-minded Easterners, that a cowboy was a kind of mythic hero. I idolized those scrawny little red-nosed hired hands in their tight jeans, funny boots, and comical hats.

Like other new arrivals in the West, I could imagine nothing more romantic than becoming a cowboy. Nothing more glorious than owning my own little genuine working cattle outfit. About the only thing better, I thought, was to be a big-league baseball player. I never dreamed that I'd eventually sink to writing books for a living. Unluckily for me—coming from an Appalachian hillbilly background and with a poor choice of parents—I didn't have much money. My father was a small-time logger. He ran a one-man sawmill and a submarginal side-hill farm. There wasn't any money in our family, no inheritance you could run ten thousand cattle on. I had no trust to back me up. No Hollywood movie deals to finance a land acquisition program. I lived on what in those days was called the GI Bill, which paid about $150 a month while I went to school. I made that last as long as I could—five or six years. I couldn't afford a horse. The best I could do in 1947 and '48 was buy a third-hand Chevy sedan and roam the West, mostly the Southwest, on holidays and weekends.

I had a roommate at the University of New Mexico. I'll just call him Mac. I don't want him to come looking for me. Mac came from a little town in southwest New Mexico where his father ran a feed store. Mackie was a fair bronc rider, eager to get into the cattle-growing business. And he had some money, enough to buy a little cinder-block house and about forty acres in the Sandia Mountains east of Albuquerque, near a town we called Landfill. Mackie fenced those forty acres, built a corral, and kept a few horses there, including an occasional genuine bronco for fun and practice.

I don't remember exactly how Mackie and I became friends in the first place. I was majoring in classical philosophy. He was majoring in screw-worm management. But we got to know each other through the mutual pursuit of a pair of nearly inseparable Kappa Kappa Gamma girls. I lived with him in his little cinder-block house. Helped him meet the mortgage payments. Helped him meet the girls. We were both crude, shy, ugly, obnoxious—like most college boys.

My friend Mac also owned a 1947 black Lincoln convertible, the kind with the big grill in front, like the cowcatcher on a locomotive, chrome-plated. We used to race to classes in the morning, driving the twenty miles from his house to the campus in never more than fifteen minutes. Usually Mac was too hung over to drive, so I'd operate the car, clutching the wheel while Mac sat beside me waving his big .44, taking potshots at jackrabbits and road signs and billboards and beer bottles. Trying to wake up in time for his ten o'clock class in brand inspection.

I'm sorry to say that my friend Mac was a little bit gun-happy. Most of his 6 forty acres was in tumbleweed. He fenced in about half an acre with chicken wire and stocked that little pasture with white rabbits. He used it as a target range. Not what you'd call sporting, I suppose, but we did eat the rabbits. Sometimes we even went deer hunting with handguns. Mackie with his revolver, and me with a chrome-plated Colt .45 automatic I had liberated from the U.S. Army over in Italy. Surplus government property.

On one of our deer-hunting expeditions, I was sitting on a log in a big 7 clearing in the woods, thinking about Plato and Aristotle and the Kappa Kappa Gamma girls. I didn't really care whether we got a deer that day or not. It was a couple of days before opening, anyway. The whole procedure was probably illegal as hell. Mac was out in the woods somewhere looking for deer around the clearing. I was sitting on the log, thinking, when I saw a chip of bark fly away from the log all by itself, about a foot from my left hand. Then I heard the blast of Mac's revolver—that big old .44 he'd probably liberated from his father. Then I heard him laugh.

"That's not very funny, Mackie," I said.

"Now don't whine and complain, Ed," he said. "You want to be a real hunter like me, you gotta learn to stay awake."

We never did get a deer with handguns. But that's when I had my first 8 little doubts about Mackie, and about the cowboy type in general. But I still loved him. Worshipped him, in fact. I was caught in the grip of the Western myth. Anybody said a word to me against cowboys, I'd jump down his throat with my spurs on. Especially if Mac was standing nearby.

Sometimes I'd try to ride those broncs that he brought in, trying to prove 9 that I could be a cowboy too. Trying to prove it more to myself than to him. I'd be on this crazy, crackpot horse going up, down, left, right, and inside out. Hanging on to the saddle horn with both hands. And Mac would sit on the corral fence, throwing beer bottles at us and laughing. Every time I got thrown off, Mac would say, "Now get right back on there, Ed. Quick, quick. Don't spoil'im."

It took me a long time to realize I didn't have to do that kind of work. 10 And it took me another thirty years to realize that there's something wrong at the heart of our most popular American myth—the cowboy and his cow.

You may have guessed by now that I'm thinking of criticizing the live- 11 stock industry. And you are correct. I've been thinking about cows and sheep for many years. Getting more and more disgusted with the whole business. There are some Western cattlemen who are nothing more than welfare parasites. They've been getting a free ride on the public lands for over a century, and I think it's time we phased it out. I'm in favor of putting the public-lands livestock grazers out of business.

First of all, we don't need the public lands beef industry. Even beef lov- 12 ers don't need it. According to most government reports (Bureau of Land Management, Forest Service), only about 2 percent of our beef, our red meat, comes from the eleven Western states. By those eleven I mean Montana, Nevada, Utah, Colorado, New Mexico, Arizona, Idaho, Wyoming, Oregon,

Washington, and California. Most our beef, aside from imports, comes from the Midwest and the East, especially the Southeast—Georgia, Alabama, Florida—and from other private lands across the nation. More than twice as many beef cattle are raised in the state of Georgia than in the sagebrush empire of Nevada. And for a very good reason: back East, you can support a cow on maybe half an acre. Out here, it takes anywhere from twenty-five to fifty acres. In the red rock country of Utah, the rule of thumb is one section—a square mile—per cow.

Since such a small percentage of the cows are produced on public lands in the West, eliminating that part of the industry should not raise supermarket beef prices very much. Furthermore, we'd save money in the taxes we now pay for various subsidies to these public lands cattlemen. Subsidies for things like "range improvement"—tree chaining, sagebrush clearing, mesquite poisoning, disease control, predator trapping, fencing, wells, stock ponds, roads. Then there are the salaries of those who work for government agencies like the BLM and the Forest Service. You could probably also count in a big part of the salaries of the overpaid professors engaged in range-management research at the Western land-grant colleges. 13

Moreover, the cattle have done, and are doing, intolerable damage to our public lands—our national forests, state lands, BLM-administered lands, wildlife preserves, even some of our national parks and monuments. In Utah's Capital Reef National Park, for example, grazing is still allowed. In fact, it's recently been extended for another ten years, and Utah politicians are trying to make the arrangement permanent. They probably won't get away with it. But there we have at least one case where cattle are still tramping about in a national park, transforming soil and grass into dust and weeds. 14

Overgrazing is much too weak a term. Most of the public lands in the West, and especially in the Southwest, are what you might call "cowburnt." Almost anywhere and everywhere you go in the American West you find hordes of these ugly, clumsy, stupid, bawling, stinking, fly-covered, shit-smeared, disease-spreading brutes. They are a pest and a plague. They pollute our springs and streams and rivers. They infest our canyons, valleys, meadows, and forests. They graze off the national bluestem and grama and bunch grasses, leaving behind jungles of prickly pear. They trample down the native forbs and shrubs and cacti. They spread the exotic cheatgrass, the Russian thistle, and the crested wheat grass. *Weeds*. 15

Even when the cattle are not physically present, you'll see the dung and the flies and the mud and the dust and the general destruction. If you don't see it, you'll smell it. The whole American West stinks of cattle. Along every flowing stream, around every seep and spring and water hole and well, you'll find acres and acres of what range-management specialists call "sacrifice areas"—another understatement. These are places denuded of forage, except for some cactus or a little tumbleweed or maybe a few mutilated trees like mesquite, juniper, or hackberry. 16

I'm not going to bombard you with graphs and statistics, which don't make much of an impression on intelligent people anyway. Anyone who goes beyond the city limits of almost any Western town can see for himself that the land is overgrazed. There are too many cows and horses and sheep out 17 there. Of course, cattlemen would never publicly confess to overgrazing, any more than Dracula would publicly confess to a fondness for blood. Cattlemen are interested parties. Many of them will not give reliable testimony. Some have too much at stake: their Cadillacs and their airplanes, their ranch resale profits and their capital gains. (I'm talking about the corporation ranches, the land-and-cattle companies, the investment syndicates.) Others, those ranchers who have only a small base property, flood the public lands with their cows. About 8 percent of the federal land permittees have cattle that consume approximately 45 percent of the forage on the government rangelands.

Beef ranchers like to claim that their cows do not compete with deer. 18 Deer are browsers, cows are grazers. That's true. But when a range is overgrazed, when the grass is gone (as it often is for seasons at a time), then cattle become browsers too, out of necessity. In the Southwest, cattle commonly feed on mesquite, cliff rose, cactus, acacia, or any other shrub or tree they find biodegradable. To that extent, they compete with deer. And they tend to drive out other and better wildlife. Like elk, or bighorn sheep, or pronghorn antelope.

How much damage have cattle done to the Western rangelands? Large- 19 scale beef ranching has been going on since the 1870s. There's plenty of documentation of the effects of this massive cattle grazing on the erosion of land, the character of the land, the character of the vegetation. Streams and rivers that used to flow on the surface all year round are now intermittent, or underground, because of overgrazing and rapid runoff.

Our public lands have been overgrazed for a century. The BLM knows it; 20 the Forest Service knows it. The Government Accounting Office knows it. And overgrazing means eventual ruin, just like stripmining or clear-cutting or the damming of rivers. Much of the Southwest already looks like Mexico or southern Italy or North Africa: a cowburnt wasteland. As we destroy our land, we destroy our agricultural economy and the basis of modern society. If we keep it up, we'll gradually degrade American life to the status of life in places like Mexico or southern Italy or Libya or Egypt.

In 1984 the Bureau of Land Management, which was required by Con- 21 gress to report on its stewardship of our rangelands—the property of all Americans, remember—confessed that 31 percent of the land it administered was in "good condition," 42 percent in "fair condition," and 18 percent in "poor condition." And it reported that only 18 percent of the rangelands were improving, while 68 percent were "stable" and 14 percent were getting worse. If the BLM said that, we can safely assume that range conditions are actually much worse.

What can we do about this situation? This is the fun part—this is the part 22 I like. It's not easy to argue that we should do away with cattle ranching. The cowboy myth gets in the way. But I do have some solutions to overgrazing.

I'd begin by reducing the number of cattle on public lands. Not that 23 range managers would go along with it, of course. In their eyes, and in the eyes of the livestock associations they work for, cutting down on the number of cattle is the worst possible solution—an impossible solution. So they propose all kinds of gimmicks. More cross-fencing. More wells and ponds so that more land can be exploited. These proposals are basically a maneuver by the Forest Service and the BLM to appease their critics without offending their real bosses in the beef industry.

I also suggest that we open a hunting season on range cattle. I realize that beef cattle will not make sporting prey at first. Like all domesticated animals (including most humans), beef cattle are slow, stupid, and awkward. But the breed will improve if hunted regularly. And as the number of cattle is reduced, other and far more useful, beautiful, and interesting animals will return to the rangelands and will increase. [24]

Suppose, by some miracle of Hollywood or inheritance or good luck, I should acquire a respectable-sized working cattle outfit. What would I do with it? First, I'd get rid of the stinking, filthy cattle. Every single animal. Shoot them all, and stock the place with real animals, real game, real protein: elk, buffalo, pronghorn antelope, bighorn sheep, moose. And some purely decorative animals, like eagles. We need more eagles. And wolves. We need more wolves. Mountain lions and bears. Especially, of course, grizzly bears. Down in the desert, I would stock every water tank, every water hole, every stockpond, with alligators. [25]

You may note that I have said little about coyotes or deer. Coyotes seem to be doing all right on their own. They're smarter than their enemies. I've never heard of a coyote as dumb as a sheepman. As for deer, especially mule deer, they, too are surviving—maybe even thriving, as some game and fish departments claim, though nobody claims there are as many deer now as there were before the cattle industry was introduced in the West. In any case, compared to elk the deer is a second-rate animal, nothing but a giant rodent—a rat with antlers. [26]

I've suggested that the beef industry's abuse of our Western lands is based on the old mythology of the cowboy as natural nobleman. I'd like to conclude this diatribe with a few remarks about this most cherished and fanciful of American fairy tales. In truth, the cowboy is only a hired hand. A farm boy in leather britches and a comical hat. A herdsman who gets on a horse to do part of his work. Some ranchers are also cowboys, but many are not. There is a difference. There are many ranchers out there who are big-time farmers of the public lands—our property. As such, they do not merit any special consideration or special privileges. There are only about 31,000 ranchers in the whole American West who use public lands. That's less than the population of Missoula, Montana. [27]

The rancher (with a few honorable exceptions) is a man who strings barbed wire all over the range; drills wells and bulldozes stockponds; drives off elk and antelope and bighorn sheep; poisons coyotes and prairie dogs; shoots eagles, bears, and cougars on sight; supplants the native grasses with tumbleweed, snakeweed, povertyweed, cowshit, anthills, mud, dust, and flies. And then leans back and grins at the TV cameras and talks about how much he loves the American West. Cowboys also are greatly overrated. Consider the nature of their work. Suppose you had to spend most of your working hours sitting on a horse, contemplating the hind end of a cow. How would that affect your imagination? Think what it does to the relatively simple mind of the average peasant boy, raised amid the bawling of calves and cows in the splatter of mud and the stink of shit. [28]

Do cowboys work hard? Sometimes. But most ranchers don't work very hard. They have a lot of leisure time for politics and bellyaching. Anytime you go into a small Western town you'll find them at the nearest drugstore, sitting around all morning drinking coffee, talking about their tax breaks.

Is a cowboy's work socially useful? No. As I've already pointed out, subsidized Western range beef is a trivial item in the national beef economy. If all of our 31,000 Western public-land ranchers quit tomorrow, we'd never miss them. Any public school teacher does harder work, more difficult work, more dangerous work, and far more valuable work than the cowboy or rancher. The same thing applies to registered nurses and nurses' aides, garbage collectors, and traffic cops. Harder work, tougher work, more necessary work. We need those people in our complicated society. We do not need cowboys or ranchers. We've carried them on our backs long enough.

"This Abbey," the cowboys and their lovers will say, "this Abbey is a wimp. A chicken-hearted sentimentalist with no feel for the hard realities of practical life." Especially critical of my attitude will be the Easterners and Midwesterners newly arrived here from their Upper West Side apartments, their rustic lodges in upper Michigan. Our nouveau Westerners with their toy ranches, their pickup trucks with the gun racks, their pointy-toed boots with the undershot heels, their gigantic hats. And, of course, their pet horses. The *instant rednecks*.

To those who might accuse me of wimpery and sentimentality, I'd like to say this in reply. I respect real men. I admire true manliness. But I despise arrogance and brutality and bullies. So let me close with some nice remarks about cowboys and cattle ranchers. They are a mixed lot, like the rest of us. As individuals, they range from the bad to the ordinary to the good. A rancher, after all, is only a farmer, cropping the public rangelands with his four-legged lawnmowers, stashing our grass into his bank account. A cowboy is a hired hand trying to make an honest living. Nothing special.

I have no quarrel with these people as fellow human beings. All I want to do is get their cows off our property. Let those cowboys and ranchers find some harder way to make a living, like the rest of us have to do. There's no good reason why we should subsidize them forever. They've had their free ride. It's time they learned to support themselves.

In the meantime, I'm going to say good-bye to all you cowboys and cowgirls. I love the legend too—but keep your sacred cows and your dead horses off of my elk pastures.

—*Harper's*, January 1986

Profile   In "Even the Bad Guys Wear White Hats" Edward Abbey argues passionately against laws that allow grazing on public lands, at bargain rates. To make his case, he assumes a familiar Western identity, that of a feisty, yarn-spinning old-timer not afraid to speak his piece (actually, the identity Abbey assumes in most of his essays). Thus, to establish his credentials on the issue, he begins autobiographically, telling how he came West as someone typically enchanted by the myth of the cowboy, befriended one, tried bronc taming, and eventually became disillusioned with the cowboy breed as exemplified by his reckless friend.

In keeping with the writer's personality, the tone of the essay ranges between the familiar and the colloquial (responding to the latter, one respondent in *Harper's* complained of Abbey's "*coprophobic* view of cattle"). It is this tone that distinguishes the piece from most argumentative essays. Instead of making his case dispassionately, marshaling his evidence and letting it speak for itself, he composes an angry and entertaining diatribe, that of a fighting environmentalist unafraid of upsetting those he described elsewhere as "moral jellyfish." Thus, he is free with profanity, humor, name-calling (deer are rats with antlers), far-fetched proposals (alligators in stock ponds), and even sentence fragments. The results are lively and stimulating if not entirely diplomatic.

The Uses of the Personal   Abbey could have written unemotionally and impersonally, arguing soberly, letting reason and data carry his message. Such an approach, if less colorful, has the advantage of sounding cool, temperate, judicious. In such argumentation the personality of the writer is usually that of a calm logician, someone informed, reliable, and concerned for the common interest. Such an arguer represses personal eccentricities, since any display of egotism may suggest self-involvement rather than civic-mindedness. Abbey, though, writes to provoke, so he stands in the forefront, drawing on his own experience as evidence for his case (an attack on cowboys and ranchers is easier to accept from a former would-be cowboy). If he seems angry, the implication is that it is for good reason. As a defender of the disappearing West, he has a public as well as a personal stake in the issue (these are public lands being ravaged, our lands). If he seems shrill, the implication is that his anger is the only appropriate response to an intolerable abuse—and the only one for a concerned citizen. He is the indignant champion of the endangered West—belligerent, confrontational, fearless (he delivered this essay as a speech at the University of Montana—to hoots and interruptions).

In making an argument, we take risks by displaying our feelings, especially anger, so visibly. Whatever may be gained by showing passion and dedication, commitment and sincerity, may be lost by the apparent lack of objectivity, the suspicion that we are egotistical, opinionated, unwilling to be fair to the evidence. Thus, as concerned an environmentalist as Gretel Ehrlich ("A Storm, the Cornfield, and Elk") termed Abbey's essay "nasty and unconstructive." On the other hand, calm rationality may convince only abstractly. Dispassionate appeals sometimes produce dispassionate audiences, that is, audiences neutral, indifferent, unmoved to act. A tactic like Abbey's, then, will attract some readers even as it repels others: those on the opposing side, those who cling to their apathy, or even a few of the potentially sympathetic, like Ehrlich. If such passion has mixed results, it at least signals the urgency and importance of one's cause. In other words, it is a tactic of *emphasis*.

Using Fragments   Technically, *fragments* are parts of sentences (single words, phrases, or clauses) treated as complete sentences—with capital letters and terminal punctuation. In formal and academic writing they are usually considered inappropriate. In the work of professional writers, though, intentional fragments are appearing with increasing frequency. Instinctively, many writers recognize that such structures are not true fragments—detached, isolated elements. The paragraph, they know, is the basic unit of written expression, and within the paragraph most fragments are not detached but have an obvious relationship with surrounding sentences. The reader is expected to see (and make) the connections. Differently punctuated, the fragments could easily be absorbed into other sentences, but with a loss of emphasis. Abbey's essay illustrates the force of intentional fragments. Thus,

> Like other new arrivals in the West I could imagine nothing more romantic than becoming a cowboy. *Nothing more glorious than owning my own little genuine working cattle outfit.*

Or,

> I had no trust to back me up. *No Hollywood movie deals to finance a land acquisition program.*

Or,

> I have been thinking about cows and sheep for many years. *Getting more and more disgusted with the whole business.*

The attentive reader connects such structures to the previous sentence. At the same time, the content of the "fragments" has some of the force of separate statements. Out of context they are not grammatically complete, but within the paragraph they have a clear relationship to their surroundings. Perhaps writers are using intentional fragments as another form of punctuation, an emphatic device that engages the reader more actively in the making as well as the finding of meaning.

Revision Strategies   In "Even the Bad Guys Wear White Hats" the selection, arrangement, and presentation of details flow from Abbey's decision to present a highly personalized argument. His authority derives primarily from his own experience, although he mentions that government data will substantiate his claims about the damage done to public lands. Under the guise of the crusty Westerner standing up for his beliefs, he not only blasts the bureaucratic policies that allow such misuse of the land, but wages a personal attack on cowboys and ranchers. Since the wise arguer will alienate as few people as possible, why does he resort to such confrontation? Because he believes that public and legislative inaction stems from America's love affair with the cowboy. Buying into the myth of the cowboy, Americans tolerate ruination of their public lands. Granted, the attack is more acceptable coming from a one-time king of the cowboy lovers, but Abbey's tone struck some as rabid and intemperate, alienating even potential sympathizers.

Student Revision

The following attempts a calmer presentation of Abbey's case. The "author" is Abbey's wife, a person who is in basic sympathy with the attack on public lands grazing, but who has had much practice smoothing feathers that her husband has ruffled. In other words, she knows that Ed has gone overboard in his essay but wants to salvage his argument for those who have been put off by his manner. In the process the writer creates an entire new personality, one suiting the fictional wife and apologist for her husband. The introduction also illustrates how different a story sounds when someone else tells it.

When I first arrived out West as a young girl in 1943, I used to dream about riding horses—tall, spotted horses with long tails that wandered the range beyond my backyard. Like most little girls, I was enamored with horses and those rugged dirt-caked men who used to ride them.

My greatest fantasy was that some day one of those mysterious cowboys would come riding up on the tallest, prettiest horse, pull me up behind his saddle, and gallop off across the prairie. Of course that never happened. And the most I can say about being swept away by an unknown cowboy is I married his best friend. I never dreamed that I'd eventually fall in love with a man who wrote about cowboys for a living. Unluckily for me—coming from a generation of women who went to college to get their "MRS" degree—I didn't have much choice. My father was a truck driver, gone for three weeks at a time. My mother was too busy raising seven children to worry about whom I dated. And even though those horses were only ten yards from my bedroom window, there wasn't any money for lessons so I could learn how to ride one. The best I could do in 1947 and '48 was get a job helping out on a cattle ranch in the Sandia Mountains east of Albuquerque. That's where I met Ed.

The guy who owned the forty-acre ranch where I worked thought he was a "real" cowboy. His friend Ed called him "Mackie," even though that wasn't his real name. Mac thought he was a great bronc rider and used to carry a big .44 revolver everywhere he went. If you want to know the truth, I thought they were both obnoxious college boys who couldn't get from one end of the day to the other without having a female pick up after them. They thought they were doing me a huge favor by paying me $20 a week to come in and cook and clean. I used to stand on the porch and shake my head every time they got in Mac's '47 black Lincoln convertible to go into town and "buy feed" for the cattle (What they really meant was they were going to Rocky's to drink cheap beer on tap and check out "the cattle" in high heels).

Ed was more of a "wannabe" cowboy. He'd ride around with Mac and do most anything he was told, but deep down I think he was pretty leery of Mackie. I'm sorry to say that Mac was a little bit gun-happy. About half an acre of his tumbleweed ranch was fenced in with chicken wire and stocked with little white rabbits. He liked to brag that he used it as a target range. Some nights he'd bring in one of those soft, white-furred bunnies hanging limp from one hand while he spun his .44 around the forefinger of his other hand and announce he had hunted us up some dinner. I always told him,

"You want to eat it, you want me to cook it, then you have to skin it." Once, when Mackie and Eddie were out tearing up the town, I'd snipped a corner of the chicken wire before I went home and watched half a dozen of white, furry cottontails bounce off into the sunset.

Ed had a gun as well. An army model Colt .45. He said he found it while he was stationed in Italy with the U.S. Army. I never saw him use it much, except once—when he and Mac went on what they used to call deer hunting expeditions. They never managed to shoot a deer with either one of their handguns, but Ed said that something had happened the time he and Mackie went into the wilderness for three days. He never said what happened exactly. But I think Mackie got carried away during target practice because after that Ed would always walk away whenever Mac started taking potshots at jackrabbits, road signs, billboards, or beer bottles.

It was during one of Mac's gun-happy episodes that Ed and I started really talking. Ed told me how much he admired Mackie. Worshipped him, in fact. If anyone had ever said a word against Mac (or cowboys, for that matter), Ed would have jumped right down their throat. But he also told me he had doubts about Mackie. Mackie was one of those people you could never read with absolute certainty.

I couldn't stop Ed, though, from trying to ride those broncos, trying to prove that he could be a cowboy too. He'd be on this crazy little horse, going up, down, left, right, and inside out, hanging on to the saddle horn with both hands. And Mac would sit on the corral fence, throwing beer bottles at him and laughing. Every time Ed would get thrown off, Mac would shout, "Now get right back on there, Ed! Don't whine and complain! You want to be a real cowboy like me, you gotta learn to stay in the saddle."

It took Ed a long time to realize that he didn't have to prove himself that way. And it took him longer to escape the fantasy he was living out on Mac's ranch. All that really matters is that, when he finally left, he took me with him. Now I'm married to an ex-wannabe cowboy who's writing articles about the American West.

Recently Ed got a burr in his sock about the livestock industry. He's been thinking about cows and sheep ever since we left Mac's cinder block house in Landfill, New Mexico. He says he's disgusted with Western cattlemen. That they've been getting a free ride on the public lands for over a century, and that it's time to phase out the program. He even says he's in favor of putting the public lands livestock grazers out of business. You know what I think? I think he's jealous.

Last month Mac paid Ed an unexpected visit after two decades of hit-and-miss Christmas cards. Mac flew into town in a private jet, rented a brand new Lincoln Town Car, and arrived on the front steps of our house with his third wife—a former "Miss Texas" runner-up half his age. The five kids from his first two marriages are all attending private schools and colleges. Mackie and Elois could only stay a few hours. (They were on their way to their vacation home in Maui and don't like flying their private jet over the ocean at night.) Ed started in after they left, calling Mac a "welfare parasite."

He said, according to most government reports (Bureau of Land Management, Forest Service), only about two percent of our beef comes from the eleven Western states—Oregon, Washington, California, Montana, Idaho, Wyoming, Nevada, Utah, Colorado, Arizona, and New Mexico. Ed says most of our beef comes from the Midwest and the East, especially the Southeast— Georgia, Alabama, Florida—and from other private lands across the nation. For more than an hour, I had to listen to him go on and on about the ratio of cattle per square mile in Georgia as compared to the ratio of cattle per square mile in Utah.

Ed believes that since such a small percentage of the cows are produced on public lands in the West, eliminating that industry should not raise super-market beef prices very much. He said we'd save money in taxes we now pay for various subsidies like "range improvements" (whatever that is). He also mentioned the money we'd save for salaries of those who work for government agencies like the BLM and the Forest Service. When he started in about the salaries of the professors who assisted Mac in getting his range-management degree at the University of New Mexico, I got up to fix us dessert.

Ed went on when I got back to say that the cattle have done, and are doing, intolerable damage to our public lands. I started thinking about our national forests, wildlife preserves, even some of our national parks and monuments, and that's when I got interested in all those reports Ed had strewn all over the dining room table. Did you know that in Utah's Capital Reef National Park, for instance, grazing is still allowed? In fact, it's recently been extended for another ten years, and Utah's government is trying to make the arrangement permanent. Ed says they won't get away with it, but the issue still gets him worked up because, in the meantime, the cattle are still tramping about a national park, transforming soil and grass into dust and weeds.

Now whenever I mention the subject of cattle or Mac's cattle range, Eddie's response is, "You mean those ugly, clumsy, stupid, bawling, stinking, fly-covered, shit-smeared, disease-spreading brutes?" He thinks they're a pest and a plague. He says they pollute our springs and streams and rivers. They infest our canyons, valleys, meadows, and forests. They graze off the native grasses, leaving behind jungles of prickly pear. His favorite term for their destruction is "cow burnt." He says what they leave behind in the wake of their grazing is *weeds*.

Whenever we take a scenic drive over I-80, he likes to point out the dung and the flies and the mud and the dust on the cattle lands we pass. Ed thinks the whole American West stinks of cattle. I've never seen him so excited as when we passed by a strip of land he said range-management specialists had designated as "sacrifice areas." It was one of those rural wastelands. The only foliage I saw for miles was some cactus or a little tumbleweed or maybe a few scrawny trees.

Can you imagine driving across the state in the middle of summer listening to a man behind the wheel exclaim, "Anyone who has any sense can see for themselves that the land is overgrazed"? I've even heard him use "Dracula" in the same sentence as "Cattlemen." By the time he starts calling them liars and seething about their Cadillacs and their airplanes, their ranch resale profits and their capital gains, I resort to reading my *Sunset* magazine or pretending like I'm taking a cat nap.

I get a kick out of Eddie's argument about which species is better, cattle or deer. He really doesn't care for either of them. The last time I overheard him discussing deer with one of his hunting buddies, he called them giant rodents—rats with antlers. If the truth be told, he'd propagate elk and antelope before he'd let deer *or* cattle graze on his own piece of land.

He's reminded me over and over again about the damage cattle have done to the Western rangelands. I guess large-scale beef ranching has been going on since the 1870s. Ed has shown me plenty of documentation of the effects of this massive cattle grazing on the erosion of the land, the character of the land, and the character of the vegetation. Streams and rivers that used to flow on the surface all year round are now intermittent, or underground, because of overgrazing and the subsequent rapid runoff.

But if our public lands have been overgrazed for a century, and the BLM knows it, and the Forest Service knows it, how are we going to change the course of history by talking about it? I'd like to support Ed in finding a solution so the eleven Western states don't end up looking like parts of Italy, northern Africa, or Mexico. I personally think Ed's taking this cattle grazing thing a bit too far when he says, "As we destroy our land, we destroy our agricultural economy and the basis of modern society." I mean, where are all these cattle going to go if they can't graze on public lands? Besides, I'd hate to think of what the drive over I-80 would look like if there wasn't a cluster of cattle dotting the landscape every fifteen miles or so.

I asked Eddie what he thought we should do. He said that's the fun part, the part he likes best. He said we can't get away with prohibiting cattle ranching. He said Mac would fly out in his private jet within the hour to set him straight. But he did have some crazy solutions to overgrazing on public lands.

The first one seemed obvious: he would begin by reducing the number of cattle on public lands. He listed all the reasons why range managers would not go along with this idea. He said they would think this was the worst possible solution. Somehow I think Ed was still trying to protect himself from a visit from Mackie and his cattle friends.

The next day he suggested we should open a hunting season on range cattle. I looked at him the way I do when he promises to mow the grass every Saturday for the rest of his natural days (without being asked) if I let him watch this one football game that particular Saturday. He said he realizes that beef cattle would not make very sporting prey at first but he insisted they would improve with each passing season.

Then he launched into a tirade about how "If I had enough money to buy respectable-sized working cattle outfit (like Mac's) I'd . . ." What *would* he do with it? First, he'd get rid of all the "stinking, filthy" cattle. Every single one of them. I won't say how. We've already covered that. Then he'd stock the place with "real" protein (as he likes to think of it): elk, buffalo, pronghorn antelope, bighorn sheep, moose. He also said he'd have some purely decorative animals, like eagles. I agreed. We need more eagles. And wolves. Well, okay, we do need more wolves. Then he got going about mountain lions and bears. Suddenly I felt like Dorothy in the forest on the way to Oz. He said down in the desert he'd stock every water tank, every water hole, every stock pond, with alligators. Alligators!

That's when I told him I had a few ideas of my own. I had never confessed to being an accomplice to the rabbits' escape on the ranch forty years ago. But I thought, hey, if it worked with fluffy white bunnies, why wouldn't it work with endearing brown cows. We could start a neighborhood adoption agency for cows and the people who love them. We might even get on the Oprah Winfrey show. Besides, I said, Margaret down the street just bought a dog the size of a large calf and I'm certain it eats twice as much food as any cow would. Eddie turned and looked at me with the same expression he gives me whenever I come home from Macy's and tell him I bought only one thing—on sale.

He quickly changed the subject and started uttering slander about Mac and his rancher friends. He said that the rancher (with few exceptions) is a man who strings barbed wire all over the range; drills wells and bulldozes stock ponds; drives off elk and antelope and bighorn sheep; poisons coyotes and prairie dogs; shoots eagles, bears, and cougars on sight; supplants the native grasses with tumbleweed, snakeweed, povertyweed, cowshit, anthills, mud, dust, and flies. And then he leans back and grins at the TV cameras and talks about how much he loves the American West. "And one of them is your best friend," I said. *Was*—Ed reminded me—*was*.

He said it's hard to respect someone who doesn't work very hard for a living and makes a lot of money off of taxpayers like you and me. Ed thinks ranchers have a lot of leisure time for politics and bellyaching. He questions the social value of their work, particularly since 31,000 of them occupy some of the finest land west of the corn belt. No one needs to convince me that any public school teacher does harder work, more difficult work, more dangerous work, and far more valuable work than any cowboy or rancher. The same thing applies to registered nurses and nurses' aides, garbage collectors, and traffic cops. We need *those* people in our complicated society, not more cowboys or ranchers.

You have to understand that my husband is a passionate man. That's one of the things I like best about him. He gets carried away from time to time but, generally speaking, his perspective is well thought out and fair. I wouldn't take his ideas about open season on range cattle very seriously. It's not like this problem warrants a simple solution. And as far as his attitude towards cattle ranchers, I think our prodigal friend Mac needs to plan his visits more carefully. I still can't believe he brought that woman with him. In the middle of May, she arrived wearing a fur coat.

—Jodi A. Edwards

Revision Assignments   Select one of the following revision strategies (or find one of your own), and rewrite Abbey's essay. Include a brief statement of your choice and its effect on the arrangement and presentation of detail.

1. Revise the essay as Abbey might have written it *when on his best behavior*— that is, for an audience that would not tolerate his profanity, name-calling, and general cantankerousness. Imagine Ed trying to persuade without giving offense, a pussyfooting Ed.

2. Rewrite the essay as an interview with Edward Abbey, either (a) opening with a paragraph of background information, then following with a

straight question-and-answer format, or (b) enclosing the interview in a story (by playing the role of an intermediary, you can cushion some of Abbey's bluntness by embedding his views in your own more temperate narration).

3. Revise the essay as your testimony before a legislative committee on public lands use, submerging your personal anger and presenting your information calmly and objectively (no remarks about scrawny, red-nosed cowboys and Cadillac-driving, tax-dodging ranchers).

Writing Assignments

1. Reply to Abbey's essay, either to the issue itself, agreeing or disagreeing with his position, or to his manner of argumentation—intemperate, fanatical, "counter productive."

2. Compose an ironical response to Abbey. Your pose is that of an apathetic citizen, one who resents Abbey's summons to action. He has challenged your indifference, been judgmental (see Carol Bly, "A Mongoose Is Missing"). Defend yourself.

3. Abbey wants to make his audience hopping mad. Write an argumentative essay in a similarly impassioned voice. Choose a "public" issue, perhaps one in which the law protects and even encourages behavior that seems to endanger the public welfare (gun control? government subsidies for tobacco growers? mining on public lands?). Use the first-person pronoun, draw on personal observations, and appeal to your audience's civic-mindedness. Don't be afraid to make some readers angry (in other words, don't be a moral jellyfish).

Shortest Route to the Mountains

RICK BASS

The trouble with buying a strawberry milkshake from the Lake Providence, Louisiana, Sonic Drive-In on the left side of Highway 65 going north through the Delta, north to Hot Springs, Arkansas, is that you have got to tag the bottom with your straw and then come up a good inch or so if you want to get anything, the reason being that the Lake Providence Sonic uses real strawberries and lots of them in their shakes. You stick your straw down to the bottom the way you do with other shakes and you won't get anything—your straw gets mired and plugged up in an inch or so of fresh-cut strawberries. So to get the actual shake itself moving up the straw and into your mouth you've got to raise the straw an inch off the bottom, sometimes more, depending on who made the shake. If you've got a lot of time to kill, the best thing to do is to pull into the parking lot under the shade of the big live oak that sprawls over and cools all of the Lake Providence First Baptist Church and most of Highway 65 as well. (Years ago, the phone company had planned to nip some of the larger limbs back away from the highway because a storm might knock them down onto the phone wire, but a petition was quickly circulated and signed that requested the phone company not cut the limbs; the townspeople would, said the petition, rather do without phone service for a day or two than have the big tree's limbs pruned. There were 1,217 signatures on the petition; Lake Providence and the surrounding hamlets of Oak Grove, Louise, and Rolling Fork have a combined population of 1,198. The limbs were spared.)

Parked under the big oak, you can still keep an eye out on the Sonic because it is right across the street. The reason you want to keep an eye on the Sonic is so you will know when the lady who puts more strawberries in the shakes than the other ladies comes on duty. The tag on her red-and-white uniform says "Hi, my name is Ellen." You will know it is her when she drives up because she drives an old white Dodge Dart with license plates that say "Ellen."

The best thing to do once you have ordered, paid for, and received your milkshake is to walk back over to the big oak and enjoy it over there—early August is the best month to do this. But if you are in a hurry to be off, if you are in a hurry to get to the mountains, you roll your window up after paying Ellen (you stay in your car and order through a loudspeaker—she brings it out to you and then waves good-bye and says "Come back again" when you drive off) and you move on, drinking the shake as you roll once more through the Delta, ducking involuntarily every now and then as a crop duster swoops head level across the highway. It is not the fastest route to the mountains, nowhere near it—the quickest and most efficient path is to jump up on the interstate and set the cruise control and rocket out of Jackson through Monroe Ruston Shreveport Tyler Dallas Fort Worth Wichita Falls AbileneAmarilloRatonPassDenver. But this year I was not in a hurry to get to the

"Shortest Route to the Mountains," from *Wild to the Heart* by Rick Bass. Reprinted by permission of Stackpole Books.

mountains, because I had saved up all of my vacation and was going to squander it all on this one trip; two week's worth of freedom in the state that I love most but that is, unfortunately, the least realistic state for me to make a living in. So I took the route up through the Delta. It is not the fastest route to the mountains, but it is the shortest, the best.

Even after Lake Providence is long ago a speck in the rearview mirror, the pleasant strawberry taste of the milkshake lingers, and my stomach continues to make contented little strawberry-tasting rumbles. It is sinfully pleasurable to drive through this part of the country in August with the windows up and the air conditioner on and one of Ellen's milkshakes empty in the little bag in the front seat. Because in August the north Louisiana/Mississippi/south Arkansas Delta is the most unbearable spot on the face of the earth. The humidity remains at one hundred percent twenty-four hours a day, and the temperatures never dip below 105 until after the sun goes down.

With the exception of the lean, gaunt, anchored-to-tractors farmers who grow soybeans and cotton out of the rich floodplain deposits, in August the human race disappears. Even the wildlife is missing in August; only the toughest, most ancient life forms remain. Dragonflies buzz in one place over a small irrigation ditch, sometimes just hovering, waiting for the summer to end. And like interlopers, domesticated outcasts who have no business being in this hellhole, stocky black Angus stand motionless in the few fields that do not grow soybeans; except for the ever-swishing tails, when viewed from a distance, the cattle look like stout china imitations placed out in the fields to break the monotony (the monotony of money—this is the richest farmland on the planet). Only the reptiles flourish, as they always have. Red-eared sliders scramble across the sun-baked asphalt, wishing (as much as is possible for turtles to wish) that they could stop and bask an hour or two on the warm road but knowing they can't, that if they do then after about thirty minutes a big truck coming up from Jackson or New Orleans carrying a load of fryers to Little Rock (white feathers trailing behind it, swirling and fluttering in its wake) will come pounding down the highway, screaming and rattling and roaring and double-clutching and shaking the heat-buckled narrow two-lane that is already as warped as a Burma bridge, hell-bent for Eudora or McGehee or Star City or any other little town that is fortunate enough to get in its way. The turtles have learned (as much as it is possible for turtles to learn) that those of their numbers who stay and bask in the pleasant August torpor of Highway 65 are almost inevitably flattened. A few of the luckier ones are only struck on the side-rim of their flat low-slung mossy carapaces by the truck's hub, and these are the ones that, rather than being squashed, are instead sent skittering head-over-teacups off the road and back into the ditch with only superficial injuries, where, with luck, they live to snap at dragonflies another day.

There is a great deal of satisfaction to be experienced racing past the half-turned fields of cotton and soybeans barefooted in shorts and tee shirt at two-thirty in the afternoon on your vacation, on your way through the Delta, on your way to the mountains, being able to watch the rest of the world at work while you and only you flaunt your two week's exempt status like a hard-earned badge, like a reward. It is as if you have escaped from a prison in some clever, cunning manner; it is a good feeling.

There is also satisfaction to be had in driving past the fields and watching   7
the tractors raising clouds of dust that, if you are lucky and are on the tail end
of an early Indian summer front, drift slowly through Jackson and New Orleans under an exhilarating mock-October royal blue sky, even in August.
But more years than not, the year's first crispness doesn't come until Thanks-
giving weekend, the weekend of the big games, and on August Friday after-
noons like this one the dust clouds raised by the tractors blow hot and dry toward Little Rock and Memphis, or at best mushroom up around the tractor
like thick fog before wisping straight up into nothing. Going north to the
mountains through Lake Providence, Louisiana, is not the fastest route to
the mountains, but it is the best. It gives you time to think and to prepare for
their beauty. It makes them seem more beautiful when you finally do get
there.

Reed, population 403. Junction City, 377. Tillar, 273. There is a state   8
park a few miles west of Tillar, but if you have left Jackson at noon and
stopped for the strawberry shake in Lake Providence, then by now it will be
getting close to four o'clock in the afternoon—sullen purple clouds will be
pouting overhead where before, earlier in the day, there were no clouds—
and it will be only an hour or two away from the hottest part of the day in the
Delta—so you drive on.

Arkansas City, Arkansas, where, if you are still speeding north on the   9
same flattened-turtle-shell-littered, flat-but-warped two-lane Highway 65
around four-thirty in the afternoon, lost in a song on the radio and half
asleep, half hypnotized by the hum of your wheels and by the fast flat
stretch of narrow Delta road, likely as not you can suddenly look up and
focus on the battered rear end of an old farm truck's tailgate that is looking
back at you and getting bigger fast. The truck's turn indicator lights will
have been broken out many years ago, many many years ago, during the
loading of an unruly Brahman bull calf into the back to take to auction,
else they would be signaling a left turn. Your shoulders will widen and tense,
your whitened knuckles gripping the steering wheel like a tourniquet, and
on this particular stretch of 65 a few miles north of Mitchelville (494), almost in the Arkansas City limits, if the driver of the old farm truck notices
that you are bearing down on him, he will, likely as not, stop in the middle
of his abbreviated left turn and gape into this rearview mirror, fascinated, as if
not realizing it is he and not some stranger that is about to be rear-ended.
The reason he is fascinated is that by and large, with few exceptions, an
accident is a big event in Arkansas City, even if the person watching the accident is involved in it himself. Anything is welcome as long as it breaks the
horrible monotony that sets in around August as they near the end of a long
hard planting-and-harvesting season, a monotony spawned by almost six
months of working dawn till dark in weather that never goes below one hundred degrees. So that others may eat. A car wreck, even your own, is much
better than another day of work, come August and the end-of-summer
fatigue.

But on this particular stretch of Highway 65 you come out of your hypno-   10
sis just in time; you whip the steering wheel around and pass on the right, on
the shoulder, with inches to spare, and loose gravel scrambles out from under
the tires and clatters up against the sides of your car, and then you are back

up on the road again and the stopped truck is in your rearview mirror, its driver watching open-mouthed as you race north toward the mountains, no longer sleepy . . .

The scenery is hot. It is flat and drab, and you look at your road map for 11 the fifth time in thirty minutes to see if you can look ahead and tell where it will end. You yawn and sing along with the radio even if you have never before heard the song that is playing; you do isometric exercises against the steering wheel; you roll the window down and then roll it back up again just to be moving. You read the billboards when you are lucky enough to pass one.

Sammie's Bait and Groceries—Mealworms, Earthworms, Cold Beer, and 12 Crickets. Stuttgart, Arkansas—Duck Hunting Capital of the World. Dumas, Arkansas—Home of the '75–'76 State 2A Champs. All along the road on either side there stand large metal buildings that sell and service tractors old and new. There are tractor stores on Highway 65 the way there are casinos in Las Vegas. Massey-Ferguson, International Harvester, Stribling-Puckett. John Deere. Caterpillar. Cat. They are great strong red beasts (sometimes green) that, along with the men who run them, work from two hours before dawn until two hours after dusk six days a week for the rest of their lives with only an occasional oil change or a day off for maintenance.

North of Dumas the landscape is broken up a little by numerous small 13 square muddy stock tanks. Catfish. Humphreys County, Mississippi—Catfish Capital of the World. Cotton is no longer king; cotton and cattle have been replaced by soybeans and catfish. Except for rabbits, I am told there is no other more efficient assimilator of protein than a channel catfish. University professors at agricultural schools throughout the South have estimated that by the year 2000, catfish will be the number one food crop in the United States, the number one food crop in the world. The land will be given a breather as crops are turned under a few years so that stock tanks can be dozed up. Towns like Dumas will be rich. So say the scientists. In the meantime, Dumas waits. And grows catfish. Big catfish. But the catfish stay submerged, sulking down in the mud, getting fat on corn meal and cottonseed and rarely if ever showing themselves; the scenery remains drab. You start yawning again.

Dooville, Arkansas, pop. 525. Where, upon filling the order for the three- 14 piece dinner at the Dooville Chicken Basket, the woman at the counter puts not one and not two but five of the little doubled-barreled paper break-open vials of salt in the sack along with your order, since the news that salt causes high blood pressure has yet to reach Dooville. There are a lot of things that have yet to reach Dooville, a lot of things that probably never will, including high blood pressure itself.

Tamo. The Tamo water tower is somewhat unique from other water tow- 15 ers across the United States in that it has no graffiti on it, no Jerry-loves-Ginny, no Srs. of '76, no Tamo-Wildcats-Number-One. The reason for this is that there are no Tamo Wildcats. Tamo, Arkansas, has exactly seven (7) school-aged children, three of whom will graduate high school next year: two are going out to Texas to work on oil rigs, the third is going to the University of Arkansas on a basketball scholarship. The Tamo Seven attend school in Dooville, a fifteen-minute bus ride.

Other than the schoolchildren, the next-youngest people in Tamo are 16
Gary and Shirley. They own Gary and Shirley's Grocery, one of six business
establishments in the town of Tamo. Gary is thirty-three, Shirley thirty-four.
Tamo, too, waits for the catfish boom.

Finally, at long last, the metropolis of Pine Bluff. Fifty-seven thousand 17
plus. An Oasis of culture in the Arkansas wilderness. Mobile homes, the Silver Shocker Disco, Pat Kreeton Figure Salon, and the Giant Water Slide
(Fastest in Arkansas!). Have a Coke and a Smile. A-1 Muffler Shop.

It would be easy to dislike Pine Bluff with its big-city sprawl of billboards 18
and stop lights in the otherwise-relaxing south Arkansas farmland, but I notice that when I stop for gas at one of the local service stations—and this is
more than I can say for the service stations in New York, Chicago, Los Angeles, and Cincinnati—the restroom is immaculate. Still, I hurry through Pine
Bluff as fast as I can, getting lost and turned around in the wrong direction
only twice. The last time I get lost pretty good, so that I finally end up not
even knowing how to backtrack, and I stop and ask for directions outside a
Kroger grocery store. Three old men with gray-stubble beards, retired farmers with all their daughters married off and their sons-left-home-too and
nothing much to do are sitting out front as if waiting for someone to come by
and ask them for directions.

A light rain has started falling, the kind that falls every day at this time 19
in Pine Bluff in the summer—the fat pregnant purple heat-spawned thun-
derclouds build up all day long and then sprinkle down just enough each
day to make the crops grow—and we stand there in the rain discussing my
roots, because they ask me where I am from before I can get the question
out. "From Jackson," I tell them. This makes no impression on them, and I
realize that they are not familiar with Jackson. "From the South," I add.
They mull this over; it seems to be inconceivable to them that I could
have gotten lost. It occurs to me that this could very well be the first time
anyone has ever gotten lost in their town and asked them for directions.
They look at each other bemusedly, glad that it is I and not they who are
lost, having no more idea than a hoot owl where 270 West is, or even if there
is such a beast.

"I jes' get on the free-way and go," one of them chuckles to another, wav- 20
ing his arm in a wild carefree half circle that takes in a sweep of country
somewhere roughly between Tacoma, Washington, and Minneapolis–St.
Paul. I grimace, try to smile politely, thank them, climb back in my car, and
take off in the general direction of the arc.

7:30 P.M. Skies are blue again, with only a few thin white wisps of clouds 21
above. Already, however, they are building, and I know that by tomorrow
evening they will once again be bunched together, fat and purple and bulg-
ing with rain, but this doesn't concern me; tomorrow I will be in the mountains, on vacation, where it never rains.

Dusk. Dragonflies from out of nowhere career off my windshield like 22
soft-bodied bullets, speckling it green when they hit, colliding with such impact that, until you are conditioned to them, you wince at first and flinch
each time one hits, as if it were something real and living you had just struck
and not just an old dragonfly. But you get used to it.

Fairfield, Arkansas. No names on the Fairfield water tower, either. 23

Twilight, almost dark, and every small-town radio station in the South can be picked up now under the cover of darkness. You reach the outskirts of Hot Springs three hours later, where, bone weary and bleary eyed, you pull off the road to nap for a couple of hours before starting up again. You fall asleep dreaming summertime dreams of a girl you knew in high school a long time ago. This time tomorrow you will be in the mountains.

It is not the fastest route to the mountains, but it is the shortest.

1987

Profile In "The Shortest Way to the Mountains" Rick Bass presents a travel narrative, an account of a day's drive through the heat and humidity of August up Highway 65 from Lake Providence, Louisiana, to Hot Springs, Arkansas. Writing as an escapee from the city, Bass alternates freely between the first and second persons. The subjective first-person voice (*I*) allows him to interpret even as he records, mixing *expressive* with *representational* detail (see below). The second person (*you*) engages the reader, inviting us at least to witness if not participate in the experience. Rhetorically, his principal motive is to evoke the atmosphere of the region, to convey a sense of life as it is lived in the Mississippi Delta, but life as experienced by a certain kind of traveler, one in a particularly receptive mood—relaxed, lazily attentive, and almost decadently committed to enjoying little pleasures (like fresh strawberry milkshakes). To capture this sense, he focuses on the details of place: its landscape, its weather, its wildlife, its relentless economic activity even in the sweltering August heat, its talkative small-town citizens (where but at Gary and Shirley's Grocery could he have learned about Tamo's schoolchildren?). To further invite reader participation, Bass also exploits the immediacy of the present tense ("Even after Lake Providence *is* a speck in the rearview mirror," not "Even after Lake Providence *was* a speck in the mirror").

But if Bass uses the present tense and follows a chronological order, his account is not continuous. There are gaps in his narrative, the kind caused by heat and fatigue and monotony, lapses of attention from which the driver must snap himself to execute a panic maneuver to avoid a rear-end collision. The final effect is a re-creation, a vivid and suggestive chronicle of an experience that is both an ordeal and a pleasure.

Representation vs. Expression In reporting our experiences and observations, we often balance two sometimes conflicting impulses: to give an accurate rendering, a faithful account, and to communicate our responses or impressions. The first we call *representational* writing, the second *expressive*. Most writing will mix both elements, although informational writing stresses the former, playing down the writer's subjectivity lest it interfere with accuracy. Bass integrates representation and expression, using close observation and vivid detail to depict the Delta, and subjective, interpretive language to communicate the *experience* of the Delta—especially, what it feels like to drive through on a hot August day. Thus, on the one hand, we have dragonflies buzzing in place over irrigation ditches, red-eared sliders scrambling across sun-baked asphalt, tractors trailing clouds of dust, billboard messages, and the numerically precise accounting for Tamo's schoolchildren (at the same time, these details tell something about the person who notices them). On the other, we have the "contented little strawberry-tasting rumbles," "sullen purple clouds," "an exhilarating mock-October royal blue sky," and cattle that "look like stout china imitations placed out in the fields to break the monotony." The latter outweigh the former, with emotionally loaded adjectives and imaginative comparisons overpowering the neutral language. The essay is less about the Delta than about Bass's response to it.

Using the Second Person   We have several uses for the second-person pronoun *you*. In speech it refers to those whom we are addressing ("Ellen, would *you* please fix me one of your strawberry milkshakes?"). In letters or other communications to specific audiences, it often has the same use. In speech and informal writing, though, *you* may mean something else. Often, it is the *indefinite "you"*—referring to everyone and no one ("*You* can't win 'em all!"). This use is generally frowned on in academic or other formal writing (perhaps because we don't want student writers to become too comfortable).

Writing almost conversationally, Bass exploits both uses of the second person. At first, he uses the indefinite form, in places where a more formal writer might try *one* or even *the traveler*: "Parked under the big oak, *you* can still keep an eye out on the Sonic because it is right across the street." As Bass warms to his story, the indefinite *you* begins to shade into the particular *you*, referring to someone halfway between the reader and the writer: "But on this particular stretch of Highway 65 *you* come out of *your* hypnosis just in time; *you* whip the steering wheel around and pass on the right . . . and then *you* are back up on the road again . . ." Of course, he is telling about an accident that almost befell himself, and *you* could be *I*, but by this time he is using the second person to invite the reader's identification. This identification is further aided by the immediacy of the present tense. Compare: "But on this particular stretch of Highway 65 *I* came out of *my* hypnosis just in time; *I* whipped the steering wheel around and passed on the right . . . and then *I* was back up on the road again." *You* and the present tense occur frequently in travel writing, a form that invites the vicarious participation of armchair travelers.

Unconventional Punctuation   In keeping with the colloquial informality of his essay, Bass takes more liberties than simply speaking directly to his readers. As noted previously, he writes both representationally and expressively, sometimes striving for an accurate depiction of his subject, sometimes communicating his impressions. To accomplish the latter, he stretches the usual rules of punctuation. Consider the more convenient route to Denver:

> . . . the quickest and most efficient path is to jump on the interstate and set the cruise control and rocket out of Jackson through *Monroe Ruston Shreveport Tyler Dallas Fort Worth Wichita Falls AbileneAmarilloRatonPassDenver.*

Notice how differently the list reads with conventional punctuation: "out of Jackson through Monroe, Ruston, Shreveport, Tyler, Dallas, Fort Worth, Wichita Falls, Abilene, Amarillo, and Raton Pass, to Denver." The twelve-item itinerary suggests some of the journey's length, but it falls far short of

Bass' re-creation of a driving marathon, one of those mind-numbing ordeals when we log town after town, until we are fighting fatigue and highway hypnosis, and the towns begin to run together.

In standard informational writing one function of commas is to separate items in a series (such as a list of towns). The object is to isolate each for the reader's attention. If we omit the commas, we eliminate the boundaries between the items. They run together and blur, and this is the effect Bass wants. He is not writing representationally, being faithful to the separate reality of each location. He is writing expressively, re-creating the impressions of a weary motorist.

Paradoxically, even as he departs from the usual conventions of punctuation, Bass exploits our grammatical conditioning. In our understanding of what the presence of certain punctuation accomplishes, we have the basis to appreciate the effect of its absence.

Revision Assignments   Select one of the following revision strategies (or find one of your own) and rewrite Bass's essay. Include a brief statement of your choice and its effect on the arrangement and presentation of detail.

1. Revise Bass's piece as a conventional article for a regional magazine or the Sunday travel section of a newspaper. You should consult examples, but you will probably want to take fewer liberties with subjectivity, fragments, shifts between first and second person, and so on.

2. By using the present tense and alternating between the first and second person, Bass re-creates the experience of driving through the Delta in August; in other words, he writes about a generic and repeatable experience. Using a first-person narrator and the past tense, revise "Shortest Route to the Mountains" as the account of one specific journey.

Writing Assignments

1. In "Shortest Route to the Mountains," Bass does what storytellers have done for thousands of years—uses a story to carry information. Thus, in pondering his motive for writing the essay, we can weigh two possibilities: Bass exploits the Delta as a backdrop for his own actions, or he exploits his actions as a device to present the Delta. So interfused are narration and description, his account of his own movements and his presentation of the region, that we can barely separate them. Employ the same technique to present an area with which you are familiar, following your movement along a route (whether on foot, on a bike, or in a car) to let the reader "see" what the place is like. Part of your objective is to capture a distinct sense of place, to convey a sense of how life is lived there. You want to invoke its spirit and feeling as the sum total of many concrete and often minor details, using the present tense and a first- or second-person narrator (or, like Bass, both).

2. Bass writes: "Going north to the mountains through Lake Providence, Louisiana, is not the fastest route to the mountains, but it is the best. It gives you time to think and to prepare for their beauty. It makes them seem more beautiful when you get there."

Bass purposely follows a more grueling route, in part to reexperience the character of the land but also to intensify his enjoyment of his destination. His essay, then, is also about simple pleasures, about the way we sometimes vary our routines and carefully plan out our experiences so that we get the most out of them. Write about some such routine of your own, explaining the background, discussing the steps you take, and describing the satisfaction you receive.

3. "It is sinfully pleasurable to drive through this part of the country in August with the windows up and the air conditioner on and one of Ellen's milkshakes empty in the little bag in the front seat." Write about an experience that you regard as "sinfully pleasurable," detailing its attractions and the circumstances under which you enjoy it.

The Pleasures of Eating

WENDELL BERRY

Many times, after I have finished a lecture on the decline of American farm- 1
ing and rural life, someone in the audience has asked, "What can city people
do?"

"Eat responsibly," I have usually answered. Of course, I have tried to ex- 2
plain what I meant, but afterwards I have invariably felt that there was more
to be said than I had been able to say. Now I would like to attempt a better
explanation.

I begin with the proposition that eating is an agricultural act. Eating ends 3
the annual drama of the food economy that begins with planting and birth.
Most eaters, however, are no longer aware that this is true. They think of
food as an agricultural product, perhaps, but they do not think of themselves
as participants in agriculture. They think of themselves as "consumers." If
they think beyond that, they recognize that they are passive consumers.
They buy what they want—or what they have been persuaded to want—
within the limits of what they can get. They pay, mostly without protest,
what they are charged. And they ignore certain critical questions about the
quality and the cost of what they are sold: How fresh is it? How pure or clean
is it, how free of dangerous chemicals? How far was it transported, and what
did transportation add to the cost? How much did manufacturing or packaging or advertising add to the cost? When the food product has been "manufactured" or "processed" or "precooked," how has that affected its quality or
nutritional value?

Most urban shoppers would tell you that food is produced on farms. But 4
most of them do not know on what farms, or what kinds of farms, or where
the farms are, or what knowledge or skills are involved in farming. They apparently have little doubt that farms will continue to produce, but they do
not know how or over what obstacles. For them, then, food is pretty much an
abstract idea—something they do not know or imagine—until it appears on
the grocery shelf or on the table.

The specialization of production induces specialization of consumption. 5
Patrons of the entertainment industry, for example, entertain themselves less
and have become more and more passively dependent on commercial suppliers. This is certainly also true of patrons of the food industry, who have
tended more and more to be *mere* consumers—passive, uncritical, and dependent. Indeed, this sort of consumption may be said to be one of the chief
goals of industrial production. The food industrialists have by now persuaded
millions of consumers to prefer food that is already prepared. They will grow,
deliver, and cook your food for you and (just like your mother) beg you to eat
it. That they do not yet offer to insert it, prechewed, into your mouth is only
because they have found no profitable way to do so. We may rest assured
that they would be glad to find such a way. The ideal industrial food consumer would be strapped to a table with a tube running from the food factory

directly into his or her stomach. (Think of the savings, the efficiency, and the effortlessness of such an arrangement!)

Perhaps I exaggerate, but not by much. The industrial eater is, in fact, one who does not know that eating is an agricultural act, who no longer knows or imagines the connections between eating and the land, and who is therefore necessarily passive and uncritical—in short, a victim. When food, in the minds of eaters, is no longer associated with farming and with the land, then the eaters are suffering a kind of cultural amnesia that is misleading and dangerous. The current version of the "dream home" of the future involves "effortless" shopping from a list of available goods on a television monitor and heating precooked food by remote control. Of course, this implies, and indeed depends on, a perfect ignorance of the history of the food that is consumed. It requires that the citizenry should give up their hereditary and sensible aversion to buying a pig in a poke. It wishes to make the selling of pigs in pokes an honorable and glamorous activity. The dreamer in this dream home will perforce know nothing about the kind or quality of this food, or where it came from, or how it was produced and prepared, or what ingredients, additives, and residues it contains. Unless, that is, the dreamer undertakes a close and constant study of the food industry, in which case he or she might as well wake up and play an active and responsible part in the economy of food. 6

There is, then, a politics of food that, like any politics, involves our freedom. We still (sometimes) remember that we cannot be free if our minds and voices are controlled by someone else. But we have neglected to understand that neither can we be free if our food and its sources are controlled by someone else. The condition of the passive consumer of food is not a democratic condition. One reason to eat responsibly is to live free. 7

But, if there is a food politics, there is also a food aesthetics and a food ethics, neither of which is disassociated from politics. Like industrial sex, industrial eating has become a degraded, poor, and paltry thing. Our kitchens and other eating places more and more resemble filling stations, as our homes more and more resemble motels. "Life is not very interesting," we seem to have decided. "Let its satisfactions be minimal, perfunctory, and fast." We hurry through our meals to go to work and hurry through our work in order to "recreate" ourselves in the evenings and on weekends and vacations. And then we hurry, with the greatest possible speed and noise and violence, through our recreation—for what? To eat the billionth hamburger at some fast-food joint hell-bent on increasing the "quality" of our life. And all this is carried out in a remarkable obliviousness of the causes and effects, the possibilities and the purposes of the life of the body in this world. 8

One will find this obliviousness represented in virgin purity in the advertisements of the food industry, in which the food wears as much makeup as the actors. If one gained one's whole knowledge of food—as some presumably do—from these advertisements, one would not know that the various edibles were ever living creatures, or that they all come from the soil, or that they were produced by work. The passive American consumer, sitting down to a meal of pre-prepared or fast food, confronts a platter covered with inert, anonymous substances that have been processed, dyed, breaded, sauced, gravied, ground, pulped, strained, blended, prettified, and sanitized beyond 9 resemblance to any part of any creature that ever lived. The products of nature and agriculture have been made, to all appearances, the products of industry. Both eater and eaten are thus in exile from biological reality. And the result is a kind of solitude, unprecedented in human experience, in which the eater may think of eating as, first, a purely commercial transaction between him and a supplier, and then as a purely appetitive transaction between him and his food.

And this peculiar specialization of the act of eating is, again, of obvious 10 benefit to the food industry, which has good reason to obscure the connection between food and farming. It would not do for the consumer to know that the hamburger she is eating came from a steer that spent much of its life standing deep in its own excrement in a feedlot, helping to pollute the local streams, or that the calf that yielded the veal cutlet on her plate spent its life in a box in which it did not have room to turn around. And, though her sympathy for the coleslaw might be less tender, she should not be encouraged to meditate on the hygienic and biological implications of mile-square fields of cabbage, for vegetables grown in huge monocultures are dependent on toxic chemicals just as animals in close confinement are dependent on antibiotics and other drugs.

The consumer, that is to say, must be kept from discovering that, in the 11 food industry—as in any other industry—the overriding concerns are not quality and health but volume and price. For decades now the entire industrial food economy, from the large farms and feedlots to the chains of fast-food restaurants and supermarkets, has been obsessed with volume. It has relentlessly increased scale in order to increase volume in order (presumably) to reduce costs. But, as scale increases, diversity declines; as diversity declines, so does health; as health declines, the dependence on drugs and chemicals necessarily increases. As capital replaces labor, it does so by substituting machines, drugs, and chemicals for human workers and for the natural health and fertility of the soil. The food is produced by any means or any shortcuts that will increase profits. And the business of the cosmeticians of advertising is to persuade the consumer that food so produced is good, tasty, healthful, and a guarantee of marital fidelity and long life.

It is, then, indeed possible to be liberated from the husbandry and wifery 12 of the old household food economy. But one can thus be liberated only by entering a trap—unless one sees ignorance and helplessness, as many people apparently do, as the signs of privilege. The trap is the ideal of industrialism: a walled city surrounded by valves that let merchandise in but no consciousness out. How does one escape this trap? Only voluntarily, the same way that one went in—by restoring one's consciousness of what is involved in eating, by reclaiming responsibility for one's own part in the food economy. One might begin with Sir Albert Howard's illuminating principle that we should understand "the whole problem of health in soil, plant, animal, and man as one great subject." Eaters, that is, must understand that eating takes place inescapably in the world, that it is inescapably an agricultural act, and that how we eat determines, to a considerable extent, the way the world is used. This is a simple way of describing a relationship that is inexpressibly complex. To eat responsibly is to understand and enact, as far as one can, this complex relationship.

What can one do? Here is a list, probably not definitive:

Participate in food production to the extent that you can. If you have a yard or even just a porch box or a pot in a sunny window, grow something to eat in it. Make a little compost of your kitchen scraps, and use it for fertilizer. Only by growing some food for yourself can you become acquainted with the beautiful energy cycle that revolves from soil to seed to flower to fruit to food to offal to decay, and around again. You will be fully responsible for any food that you grow for yourself, and you will know all about it. You will appreciate it fully, having known it all its life.

Prepare your own food. This means reviving in your own mind and life the arts of kitchen and household. This should enable you to eat more cheaply and give you a measure of "quality control." You will have some reliable knowledge of what has been added to the food you eat.

Learn the origins of the food you buy, and buy the food that is produced closest to your home. The idea that every locality should be, as far as possible, the source of its own food makes several kinds of sense. The locally produced food supply is the most secure, the freshest, and the easiest for local consumers to know about and to influence.

Whenever you can, deal directly with a local farmer, gardener, or orchardist. All the reasons listed for the previous suggestion apply here. In addition, by such dealing, you eliminate the whole pack of merchants, transporters, processors, packagers, and advertisers who thrive at the expense of both producers and consumers.

Learn, in self-defense, as much as you can of the economy and technology of industrial food production. What is added to food that is not food, and what do you pay for these additions?

Learn what is involved in the *best* farming and gardening.

Learn as much as you can, by direct observation and experience if possible, of the life histories of the food species.

The last suggestion seems particularly important to me. Many people are now as much estranged from the lives of domestic plants and animals (except for flowers and dogs and cats) as they are from the lives of the wild ones. This is regrettable, for these domestic creatures are in diverse ways attractive; there is much pleasure in knowing them. And, at their best, farming, animal husbandry, horticulture, and gardening are complex and comely arts; there is much pleasure in knowing them, too.

And it follows that there is great displeasure in knowing about a food economy that degrades and abuses those arts and those plants and animals and the soil from which they come. For anyone who does know something of the modern history of food, eating away from home can be a chore. My own inclination is to eat seafood instead of red meat or poultry when I am traveling. Though I am by no means a vegetarian, I dislike the thought that some animal has been made miserable in order to feed me. If I am going to eat meat, I want it to be from an animal that has lived a pleasant, uncrowded life outdoors, on bountiful pasture, with good water nearby and trees for shade. And I am getting almost as fussy about food plants. I like to eat vegetables and fruits that I know have lived happily and healthily in good soil—not the products of the huge, bechemicaled factory-fields that I have seen, for example, in the Central Valley of California. The industrial farm is said to have been patterned on the factory production line. In practice, it invariably looks more like a concentration camp.

The pleasure of eating should be an *extensive* pleasure, not that of the mere gourmet. People who know the garden in which their vegetables have grown and know that the garden is healthy will remember the beauty of the growing plants, perhaps in the dewy first light of morning when gardens are at their best. Such a memory involves itself with the food and is one of the pleasures of eating. The knowledge of the good health of the garden relieves and frees and comforts the eater. The same goes for eating meat. The thought of the good pasture, and of the calf contentedly grazing, flavors the steak. Some, I know, will think it blood-thirsty or worse to eat a fellow creature you have known all its life. On the contrary, I think, it means that you eat with understanding and gratitude. A significant part of the pleasure in eating is in one's accurate consciousness of the lives and the world from which the food comes. The pleasure of eating, then, may be the best available standard of our health. And this pleasure, I think, is pretty fully available to the urban consumer who will make the necessary effort. 16

I mentioned earlier the politics, aesthetics, and ethics of food. But to speak of the pleasure of eating is to go beyond those categories. Eating with the fullest pleasure—pleasure, that is, that does not depend on ignorance—is perhaps the profoundest enactment of our connection with the world. In this pleasure we experience and celebrate our dependence and our gratitude, for we are living from mystery, from creatures we did not make and powers we cannot comprehend. When I think of the meaning of food, I always remember these lines by the poet William Carlos Williams, which seem to me merely honest: 17

> There is nothing to eat,
>> seek it where you will,
>>> but the body of the Lord.
> The blessed plants
>> and the sea, yield it
>>> to the imagination
> intact.

1992

Profile   "I am eating misery," declares Alice Walker, and spits out her steak (in "Am I Blue"). Whether dining on beef or cauliflower from the local supermarket, Wendell Berry would answer as quickly, "I am eating my freedom," and he justifies his belief in "The Pleasures of Eating." In a series of ringing pronouncements, he wades into America's industrialized system of food production, urging his readers to set aside their ignorance and passivity and recognize "eating as an agricultural act." Contrary to what the average "industrial eater" would like to think, eating is not a purely private matter, something only between oneself, one's pocketbook, and one's palate. Rather, it is a public and political act connecting one with the land and those who work it, the "annual drama of the food economy that begins with planting and birth." By purchasing whatever the food industry offers us, accepting a standard that prizes volume and ease of preparation over quality and health, we forfeit control over a vital part of our lives, and we contribute to the decline of a way of life. Agribusiness, with its "huge, bechemicaled factory-fields," not only is selling us tasteless food saturated with chemical additives and residues, it is driving the small family farm into extinction and depopulating rural communities.

Himself the owner of a small working farm in Kentucky, Berry can take the moral and ecological high ground, practicing what he preaches. While working his own farm, he finds time to write essays on agricultural topics from farming in such unlikely locales as the arid Southwest and the Peruvian Andes, to the problems of soil erosion, water pollution, and general ecological deterioration caused by agribusiness and its overreliance on mechanized farming. His preference is for small-scale farming, for agriculture that preserves the connection between farmer and soil. His aversion is for hired hands driving air-conditioned, stereo-equipped monster tractors around factory-fields. He has even argued for the return of horse-drawn machinery and other labor-intensive changes that would turn back the technological clock (among other modern gadgets, he refuses to use a word processor).

"The Pleasures of Eating" is an argumentative essay with a strenuous design on our understandings. It begins with a clear proposition ("eating is an agricultural act"), defines a problem, explores its nature and consequences, then concludes with a solution, a plan of action for the principled consumer. Refraining from humor or anecdotes, Berry delivers a stern lecture, insisting that eating, like other forms of consumption, is a public, and thus a political and moral, act. He challenges American consumers to abandon their ignorance and indifference, and summons them to a more conscious and responsible life. Many will recoil from such a summons, but Berry addresses the most earnest readers, those who take matters to heart, those who worry about the impact of their behavior on other lives. As for the others, those who place comfort before conscience, they are not his primary audience. They will not listen anyway. Impatient with levity, he means business.

The Limits of Humor   Wendell Berry is every bit as earnest about his subject as Edward Abbey ("Even the Bad Guys Wear White Hats"), but without the sense of humor. Where Abbey softens up his audience by tickling its funny bone, Berry presents a series of angry assertions. But while Abbey is being witty and perverse, he is also being theatrical and outrageous, almost visibly enjoying his outlandish proposals. Some readers will wonder if Abbey is sacrificing truth and accuracy for entertainment. Not so with Berry. From the first sentence he strikes the tone of a physician lecturing a chain-smoker. If Abbey sometimes sacrifices plausibility for humor (alligators in stock ponds!), Berry never relieves his sermon with a moment of levity, never relaxes from his tone of high moral severity.

Each reader will respond differently to Berry's tactic. Some will take him at his word, convinced that the situation is as critical as he claims. Others will dismiss him as a purist, an environmental extremist, someone urging an impractical standard of behavior (not everyone will sympathize with coleslaw and worry about concentration camps for cabbages). And many in between will at least be disturbed by his message, even if they are not prepared to embrace the strenuous life. Whichever way we respond, we recognize his argumentative stance, one that presents the reader with a clear imperative, an obligation to act: Become conscious, change your behavior, or pay the consequences. Such a stance does not worry about making some readers uncomfortable; in their discomfort some may alter their positions.

In persuasive writing, humor signals goodwill and lessens the distance between reader and writer (after all, we are sharing a good laugh). It acknowledges that most of us are grateful for a little entertainment, even as we are being informed and enlightened. It recognizes that many of us do not have the stomach for a straight diet of information and close reasoning. At the same time, unless controlled, humor can upstage the message it is meant to serve. It can degenerate into the type of monologue we are familiar with from late-night talk shows, where the most serious news of the day is reduced to fodder for one-liners. In striking a balance between seriousness and humor, we must consider our subject, the occasion, and the temperament of our audience. A strict, no-nonsense approach can seem cold and off-putting, but it also signals that we mean business, that the issue deserves audience's most serious consideration. By contrast, while humor reassures with the promise of further comic relief, it also may suggest to some that we take our subject lightly.

Pronouns and Coherence   A piece of writing that is *coherent*, that coheres, is one whose parts "cling together." The manner of the clinging varies, from logical connection of ideas, to chronological sequence of actions, to spatial arrangement of details, to transition terms, to patterns of repetition and parallelism in phraseology, and more—in combinations, arrangements, and rhythms. Every time a talented writer composes a new work, he or she finds a new way to achieve coherence. There is no set formula, no mechanical process, no one coherence-mold into which to pour one's material. Each new writing task demands rediscovery of what coherence will mean *here*.

Personal pronouns (*I, you, he, she, it, we, they*) take their meaning from *antecedents* (to go before), from words in earlier sentences and paragraphs. Thus, while nouns signify by themselves, personal pronouns ask the reader to remember their antecedents. At the same time, they are less intrusive than nouns, less insistent, so they can bear greater repetition. Pronouns, then, make a unique contribution to coherence, holding together successive statements with strings of words sharing the same antecedents. Consider Berry's third paragraph:

> I begin with the proposition that eating is an agricultural act. Eating ends the annual drama of the food economy that begins with planting and birth. Most eaters, however, are no longer aware that this is true. *They* think of food as an agricultural product, perhaps, but *they* do not think of themselves as participants in agriculture. *They* think of themselves as "consumers." If *they* think beyond that, *they* recognize that *they* are passive consumers. *They* buy what *they* want—or what *they* have been persuaded to want—within the limits of what *they* can get. *They* pay,

mostly without protest, what *they* are charged. And *they* ignore certain critical questions about the quality and the cost of what *they* are sold: How fresh is *it*? How pure or clean is *it*, how free of dangerous chemicals? How far was *it* transported, and what did transportation add to the cost? How much did manufacturing or packaging or advertising add to the cost? When the food product has been "manufactured" or "processed" or "precooked," how has that affected its quality or nutritional value?

Berry "sticks together" the first two-thirds of his paragraph with a chain of *they*'s, all referring back to "most eaters." This repetition (or what Gertrude Stein called *insistence*) drives home the unenlightenment of passive consumers: They select, they pay, they ignore. The result is a stirring indictment. And then he concludes with a series of questions, the ones industrial eaters never ask, drawing them together by the repetition of *it* (referring to "the quality and cost of what they are sold"). He further reinforces this final coherence by beginning each question with the same word, *how* (a device called *anaphora*).

In revising our own work, then, one useful practice is to circle the pronouns in each paragraph, looking for patterns of repetition and the opportunity to strengthen them.

Writing with Gender   Until recently, custom dictated that the pronoun *he* referred not only to someone masculine but, in some circumstances, to anyone of either gender ("*He*'s a fool who makes *his* doctor *his* heir"). *He*, in other words, was the generic gender pronoun. Now, such use offends many because it suggests that males set the standard for certain universalizing statements, that women are included only secondarily. To avoid such bias, one alternative is to use *he or she*, but this solution can become cumbersome ("*He or she* is a fool who makes *his or her* doctor *his or her* heir"). Another alternative is to use the plural, but it is often too general for our purposes ("*They* are fools who make *their* doctors *their* heirs"). Sometimes we want to refer to that hypothetical individual case, to the unique experience of one lonely individual, to that one fool.

So how do we avoid offensive gender references and enjoy the option of using the singular? We adopt the practice now followed by many professional writers: We use the feminine as well as the masculine pronoun to refer to both genders, as Berry illustrates:

> It would not do for the consumer to know that the hamburger *she* is eating came from a steer that spent much of its life standing deep in its own excrement in a feedlot, helping to pollute local streams, or that the calf that yielded the veal cutlet on *her* plate spent its life in a box in which it did not have room to turn around. And, though *her* sympathy for the coleslaw might be less tender, *she* should not be encouraged to meditate on the hygienic and biological implications of mile-square fields of cabbage . . .

Some writers will use the feminine pronoun exclusively where custom once called for the masculine, while others simply alternate masculine and feminine in alternate paragraphs or sections.

Revision Assignments   Select one of the following strategies and revise "The Pleasures of Eating." Include a brief statement explaining your choice and its effect on the arrangement and presentation of material.

1. "We are a nation of industrial eaters." Beginning with this statement, write a new introduction for Berry's essay (one containing three or four Berry-length paragraphs).

2. To make Berry's argument more accessible to casual readers (say, of a magazine section of a Sunday newspaper), present his case in a question-and-answer format. Write a brief opening to introduce the interviewee and establish the setting; then present Berry's case in a more dramatic, lively fashion.

3. Revise "The Pleasures of Eating" by changing the personality of the speaker or writer. Mellow him out; make him more of a moderate, someone who sympathizes with our desire to avoid drudgery even as he wishes to paint the consequences of making a fetish out of convenience. Berry's essay reads like a sermon to the already converted, or at least to those susceptible to a demanding challenge. Address a less receptive audience, an audience that must be won over, an audience that does not wish to be scolded or asked to do too much.

4. Revise several paragraphs to make them sound more like Edward Abbey or some other more humorous writer. Find laughs in the subject. Call names (creatively). Give outrageous descriptions (deer as rats with antlers). Use ridicule to awaken the reader to consciousness and action.

Writing Assignments

1. Berry accepts as axiomatic that "we cannot be free if our minds and voices are controlled by someone else." Such is the consequence of being passive, of acquiescing while others tell us what we want and need, of allowing others to usurp the right to interpret our needs for us. Write about another area of American (or Canadian, Mexican, Taiwanese) life where you believe people are forfeiting their freedoms by living passive, uninformed, unexamined existences.

2. "Eating is an agricultural act," one that involves us in the lives of many others. By our unconscious styles of consumption, we affect human and nonhuman alike, not to mention undermine our own health. Using Sallie Tisdale's "Shoe and Tell," write a Berry-esque discussion of athletic shoes, another product that Americans consume without thought to the nature of production and distribution. You may personalize the subject, relating your own quests to find good buys (but what about buys that do not exploit those who assemble the product?). Begin with a proposition, describe the American practice of buying shoes or other attire, explain the evils of separating our purchase from a knowledge of the product's origin, discuss the advantages and disadvantages to the consumer, then give a practical answer to the question, "What can I do to purchase shoes and clothing without contributing to the exploitation of others?"

3. Many readers will find Berry to be extremely earnest and intense, making most of us seem frivolous in our attitudes and conduct (notice that he sees the latter as an inevitable product of the former, suggesting that we must take our belief system more seriously). It is probably safe to say that most Americans do not confront life with such an exaggerated sense of responsibility, do not embrace such a strenuous existence. By comparison with Berry, most of us lead relatively unaware, self-indulgent existences, assigning less ponderous significance to our behavior. Using other individuals in your life, private and public, discuss your own approach to life. If, on a scale of one to ten, Berry scores a ten in moral earnestness, where do you fit?

A Mongoose Is Missing

CAROL BLY

> Great men, to be heroes, need our idealization, and what is new in the modern age is
> the refusal to idealize.
>
> —Henry Fairlie in "Too Rich for Heroes"
> *Harper's*, November 1978

> [The cobra] spread out his hood more than ever, and Rikki-tikki saw the spectacle-
> mark on the back of it that looks exactly like the eye part of a hook-and-eye fasten-
> ing. He was afraid for the minute; but it is impossible for a mongoose to stay fright-
> ened for any length of time, and though Rikki-tikki had never met a live cobra
> before, his mother had fed him on dead ones, and he knew that all a grown mon-
> goose's business in life was to fight and eat snakes. . . .
>
> Rikki-tikki had a right to be proud of himself; but he did not grow too proud, and
> he kept that garden as a mongoose should keep it, with tooth and jump and spring
> and bite, till never a cobra dared show its head inside the walls.
>
> —Rudyard Kipling, "Rikki-Tikki Tavi"[1]

At last there is a way in which unsophisticated country people are *less* re-   1
pressed than sophisticated urban people. For over a decade it has been axiomatic that educated urban elements have learned to face their feelings better than small-town people; they use available psychotherapeutic services
with elan; they belong to Group, not American Lutheran Church Women's
Circle; they know the right things to say—such as *we* are not always right and
they always wrong. Their conversations are jeweled with smooth stones like
"You know, when you're that angry at someone, it's usually that very thing
inside yourself that you're *really* angry at." They know all about projection
and association, and usually have a little repertoire of stories illustrating a colleague's lack of individuation. Yet there is one form of major repression of
the 1970s to which psychological sophisticates are more subject than are
Minnesota rural people: it is repression of the ancient, infinitely practical instinct to isolate ignobility from the community.

Nobility itself is a little out of style, like Kipling and more recently Hem-   2
ingway, who dreamed about it. Humankind is a partisan, right-and-wrong-
thinking race, so we don't just peaceably let something slip out of style: we
stomp it on its way. Bloomsbury[2] finished off Kipling ages ago with "O dear,
straight British Empire, best beloved!" and similar sarcasm. Our helping pro-
fessions have developed and proliferated a special set of pejorative language
just for people who try to identify ignobility and then pay attention to it: The

[1] From Kipling's *The Jungle Book* (1894), a collection of animal stories for children taking place in nineteenth-
century India. The hero of this story is Rikki-Tikki-Tavi (pronounced *TAR-vee*), a valiant mongoose who
saves a family from two murderous cobras. (A mongoose is a weasel-like mammal whose speed and agility enable it to kill cobras and other deadly snakes.)

[2] A prominent group of English writers and intellectuals (Virginia Woolf, E. M. Forster, and others) whose influence helped end Rudyard Kipling's reign as England's most popular writer.

best-known words of this language are *judgmental, rigid,* (or *inflexible*), and *punitive.*

In my town, at least, we are still judgmental, rigid, and punitive about bad behavior. We still do the classic American small-town process of slightly isolating anyone who is practicing selfishness at others' expense. We don't ostracize them (we haven't that luxury—sooner or later we shall have to do daily business with them: sell them things, help their kids learn lay-ups, let them fill our teeth, as the case may be); we don't exactly drop them. We see them less.

To a therapy-oriented world this sounds provincial indeed. In fact, it is practical. Immorality is something of a contagion. If cheats and liars associate freely with those trying at some cost to themselves *not* to cheat and lie, the simple result is that the latter won't try so hard in future. Any school headmaster knows enough to write home if someone's son or daughter "is keeping undesirable company." We edge away, in our towns, we do not keep company, with people committing embezzlement, adultery, and crooked figuring of hours spent in repair work.

We edge away from a plumber who tells Mrs. Hofstad, "I have to go back to town to get a part for that," and then takes the pickup over to Mrs. Beske's house, puts in a half hour there, and then explains to her, "We're going to have to get a gasket for that," and then returns to Mrs. Hofstad's, and subsequently charges both women for all the time involved. We spread the word about such behavior in a rigid, judging, and punitive way: that kind of behavior is bad.

If moral division is natural to our species at this era of our evolution, then we not only need to do it, but we simply will do it. When we do it well, it will be our genius for discernment; when we do it poorly, we will be wrongheaded and name callers—but for better or worse that faculty is at work. If psychological fashion declares dividing good from bad to be archaic, we are likely to be daunted and try to repress the instinct. After all, the psychological communities are daunting to most of us: they are better-dressed and more authoritative and they know our sexual secrets and God knows what all else besides. They have offices with true slimers[3] outside the doors who say things like "Doctor will see you now." If we have anything of the social climber in us we are likely to believe them when they say right and wrong are archaic concepts; we too may start using expressions like "irresponsible" instead of "cruel" or "crooked." We may repress right and wrong. So down into the unconscious it goes. And, to the parent who had abandoned his or her five children in favor of a fulfilling mid-life crisis, we smile cordially and ask, "Are you coping? Are you all right?"

If the instinct to judge and isolate has gone down into the unconscious, where will it show up? It is useful to define *isolating.* To isolate someone is to refuse to participate in his destiny, and to refuse to take his needs to heart. Then the questions to ask are: Whose destiny do Americans tend to refuse to participate in? And whose needs do we proverbially fail to take to heart?

We are a money-making culture, with a minor in recreational sex—to put us in our worst light. People who do not make money and who do not

[3] Presumably, those who slime.

practice recreational sex include children, the aged, and the dying. Those whose destiny we do not participate in enough are children, the aged, and the dying. We are famous, in everyone's sociology, for not taking their needs to heart—but there is something worse about it: not only do we not take their needs to heart, but we practice behavior modification on all three groups. They are the subjects of our experimentation. However harmless the experimentation, being a subject is still being a subject. It is as if the coarsest kind of vengeance were working itself out in our unconscious: The children, the old, the dying fail us as colleagues in money-making and recreational sex; we retaliate by making them lab subjects, not human beings.

Sometimes this unconscious hostility is practiced only as negligence of their best interests. For example, as a society we have done very little to cut down children's television-watching, although an appalling relationship has been established between TV and dyslexia in male children. TV (as opposed to film screen) disallows a certain normal eye-muscle response, so a child watching a lot of TV is engaging for the first time in physiological history in stationing the eye. A result is dyslexia. Two very recent reports which point out our responsibility in this new crisis are *The TV Report* by Robert W. Morse, Regional Religious Educational Coordinators of the Episcopal Church, 815 Second Avenue, New York, N.Y. 10007; and Marshall McLuhan's speech on KSJB (Minnesota Public Radio), November 18, 1978, available on cassette from Minnesota Public Radio, 400 Sibley Street, St. Paul, Minnesota 55101. Our unconscious hostility, in this case idly landing on the children, explains why we allow TV watching to continue in homes where there are small children. Indeed, we have brought TV into our schools.

I think we would be on a kinder course if we criticized openly those who threaten us. The 1960s produced a new permissive attitude toward crimes of all kinds, and it produced the most disturbing trend in children's books in a long time. A new genre of children's picture book appeared, in which death was the subject, and the drawings were large and spooky, and in the end the protagonist died with a lot of affected psycho-slime attached. In one book, the man gave away his heart and his mind and his other vital parts until he was all given away. It seemed like such a touching book, so sensitive, so marvelously taking children at their intuitive, able-to-cope-with-serious-things level—until you finished reading it and realized it was simply trendy sadism. The children listening directly experienced the horrors, in aid of nothing in particular. These books all had minimal plots, and a spacy sort of Marin County Weltanschauung[4] about them. How very different their "sensitivity" is from the pure, straight affection of Kipling's calling his readers Best Beloved on the one hand and killing off both cobras, without any nonsense. It is an act of hostility to pretend to tell a story and then not supply a plot. It takes energy, though, to write a plot for children. Perhaps Kipling's yarn about Rikki-tikki-tavi is so thoroughgoing a story because the author didn't waste energy suppressing a natural dislike of cobras. He didn't tell himself that

[4] Marin County—an affluent community just north of San Francisco famous for its sophisticated trendiness and where psychological therapy has been described as "a light industry." *Weltanschauung*—world view (German).

cobras need understanding, perhaps therapy, even. E. B. White—also a generous plotter, whose psychology has no slickness—never suggests to children that Templeton the rat is "fulfilling himself."[5] He suggests to children that Templeton the rat has a revolting, abysmally selfish personality and never does anything decent unless bribed to the barn roof. The great children's writers, such as Kipling, Rumer Godden, E. Nesbit, E. B. White, and Ted Hughes, know for one thing that an open battle between good and bad is the birthplace of humor.

It takes energy to suppress a natural dislike of adultery and robbery, avarice and treachery. All this open-mindedness! And such strictures it lays on us: you must hate the sin, but love the sinner! That particular piece of medieval Christianity has been strangely resurrected by current psychology; it is tottering about like something from a Regensburg lab[6] in the horror movies. Whoever heard of hating snakebites and loving cobras? 11

If we continue to suppress judgment, rigidity, and punitiveness, wrongdoing will thunder closer and closer to the center of civilization. Then there will be rage about it; more books will be written about lying in high places, surprising corruptions, amazing treachery unsuspected for decades, and if society itself can be said to feel self-hatred it will feel it more and more, but it will be an ever more unconscious sort of shimmering, unclear hatred, hard to identify. And in this thunder of greed and fear, the children, the sick, and the old will fly off into something like total psychic isolation, like people flung out into space at night. Since good and bad will be out of style, we will fail children by not reading them literature about courageous mongooses. In fact, we are already failing our children that way. 12

1979

Profile   In her *Letters From the Country* Carol Bly writes from the perspective of small-town America, or the "lost Swede towns" of Minnesota, as one American novelist described them. In particular, she confronts the split "between Middle America and educated or enlightened America." This division opposes two sets of values, two ways of confronting life, each antagonistic to the other and neither without its limitations. Thus, Bly can regret the emotional restraint of her fellow townspeople, reflected in their tame amusements and their subdued responses to tragedy, because she believes that feeling strengthens, not weakens. On the other hand, she agrees with them that "the soul cannot live on fun alone." As for "educated and enlightened America," with its condescending attitude toward country ways, Bly points to its loss of a communal sense and the resulting disintegration of the cities. "Educated urban elements," with their fashionable enthusiasms and trendy cynicisms, have too many troubles of their own to turn up their noses at small-town America.

In her essay Bly examines trends in children's literature as a window on American ethical attitudes. Her point of reference is Rudyard Kipling's neglected classic, "Rikki-Tikki-Tavi," a story of good and evil in which a

---

[5] The reference, of course, is to White's children's classic, *Charlotte's Web* (1952), in which the clever and kindhearted spider Charlotte must outwit the selfish rat Templeton to save the life of Wilbur the pig.

[6] An ancient city in southeastern Germany. In this case, a stock movie setting.

fearless mongoose saves a human family from the murderous designs of a pair of cobras. The mongoose is noble and self-sacrificing, the cobras unrelentingly evil. There is only one way to save the family; the cobras will not move out of the neighborhood. By contrast, current stories—in Bly's opinion—drip with "sensitivity" and "psycho-slime," and often lack plots because they sidestep the confrontation of good and evil, of socially acceptable and socially unacceptable behavior.

Given Bly's assumptions, her strenuous commitment to community-preserving values, we can appreciate her tone. She assumes the role of an indignant public defender, someone justifiably angry with the attitudes that erode public consensus. Thus, she pulls no punches, displaying the clear sense of right and wrong that she endorses, using emotionally freighted language ("slimers," "psycho-slime"). Like Wendell Berry's ("The Pleasures of Eating"), Bly's tone will disturb some readers, especially those who resist summonses to strenuous action. Others, though, even those who suspect that she is oversimplifying complex behavioral issues, will at least sympathize with her effort to reaffirm human interconnectedness. We are in one another's lives, she would say, whether we like it or not, and by our choice of conduct we help or harm one another. We have an investment in one another, an investment in upholding one another's "nobility."

Writing About Values   To write about values—about our moral principles and standards—is often to write to the already converted. If we wish to persuade, to move our readers to a particular course of action, our best hope is to appeal to dormant, shared values from which they might have lapsed. Usually, though, all we can do is define our position and signal that we are of goodwill. The reason, of course, lies in the nature of value systems themselves, systems that rely upon debatable assumptions, all-but-unprovable beliefs about human nature and its needs.

Because opinions on right behavior are so unsettled, we are, if only for practical purposes, entitled to begin with our assumptions in place. Our only obligation is to make them clear and then to be consistent in applying them. Carol Bly, writing from the vantage point of small-town life and remarking on the contemporary phobia of being "judgmental," does both.

Bly begins with the assumption that human beings are social creatures. And as social creatures, we have evolved time-tested and community-preserving moral codes, codes that reinforce socially constructive behavior, codes that are intelligible or knowable. "Humankind is a partisan, right-and-wrong thinking race," something not forgotten in the country where people continue to be "judgmental, rigid, and punitive about bad behavior." It is our instinct, Bly believes, to define terms like *right* and *wrong*, *nobility*, and *ignobility*, and to censure those "practicing selfishness at someone else's expense." Caring citizens recognize an active obligation to uphold this code by making value judgments and isolating wrongdoers.

The current threat to the code comes from "sophisticated urban people," those who scorn "archaic" notions of right and wrong and, in their avoidance of moral censure, have forgotten "the ancient, infinitely practical instinct to isolate ignobility from the community." One piece of evidence rests in the new taste in children's literature. In the "therapy-oriented" world people do not censure immorality (like cheating and lying), so there is no social reinforcement of honesty, resulting in moral chaos and social disintegration. In the country (or at least in Bly's small Minnesota town), dishonesty is remarked and punished, usually by partial ostracism.

If being judgmental, though, is the duty of socially concerned citizens, it requires judgment in the best sense: "When we do it well, it will be our genius for discernment; when we do it poorly, we will be wrong-headed and name callers." Being effective, then, requires more than an instinct to preserve the community; it requires a "genius for discernment." Applying values, in other words, requires wisdom and experience.

Transitions and Digressions   Bly's essay develops a clear theme: what she perceives to be the contemporary reluctance to "isolate ignobility from the community," and the aversion to moral evaluation. In small-town America, such evaluation continues, as it does in the best children's literature. In small towns neighbors edge away from those practicing selfishness at others' expense, and in the better children's books evil is clearly identified and confronted. "Moral division is natural to our species," insists Bly, and our instinct is to isolate wrongdoers, but the psychological community represses that community-preserving instinct, at least in the cities.

So far so good. Whether we agree with her or not, we can recognize Bly's assumptions and follow her reasoning, at least for the first six paragraphs. But in paragraphs 7–9, she seems to wander off the main track, using as a point of departure the idea of isolation:

> If the instinct to judge and isolate has gone down into the unconscious, where will it show up? It is useful to define *isolating*. To isolate someone is to refuse to participate in his destiny, and to refuse to take his needs to heart. Then the questions to ask are: Whose destiny do Americans tend to refuse to participate in? And whose needs do we proverbially fail to take to heart?
>
> We are a money-making culture, with a minor in recreational sex—to put us in our worst light. People who do not make money and who do not practice recreational sex include children, the aged, and the dying. Those whose destiny we do not participate in enough are children, the aged, and the dying. We are famous, in everyone's sociology, for not taking their needs to heart . . .

Then Bly is off into the neglect of children, especially the failure to limit their television viewing and the resultant dyslexia in male children. Not until paragraph 10 is she back on track:

> I think we would be on a kinder course if we criticized openly those who threaten us. The 1960s produced a new permissive attitude toward crimes of all kinds, and it produced the most disturbing trend in children's books in a long time. . . .

Some readers will be comfortable with Bly's digression, accepting her use of isolation as a transition point: If we have repressed the instinct to isolate wrongdoers, then it will surface elsewhere, in this case, the "isolation" of children, the aged, and the dying. This enables Bly to introduce her views on our cultural neglect of children and the elderly, which could be the subject of another essay. Others, though, will find this transition a stretch and her reasoning thin (if we can't censure wrongdoers, we will take it out on the dying?).

Mild digressions, briefly addressing tangential issues, can suggest that our topic is a large and complex one, one with innumerable applications—but only if they are convincingly introduced. If they are not, we appear to have become sidetracked, and we arouse the suspicion that we are not in control of our discussion, especially if a digression occupies three paragraphs of a twelve-paragraph essay. If we omit paragraphs 7–9, we will improve the unity, coherence, and emphasis of "A Mongoose Is Missing"—unity because the essay will then restrict itself to the issue of identifying and isolating ignobility, coherence because the line of development will be unbroken, and emphasis because nothing will interrupt our concentration on the main point.

Revision Assignments   Select one of the following strategies and revise "A Mongoose Is Missing." Include a brief statement explaining your choice and its effect on the arrangement and presentation of material.

1. Between digression and repetition, the latter sometimes for emphasis, Bly stretches a simple point to a dozen paragraphs. Tighten her discussion into a six-paragraph essay, preserving as much emphasis as possible.

2. Bly's essay follows a general-to-specifics organization. Reverse this pattern so that it begins with the specific: "In my small town in Minnesota, we edge away from a plumber who . . ." Write the first three paragraphs, then give a brief outline of the remainder.

Writing Assignments

1. Among "educated urban elements . . . [n]obility itself is out of style," observes Bly. No self-respecting city dweller would be so unsophisticated as to pass judgment on someone "practicing selfishness at others' expense." Do you agree with Bly's assessment? Is she being too simplistic, or does she have a point? Do you see areas of American life where you believe we are too tolerant of antisocial behavior? Is Bly calling for an era of responsible community involvement, or inviting one of rigidity and intolerance? Use examples from your own observations and experience to support or refute Bly's position.

2. Writing as a member of "the therapy crowd," challenge Bly's argument. Bly, after all, is writing about small, homogeneous communities, small towns where "everyone knows everyone else" and is thus susceptible to social pressure, not to mention where values are widely shared. What are some of the problems of trying to implement Bly's plan in large cities with mixed populations and almost total anonymity? And what are some of the prospects for success?

3. In "The Tucson Zoo," Lewis Thomas raises the possibility that human beings are genetically coded for social cooperation. Carol Bly makes a similar suggestion ("moral division," or differentiation between right and wrong, "is natural to our species at this stage in our evolution"). Evaluate their two arguments; then state your own conclusions, drawing on your own experience and observations for support.

Think About It

FRANK CONROY

When I was sixteen I worked selling hotdogs at a stand in the Fourteenth   1
Street subway station in New York City, one level above the trains and one
below the street, where the crowds continually flowed back and forth. I
worked with three Puerto Rican men who could not speak English. I had no
Spanish, and although we understood each other well with regard to the tasks
at hand, sensing and adjusting to each other's body movements in the extremely confined space in which we operated, I felt isolated with no one to
talk to. On my break I came out from behind the counter and passed the
time with two old black men who ran a shoeshine stand in a dark corner of
the corridor. It was a poor location, half hidden by columns, and they didn't
have much business. I would sit with my back against the wall while they
stood or moved around their ancient elevated stand, talking to each other or
to me, but always staring into the distance as they did so.

As the weeks went by I realized that they never looked at anything in   2
their immediate vicinity—not at me or their stand or anybody who might
come within ten or fifteen feet. They did not look at approaching customers
once they were inside the perimeter. Save for the instant it took to discern
the color of the shoes, they did not even look at what they were doing while
they worked, but rubbed in polish, brushed, and buffed by feel while looking
over their shoulders, into the distance, as if awaiting the arrival of an important person. Of course there wasn't all that much distance in the underground station, but their behavior was so focused and consistent they seemed
somehow to transcend the physical. A powerful mood was created, and I
came almost to believe that these men could see through walls, through gird-
ers, and around corners to whatever hyperspace it was where whoever it was
they were waiting and watching for would finally emerge. Their scattered
talk was hip, elliptical, and hinted at mysteries beyond my white boy's ken,
but it was the staring off, the long, steady staring off, that had me hypnotized. I left for a better job, with handshakes from both of them, without understanding what I had seen.

Perhaps ten years later, after playing jazz with black musicians in various   3
Harlem clubs, hanging out uptown with a few young artists and intellectuals,
I began to learn from them something of the extraordinarily varied and complex riffs[1] and rituals embraced by different people to help themselves get
through life in the ghetto. Fantasy of all kinds—from playful to dangerous—
was in the very air of Harlem. It was the spice of uptown life.

Only then did I understand the two shoeshine men. They were trapped   4
in a demeaning situation in a dark corner in an underground corridor in a
filthy subway system. Their continuous staring off was a kind of statement, a
kind of dance. Our bodies are here, went the statement, but our souls are receiving nourishment from distance sources only we can see. They were

[1]A short rhythmic phrase, especially one used in improvisations. Here, of course, the term is used as a figure
of speech.

powerful magic dancers, sorcerers almost, and thirty-five years later I can still feel the pressure of their spell.

The light bulb may appear over your head, is what I'm saying, but it may be a while before it actually goes on. Early in my attempts to learn jazz piano, I used to listen to recordings of a fine player named Red Garland, whose music I admired. I couldn't quite figure out what he was doing with his left hand, however; the chords eluded me. I went uptown to an obscure club where he was playing with his trio, caught him on his break, and simply asked him. "Sixths," he said cheerfully. And then he went away.

I didn't know what to make of it. The basic chord is the seventh, which comes in various configurations, but it is what it is. I was a self-taught pianist, pretty shaky on theory and harmony, and when he said sixths I kept trying to fit the information into what I already knew, and it didn't fit. But it stuck in my mind—a tantalizing mystery.

A couple of years later, when I began playing with a bass player, I discovered more or less by accident that if the bass played the root and I played a sixth based on the fifth note of the scale, a very interesting chord involving both instruments emerged. Ordinarily, I suppose I would have skipped over the matter and not paid much attention, but I remembered Garland's remark and so I stopped and spent a week or two working out the voicings, and greatly strengthened my foundations as a player. I had remembered what I hadn't understood, you might say, until my life caught up with the information and the light bulb went on.

I remember another, more complicated example from my sophomore year at a small liberal-arts college outside Philadelphia. I seemed never to be able to get up in time for breakfast in the dining hall. I would get coffee and a doughnut in the Coop instead—a basement area with about a dozen small tables where students could get something to eat at odd hours. Several mornings in a row I noticed a strange man sitting by himself with a cup of coffee. He was in his eighties, perhaps, and sat straight in his chair with very little extraneous movement. I guessed he was some sort of distinguished visitor to the college who had decided to put in some time at a student hangout. But no one ever sat with him. One morning I approached his table and asked if I could join him.

"Certainly," he said, "please do." He had perhaps the clearest eyes I had ever seen, like blue ice, and to be held in the their steady gaze was not, at first, an entirely comfortable experience. His eyes gave nothing away about himself while at the same time creating in me the eerie impression that he was looking directly into my soul. He asked a few quick questions, as if to put me at my ease, and we fell into conversation. He was William O. Douglas from the Supreme Court, and when he saw how startled I was he said, "Call me Bill. Now tell me what you're studying and why you get up so late in the morning." Thus began a series of talks that stretched over many weeks. The fact that I was an ignorant sophomore with literary pretensions who knew nothing about the law didn't seem to bother him. We talked about everything from Shakespeare to the possibility of life on other planets. One day I mentioned that I was going to have dinner with Judge Learned Hand. I explained that Hand was my girlfriend's grandfather. Douglas nodded, but I could tell he was surprised at the coincidence of my knowing the chief judge of the most important court in the country save the Supreme Court itself. After fifty years on the bench Judge Hand had become a famous man, both in and out of legal circles—a living legend, to his own dismay. "Tell him hello and give him my best regards," Douglas said.

Learned Hand, in his eighties, was a short, barrel-chested man with a large, square head, huge, thick, bristling eyebrows, and soft brown eyes. He radiated energy and would sometimes bark out remarks or questions in the living room as if he were in court. His humor was sharp, but often leavened with a touch of self-mockery. When something caught his funny bone he would burst out with explosive laughter—the laughter of a man who enjoyed laughing. He had a large repertoire of dramatic expressions involving the use of his eyebrows—very useful, he told me conspiratorially, when looking down on things from behind the bench. (The court stenographer could not record the movement of his eyebrows.) When I told him I'd been talking to William O. Douglas, they first shot up in exaggerated surprise, and then lowered and moved forward in a glower. [10]

"*Justice* William O. Douglas, young man," he admonished. "Justice Douglas, if you please." About the Supreme Court in general, Hand insisted on a tone of profound respect. Little did I know that in private correspondence he had referred to the Court as "The Blessed Saints, Cherubim and Seraphim," "The Jolly Boys," "The Nine Tin Jesuses," "The Nine Blameless Ethiopians," and my particular favorite, "The Nine Blessed Chalices of the Sacred Effluvium." [11]

Hand was badly stooped and had a lot of pain in his lower back. Martinis helped, but his strict Yankee wife approved of only one before dinner. It was my job to make the second and somehow slip it to him. If the pain was particularly acute he would get out of his chair and lie flat on the rug, still talking, and finish his point without missing a beat. He flattered me by asking for my impression of Justice Douglas, instructed me to convey his warmest regards, and then began talking about the Dennis case, which he described as a particularly tricky and difficult case involving the prosecution of eleven leaders of the Communist party. He had just started in on the First Amendment and free speech when we were called in to dinner. [12]

William O. Douglas loved the outdoors with a passion, and we fell into the habit of having coffee in the Coop and then strolling under trees down toward the duck pond. About the Dennis case, he said something to this effect: "Eleven Communists arrested by the government. Up to no good, said the government; dangerous people, violent overthrow, etc. First Amendment, said the defense, freedom of speech, etc." Douglas stopped walking. "Clear and present danger." [13]

"What?" I asked. He often talked in a telegraphic manner, and one was expected to keep up with him. It was sometimes like listening to a man thinking out loud. [14]

"Clear and present danger," he said. "That was the issue. Did they constitute a clear and present danger? I don't think so. I think everybody took the language pretty far in Dennis." He began walking, striding along quickly. Again, one was expected to keep up with him. "The FBI was all over them. Phones tapped, constant surveillance. How could it be clear and present [15] danger with the FBI watching every move they made? That's a ginkgo," he said suddenly, pointing at a tree. "A beauty. You don't see those every day. Ask Hand about clear and present danger."

I was in fact reluctant to do so. Douglas's argument seemed to me to be crushing—the last word, really—and I didn't want to embarrass Judge Hand. But back in the living room, on the second martini, the old man asked about Douglas. I sort of scratched my nose and recapitulated the conversation by the ginkgo tree.

"What?" Hand shouted. "Speak up, sir, for heaven's sake."

"He said the FBI was watching them all the time so there couldn't be a clear and present danger," I blurted out, blushing as I said it.

A terrible silence filled the room. Hand's eyebrows writhed on his face like two huge caterpillars. He leaned forward in the wing chair, his face settling, finally, into a grim expression. "I am astonished," he said softly, his eyes holding mine, "at Justice Douglas's newfound faith in the Federal Bureau of Investigation." His big, granite head moved even closer to mine, until I could smell the martini. "I had understood him to consider it a politically corrupt, incompetent organization, directed by a power-crazed lunatic.[2] I realized I had been holding my breath throughout all this, and as I relaxed, I saw the faintest trace of a smile cross Hand's face. Things are sometimes more complicated than they first appear, his smile seemed to say. The old man leaned back. "The proximity of the danger is something to think about. Ask him about that. See what he says."

I chewed the matter over as I returned to campus. Hand had pointed out some of Douglas's language about the FBI from other sources that seemed to bear out his point. I thought about the words "clear and present danger," and the fact that if you looked at them closely they might not be as simple as they had first appeared. What degree of danger? Did the word "present" allude to the proximity of the danger, or just the fact that the danger was there at all—that it wasn't an anticipated danger? Were there other hidden factors these great men were weighing of which I was unaware?

But Douglas was gone, back to Washington. (The writer in me is tempted to create a scene here—to invent one for dramatic purposes—but of course I can't do that.) My brief time as a messenger boy was over, and I felt a certain frustration, as if, with a few more exchanges, the matter of *Dennis vs. United States* might have been resolved to my satisfaction. They'd left me high and dry. But, of course, it is precisely because the matter did not resolve that has caused me to think about it, off and on, all these years. "The Constitution," Hand used to say to me flatly, "is a piece of paper. The Bill of Rights is a piece of paper." It was many years before I understood what he meant. Documents alone do not keep democracy alive, nor maintain the state of law. There is no particular safety in them. Living men and women, generation after generation, must continually remake democracy and the law, and that involves an ongoing state of tension between the past and the present which will never completely resolve.

[2]A reference, of course, to J. Edgar Hoover, Director of the FBI from 1924 until his death in 1972.

Education doesn't end until life ends, because you never know when you're going to understand something you hadn't understood before. For me, the magic dance of the shoeshine men was the kind of experience in which understanding came with a kind of click, a resolving kind of click. The same with the experience at the piano. What happened with Justice Douglas and Judge Hand was different, and makes the point that understanding does not always mean resolution. Indeed, in our intellectual lives, our creative lives, it is perhaps those problems that will never resolve that rightly claim the lion's share of our energies. The physical body exists in a constant state of tension as it maintains homeostasis,[3] and so too does the active mind embrace the tension of never being certain, never being absolutely sure, never being done, as it engages the world. That is our special fate, our inexpressibly valuable condition.

1988

Profile   "Think About It" is a personal essay in the vein of Orwell's "Shooting an Elephant," Lewis Thomas's "Tucson Zoo," and Alice Walker's "Am I Blue?" But Orwell, Thomas, and Walker are interested in telling us where they've gotten, Conroy in how we can get there. The first three want to disclose specific insights: what they've learned respectively about the mutually corrupting effects of colonialism, the possibility that we humans are coded for social cooperation, and the rights of "nonhuman animals." Conroy wants to explore how we arrive at such understandings, especially those beginning in puzzlement and taking years to resolve.

Being less interested in specific insights than in the process leading to them, Conroy develops his essay in three parts: the episodes about the shoeshine men and Red Garland, the "more complicated example" involving William O. Douglas and Learned Hand, and the conclusion. The first part introduces his insight, the longer second part refines it, and the conclusion discusses its significance.

After Conroy resolves the mysteries of the shoeshine men and Red Garland's sixths, he makes his relatively simple point about delayed understandings: "I had remembered what I hadn't understood, you might say, until my life caught up with the information and the light bulb went on." So why doesn't he write a tidy paragraph explaining the value of his insight? Instead, he uses his first two experiences as a prologue to a much more complicated one. Thus, he sets the stage by introducing the two judicial contestants, describes them in detail, and meticulously records their utterances. As useful as his insight had been, he had come to premature closure. He had decided, implicitly, that life hands us two kinds of problems: those we solve right away and those that take longer. Thus, when Hand leaves him with an enigmatic pronouncement—("The Constitution . . . is a piece of paper")—he seems to be dealing again with the second kind. Give him some time, even years, and he will puzzle it out, and he does:

> Documents alone do not keep democracy alive, nor maintain the state of law. There is no particular safety in them. Living men and women, generation after

[3] "The ability or tendency of an organism or a cell to maintain internal equilibrium by adjusting its physiological processes." —*American Heritage Dictionary*, 3rd ed.

generation, must continually remake democracy and the law, and that involves an ongoing state of tension between the past and the present which will never completely resolve.

The law, then, is never fully resolved, but is in a continually dynamic state as successive generations attempt to define it. The same is true of our best personal understandings: We never reach a state of complete and final enlightenment.

Sometimes, if only after years, we close the case on certain issues, as Conroy did with "the magic dance of the shoeshine men" and the riddle of sixths, or even Hand's point about the unending process of unveiling the law. And so we get the inspirational opening sentiment of the last paragraph: "Education doesn't end until life ends, because you never know when you're going to understand something you hadn't understood before." But some of our understandings are like the law itself. Hand had added a crucial amendment to his insight: "that understanding does not always mean resolution." And it is the problems we never solve that may stimulate our deepest thinking and our best work. Living with uncertainty is the price of leading an active mental life: "That is our special fate, our inexpressibly valuable condition."

Loose vs. Periodic Sentences   The average sentence opens with a main clause, followed by modifying elements, like this one. Such a sentence, termed a *loose* sentence, most often sequences information by moving from general to particular, with the opening main clause making a relatively broad statement that the trailing modifiers then narrow by description, or illustration, or some other form of commentary:

> *I left for a better job*, with handshakes from both of them, without understanding what I had seen.

> *He began walking*, striding along quickly.

> *His humor was sharp*, often leavened with a touch of self-mockery.

> *He leaned forward in the wing chair*, his face settling, finally, in a grim expression.

> *Education doesn't end until life ends*, because you never know when you're going to understand something you hadn't understood before.

In each case the additional detail adds precision and concreteness to the opening statement. More is less, the supplementary material limiting the range of the opening clause, narrowing its focus. Read without the trailing modifiers, each main clause remains bare ("He began walking"), even meaningless (why doesn't education end until life ends?). We might say that often the main clause only makes a promise, which the trailing detail then keeps.

Another kind of structure, the *periodic* sentence, sequences information in the opposite manner, beginning with qualifying details and postponing the main clause. Since the principal structural work of a sentence is completed in the main clause (or clauses), a periodic sentence creates suspense while suggesting that the central statement rests upon prefatory details or conditions. The opening qualifications, in other words, lay the groundwork for the main statement, which may otherwise be meaningless or irrelevant. In modern American prose periodic sentences appear much less frequently than loose sentences, but like any other tools, they are especially suited for certain kinds of work, as Conroy illustrates in the first section of his essay:

> Perhaps ten years later, after playing jazz with black musicians in various Harlem clubs, hanging out uptown with a few young artists and intellectuals, *I began to learn from them something of the extraordinarily varied and complex riffs and rituals embraced by different people to help themselves get through life in the ghetto.*

> A couple of years later, when I began playing with a bass player, *I discovered more or less by accident that if the bass played the root and I played a sixth based on the fifth note of the scale, a very interesting chord involving both instruments emerged.*

And earlier in his essay, Conroy uses a similar structure to delay the second main clause of a sentence:

> *I had no Spanish,* and although we understood each other well with regard to the tasks at hand, sensing and adjusting to each other's body movements in the extremely confined space in which we operated, *I felt isolated with no one to talk to.*

Given the subject of Conroy's essay—the postponement of understanding, the period of additional living that must elapse before experience catches up with knowledge—the periodic structure seems especially apt. As one astute observer remarked, "Attention to *how to say* helps writers find *what to say*," and vice-versa.

Revision Assignments   Select one of the following strategies and revise "Think About It." Include a brief statement explaining your choice of strategy and its effect on the arrangement and presentation of material.

1. The essay moves *inductively*, from particulars to generality, from anecdote to interpretation, from evidence to conclusion. Compose a deductive opener for the essay, beginning with a good thesis statement (the point you wish to make), and then present the evidence (personal experience). You may also do this in two parts as Conroy did (two simple experiences, conclusion; one complex experience, expanded conclusion). Or, you may begin with your point, give all three examples, then expand on your point.

2. Conroy could have reduced the debate between Douglas and Hand to the arguments themselves. Instead, he treats the combatants as if they were characters in a novel, recording their settings, their appearances, their gestures, their precise words. What does he accomplish with this approach? To answer, reduce paragraphs 8–21 down to the bare basics, being as economical as Conroy was in relating the Red Garland anecdote. How does the essay then read?

Writing Assignments

1. "Education doesn't end until life ends, because you never know when you're going to understand something you hadn't understood before." Discuss at least one such event, or series of events, in your own life when

your experience "caught up with the information and the light bulb went on." Perhaps it was a puzzling behavior that took you weeks, months, or perhaps years to understand, or a piece of advice that at first seemed pointless, abstract, but that later made sense in light of your experience. As a child perhaps you observed puzzling adult behavior that you did not understand until you had yourself become an adult.

2. "The light bulb may appear over your head, is what I'm saying, but it may be a while before it actually goes on." Write about such a light bulb over your own head, something you have experienced and not yet understood but that you feel needs resolution. Your goal here will be to capture what you understand to be the relevant circumstances.

3. Compare and contrast Frank Conroy's "Think About It" with Alan Dershowitz's "Shouting 'Fire!'" Both deal with First Amendment cases involving Supreme Court decisions (*Schenck v. United States* and *Dennis v. United States*). Given what you know of the cases from reading these two essays, or even from doing some outside research, discuss the issues, perhaps relating them to some current First Amendment controversy, such as the struggle to limit the rights of anti-abortion protesters to demonstrate before abortion clinics or the proposal to place legal limitations on the amount of violence in movies and television programs (see Lewis Lapham's "Burnt Offerings").

Shouting "Fire!"

ALAN M. DERSHOWITZ

When the Reverend Jerry Falwell learned that the Supreme Court had re- 1
versed his $200,000 judgment against *Hustler* magazine for emotional distress
that he had suffered from an outrageous parody, his response was typical of
those who seek to censor speech: "Just as no person may scream 'Fire!' in a
crowded theater when there is no fire, and find cover under the First Amendment,[1] likewise, no sleazy merchant like Larry Flynt should be able to use
the First Amendment as an excuse for maliciously and dishonestly attacking
public figures, as he has so often done."

Justice Oliver Wendell Holmes's classic example of unprotected 2
speech—falsely shouting "Fire!" in a crowded theater—has been invoked so
often, by so many people, in such diverse contexts, that it has become part of
our national folk language. It has even appeared—most appropriately—in the
theater: in Tom Stoppard's play *Rosencrantz and Guildenstern Are Dead* a character shouts at the audience, "Fire!" He then quickly explains: "It's all
right—I'm demonstrating the misuse of free speech." Shouting "Fire!" in
the theater may well be the only jurisprudential analogy that has assumed
the status of folk argument. A prominent historian recently characterized it as
"the most brilliantly persuasive expression that ever came from Holmes'
pen." But in spite of its hallowed position in both the jurisprudence of the
First Amendment and the arsenal of political discourse, it is and was an inapt
analogy, even in the context in which it was originally offered. It has lately
become—despite, perhaps even because of, the frequency and promiscuous-
ness of its invocation—little more than a caricature of logical argumentation.

The case that gave rise to the "Fire!"-in-crowded-theater analogy, *Schenck* 3
v. United States, involved the prosecution of Charles Schenck, who was the
general secretary of the Socialist party in Philadelphia, and Elizabeth Baer,
who was its recording secretary. In 1917 a jury found Schenck and Baer guilty
of attempting to cause insubordination among soldiers who had been drafted
to fight in the First World War. They and other party members had circulated leaflets urging draftees not to "submit to intimidation" by fighting in a
war being conducted on behalf of "Wall Street's chosen few."

Schenck admitted, and the court found, that the intent of the pamphlet's 4
"impassioned language" was to "influence" draftees to resist the draft. Interestingly, however, Justice Holmes noted that nothing in the pamphlet suggested that the draftees should use unlawful or violent means to oppose con-
scription: "In form at least [the pamphlet] confined itself to peaceful
measures, such as a petition for the repeal of the act" and an exhortation to
exercise "your right to assert your opposition to the draft." Many of its most
impassioned words were quoted directly from the Constitution.

Justice Holmes acknowledged that "in many places and in ordinary times 5
the defendants, in saying all that was said in the circular, would have been

Reprinted by permission.

[1] "Congress shall make no law respecting an establishment of religion, or prohibiting the free exercise thereof;
or *abridging the freedom of speech, or of the press*, or the right of people peaceably to assemble, and to petition the
Government for a redress of grievances."

within their constitutional rights." "But," he added, "the character of every act depends upon the circumstances in which it is done." And to illustrate that truism he went on to say:

> The most stringent protection of free speech would not protect a man in falsely shouting fire in a theater, and causing a panic. It does not even protect a man from an injunction against uttering words that may have all the effect of force.

Justice Holmes then upheld the convictions in the context of a wartime draft, holding that the pamphlet created "a clear and present danger" of hindering the war effort while our soldiers were fighting for their lives and our liberty.   6

The example of shouting "Fire!" obviously bore little relationship to the facts of the Schenck case. The Schenck pamphlet contained a substantive political message. It urged its draftee readers to *think* about the message and then—if they so chose—to act on it in a lawful and nonviolent way. The man who shouts "Fire!" in a crowded theater is neither sending a political message nor inviting his listener to think about what he has said and decide what to do in a rational, calculated manner. On the contrary, the message is designed to force action *without* contemplation. The message "Fire!" is directed not to the mind and the conscience of the listener but, rather, to his adrenaline and his feet. It is a stimulus to immediate *action*, not thoughtful reflection. It is—as Justice Holmes recognized in his follow-up sentence—the functional equivalent of "uttering words that may have all the effect of force."   7

Indeed, in that respect the shout of "Fire!" is not even speech, in any meaningful sense of that term. It is a *clang* sound, the equivalent of setting off a nonverbal alarm. Had Justice Holmes been more honest about his example, he would have said that freedom of speech does not protect a kid who pulls a fire alarm in the absence of a fire. But that obviously would have been irrelevant to the case at hand. The proposition that pulling an alarm is not protected speech certainly leads to the conclusion that shouting the word "fire!" is also not protected. But the core analogy is the nonverbal alarm, and the derivative example is the verbal shout. By cleverly substituting the derivative shout for the core alarm, Holmes made it possible to analogize one set of words to another—as he could not have done if he had begun with the self-evident proposition that setting off an alarm bell is not free speech.   8

The analogy is thus not only inapt but also insulting. Most Americans do not respond to political rhetoric with the same kind of automatic acceptance expected of schoolchildren responding to a fire drill. Not a single recipient of the Schenck pamphlet is known to have changed his mind after reading it. Indeed, one draftee, who appeared as a prosecution witness, was asked whether reading a pamphlet asserting that the draft law was unjust would make him "immediately decide that you must erase that law." Not surprisingly, he replied, "I do my own thinking." A theatergoer would probably not respond similarly if asked how he would react to a shout of "Fire!"   9

Another important reason why the analogy is inapt is that Holmes emphasizes the factual falsity of the shout "Fire!" The Schenck pamphlet,   10 however, was not factually false. It contained political opinions and ideas about the causes of the war and about appropriate and lawful responses to the draft. As the Supreme Court recently reaffirmed (in *Falwell v. Hustler*), "The First Amendment recognizes no such thing as a 'false' idea." Nor does it recognize false opinions about the causes of or cures for war.

A closer analogy to the facts of the Schenck case might have been provided by a person's standing outside a theater, offering the patrons a leaflet advising them that in his opinion the theater was structurally unsafe, and urging them not to enter but to complain to the building inspectors. That analogy, however, would not have served Holmes' argument for punishing Schenck. Holmes needed an analogy that would appear relevant to Schenck's political speech but that would invite the conclusion that censorship was appropriate.

Unsurprisingly, a war-weary nation—in the throes of a know-nothing hysteria over immigrant anarchists and socialists—welcomed the comparison between what was regarded as a seditious political pamphlet and a malicious shout of "Fire!" Ironically, the "Fire!" analogy is nearly all that survives from the Schenck case; the ruling itself is almost certainly not good law. Pamphlets of the kind that resulted in Schenck's imprisonment have been circulated with impunity during subsequent wars.

Over the past several years I have assembled a collection of instances— cases, speeches, arguments—in which proponents of censorship have maintained that the expression at issue is "just like" or "equivalent to" falsely shouting "Fire!" in a crowded theater and ought to be banned, "just as" shouting "Fire!" ought to be banned. The analogy is generally invoked, often with self-satisfaction, as an absolute argument-stopper. It does, after all, claim the high authority of the great Justice Oliver Wendell Holmes. I have rarely heard it invoked in a convincing, or even particularly relevant way. But that, too, can claim lineage from the great Holmes.

Not unlike Falwell, with his silly comparison between shouting "Fire!" and publishing an offensive parody, courts and commentators have frequently invoked "Fire!" as an analogy to expression that is not an automatic stimulus to panic. A state supreme court held that "Holmes' aphorism . . . applies with equal force to pornography"—in particular to the exhibition of the movie *Carmen Baby* in a drive-in theater in close proximity to highways and homes. Another court analogized "picketing . . . in support of a secondary boycott" to shouting "Fire!" because in both instances "speech and conduct are brigaded." In the famous Skokie case one of the judges argued that allowing Nazis to march through a city where a large number of Holocaust survivors live "just might fall into the same category as one's 'right' to cry fire in a crowded theater."

Outside court the analogies become even more badly stretched. A spokesperson for the New Jersey Sports and Exposition Authority complained that newspaper reports to the effect that a large number of football players had contracted cancer after playing in the Meadowlands—a stadium atop a landfill—were the "journalistic equivalent of shouting fire in a crowded theater." An insect researcher acknowledged that his prediction that a certain amusement park might become roach infested "may be tantamount to shouting fire in a crowded theater." The philosopher Sidney Hook, in a letter to the *New York Times* bemoaning a Supreme Court decision that required a plaintiff in a defamation action to prove that the offending statement was actually false, argued that the First Amendment does not give the press carte blanche to accuse innocent persons "any more than the First Amendment protects the right of someone falsely to shout fire in a crowded theater."

Some close analogies to shouting "Fire!" or setting off an alarm are, of course, available: calling in a false bomb threat; dialing 911 and falsely describing an emergency; making a loud, gun-like sound in the presence of the President; setting off a voice-activated sprinkler system by falsely shouting "Fire!" In one case in which the "Fire!" analogy was directly to the point, a creative defendant tried to get around it. The case involved a man who calmly advised an airline clerk that he was "only there to hijack the plane." He was charged, in effect, with shouting "Fire!" in a crowded theater, and his rejected defense—as quoted by the court—was as follows: "If we built fire-proof theaters and let people know about this, then the shouting of "Fire!" would not cause panic." 16

Here are some more-distant but still related examples: the recent incident of the police slaying in which some members of an onlooking crowd urged a mentally ill vagrant who had taken an officer's gun to shoot the officer; the screaming of racial epithets during a tense confrontation; shouting down a speaker and preventing him from continuing his speech. 17

Analogies are, by their nature, matters of degree. Some are closer to the core example than others. But any attempt to analogize political ideas in a pamphlet, ugly parody in a magazine, offensive movies in a theater, controversial newspaper articles, or any of the other expressions and actions catalogued above to the very different act of shouting "Fire!" in a crowded theater is either self-deceptive or self-serving. 18

The government does, of course, have some arguably legitimate bases for suppressing speech which bear no relationship to shouting "Fire!" It may ban the publication of nuclear-weapon codes, of information about troop movements, and of the identity of undercover agents. It may criminalize extortion threats and conspiratorial agreements. These expressions may lead directly to serious harm, but the mechanisms of causation are very different from that at work when an alarm is sounded. One may also argue—less persuasively, in my view—against protecting certain forms of public obscenity and defamatory statements. Here, too, the mechanisms of causation are very different. None of these exceptions to the First Amendment's exhortation that the government "shall make no law . . . abridging the freedom of speech, of the press" is anything like falsely shouting "Fire!" in a crowded theater; they all must be justified on other grounds. 19

A comedian once told his audience, during a stand-up routine, about the time he was standing around a fire with a crowd of people and got in trouble for yelling "Theater, theater!" That, I think, is about as clever and productive a use as anyone has ever made of Holmes' flawed analogy. 20

Atlantic Monthly, January 1989

Profile   In "Shouting 'Fire!'" Alan M. Dershowitz offers a classic example of how to refute an argument based on a false analogy or misleading comparison. An *analogy* is a comparison based on similarity, and for it to be valid, the similarities must be relevant and significant, and they must not be overwhelmed by dissimilarities between the objects being compared. In this case the comparison is between expressing an opinion in public and shouting "Fire!" in a theater, the idea being that some ideas are dangerous because they have a power equivalent to that of a false alarm to stampede an audience into self-destructive panic. To construct his refutation of the false analogy, he opens by establishing the topicality of his subject, citing a recent occasion of its use as well as its long-standing popularity. Then he gives its history, explains how the stated similarity is overpowered by differences, and suggests a few limited circumstances where the comparison might apply.

A common justification for censoring speech and a frequently compelling argument-stopper, the shouting-"Fire!" analogy has a long and distinguished career, beginning with its origination in a Supreme Court decision. One recent public figure to invoke the analogy was the Reverend Jerry Falwell, protesting the Supreme Court's decision to overturn his $200,000 judgment against publisher Larry Flynt for a parody of Falwell in *Hustler* magazine. Here, as elsewhere, Dershowitz argues, the analogy simply does not apply: Shouting "Fire!" is the verbal equivalent of a fire alarm, not the expression of an opinion or a calculated appeal to another's reasoning—actions protected by the First Amendment to the U.S. Constitution. Shouting "Fire!" might be compared more accurately to phoning in a false bomb threat, or dialing 911 to report a false emergency, or making a gunlike sound near the President.

Like most thought-provoking essays, "Shouting 'Fire!'" has two subjects—an immediate, specific one (the falsity of a particular analogy), and a more enduring, universal one (the nature of protected speech). The link rests in the motive behind the analogy: to limit the expression of opinion. Thus, while Dershowitz goes about the relatively easy business of poking holes in the analogy, he explores the First Amendment and the speech acts it was framed to protect. Without this exploration there would be no need for the third section of the essay. There, in paragraphs 13–20, Dershowitz presents a collection of instances where the "Fire!" analogy has been indiscriminately invoked. Had he simply wanted to establish the currency of the false analogy and thus the need for a clarification, this material (presented a little differently) could have appeared in his introduction.

Left unchallenged, the third section argues, the "Fire!" analogy has been stretched to embrace an ever-wider range of expression, none of it qualifying as "an automatic stimulus to panic." Users of the analogy have attempted to censor everything from sexually explicit films, picket lines, and demonstrations, to reports of possible cancer risks and roach infestations, and—of course—magazine parodies. In only a few cases may the government legitimately suppress speech: publication of nuclear-weapon codes, information about the identity of undercover agents, extortion threats, conspiratorial agreements, and so on—all cases where the expressions may lead to serious and demonstrable harm.

As stated above, effective writing usually has two subjects, a specific and a general one, an immediate and a universal one. Effective writing also leaves the reader thinking, in this case both about the uses of analogy and the meaning and purposes of free speech.

Using Paraphrase   Because it is so closely reasoned, readers often find persuasive or argumentative writing to be dense and difficult to follow. The difficulty increases in key passages, those containing the heart of the writer's demonstration. Here is where readers fall victim to the habits formed by reading too many novels, writing in which one's instinct is to hurry on to find what happens next. In persuasive reading this impulse translates into an impatience to learn the writer's conclusions, neglecting his or her demonstration. To read critically and give ourselves a fair opportunity to understand, or to confirm or refute someone's position, we should linger over such passages, rereading them and, where necessary, restating them in our own words to make sure that we grasp their content. There are several such passages in Dershowitz's essay, and before we can validly agree or disagree with him, before we can give him more than our passive consent, we must be able to follow them closely. One test of this is our ability to state his position in our own words. Take paragraph 8:

> [1]Indeed, in that respect the shout of "Fire!" is not even speech, in any meaningful sense of the term. [2]It is a *clang* sound, the equivalent of setting off a nonverbal alarm. [3]*Had Justice Holmes been more honest about his example, he would have said that freedom of speech does not protect a kid who pulls a fire alarm in the absence of a fire.* [4]*But that obviously would have been irrelevant to the case at hand.* [5]*The proposition that pulling an alarm is not protected speech certainly leads to the conclusion that shouting the word "fire" is also not protected.* [6]*But the core analogy is the nonverbal alarm, and the derivative example is the verbal shout.* [7]*By cleverly substituting the derivative shout for the core alarm, Holmes made it possible to analogize one set of words to another—as he could not have done if he had begun with the self-evident proposition that setting off an alarm bell is not free speech.*

In sentences 3–7 Dershowitz exposes the rational sleight-of-hand whereby Judge Holmes established his false analogy. To agree critically, not merely consent passively, we must be able to restate his reasoning:

> [3]If Holmes had reasoned honestly, he would have conceded that freedom of speech does not apply to setting off false fire alarms. [4]But that concession would obviously not have fit his case. [5]If the First Amendment does not protect pulling an alarm, it does not protect shouting "Fire!" [6]The central comparison is with a nonverbal alarm, for which the verbal shout is merely a substitute. [7]By using the verbal alarm in place of the nonverbal one, Holmes was able to draw a false comparison between an alarm bell and an expression of opinion—something he could not have done if he had begun by admitting that alarm bells have nothing to do with free speech.

Paraphrase is the equivalent of viewing someone's card tricks in slow motion: We will be more likely to spot cards disappearing up sleeves.

Revision Assignments   Select one of the following strategies and revise "Shouting 'Fire!'" Include a brief statement explaining your choice and its effect on the arrangement and presentation of material.

1. "Shouting 'Fire!'" refutes a false analogy and explores the meaning of the First Amendment. Revise the essay solely as a discussion of invalid reasoning, discussing freedom of speech no more than required to expose the false analogy.

2. Revise the essay as a definition and defense of free speech, drawing as much as possible upon Dershowitz's arguments and illustrations. Deal with the falsity of the "Fire!" analogy only in passing.

Writing Assignments

1. Along with Frank Conroy's "Think About It" and Lewis Lapham's "Burnt Offerings," Dershowitz's essay addresses the First Amendment to the U.S. Constitution, a subject on which all Americans should have informed opinions. Using Dershowitz's position as a point of reference, explore a free speech issue (for example, pornography, demonstrations before abortion clinics, mandated limits to violence in movies and television, offensive speech on campuses). Give a fair hearing to opposing arguments (with or without the fire analogy, the belief that some expressions of opinion demonstrably threaten the public welfare).

2. Analogy is a popular form of argument or at least illustration. To be valid, though, as Dershowitz illustrates, an analogy must be based on a genuine and relevant similarity between the objects in question. Where the First Amendment is concerned, there is no fair comparison between setting off a fire alarm and delivering a reasoned expression of opinion. Holmes muddied the issue by substituting a verbal alarm for the mechanical one, thus seeming to introduce the idea of speech. Write your own refutation of an argument from false analogy or invalid comparison, whether citing an incident in history, the news, or even your private life. And, where relevant, explore the larger issue that the false analogy has been made to serve.

3. In a previous paragraph, paraphrase is likened to viewing card tricks in slow motion. Write a brief paper discussing the validity of this analogy. In what ways may an argumentative passage be likened to someone performing card tricks? In what ways do arguments and card tricks differ? Do the differences undermine the analogy? In what senses might the comparison work?

What Are Men Good For?

JARED DIAMOND

When I first began to work in the New Guinea highlands, I often became en- 1
raged when I saw how grossly women were abused. Along jungle trails I encountered married couples, the woman typically bent under a huge load of
firewood and vegetables, carrying an infant, while her husband sauntered
along, bearing nothing more than his bow and arrow. Men's hunting trips
seemed to be little more than male-bonding opportunities, yielding only a
few prey animals consumed on the spot by the hunters. Wives were bought,
sold, and discarded without their consent.

Later, when I had children of my own and shepherded my family on 2
walks, I felt I could better understand the New Guinea men striding beside
their families. The men were functioning as lookouts and protectors, keeping
their hands free so that they could quickly deploy their bows and arrows in
the event of an ambush by men of another tribe. But the men's hunting trips
and the sale of women as wives continue to trouble me.

The question "What are men good for?" may sound like a flip one-liner, 3
but it touches a raw nerve in our society. Women are becoming intolerant of
men's self-ascribed status and are criticizing those men who provide better
for themselves than they do for their wives and children. The question is also
a theoretical problem for anthropologists. In terms of services offered to
mates and children, males of most mammal species are good for nothing but
injecting sperm. They part from the female after copulation, leaving her to
bear the entire effort of feeding, protecting, and training the offspring. But
human males differ by (usually) remaining with mates and offspring. A widespread assumption among anthropologists is that men's familial roles contrib-
uted crucially to the evolution of our species' most distinctive features. The
reasoning is as follows.

Men's and women's economic roles differ in all surviving hunter-gatherer 4
societies, a category that encompassed all human societies until the rise of agriculture 10,000 years ago. Men invariably spend more time hunting large
animals, while women spend more time gathering plant foods, trapping small
animals, and caring for children. Anthropologists traditionally argue that this
division of labor arose because it promoted the nuclear family's joint interests
and thereby represented a sound, cooperative strategy. Men are much better
able than women to track and kill big animals, for the obvious reason that
men don't have to carry infants around to nurse them. In the view of most
anthropologists, men hunt in order to provide meat for their wives and
children.

A similar division of labor persists to some degree in modern industrial so- 5
cieties, since most women still devote more time to child care than men do.
While hunting is no longer an important male occupation and women now
work outside the home, men still provide for their spouses and children by
holding paying jobs. Thus, the expression "bringing home the bacon" has a
profound and ancient meaning.

Meat provisioning is considered a distinctive function of human males, 6
shared with only a few other mammal species, such as wolves and African
hunting dogs. Like many other primate males, men protect their mates and
their offspring, but that service is viewed as less of a net contribution by men
to society than is hunting, since men defend their families mainly from other
men. Meat provisioning is assumed to be linked to other uniquely human
features, in particular the continued association of men and women in nuclear families after copulation and the inability of human children (unlike
young apes) to obtain their own food for many years after weaning.

From this theory, the correctness of which is generally taken for granted, 7
follow two straightforward predictions about men's hunting: First, if the main
purpose of hunting is to bring meat to the hunter's family, men should pursue the hunting strategy that reliably yields the most meat. Hence the presumed explanation for men's hunting big animals is that they thereby bag, on
average, more pounds of meat per day than by hunting small animals. Second, a hunter should be expected to bring his kill to his wife and children, or
at least to share it with them preferentially. But do the two predictions
square with reality?

Surprisingly, neither assumption has been much tested. Less surprisingly, 8
perhaps, a woman anthropologist has taken the lead in testing them. Kristen
Hawkes, of the University of Utah, has studied Paraguay's Northern Ache
Indians, measuring their foraging yields in a study carried out jointly with
Kim Hill, A. Magdalena Hurtado, and H. Kaplan. In collaboration with
Nicholas Blurton Jones and James O'Connell, Hawkes conducted other tests
based on the practices of Tanzania's Hadza people.

The Northern Ache used to be full-time hunter-gatherers, and they con- 9
tinued to spend much time foraging in the forest even after they began to
settle at mission agricultural settlements in the 1970s. Ache men hunt large
mammals, such as peccaries and deer, and also collect masses of honey from
bees' nests. Women pound starch from palm trees, gather fruits and insect
larvae, and care for children. The contents of an Ache man's hunting bag vary
greatly from day to day. He brings home enough food for many people if he
kills a peccary or finds a beehive, but he gets nothing at all on one-quarter of
all days spent hunting. In contrast, women's returns vary little from day to
day because palms are abundant: how much starch a woman gets depends
mainly on how much time she spends pounding it. A woman can always
count on getting enough for herself and her children, but she can never reap
a bonanza big enough to feed many others.

The first shock resulting from the studies by Hawkes and her colleagues 10
concerned the difference between the returns achieved by men's and
women's strategies. Peak yields were, of course, much higher for men than
for women, since a man's daily bag topped 40,000 calories when he was lucky
enough to kill a peccary. However, such glorious days are greatly outnum-
bered by the humiliating days when he returns empty-handed. A man's average daily return of 9,634 calories per day proved to be lower than that of a
woman (10,356), and man's median return (4,663 calories per day) was even
lower.

Thus, Ache men would do better in the long run by sticking to the un- 11
heroic "women's job" of pounding palms than by devoting themselves to the

excitement of the chase. Since they are stronger than women, men could, if they chose to, pound even more daily calories from palm starch than can women. In going for high but very unpredictable returns, Ache men can be compared with gamblers who aim for the jackpot, even though in the long run the gamblers would do much better by putting their money in the bank and collecting the boringly predictable interest.

The other shock was that successful hunters do *not* bring meat or honey home mainly for their wives and children, but share it widely. Women share also, but not so widely as men. As a result, three-quarters of all food that an Ache consumes is acquired by someone outside the consumer's nuclear family.   12

These findings suggest that something other than the best interests of his wife and children lies behind an Ache man's preference for big-game hunting. As Kristen Hawkes described these paradoxes to me, I began to develop an awful foreboding that the true explanation might prove less noble than the necessity of bringing home the bacon. I began to feel defensive about my fellow men and searched for explanations that might restore my faith in the nobility of our strategy.   13

My first objection was that Kristen Hawkes' calculations of hunting returns were measured in calories. In reality, any nutritionally aware modern reader knows that not all calories are equal. Perhaps the purpose of big-gaming hunting lies in fulfilling our needs for protein and fat, which are more valuable to us nutritionally than are the humble carbohydrates of palm starch. However, Ache men target not only protein-rich meat but also honey, whose carbohydrates are every bit as humble as those of palm starch. While Kalahari San men (Bushmen) are hunting big game, San women are gathering and preparing mongongo nuts, an excellent protein source. While lowland New Guinea hunters are wasting their days in the usually futile search for kangaroos, their wives and children are predictably acquiring protein in the form of fish, rats, grubs, and spiders. Why don't San and New Guinea men emulate their wives?   14

I next began to wonder whether Ache men might be unusually ineffective hunters, a modern aberration among hunter-gatherers. Undoubtedly, the hunting skills of Eskimo and Arctic Indian men are indispensable, especially in winter, when little food other than big game is available. Tanzania's Hadza men, unlike the Ache, achieve higher average returns by hunting big game more than small game. But New Guinea men, like the Ache, persist in hunting even though yields are very low. And Hadza hunters persist in the face of enormous odds, since on most hunting days they bag nothing at all. A Hadza family could starve while waiting for a husband/father to win his gamble of bringing down a giraffe. In any case, from the family's point of view, it is an academic question whether big-game hunting yields higher or lower returns than alternative strategies, since all the meat occasionally bagged by a Hadza or Ache hunter isn't reserved for the family.   15

Still seeking to defend my fellow men, I then wondered: Does widespread sharing of meat and honey smooth out hunting yields, constituting a form of reciprocal altruism? That is, I expect to kill a giraffe only every twenty-ninth day, and so does each of my hunter friends, but we all go off in different directions, and each of us is likely to kill our giraffe on different   16 days. If successful hunters agree to share meat with the rest of the social group, most people will have full bellies most of the time. According to this scenario, hunters would share their catch with the best other hunters, those from whom they are most likely to receive meat in return.

In reality, though, successful Ache and Hadza hunters share their catch 17 with anyone, regardless of whether he's a good or hopeless hunter. That raises the question of why an Ache or Hadza man should bother to hunt at all, since he can claim a share of meat even if he never bags anything himself. Conversely, why should he hunt when any animal he kills is shared widely? Why doesn't he just gather nuts and rats, which he can bring to his family exclusively?

As my last defense (objection?) I hypothesized that wide sharing of meat 18 helps the hunter's whole tribe, which is likely to flourish or perish together. It's not enough to concentrate on nourishing your own family if the rest of your tribe is starving and can't fend off an attack by tribal enemies. But that line of reasoning brought me back to the original paradox: The best way for the whole Ache tribe to become well nourished is for all to humble themselves, by pounding good old reliable palm starch and collecting fruit or insect larvae. The men shouldn't waste their time gambling on the occasional peccary.

Thus collapsed all four of my efforts to defend Ache big-game hunting as 19 a sensible way for men to contribute nobly to the best interests of their wives and children. Kristen Hawkes then drove home some painful truths, reminding me that the Ache man himself (and not his wife and children) gets big benefits from his kills.

To begin with, among the Ache, as among most other peoples, extramari- 20 tal sex is not unknown. Dozens of Ache women asked to name the possible fathers (sex partners at the time of conception) of sixty-six of their children, named an average of 2.1 men per child. (Before you condemn Ache women as exceptionally loose, reflect that genetic markers show that 5 percent to 40 percent of American and British babies have been sired by a man other than the mother's spouse. And these numbers underestimate the frequency of adultery, because not every bout of adultery results in conception.) When asked about a sample of twenty-eight Ache men, women named good hunters as their lovers more often than poor hunters as their lovers, and named good hunters as possible fathers of their children.

To understand the biological significance of adultery, recall that the facts 21 of reproductive biology introduce a fundamental asymmetry into the interests of men and women. Multiple sex partners contribute nothing directly to a woman's reproductive output. Once a woman has had an ovum fertilized by a man, having sex with another man cannot lead to another baby for at least nine months, and probably for at least several years under hunter-gatherer conditions of extended lactational amenorrhea.[1] In a few adulterous minutes, though, a married man may increase his total number of children.

Now compare the reproductive outputs of two hypothetical men pursuing 22 the two different hunting strategies that Hawkes terms the "provider" strategy and the "showoff" strategy. The provider brings home foods such as

[1]Suppression of menstruation in nursing mothers.

palm starch and rats, yielding moderate but predictable returns. The showoff instead hunts for big animals, aiming at occasional bonanzas instead of higher mean returns. The provider obtains on the average the most food for his wife and children, although he never gets enough of a surplus to feed anyone else. The showoff usually brings less food to his wife and children, but does occasionally get lots of meat to share with others.

Obviously, if a woman gauges her genetic interests by the number of children she can rear to maturity, which is, in turn, a function of how much food she can provide them, she is better off marrying a provider. But she is further well served by having showoffs as neighbors, with whom she can trade occasional sex in return for extra meat for herself and her offspring. The whole tribe also likes a showoff because of the occasional bonanzas that he brings home for sharing. 23

In terms of advancing his own genetic interests, the showoff gains advantages as well as disadvantages when compared with the provider. One advantage is the extra offspring sired adulterously, as I've already explained. But the showoff also gains prestige in the tribe's eyes. Others in the tribe want him as a neighbor because of his gifts of meat, and they may reward him with their daughters as wives. For the same reason, the tribe is likely to give favored treatment to the showoff's children. Disadvantages are that the showoff's less reliable provisioning of his own family may mean that he may have fewer legitimate children reaching maturity. The showoff's wife may also philander, so some of her children may not be his. Is the showoff better off giving up the provider's certainty of fathering of a few children in return for the possibility of fathering many children? 24

The answer depends on several numbers, such as the extra number of legitimate children that a provider's wife can rear, the percentage of a provider's wife's children that are legitimate, and the potential extra survivorship that a showoff's offspring may gain from their favored status. The answer may differ among tribes, depending on the local ecology. For the Ache, Hawkes estimates that over a wide range of likely conditions, showoffs can expect to pass on their genes to more surviving children than can providers. This fact, rather than the traditionally accepted view of bringing home the bacon to wife and children, may be the motive reason behind big-game hunting. Ache men thereby do good for themselves rather than for their families. 25

Thus, men hunters and women gatherers don't always constitute a division of labor whereby the family unit most effectively promotes its joint interest. They also don't constitute an arrangement in which the work force is selectively deployed for the good of the group. Instead, the hunter-gatherer life style involves a classic conflict of interest, in which what's best for a man isn't necessarily best for a woman and vice versa. Spouses share interests but also have divergent interests. A woman is better off married to a provider, but a man is not better off being a provider. 26

Biological studies in recent decades have demonstrated many such conflicts of interest in animals and humans: not only conflicts between husbands and wives (or between mated animals) but also between parents and children and among siblings. While biologists explain the conflicts theoretically, all of us recognize them from experience, without doing any calculations of 27 genetics and foraging ecology. Conflicts of interest between spouses and close relatives are the commonest, most gut-wrenching tragedies of our lives.

How generally can these findings be applied? The conclusion of Hawkes and her colleagues await testing for other hunter-gatherers. The answers are likely to vary among tribes and even among individuals. From my experience in New Guinea, Hawkes's conclusions are likely to apply even more strongly there. New Guinea has few large animals, hunting yields are low, and empty bags are frequent. Men consume much of their catch while they are off in the jungle; and when big animals are brought home, the meat is shared widely. New Guinea hunting is hard to defend economically, but it brings obvious payoffs in status to successful hunters. 28

What about the relevance to our own society? Perhaps you're already livid because you foresaw that I'd raise that question, and you're expecting me to conclude that American men aren't good for much. Of course that's not what I conclude. I acknowledge that many (most? by far the majority of?) American men are devoted husbands, work hard to increase their income, devote that income to their wives and children, do much child care, and don't philander. 29

But alas, the Ache findings are relevant to at least some men in our society. Some American men do desert their wives and children. The proportion of divorced men who renege on their legally stipulated child support is scandalously high, so that even our government is proposing to do something about it. Single parents outnumber co-parents in the United States, and most of those single parents are women. 30

Among those men who remain married, all of us know some who take better care of themselves than of their wives and children, and who devote inordinate time, money, and energy to philandering and to male status symbols and activities, such as cars, sports, and alcohol consumption. I don't claim to have measured what percentage of American men rate as showoffs rather than providers, but the percentage of showoffs appears not to be negligible. 31

Even among devoted working couples, time budget studies show that American working women spend on the average twice as many hours on their responsibilities (defined as job plus children plus household) as do their husbands, yet women receive on the average less pay for the same jobs. When American husbands are asked to estimate the numbers of hours that they and their wives each devote to children and household, the same time-budget studies show that men tend to overestimate their hours and to underestimate their wives' hours. It's my impression that men's household and child-care contributions are on the average still lower in some other industrialized countries, such as Australia, Japan, Germany, France, and Poland, to mention a few with which I happen to be familiar. That's why the question "What are men good for?" continues to be debated within our societies, as well as among anthropologists. 32

—Natural History, May 1993

Profile   Properly speaking, "What Are Men Good For?"—like "Maya Art for the Record"—is an article, not an essay; that is, its purpose is less to explore ideas than to present information, in this case an update on anthropological theories of male usefulness. Unlike the typical article, though, it resembles a story with two plots, presenting two complementary intellectual dramas: one pitting new theories against old, and another pitting the male author against feminist accusers. And like Tristram Wyatt's "Submarine Beetles," "What Are Men Good For?" exploits a first-person narrative to spice up what could have been a plodding recital of information.

Diamond could have accomplished his purpose by dutifully summarizing the most recent findings, pitching his material to specialists, those already informed on the subject. Instead, to reach a more general audience, he writes more informally, explaining details unfamiliar to outsiders and using the first person to insert himself into the essay as an interested observer, someone with a personal as well as professional investment in the outcome: He is a poor beleaguered male trying to defend his gender.

By playing gender defender, a part that he occasionally seems to accept half-heartedly (sometimes lobbing slow, fat pitches to Kristen Hawkes), Diamond creates tension and energy where there could have been a simple listing and testing of assumptions. On one level, his essay is a model of its kind, laying out traditional theories, finding fault with them, introducing and testing new theories, pursuing a continual chain of reasoning to a fresh understanding. On another level, it is a conversion story: "How I rose above error and accepted the truth about my gender." By casting himself as an adversary, a defensive male reluctant to accept an indictment of his gender, Diamond adds a second level of interest, one complementing the first.

Addressing the Reader   As the Introduction to this text explains, reading is participatory. Following the prompts of the writer, the reader must indeed *make* sense: recognize words and structures, draw inferences, remember, anticipate. In more general terms the reader also receives prompts from sentence types themselves, which ask for three general responses. *Declarative* sentences (the sentences we use most of the time) make statements, asking the reader to accept them as true; *interrogative* sentences ask questions, expecting the reader to respond with data or at least to think about something; *imperative* sentences give an order or request and usually expect the reader to respond with some kind of action.

All three sentences engage the reader, but interrogatives and imperatives appeal more directly than declaratives. The reason? Look to the subects. A standard declarative sentence has a built-in subject (the topic about which the comment will be made): "*Some American men* do desert their wives and children." Interrogative and imperative sentences, though, have an implied or understood subject or addressee, *you* (the listener or reader): "What about the relevance to our [yours and mine] own society?" This may be a *rhetorical question*, one not literally asking the listener or reader for an answer, but it does implicitly ask the reader to think about the issue, to participate, however briefly, in considering the issues. In the context of the article, then, such a question has some of the effect of being called on in class. In this case Diamond even goes on to speak to the reader for several more sentences:

What about the relevance to our own society? Perhaps you're already livid because you foresaw that I'd raise that question, and you're expecting me to conclude that American men aren't good for much. . . .

Imperative sentences have a similar effect. Consider the two following versions:

To understand the biological significance of adultery, recall that the facts of reproductive biology introduce a fundamental asymmetry into the interests of men and women.

Adultery has an obvious biological significance because the facts of reproductive biology introduce a fundamental asymmetry into the interests of men and women.

The second version is a garden-variety declarative sentence, in the same vein as most of those preceding it. The first, Diamond's original sentence, changes pace, addressing the reader directly. You might say that he has gone from talking *at* the reader to talking *to* the reader. At the least, it is the writer's equivalent of making eye contact with the audience; at best, it is a wake-up call, an invitation for the reader to take a more active part in the discussion, to draw on his or her personal lore.

By making frequent use of questions and imperatives, Diamond provides relief from an endless string of declarative sentences, sentences asking one kind of response, a response that is relatively passive compared to that of the interrogative and the imperative. Questions do more than address the reader, though. They are excellent focusers and they make good topic sentence openers for paragraphs.

Revision Assignments   Select one of the following strategies and revise "What Are Men Good For?" Include a brief statement explaining your choice and its effect on the arrangement and presentation of material.

1. In order to give the Diamond article a more direct and dynamic structure, present its material in a question-and-answer format. You may have to take some fictional liberties, such as having Diamond provide the questions and Kristen Hawkes the answers, or you may create a third party as questioner and have Diamond give the answers. Question-and-answer formats have a dramatic advantage, making the participants seem more immediate, alive, and responsive.

2. Diamond does not simply present the latest anthropological thinking on division of labor in hunter-gatherer societies. He enters into the debate, playing the role of male gender defender. To appreciate what this tactic accomplishes, revise paragraphs 13–19 by removing the male apologist. Simply lay out the information and arguments objectively without the debate structure.

Writing Assignments

1. Do you accept Diamond's and Hawkes' conclusions about hunter-gatherer males? Are there other less damaging interpretations of the data?

Both accept, for example, that the thousands-of-years-old male hunting strategies are inefficient compared to the steady but reliable work of the women. Might not those strategies have been quite efficient until just recently, when they were disturbed by the related issues of human overpopulation and the declining availability of game?

2. Diamond argues for the relevancy of hunter-gatherer experience to modern society (or at least he seems to assume a degree of relevancy that some might challenge). Using both his own arguments and data and your own observations, discuss this relevancy. Are Hawkes and Diamond, for example, applying to hunter-gatherer societies criteria for gender relationships formed in modern, postindustrial societies?

3. Using your own observations, make an argument for men as primarily either showoffs or providers. What social encouragements do you see for men being one or the other? What about normal male socialization in which adolescents have opportunities to be showoffs well before they can be expected to be providers? How does the showoff/provider distinction affect the gender relationships that you observe? In our postindustrial society do you think providers labor under the competitive disadvantages of their counterparts in hunter-gatherer societies? Do you see inconsistencies or "conflicts of interest" in current dating or marital practices?

Marrying Absurd

JOAN DIDION

To be married in Las Vegas, Clark County, Nevada, a bride must swear she   1
is eighteen or has parental permission and a bridegroom that he is twenty-
one or has parental permission. Someone must put up five dollars for the license. (On Sundays and holidays, fifteen dollars. The Clark County Courthouse issues marriage licenses at any time of the day or night except
between noon and one in the afternoon, between eight and nine in the evening, and between four and five in the morning.) Nothing else is required.
The State of Nevada, alone among these United States, demands neither a
premarital blood test nor a waiting period before or after the issuance of a
marriage license. Driving in across the Mojave from Los Angeles, one sees
the signs way out on the desert, looming up from that moonscape of rattlesnakes and mesquite, even before the Las Vegas lights appear like a mirage
on the horizon: "GETTING MARRIED? Free license information First
Strip Exit." Perhaps the Las Vegas wedding industry achieved its peak operational efficiency between 9:00 P.M. and midnight of August 26, 1965, an
otherwise unremarkable Thursday which happened to be, by Presidential order, the last day on which anyone could improve his draft status merely by
getting married. One hundred and seventy-one couples were pronounced
man and wife in the name of Clark County and the State of Nevada that
night, sixty-seven of them by a single justice of the peace, Mr. James A.
Brennan. Mr. Brennan did one wedding at the Dunes and the other sixty-six
in his office, and charged each couple eight dollars. One bride lent her veil to
six others. "I got it down from five to three minutes," Mr. Brennan said later
of his feat. "I could've married them *en masse*, but they're people, not cattle.
People expect more when they get married."

What people who get married in Las Vegas actually do expect—what, in   2
the largest sense, their "expectations" are—strikes one as a curious and self-
contradictory business. Las Vegas is the most extreme and allegorical of
American settlements, bizarre and beautiful in its venality and in its devotion
to immediate gratification, a place the tone of which is set by mobsters and
call girls and ladies' room attendants with amyl nitrate poppers[1] in their uniform pockets. Almost everyone notes that there is no "time" in Las Vegas, no
night and no day and no past and no future (no Las Vegas casino, however,
has taken the obliteration of the ordinary time sense quite so far as Harold's
Club in Reno, which for a while issued, at odd intervals in the day and night,
mimeographed "bulletins" carrying news from the world outside); neither is
there any logical sense of where one is. One is standing on a highway in the
middle of a vast hostile desert looking at an eighty-foot sign which blinks
"STARDUST" or "CAESAR'S PALACE." Yes, but what does that explain?
This geographical implausibility reinforces the sense that what happens
there has no connection with "real" life; Nevada cities like Reno and Carson

[1]Like smelling salts, used to relieve faintness or headaches.

are ranch towns, Western towns, places behind which there is some historical imperative. But Las Vegas seems to exist only in the eye of the beholder. All of which makes it an extraordinarily stimulating and interesting place, but an odd one in which to want to wear a candlelight satin Priscilla of Boston wedding dress with Chantilly lace insets, tapered sleeves and a detachable modified train.

And yet the Las Vegas wedding business seems to appeal to precisely 3 that impulse. "Sincere and Dignified Since 1954," one wedding chapel advertises. There are nineteen such wedding chapels in Las Vegas, intensely competitive, each offering better, faster, and by implication, more sincere services than the next: Our Photos Best Anywhere, Your Wedding on a Phonograph Record, Candlelight with Your Ceremony, Honeymoon Accommodations, Free Transportation from your Motel to Courthouse to Chapel and Return to Motel, Religious or Civil Ceremonies, Dressing Rooms, Flowers, Rings, Announcements, Witnesses Available, and Ample Parking. All of these services, like most others in Las Vegas (sauna baths, payroll-check cashing, chinchilla coats for sale or rent) are offered twenty-four hours a day, seven days a week, presumably on the premise that marriage, like craps, is a game to be played when the table seems hot.

But what strikes one most about the Strip chapels, with their wishing 4 wells and stained-glass paper windows and their artificial bouvardia,[2] is that so much of their business is by no means a matter of simple convenience, of late-night liaisons between show girls and baby Crosbys.[3] Of course there is some of that. (One night about eleven o'clock in Las Vegas I watched a bride in an orange minidress and masses of flame-colored hair stumble from a Strip chapel on the arm of her bridegroom, who looked the part of the expendable nephew in movies like *Miami Syndicate*. "I gotta get the kids," the bride whimpered. "I gotta pick up the sitter, I gotta get to the midnight show." "What you gotta get," the bridegroom said, opening the door of the Cadillac Coupe de Ville and watching her crumple on the seat, "is sober.") But Las Vegas seems to offer something other than "convenience"; it is merchandising "niceness," the facsimile of proper ritual, to children who do not know how else to find it, how to make arrangements, how to do it "right." All day and evening long on the Strip, one sees actual wedding parties, waiting under the harsh lights at a crosswalk, standing uneasily in the parking lot of the Frontier while the photographer hired by "The Little Church of the West" ("Wedding Place of the Stars") certifies the occasion, takes the picture: the bride in a veil and white satin pumps, the bridegroom usually in a white dinner jacket, and even an attendant or two, a sister or best friend in hot-pink *peau de soie*, a flirtation veil, a carnation nosegay. "When I Fall in Love It Will Be Forever," the organist plays, and then a few bars of Lohengrin. The mother cries, the stepfather, awkward in his role, invites the chapel hostess to join them for a drink at the Sands. The hostess declines with a professional smile; she has already transferred her interest to the group waiting outside. One bride out, another in, and again the sign goes up on the chapel door: "One moment please—Wedding."

[2]Showy, colorful flowers.
[3]Some sons and nephews of the entertainer Bing Crosby married and then divorced Las Vegas showgirls.

I sat next to one such wedding party in a Strip restaurant the last time I 5
was in Las Vegas. The marriage had just taken place; the bride still wore her
dress, the mother her corsage. A bored waiter poured out a few swallows of
pink champagne ("on the house") for everyone but the bride, who was too
young to be served. "You'll need something with more kick than that," the
bride's father said with heavy jocularity to his new son-in-law; the ritual jokes
about the wedding night had a certain Panglossian[4] character, since the bride
was clearly several months pregnant. Another round of pink champagne, this
time not on the house, and the bride began to cry. "It was just as nice," she
sobbed, "as I hoped and dreamed it would be."

1967

Profile   Technically, Joan Didion is a journalist, a conveyor of information, an observer who "reports" on contemporary American society. But
many would call Didion a reporter with an "attitude," someone who—for all
her precise, verifiable detail—is anything but neutral. She writes informa-
tion-laden narratives, but she interprets as she reports—at least implicitly—
and invites the reader to join in, as "Marrying Absurd" illustrates. Her target
is an American society that is morally adrift, out of touch with its past and
seeking salvation in conspicuous consumption and the pursuit of power and
status.

Like a journalist Didion visits the scene, notes details, collects quotes,
and—presumably—refrains from fabrication. But unlike a conventional journalist Didion takes a moral stance. Her principal method is to select and arrange information so that it exposes and embarrasses her subject, exploiting
self-indicting or self-contradicting details ("stained-glass paper windows");
unintentionally self-revealing quotes ("'It was just as nice,' she sobbed, 'as I
hoped and dreamed it would be'"); and ironic juxtapositions (as the organist
plays "When I Fall in Love It Will Be Forever," the stepfather—himself
probably in his second or third marriage—fidgets, obviously uncomfortable
in his role). Then the hostess rushes the party out; time for the next quickie
ceremony. (And if she has job security and a good memory, she may recognize some return customers.)

By generally minimizing interpretive comments, by carefully selecting
and arranging details so that they suggest inconsistencies and absurdities,
Didion invites her readers to draw their own conclusions (which likely will
be similar to her own). At the same time, she is screening her audience, writing for insiders, those on her moral and intellectual wavelength. She is not interested in superficial *Panglossian* readers; she wants readers who are as
tough-minded and realistic as herself, people who prefer an unpleasant truth
to a pleasing fiction. The former will miss the point of the sign on the chapel
door: "One moment please—Wedding." The latter will enjoy the implications: "One moment please—Wedding (or is it *Marriage?*)."

By being open and explicit about her moral judgments, like Carol Bly in
"A Mongoose Is Missing," a writer ensures that most of her readers will understand her position. Understanding it and sharing it, though, are not

---

[4]Pangloss, a character in Voltaire's satiric novel *Candide* (1759), is an embodiment of invincible optimism. His
trademark belief is that this is "the best of all possible worlds" and that all things work out for the best.

necessarily the same thing, and Didion seems more interested in the firm assent of the few than the casual assent of the many. In other words, Didion deliberately addresses a smaller audience, one critical and sophisticated but not, she would argue, cynical. To attain this consent, Didion is willing to gamble. By withholding commentary, by selecting details and letting them speak for themselves, she knows that many readers will not hear. For the others the details do have voices, loud ones. Didion, after all, only quoted the sign outside the chapel: "One moment please—Wedding."

The method of persuasion is a sound one, equivalent to that of performing an experiment before witnesses. What, after all, can we say to the evidence of our senses? But a writer is doing more than simply presenting information. By including some details and excluding others, and by creating favorable or unfavorable sequences or juxtapositions, the act of selecting and arranging material can be as prejudicial as attaching evaluative labels and editorial opinions.

If Didion's method is rationally suspect (if one acknowledges that she is stacking the deck), it is psychologically sound. Her delivery works by appealing to our desire to be insiders, to be among the knowing few, the enlightened handful who understand what is going on. In other words, irony (and especially her irony) appeals to our sense of superiority. We "get it"; we know what she means even as we appreciate that denser folks will not.

Writing with Gaps   In their attention to craftsmanship, most writers attend closely to the *coherence* of their work. To ensure that readers can follow their reasoning, they connect their ideas openly and clearly, using devices like repetition, parallelism, transition terms, pronouns and adjectives that refer to previous terms, and so on. And Didion does often maintain this kind of coherence within and between sentences, as in paragraph 3:

> *But* what strikes one most about the Strip chapels, with *their* wishing wells and stained-glass paper windows and *their* artificial bouvardia, is that so much of *their* business is by no means a matter *of* simple *convenience, of* late-night liaison between show girls and baby Crosbys. Of course there is some of *that.* (One night about eleven o'clock in Las Vegas I watched . . .) *but* Las Vegas seems to offer something other than "*convenience*" . . .

But, consistent with her ironic method and her insider appeal to the reader, she also omits connections between segments of her material, especially within paragraphs:

> [1]To be married in Las Vegas, Clark County, Nevada, a bride must swear that she is eighteen or has parental permission and a bridegroom that he is twenty-one or has parental permission. [2]Someone must put up five dollars for the license. ([3]On Sundays and holidays, fifteen dollars. [4]The Clark County Courthouse issues marriage licenses at any time of the day or night except between noon and one in the afternoon, between eight and nine in the evening, and between four and five in the morning.) [5]Nothing else is required. [6]The State of Nevada, alone among these United States, demands neither a premarital blood test nor a waiting period before or after issuance of a marriage license. [7]Driving in across the Mojave from Los Angeles, one sees the signs way out on the desert, looming up from that

moonscape of rattlesnakes and mesquite, even before the Las Vegas lights appear like a mirage on the horizon: "GETTING MARRIED? Free License Information First Strip Exit." [8]Perhaps the Las Vegas wedding industry achieved its peak operational efficiency between 9:00 P.M. and midnight of August 26, 1965, an otherwise unremarkable Thursday which happened to be, by Presidential order, the last day on which anyone could improve his draft status merely by getting married. [9]One hundred and seventy-one couples were pronounced man and wife in the name of Clark County and the State of Nevada that night, sixty-seven of them by a single justice of the peace, Mr. James A. Brennan. [10]Mr. Brennan did one wedding at the Dunes and the other sixty-six in his office, and charged each couple eight dollars. [11]One bride lent her veil to six others. [12]"I got it down from five to three minutes," Mr. Brennan said later of his feat. [13]"I could've married them *en masse*, but they're people, not cattle. [14]People expect more when they get married."

The first six sentences announce, methodically and straightforwardly, the legal requirements for marriage in "Las Vegas, Clark County, Nevada." The dry, factual tone smacks of officialese. But sentence 7 abruptly changes direction: "Driving in across the Mojave from Los Angeles, one sees way out on the desert . . . " And then sentence 8 again changes direction: "Perhaps the Las Vegas wedding industry achieved peak operational efficiency . . ."

Without explicit transition terms the first paragraph could easily be subdivided into three paragraphs. There are implied connections, however, as the following revision illustrates:

> . . . Nothing else is required. *And Las Vegas openly capitalizes on the ease with which it ties the wedding knot.* Driving in across the Mojave from Los Angeles, one sees the signs way out on the desert, looming up from that moonscape of rattlesnakes and mesquite, even before the Las Vegas lights appear like a mirage on the horizon: "GETTING MARRIED? Free License Information First Strip Exit." *As a measure of just how streamlined the Las Vegas wedding industry has become*, it achieved its peak operational efficiency between 9:00 P.M. and midnight of August 26, 1965 . . .

Didion expects her readers to supply the connections, to understand that she is still on track and in control of her material. Just as she expects her readers to appreciate her irony, to "read between the lines," she also expects them to make broad inferential leaps, to supply connections, and to fill in large gaps.

Using Details   Type out "Marrying Absurd" and you will find yourself using the shift key over and over to make capital letters, the ones with which we identify proper nouns, the names of particular things, the most specific of all details: Las Vegas, Clark County, Nevada; the Clark County Courthouse; the Mojave; Los Angeles; Mr. James A. Brennan; Harold's Club in Reno; Priscilla of Boston; Cadillac Coupe de Ville; The Little Church of the West. And then there are the signs advertising weddings as if they were appliances or used cars: Our Photos Best Anywhere, Your Wedding on a Phonograph Record, Candlelight with Your Ceremony, Honeymoon Accommodations. Such circumstantial details abound in Didion's writing: the exact names of people and places (not just "a single justice of the peace" but Mr. James A. Brennan), exact times and dates (between 9:00 P.M. and midnight of August 26, 1965)—all the products of close observation, careful research, and exact record-keeping. To further impart a sense of accuracy, of damning evidence relentlessly accumulated, she is also numerically precise:

> *One hundred and seventy-one couples* were pronounced man and wife in the name of Clark County and the State of Nevada that night, *sixty-seven* of them by a *single-*justice of the peace, Mr. James A. Brennan. Mr. Brennan did *one* wedding at the Dunes and the other *sixty-six* in his office, and charged each couple *eight* dollars. *One* bride lent her veil to *six* others. "I got it down from *five* to *three* minutes," Mr. Brennan said later of his feat.

Didion's motive is to expose the falsity of her subject, the reduction to a flimsy counterfeit of what most cultures still regard as a vital, society-renewing ritual. Her method is to drag it out into the "harsh light" where her audience can see it for what it is. She makes the occasional offhand judgment, speaking of "the Las Vegas wedding industry," but her principal method is the recording of damning detail.

Using Dialogue Guides   We use quotation marks to identify certain material as an accurate, word-for-word report of someone else's speech or writing. A representation of speech usually has two parts, a *dialogue guide* identifying the speaker and the quote itself:

> "I got it down from five to three minutes," *Mr. Brennan said* later of his feat.

Like many fiction writers Didion often prefers to open with the quote, postponing the dialogue guide until the middle or end of the quote. The effect is usually to make the statement more abrupt, more dramatic:

> "I gotta get the kids," *the bride whimpered*. "I gotta pick up the sitter, I gotta get to the midnight show." "What you gotta get," *the bridegroom said*, opening the door of a Cadillac Coupe de Ville and watching her crumple on the seat, "is sober."

Suppose she had placed the dialogue guides first, as less experienced writers are inclined to do:

> *The bride whimpered*, "I gotta get the kids. I gotta pick up the sitter, I gotta get to the midnight show." *The bridegroom said*, "What you gotta get is sober."

Largely missing, of course, is the impact of the punch line, a product of timing, of pacing. In her version Didion begins the bridegroom's quote, then interrupts it, creating suspense, making the reader wonder what will come next. Will he say something threatening? Insulting? Humorous?

In sum, there is a rhetoric to using dialogue guides, one that Didion has mastered. Consider the following three versions:

> She sobbed, "It was just as nice as I hoped and dreamed it would be."

> "It was just as nice," she sobbed, "as I hoped and dreamed it would be."

> "It was just as nice as I hope and dreamed it would be," she sobbed.

With the dialogue guide first, the statement is definitely a quote, and more particularly, a report of a quote: She said *this*. Furthermore, the introductory dialogue guide continues the narrative, maintaining to some extent the narrator's control of the material. In other words, we are more conscious of the narrator standing between us and the speaker. In the second two versions, though, the quote breaks into the narrative; we are hearing a new voice, not the narrator's. By the time the dialogue guide does appear, identifying the source, the speaker has established his or her authority, or at least presence. Furthermore, the reader has a stronger sense of experiencing the speech directly, not second-hand through the narrator.

As for the difference between the second and third versions (the second being Didion's), the second exploits suspense. In addition, we hear "sobbed" early enough to appreciate the manner of the delivery. What good does it do to hear about it after we have read the quote, as happens in the third version ("oh, and she was crying the whole time she said this"). Notice that where Didion does identify the speaker last, the delivery is neutral: "'I got it down from five to three minutes,' Mr. Brennan said later." The importance here is the source, not the delivery. Sometimes, though, the manner dominates the content: "'Have a nice day!' *he snarled*."

Revision Assignments Select one of the following strategies and revise "Marrying Absurd." Include a brief statement explaining your choice and its effect on the arrangement and presentation of material.

1. Didion opens by citing the legal requirements for marriage in Las Vegas. Her abrupt opener identifies her subject but not her theme. Compose a more conventional thesis-first opening paragraph, then the next two paragraphs that would follow. Rearrange and re-present the material.

2. In paragraphs 3 and 4 we see (or rather hear) Didion at her most characteristic, at once ironic and relentless in recording detail. Revise the paragraphs into a more neutral, less judgmental voice—to convey information but not to invite interpretation.

Writing Assignments

1. Using Didion's style—her irony and detail and extensive quotation—write on another manifestation in American life of our moral and spiritual disorientation (where we are "looking for happiness in all the wrong places").

2. Write a first-person narrative of a Las Vegas wedding, using the details supplied by Didion but omitting the criticism and irony. Your narrator should be an innocent, someone not terribly reflective, someone who likes to think happy thoughts. Perhaps she is the bride in the last paragraph.

3. Focusing on technique as well as theme, compare and contrast "Marrying Absurd" with Carol Bly's "A Mongoose Is Missing." What common assumptions (or conclusions) do they seem to share? Where might they differ? (You might handle this using a joint question-and-answer format

with both Didion and Bly being interviewed on "The State of Morality in These United States.")

4. In "Marrying Absurd" Didion portrays assembly-line wedding chapels as offering shabby facsimiles of the real thing. Recount another area of American life where people seem willing to settle for poor imitations (say, amusement or "theme" parks).

In the Jungle

ANNIE DILLARD

Like any out-of-the-way place, the Napo River in the Ecuadorian jungle 1
seems real enough when you are there, even central. Out of the way of *what*?
I was sitting on a stump at the edge of a bankside palm-thatch village, in the
middle of the night, on the headwaters of the Amazon. Out of the way of human
life, tenderness, or the glance of heaven?

A nightjar in deep-leaved shadow called three long notes, and hushed. 2
The men with me talked softly in clumps: three North Americans, four
Ecuadorians who were showing us the jungle. We were holding cool drinks
and idly watching a hand-sized tarantula seize moths that came to the lone
bulb on the generator shed beside us.

It was February, the middle of summer. Green fireflies spattered lights 3
across the air and illumined for seconds, now here, now there, the pale trunks
of enormous, solitary trees. Beneath us the brown Napo River was rising, in
all silence; it coiled up the sandy bank and tangled its foam in vines that
trailed from the forest and roots that looped the shore.

Each breath of night smelled sweet, more moistened and sweet than any 4
kitchen, or garden, or cradle. Each star in Orion seemed to tremble and stir
with my breath. All at once, in the thatch house across the clearing behind us,
one of the village's Jesuit priests began playing an alto recorder, playing a
wordless song, lyric, in a minor key, that twined over the village clearing, that
caught in the big trees' canopies, muted our talk on the bankside, and wandered over the river, dissolving downstream.

This will do, I thought. This will do, for a weekend, or a season, or a 5
home.

Later that night I loosed my hair from its braids and combed it smooth— 6
not for myself, but so the village girls could play with it in the morning.

We had disembarked at the village that afternoon, and I had slumped on 7
some shaded steps, wishing I knew some Spanish or some Quechua so I
could speak with the ring of little girls who were alternately staring at me and
smiling at their toes. I spoke anyway, and fooled with my hair, which they
were obviously dying to get their hands on, and laughed, and soon they were
all braiding my hair, all five of them, all fifty fingers, all my hair, even my
bangs. And then they took it apart and did it again, laughing, and teaching
me Spanish nouns, and meeting my eyes and each other's with open delight,
while their small brothers in blue jeans climbed down from the trees and began kicking a volleyball around with one of the North American men.

Now, as I combed my hair in the little tent, another of the men, a free- 8
lance writer from Manhattan, was talking quietly. He was telling us the tale
of his life, describing his work in Hollywood, his apartment in Manhattan, his
house in Paris.... "It makes me wonder," he said, "what I'm doing in a tent
under a tree in the village of Pompeya, on the Napo River, in the jungle of

Ecuador." After a pause he added, "It makes me wonder why I'm going *back*."

The point of going somewhere like the Napo River in Ecuador is not to 9
see the most spectacular anything. It is simply to see what is there. We are
here on the planet only once, and might as well get a feel for the place. We
might as well get a feel for the fringes and hollows in which life is lived, for
the Amazon basin, which covers half a continent, and for the life that—there,
like anywhere else—is always and necessarily lived in detail: on the tributaries, in the riverside villages, sucking this particular white-fleshed guava in
this particular pattern of shade.

What is there is interesting. The Napo River is wide (I mean wider than 10
the Mississippi at Davenport) and brown, opaque, and smeared with floating
foam and logs and branches from the jungle. White egrets hunch on shoreline deadfalls and parrots in flocks dart in and out of the light. Under the
water in the river, unseen, are anacondas—which are reputed to take a few
village toddlers every year—and water boas, stingrays, crocodiles, manatees,
and sweet-meated fish.

Low water bares gray strips of sandbar on which the natives build tiny 11
palm-thatch shelters, arched, the size of pup tents, for overnight fishing trips.
You see these extraordinarily clean people (who bathe twice a day in the
river, and whose straight black hair is always freshly washed) paddling down
the river in dugout canoes, hugging the banks.

Some of the Indians of this region, earlier in the century, used to sleep 12
naked in hammocks. The nights are cold. Gordon MacCreach, an American
explorer in these Amazon tributaries, reported that he was startled to hear
the Indians get up at three in the morning. He was even more startled, night
after night, to hear them walk down to the river slowly, half asleep, and bathe
in the water. Only later did he learn what they were doing: they were getting
warm. The cold woke them; they warmed their skins in the river, which was
always ninety degrees; they returned to their hammocks and slept through
the rest of the night.

The riverbanks are low, and from the river you see an unbroken wall of 13
dark forest in every direction, from the Andes to the Atlantic. You get a taste
for looking at trees: trees hung with the swinging nests of yellow troupials,
trees from which seven-colored tanagers flutter, coral trees, teak, balsa and
breadfruit, enormous emergent silk-cotton trees, and the pale-barked *samona*
palms.

When you are inside the jungle, away from the river, the trees vault out 14
of sight. It is hard to remember to look up the long trunks and see the fans,
strips, fronds, and sprays of glossy leaves. Inside the jungle you are more
likely to notice the snarl of climbers and creepers round the trees' boles, the
flowering bromeliads and epiphytes in every bough's crook, and the fantastic
silk-cotton tree trunks thirty or forty feet across, trunks buttressed in flanges
of wood whose curves can make three high walls of a room—a shady, loamy-
aired room where you would gladly live, or die. Butterflies, iridescent blue,
striped, or clear-winged, thread the jungle paths at eye level. And at your feet
is a swath of ants bearing triangular bits of green leaf. The ants with their
leaves look like a wide fleet of sailing dinghies—but they don't quit. In

either direction they wobble over the jungle floor as far as the eye can see. I followed them off the path as far as I dared, and never saw an end to ants or to those luffing chips of green they bore.

Unseen in the jungle, but present, are tapirs, jaguars, many species of snake and lizard, ocelots, armadillos, marmosets, howler monkeys, toucans and macaws and a hundred other birds, deer, bats, peccaries, capybaras, agoutis, and sloths. Also present in this jungle, but variously distant, are Texaco derricks and pipelines, and some of the wildest Indians in the world, blow-gun-using Indians, who killed missionaries in 1956 and ate them.

Long lakes shine in the jungle. We traveled one of these in dugout canoes, canoes with two inches of freeboard, canoes paddled with machete-hewn oars chopped from buttresses of silk-cotton trees, or poled in the shallows with peeled cane or bamboo. Our part-Indian guide had cleared the path to the lake the day before; when we walked the path we saw where he had impaled the lopped head of a boa, open-mouthed, on a pointed stick by the canoes, for decoration.

This lake was wonderful. Herons, egrets, and ibises plodded the sawgrass shores, kingfishers and cuckoos clattered from sunlight to shade, great turkeylike birds fussed in dead branches, and hawks lolled overhead. There was all the time in the world. A turtle slid into the water. The boy in the bow of my canoe slapped stones at birds with a simple sling, a rubber thong and leather pad. He aimed brilliantly at moving targets, always, and always missed; the birds were out of range. He stuffed his sling back in his shirt. I looked around.

The lake and river waters are as opaque as rain-forest leaves; they are veils, blinds, painted screens. You see things by their effects. I saw the shoreline water roil and the sawgrass heave above a thrashing *paichi*, an enormous black fish of these waters; one had been caught the previous week weighing 430 pounds. Piranha fish live in the lakes, and electric eels. I dangled my fingers in the water, figuring it would be worth it.

We would eat chicken that night in the village, and rice, yucca, onions, beets, and heaps of fruit. The sun would ring down, pulling darkness after it like a curtain. Twilight is short, and the unseen birds of twilight wistful, uncanny, catching the heart. The two nuns in their dazzling white habits—the beautiful-boned young nun and the warm-faced old—would glide to the open cane-and-thatch schoolroom in darkness, and start the children singing. The children would sing in piping Spanish, high-pitched and pure; they would sing "Nearer My God to Thee" in Quechua, very fast. (To reciprocate, we sang for them "Old MacDonald Had a Farm"; I thought they might recognize the animal sounds. Of course they thought we were out of our minds.) As the children became excited by their own singing, they left their log benches and swarmed around the nuns, hopping, smiling at us, everyone smiling, the nuns' faces bursting in their cowls, and the clear-voiced children still singing, and the palm-leafed roofing stirred.

The Napo River: it is not out of the way. It is *in* the way, catching sunlight the way a cup catches poured water; it is a bowl of sweet air, a basin of greenness, and of grace, and, it would seem, of peace.

1982

Profile   This essay is not just about a place, but about a person *in* a place, a person responding, thinking. Dillard is there as witness and participant, our proxy, our stand-in. It is her active connection with the scene that brings it alive. She dramatizes what it is like to *be* there, fully and completely, in a way that most of us experience infrequently, if at all. To begin with, the first paragraph establishes the same kind of attentiveness that Virginia Woolf introduces in "The Death of the Moth," the same absorption that William Saroyan reported in reading "The Bell." She opens with a quiet moment: The river is flowing by, the men are talking quietly, a jungle bird calls out three times and hushes. It is one of those rare and valuable moments when life has slowed down, when we are relaxed but also keenly aware, noticing and enjoying what would normally escape us. It is the quietest time of the day in a quiet part of the world, a place free from the sensory overload of urban life.

And that contrast between urban and jungle life is stark, so stark that it compels the writer to meditate on its implications. Viewed from the perspective of an American city dweller, villages in the Ecuadorian jungle are backwaters—unsophisticated, stagnant, backward places where nothing significant happens. They are places one escapes to, or perhaps visits in a spirit of condescension and cultural superiority. But Dillard senses no privation, no inadequacy. The inhabitants seem peaceful, serene, content. They show no signs of missing the conveniences of modern city living, of believing that their simpler circumstances hinder their enjoyment of life or the conduct of their relationships.

If Gertrude Stein did say of Oakland, California, that "There is no there there," it would seem to be even truer of this village on the Napo, but Dillard would disagree. Life there is lived very much as it is anywhere else, "in detail"—that is, "sucking on this particular white-fleshed guava in this particular pattern of shade." And "What is there is interesting," which is probably true of most places if we take the trouble to study them. But such familiarity and appreciation owe as much to one's openness as to the merits of the place itself, and Dillard has arrived in a mode of attentiveness and receptivity. She has brought a certain state of mind to the scene, to her subject, receiving as well as endowing. Properly speaking, then, the essay is not simply about life on the Napo, but about Annie Dillard thinking about life on the Napo. She could present reflections of a similar quality in any other setting, including the heart of a large American city. And that is one of her points. There is as much of a *there* in that village on the Napo as there is anywhere else. And its inhabitants are as fully alive as those living in any modern city.

Composing Openers   The standard action movie now begins in the middle of a chase, a fight, some kind of disaster. Viewers are barely in their seats before they are on the edge of them. An accelerated pulse rate measures the effectiveness of such entertainment. The goal is to provide not a cerebral experience but, as reviewer Pauline Kael has suggested, "jolts for jocks." The equivalent opening for an essay would be a narrative or anecdote, a little piece of action to set up an explanation, like Frank Conroy's "Think About

It" or even June Kinoshita's "Maya Art for the Record." We all like stories; they have energy and they generally lead somewhere.

But consider the opening paragraphs of "In the Jungle":

> Like any out-of-the-way place, the Napo River in the Ecuadorian jungle seems real enough when you are there, even central. Out of the way of *what*? I was sitting on a stump at the edge of a bankside palm-thatch village, in the middle of the night, on the headwaters of the Amazon. Out of the way of human life, tenderness, or the glance of heaven?
>
> A nightjar in deep-leaved shadow called three long notes, and hushed. The men with me talked softly in clumps: three North Americans, four Ecuadorians who were showing us the jungle. We were holding cool drinks and idly watching a hand-sized tarantula seize moths that came to the lone bulb on the generator shed beside us.

This opening is deliberately slow (in an action movie, of course, this would only be the calm before the storm). Dillard begins with a thought, then sets a quiet scene. Individual sounds stand out; people speak softly, clutch cool drinks, are composed, thoughtful. Of course, she is being faithful to the setting, is being circumstantially accurate, but she is also composing the reader, preparing the reader to be receptive, as Virginia Woolf does with her opening to "The Death of the Moth." "In the Jungle" is less a travel essay than a meditation on life lived at a slower pace, a life conducive to attentiveness and engagement and appreciation.

Dillard could have begun her essay more energetically: the afternoon arrival by boat, the excited children, the memory of the river trip, a litany of all the wild life. Instead, she wants to prepare the reader, to put the reader in a mood to "get a feel for the place," to appreciate how life is lived in detail, to notice "the particular white-fleshed guava in this particular pattern of shade." When we live our lives, physically or mentally, on fast forward, we do not notice particular patterns of shade, even in our own backyards. The details slide. So Dillard writes a slow-motion opener, a quiet, meditative beginning for what will be a mental experience, not a physical adventure.

Transitions   *Transition* comes from a word meaning "to go across." In other words, a transition is a passage, from one place to another, one subject to another, one theme to another. In writing, such a passage suggests connection or coherence. To see how Annie Dillard handles transitions, consider the middle section of "In the Jungle":

> Later that night I loosed my hair from its braids and combed it smooth—not for myself, but so the village girls could play with it in the morning.
>
> We had disembarked at the village that afternoon, and I had slumped on some shaded steps, wishing I knew some Spanish or some Quechua so I could speak with the ring of little girls who were alternately staring at me and smiling at their toes. I spoke anyway, and fooled with my hair, which they were obviously dying to get their hands on, and laughed, and soon they were all braiding my hair, all five of them, all fifty fingers, all my hair, even my bangs. And then they took it apart and did it again, laughing, and teaching me Spanish nouns, and meeting my

eyes and each other's with open delight, while their small brothers in blue jeans climbed down from the trees and began kicking a volleyball around with one of the North American men.

Now, as I combed my hair in the little tent, another of the men, a free-lance writer from Manhattan, was talking quietly. He was telling us the tale of his life, describing his work in Hollywood, his apartment in Manhattan, his house in Paris. . . . "It makes me wonder," he said, "what I'm doing in a tent under a tree in the village of Pompeya, on the Napo River, in the jungle of Ecuador." After a pause he added, "It makes me wonder why I'm going *back*."

The section is both self-contained and parallel with the first passage, each ending with affirmations of life on the Napo ("This will do, I thought. This will do, for a weekend, or a season, or a home."; " 'It makes me wonder why I'm going *back*.' "). The first paragraph opens with a transition phrase, "Later that night": Later that night Dillard is loosening her hair from its braids, an act—it works out—pointing both forward and back. She is loosening her hair so the little girls from the village can play with it in the morning. But this ritual had begun that afternoon after her arrival, as she sat slumped on the steps wishing she could speak one of the local languages, but then found that her hair provided a way to communicate with the little girls from the village, who in turn taught her Spanish nouns while they played hairdresser.

With "now as I combed my hair," paragraph 3 jumps back to the moment established in the first paragraph of the section. While she combs she listens to the free-lance writer from Manhattan quietly telling the tale of his busy life, his work and homes in *in-the-way* places, and his final admission that he has fallen under the spell of the Napo. One is tempted to say that she uses her hair as a continuous strand to tie the present moment to her anticipation of the morning and to her memory of her arrival.

Revision Assignment   Use the following strategy to revise "In the Jungle," including a brief statement explaining its effect on the arrangement and presentation of material.

Rewrite at least the first part of "In the Jungle" as a third-person narrative: "*She* was sitting on a stump . . . " But do more than substitute one pronoun for another. Use a third-person *subjective* narrator, that is, a narrator who focuses on one character and reports what he or she is thinking (in this case, obviously, Dillard): "She wondered for a moment why some people called places like this out-of-the-way." This choice will also require you to reconsider the sequence of events. Do you reconstruct the events in a linear, sequential fashion, or do you work retrospectively, with flashbacks ("She remembered how she felt when they had first disembarked earlier that afternoon . . . ").

Writing Assignments

1. Although by conventional standards the Napo River in the Ecuadorian jungle is out of the way, Annie Dillard insists that, ultimately, it is not. It is "real enough when you are there, even central" and life there, as elsewhere, "is always and necessarily lived in detail . . . sucking this

particular white-fleshed guava in this particular pattern of shade." Write about some "out-of-the-way" place with which you are familiar, that is, a place not usually acknowledged for being glamorous, important, interesting—a place where one will not find "the most spectacular anything," but a place that is still "central." Focus especially on the specifics, on how life is lived there in detail, on its reality for the person who is thoroughly and attentively *there*. And use all the senses: What are the sights? The sounds? The smells? The textures? The tastes?

2. Dillard's essay deals in part with the quiet pace of life on the Napo as contrasted with the harried pace of modern urban life. Explore the pace of living in your own life, contrasting the busiest, most stressful moments with those when you are able to slow down, savor some of life's simpler pleasures, and take some time to think.

3. Dillard writes with an acute sense of place, a distinct sense and appreciation of what makes the Napo River and the life there so unique. At the same time, she locates herself firmly in the scene: She sits on a stump in the moonlight and watches the brown Napo roll by; village girls braid and rebraid her hair. Compare and contrast her treatment of the Napo River with Rick Bass's treatment of the Arkansas Delta in "Shortest Route to the Mountains." How does each communicate "a sense of place"?

Talking in Couples

BARBARA EHRENREICH

Some time ago, *Ms* magazine carried an article on how to talk to a man in   1
bed. My only disappointment was that it was not followed up by a series of
articles on how to talk to a man in other settings and on other items of furniture: "Talking in Living Rooms," for example, "Talking in Dinettes," and
"Talking on Straight-Backed Chairs." For it is my conviction, based on years
of what sociologists call participant observation, that far more male-female relationships die in the dining room than in the bedroom. And the problem is
not the cuisine, it's the conversation.

The fact is that we are going through a profound Crisis in Intersex Con-   2
versation, and that this crisis has been the subject of a vast, systematic
coverup. I am not referring to the well-known difficulty of maintaining equity in public discourse—meetings, cocktail parties, seminars, and the like—
a problem amply documented by our feminist foresisters in the late sixties. I
am referring to the much more insidious problem of intimate conversation
between consenting adults of different sexes. Television evangelists alert us
daily to new threats to the family, ranging from sex education to secular hu-
manism. No one, however, mentions the crisis in conversation, which is far
more serious. It threatens not only the family, but also the casual affair, the il-
licit liaison, and possibly the entire institution of heterosexuality.

I can understand that there are solid artistic and commercial reasons for   3
the coverup. If art were forced to conform to conversational reality, *A Man
and a Woman* would have been done as a silent film, and the Broadway hit
The Lunch Hour would have been condensed, quite adequately, into *The Coffee
Break*. Imagine, for example, what would happen if Gothic novels were required to meet truth-in-conversation standards:

> She: Now that we are alone, there is so much to talk about! I am filled
>   with such confusion, for I have never told you the secrets of my
>   origins. . . .
> He: Hmmm.
> She: The truth about my identity and my true relationship to the Earl of
>   D'Arcy, not to mention the real reason why the uppermost room in
>   the far turret of Weathermore Manor has been sealed for thirty
>   years!
> He: Uh-huh.
> She: You know the room at the top of the spiral staircase over the
>   stables? Well, there's something so terrifying, so abominable, so
>   *evil* . . .
> He: Hey, will you look at that? It stopped raining.

Nevertheless, the truth about male-female conversations has been leak-   4
ing out. In her book *On Loving Men*, Jane Lazarre recounts a particularly
disastrous conversational attempt with one of the objects of her love. Jane has

just spent a long phone call consoling her recently widowed mother-in-law, who is hysterical with grief. She tells her husband about the call (after all, it was *his* mother), "after which we both lie there quietly." But she is still—understandably—shaken, and begins to fantasize losing her own husband:

> Crying by now, due to the reality of my fantasy as well as the full comprehension of my mother-in-law's pain, I turn to James, then intrude upon his perpetual silence and ask, "What are you thinking?" hoping for once to be answered from some vulnerable depth. . . . And he admitted (it was an admission because he was incredulous himself at the fact): "I was thinking about the Knicks. Wondering if they were going to trade Frazier."

Jane Lazarre attributes her husband's talent for aborting conversations to some "quality of character" peculiar to him and, in the book, goes off in search of more verbose companionship. Thousands of other women have also concluded that theirs was an individual problem: "*He* just doesn't listen to me," "I just can't talk to him," and so forth. This, however, is a mistake. We are not dealing with individual problems—unfortunate conversational mismatches—but with a crisis of genderwide proportions. 5

Much of the credit for uncovering the crisis must go to a few stealthy sociologists who have devoted themselves to listening in on male-female conversations. Pamela Fishman planted tape recorders in the homes of three couples and recorded (with their permission) more than fifty hours of real-life chitchat. The picture that emerges from Fishman's work is that of women engaged in more or less solitary battle to keep the conversational ball rolling. Women nurture infant conversations—throwing out little hookers like "you know?" in order to enlist some help from their companions. Meanwhile, the men are often working at cross-purposes, dousing conversations with "ummms," non sequiturs, and unaccountable pauses. And, in case you're wondering, the subjects that Fishman's women nourished and men killed were neither boringly trivial nor threateningly intimate: they were frequently about current events, articles read, work in progress. Furthermore, the subjects of Fishman's research were couples who described themselves as "liberated" from sex roles. One can only wonder what she might have found by leaving her tape recorder in the average Levittown breakfast nook. 6

The problem is not that men are so taken with the strong, silent look that they *can't* talk. Sociologists Candace West and Donald Zimmerman did some extensive eavesdropping at various sites around the University of California campus at Santa Barbara and found that men interrupt women much more often than they interrupt other men and that they do so more often than women interrupt either men or other women. In analyzing her tapes of men and women who live together, Pamela Fishman found that topics introduced by men "succeeded" conversationally 96 percent of the time, while those introduced by women succeeded only 36 percent of the time and fell flat the rest of the time. Men can and will talk—if they can set the terms. 7

There are all kinds of explanations for the conversational mismatch between the sexes, none of which require more than a rudimentary feminist analysis. First, there's the fact that men are more powerful as a class of 8 people, and expect to dominate in day-to-day interactions, verbal or other-wise. Take any intersex gathering and—unless a determined countereffort is undertaken—the basses and tenors quickly overpower the altos and sopranos.

For most men, public discourse is a competitive sport, in which points are 9 scored with decisive finger jabs and conclusive table poundings, while adversaries are blocked with shoulder thrusts or tackled with sudden interruptions. This style does not, of course, carry over well to the conversational private sector. As one male informant admitted to me, albeit under mild duress, "If you're just with a woman, there's not real competition. What's the point of talking?"

Male dominance is not the only problem. There's also male insecurity. 10 When men have talked honestly about talking (or about not talking), either under psychiatric pressure or the lure of royalties, they tell us they are *afraid* to talk to women. Marc Feigen Fasteau confessed in *The Male Machine* that a "familiar blankness" overcame him in conversations with his wife, resulting from an "imagined fear that spontaneous talk will reveal unacceptable feelings—almost anything that would show vulnerability or indicate that the speaker doesn't 'measure up' to the masculine ideal."

Given the cultural barriers to intersex conversation, the amazing thing is 11 that we would even expect women and men to have anything to say to each other for more than ten minutes at a stretch. The barriers are ancient—perhaps rooted, as some paleontologist may soon discover, in the contrast between the occasional guttural utterances exchanged in male hunting bands and the extended discussions of female food-gathering groups. History does offer a scattering of successful mixed-sex conversational duos—Voltaire and Madame Du Chatelet, Marie and Pierre Curie—but the *mass* expectation that ordinary men and women should engage in conversation as a *routine* activity probably dates back no further than the 1950s and the era of "togetherness." Until then, male-female conversation had served principally as an element of courtship, sustained by sexual tension and easily abandoned after the nuptials. After suburbanization threw millions of couples alone together in tiny tract houses for whole weekends at a stretch, however, media pundits decided that conversation was not only a healthy but necessary marital activity, even if the topic never rose above the level of septic tanks and aluminum siding. While I have no direct evidence, the success of these early mixed-sex conversational endeavors may perhaps be gauged by the mass influx of women into the work force and the explosive spread of feminism in the 1960s and 1970s.

It was feminism, of course, that raised women's conversational expecta- 12 tions. In consciousness-raising groups and National Organization for Women chapters, women's centers and caucuses, women discovered (or rediscovered) the possibilities of conversation as an act of collective creativity: the intimate sharing of personal experience, the weaving of the personal into the general and political, the adventure of freewheeling speculation unrestrained by academic rules or boundaries.

As men became aware of the heightened demands being placed upon 13 them, their intellectual spokesmen quickly displaced the problem into the realm of sexuality. Thus Christopher Lasch, in discussing men's response to feminism, never even touches upon the conversational crisis, but tells us that "women's sexual demands terrify men," evoking images of "the vagina which threatens to eat them alive." But we could just as well invert this overwrought Freudiana and conclude that it is women's verbal demands that terrify men and that the dread *vagina dentata* (devouring, toothed vagina) of male fantasy is in fact a *mouth* symbol, all set to voice some conversational overture such as "Don't you think it's interesting that . . . ?"

Now that the crisis is out in the open, what do we do about it? Is there   14 any way to teach a grown man, or short of that, a little one, how to converse in a manner that is stimulating, interesting, and satisfying to women? One approach might be to work through the educational system, introducing required mixed-gender courses in English Conversation. Or we might take a clinical approach, setting up therapeutic centers to treat Male Conversational Dysfunction. Various diagnostic categories leap to mind: "Conversational Impotence" (total inability to get a subject off the ground); "Premature Ejaculation" (having the answer to everything before anybody else gets a chance to utter a sentence); "Conversus Interruptus"; and so forth. It may even be necessary, in extreme cases, to provide specially trained female Conversational Surrogates.

My own intuition is that the conversational crisis will be solved only   15 when women and men—not just women—together realize their common need for both social and personal change. After all, women have discovered each other and the joy of cooperative discourse through a common political project—the feminist movement. So struck was I with this possibility that I tried it out on a male companion: "Can you imagine women and men working together in a movement that demands both social and personal transformation?" There was a long, and I hoped pregnant, pause. Then he said, "Hmmmmm."

1981

Profile   In "Talking in Couples" Barbara Ehrenreich operates on her own turf, enjoying all the advantages of writing a personal opinion column for *Ms* magazine, a flagship publication of the feminist movement. Columnists enjoy a privilege most writers lack, a familiar audience of repeat readers. Thus, syndicated newspaper columnists like Ellen Goodman and Russell Baker have established a following of loyal and tolerant readers open to opinions on a wide range of subjects. But columnists in specialized publications like *Ms*, those with clearly defined subject matters and ideologies, enjoy an even further advantage: the assurance of a more intimate audience, one more homogeneous and dedicated, one with specialized interests and shared values. In other words, Barbara Ehrenreich has the security of writing to fellow partisans, readers whose knowledge and beliefs she shares. Instead of laying a groundwork of information and opinion, she can begin with these in place, writing as insider to insiders.

If in "Talking in Couples," then, Ehrenreich sometimes seems too sure of herself, to be preaching to the already converted and basing her arguments on debatable assumptions, it is because we are responding as outsiders, as latecomers to a continuing dialogue. To us the essay should be more self-contained, able to stand on its own argumentative legs; to her regular readers, the column is only one of a series, one based not only on previous columns but on other articles and essays in *Ms* magazine. It does not have to stand by itself. It has been buttressed by a continuous line of argument and information. The readers have been conditioned to accept what she has to say. To them she does not seem to be taking liberties when she asserts, "*The fact is* [my italics] that we are going through a profound Crisis in Intersex Conversation, and that this crisis has been the subject of a vast, systematic coverup," or when she refers to "*the well-known difficulty* of maintaining equity in public discourse." She knows what her readers know, knows what they have been reading, and has long since demonstrated her reliability to them, as well as her wit and intelligence and goodwill. She has established what classical rhetoricians called her *ethical proof* and "needs no introduction."

Even given its status as a piece of insider writing and the writer's highly distinctive voice, "Talking in Couples" models a classic three-part argument: definition of problem, description of causes, proposal of solution. The first part introduces the problem of intersex communication, the "coverup" of the problem, and testimony supporting the extent and nature of the problem, focusing on the inability of males to hold intimate conversations. The second part discusses the reasons males cannot talk: their need to maintain the strong, silent image; habits of male dominance; cultural barriers to intersex communication; and even the additional stress created by the woman's movement. And the final part offers a "solution," one that only reinforces the impression that men are hopeless: the requirement in schools of mixed-gender courses in English Conversation, clinics to treat Male Conversational Dysfunction, and—Ehrenreich's final hope—spontaneous male adoption of the feminist agenda ("the conversational crisis will be solved only when women and men—not just women—together realize their common need for both personal and social change").

But Ehrenreich does not dwell solely on what is amiss with the strong, silent sex. Throughout she contrasts her depiction of male shortcomings with a recommended alternative, reassuring the readers of *Ms* magazine that women are doing it right. Both privately and publicly, women initiate and model conversations, and from them men can learn "the possibilities of conversation as an act of collective creativity," and "the joy of cooperative discourse."

Writing with Humor   Like Edward Abbey ("Even the Bad Guys Wear White Hats"), Barbara Ehrenreich appreciates the value of humor in arguing an issue. Unrelieved by humor, many topics, especially when discussed at length, may be too grim for many readers. Further, for some topics a large number of readers have already made up their minds. In these cases humor becomes a softening-up tactic, a way to encourage readers to relax their defenses, to lower their guards long enough to admit a contrary point of view. And even if such people will not alter their positions, they may at least hold them less rigidly. After all, the opposition has shown that it is friendly.

For topics that are sensitive or controversial, writers risk alienating an audience unless they handle the presentation tactfully. Potentially, "Male

Conversational Dysfunction" is one such topic. Even with the reassurance of writing for *Ms* magazine, Ehrenreich is still criticizing the fathers, brothers, husbands, and male friends of her readers. If she seems too stern and unbending, if she seems driven only by anger and scorn, she will lose some of her audience. By using humor, though, she signals flexibility and tolerance.

The most general purpose of humor, though, is to help a writer establish goodwill, to affirm solidarity with the audience, a commonality of interests and values. If to some (men?) Ehrenreich's brand of humorous ridicule seems ill-willed, to others—her prime audience—it will be a rallying call. What better way to establish commonality, after all, than to form ranks to laugh at our perceived adversaries and persecutors? At the same time, by being the subjects of humor, they will seem less powerful. Traditionally, humans have affirmed their insider status by identifying and then rejecting outsiders: We know who is in the tribe by establishing who is outside. In this case women are in the tribe and men are not (at least until they learn to behave themselves).

Ehrenreich, then, uses humor not merely to lighten her subject and soften up her readers; she uses it to muster her audience.

Revision Assignments   Select one of the following strategies and revise "Talking in Couples." Include a brief statement explaining your choice of strategy and its effect on the arrangement and presentation of material.

1. Rewrite Ehrenreich's essay (or at least the first half of it), for a men's magazine ("Let's face it, guys, you just don't know how to talk to us!"). In the original Ehrenreich addressed insiders—the already converted (confirming their worst suspicions), those with a common body of knowledge and beliefs. You will be addressing a more skeptical audience, one composed of "masculinist" brothers, an audience reluctant to think the worst of itself.

2. Ehrenreich demonstrates a few of the values of humor in persuasive writing—as a softening-up technique, a way to make a serious topic less dreary, a means of signaling her ultimate goodwill. Select several passages where her humor shines most openly, then revise her argument to be completely somber and humorless. Then compare the results.

3. Revise Ehrenreich's essay into a question-and-answer interview format. In addition to composing questions, this approach will require you to condense and rearrange Ehrenreich's remarks.

Writing Assignments

1. Using your own "participant observations" for data, discuss the accuracy of Ehrenreich's assertions about male-female communication. Do you believe that we are going through "a profound Crisis in Intersex Communication"? Do you see cultural barriers to intersex conversations? Do you believe men fear spontaneous conversation lest they reveal inner weaknesses? Do you experience frequent "conversational mismatches" with members of the other sex? Do you find one sex more willing than the other to interrupt or to correct what someone else has said? If so, have you found any exceptions? Do the conversations you have with members

of your sex differ significantly from those you have with the other? Do you find it easier to talk with the other sex in private or in public? Do you find some topics more successful with one sex than the other?

2. Take the opposite, masculinist tack: Women and men can't communicate all right, but it is the fault of women. So, *is there any way to teach a grown woman, or short of that, a young girl, how to converse in a manner that is stimulating, interesting, and satisfying to men?*

3. Ehrenreich operates on the assumption that by nature men are competitive and women cooperative. Thus, "For most men, public discourse is a competitive sport," while feminist groups have discovered "the possibilities of conversation as an act of collective creativity." And this assumption is based on another, that one can make valid "genderalizations," wide-sweeping statements about both sexes. Do you agree that we can make such statements, or do you think they require significant qualification ("in some circumstances, men are more prone to . . . ")? And if you do agree that we can at least make qualified generalizations (otherwise, we have to agree that both sexes behave pretty much the same), what do you think of the male-female, competition/cooperation statement? Again, use your own "participant observations" for data.

4. In paragraph 3, Ehrenreich has some fun presenting the kind of dialogue we might find in Gothic novels if they adhered to "truth-in-conversation standards." Write some dialogue of your own depicting communication (or miscommunication) between the sexes. Your objective is either to confirm or refute Ehrenreich's position.

A Storm, the Cornfield, and Elk

GRETEL EHRLICH

Last week a bank of clouds lowered itself down summer's green ladder and let loose with a storm. A heavy snow can act like fists: trees are pummeled, hay- and grainfields are flattened, splayed out like deer beds; field corn, jack-knifed and bleached blond by the freeze, is bedraggled by the brawl. All night we heard groans and crashes of cottonwood trunks snapping. "I slept under the damned kitchen table," one rancher told me. "I've already had one of them trees come through my roof." Along the highway electric lines were looped to the ground like dropped reins. 1

As the storm blows east toward the Dakotas, the blue of the sky intensi-fies. It inks dry washes and broad grasslands with quiet. In their most com-plete gesture of restraint, cottonwoods, willows, and wild rose engorge them-selves with every hue of ruddiness—russet, puce, umber, gold, musteline—whose spectral repletion we know also to be an agony, riding on-coming waves of cold. 2

The French call the autumn *feuille morte.*[1] When the leaves are finally cor-rupted by frost they rain down into themselves until the tree, disowning it-self, goes bald. 3

All through Autumn we hear a double voice: one says everything is ripe; the other says everything is dying. The paradox is exquisite. We feel what the Japanese call "aware"[2]—an almost untranslatable word meaning some-thing like "beauty tinged with sadness." Some days we have to shoulder against a marauding melancholy. Dreams have a hallucinatory effect: in one, a man who is dying watches from inside a huge cocoon while stud colts run through deep mud, their balls bursting open, their seed spilling into the black ground. My reading brings me this thought from the mad Zen priest Ikkyu: "Remember that under the skin you fondle lie the bones, waiting to reveal themselves." But another day, I ride in the mountains. Against rim-rock, tall aspens have the graceful bearing of giraffes, and another small grove, not yet turned, gives off a virginal limelight that transpierces every-thing heavy. 4

Fall is the end of a rancher's year. Third and fourth cuttings of hay are stacked; cattle and sheep are gathered, weaned, and shipped; yearling bulls and horse colts are sold. "We always like this time of year, but it's a lot more fun when the cattle prices are up!" a third generation rancher tells me. 5

This week I help round up their cows and calves on the Big Horns. The storm system that brought three feet of snow at the beginning of the month now brings intense and continual rain. Riding for cows resembles a wild game of touch football played on skis: cows and cowboys bang into each other, or else, as the cows run back, the horse just slides. Twice today my buckskin falls with me, crushing my leg against a steep sidehill, but the mud and snow, now trampled into gruel, is so deep it's almost impossible to get bruised. 6

[1]Dead leaf.

[2]Pronounced ah-wah-ray.

When the cattle are finally gathered, we wean the calves from the cows in portable corrals by the road. Here, black mud reaches our shins. The stock dogs have to swim in order to move. Once, while trying to dodge a cow, my feet stuck, and losing both boots in the effort to get out of the way, I had to climb the fence barefooted. Weaning is noisy; cows don't hide their grief. As calves are loaded into semis and stock trucks, their mothers—five or six hundred of them at a time—crowd around the sorting alleys with outstretched necks, their squared-off faces all opened in a collective bellowing.

On the way home a neighboring rancher who trails his steers down the mountain highway loses one as they ride through town. There's a high-speed chase across lawns and flower beds, around the general store and the fire station. Going at a full lope, the steer ducks behind the fire truck just as Mike tries to rope him. "Missing something?" a friend yells out her window as the second loop sails like a burning hoop to the ground.

"That's nothing," one onlooker remarks. "When we brought our cattle through Kaycee one year, the minister opened the church door to see what all the noise was about and one old cow just ran in past him. He had a hell of a time getting her out."

In the valley, harvest is on but it's soggy. The pinto bean crops are sprouting, and the sugar beets are balled up with mud so that one is indistinguishable from the other. Now I can only think of mud as being sweet. At night the moon makes a brief appearance between storms and laces mud with a confectionary light. Farmers whose last cutting of hay is still on the ground turn windrows to dry as if they were limp, bedridden bodies. The hay that has already been baled is damp, and after four inches of rain (in a country where there's never more than eight inches a year) mold eats its way to the top again.

The morning sky looks like cheese. Its cobalt wheel has been cut down and all the richness of the season is at our feet. The quick-blanch of frost stings autumn's rouge into a skin that is tawny. At dawn, mowed hay meadows are the color of pumpkins, and the willows, leafless now, are pink and silver batons conducting inaudible river music. When I dress for the day, my body, white and suddenly numb, looks like dead coral.

After breakfast there are autumn chores to finish. We grease head gates on irrigation ditches, roll up tarp dams, pull horseshoes, and truck horses to their winter pasture. The harvest moon gives way to the hunter's moon. Elk, deer, and moose hunters repopulate the mountains now that the livestock is gone. One young hunting guide has already been hurt. While he was alone at camp, his horse kicked him in the spleen. Immobilized, he scratched an SOS with the sharp point of a bullet on a piece of leather he cut from his chaps. "Hurt bad. In pain. Bring doctor with painkiller," it read. Then he tied the note to the horse's halter and threw rocks at the horse until it trotted out of camp. When the horse wandered into a ranch yard down the mountain, the note was quickly discovered and a doctor was helicoptered to camp. Amid orgiastic gunfire, sometimes lives are saved.

October lifts over our heads whatever river noise is left. Long carrier waves of clouds seem to emanate from hidden reefs. There's a logjam of them around the mountains, and the horizon appears to drop seven thousand feet. Though the rain has stopped, the road ruts are filled to the brim. I saw a frog jump cheerfully into one of them. Once in a while the mist clears and we can see the dark edge of a canyon or an island of vertical rimrock in the white bulk of snow. Up there, bull elk have been fighting all fall over harems. They charge with antlered heads, scraping the last of the life-giving velvet off, until one bull wins and trots into the private timber to mount his prize, standing almost humanly erect on hind legs while holding a cow elk's hips with his hooves.

In the fall, my life, too, is timbered, an unaccountably libidinous place: 14 damp, overripe, and fading. The sky's congestion allows the eye's iris to open wider. The cornfield in front of me is torn parchment paper, as brittle as bougainvillea leaves whose tropical color has somehow climbed these northern stalks. I zigzag through the rows as if they were city streets. Now I want to lie down in the muddy furrows, under the frictional sawing of stalks, under corncobs which look like erections, and out of whose loose husks sprays of bronze silk dangle down.

Autumn teaches us that fruition is also death; that ripeness is a form of   15 decay. The willows, having stood for so long near water, begin to rust. Leaves are verbs that conjugate the seasons.

Today the sky is a wafer. Placed on my tongue, it is a wholeness that has   16 already disintegrated; placed under the tongue, it makes my heart beat strongly enough to stretch myself over the winter brilliances to come. Now I feel the tenderness to which this season rots. Its defenselessness can no longer be corrupted. Death is its purity, its sweet mud. The string of storms that came across Wyoming like elephants tied tail to trunk falters now and bleeds into a stillness.

There is neither sun, nor wind, nor snow falling. The hunters are gone;   17 snow geese waddle in grainfields. Already, the elk have started moving out of the mountains toward sheltered feedgrounds. Their great antlers will soon fall off like chandeliers shaken from ballroom ceilings. With them the light of these autumn days, bathed in what Tennyson called "a mockery of sunshine," will go completely out.

1985

Profile   The title, "A Storm, the Cornfield, and Elk," names three subjects, but the essay itself contains five sections. Furthermore, Ehrlich does not observe the order suggested by her title, first devoting most of her attention to the aftermath of the storm, then treating the elk before the cornfield episode, and each of these in a half paragraph. So the questions arise: What are the parts? How do they relate? How do they connect? In other words, how do they achieve unity, coherence, and emphasis? Or are the five sections separate sketches loosely tied to the theme of Wyoming's autumn moods? Which do we make of it: some attractive scraps that Ehrlich wants to use because they contain some of her most lyrical writing, or a unified, coherent statement?

"All through autumn we hear a double voice: one says everything is ripe; the other says everything is dying," writes Ehrlich in the first section. And in her conclusion she observes, "Autumn teaches us that fruition is also death; that ripeness is a form of decay." This, then, is her theme: Autumn, especially in Wyoming, is an exquisite paradox, a season of mixed signals—everything is ripe, everything is dying; the fullness of life implies the end of life. The beautiful ruddiness of cottonwoods, willows, and wild rose is a *repletion* (abundant, from a word meaning "refilled") but also an agony, a gauge of the extreme cold. The voice of autumn speaks a message of "beauty tinged with sadness," but amidst the melancholy Ehrlich finds aspens with the graceful bearing of giraffes, and the small grove with its virginal limelight, "transpiercing" everything heavy.

The second section presents the frenzied mountain roundup necessitated by the storm. But then the roundup, for all its tragic overtones (the separation of calves from their mothers, for example), takes on a comic face: the wild game of touch football played on skis; the wild cow chase across town lawns and through flower beds; the story of the Kansas City church cow.

After the mountain roundup, the third section shifts to the harvest scene in the valley: the sugar beets suggesting balls of sweet mud; the moon appearing between storms and lacing the mud with "confectionary" light (light the color of powdered sugar?); the rows of hay cuttings looking like "limp, bedridden bodies"; the frost stinging "autumn's rouge" into one's skin (suggesting the ruddiness of the cottonwoods, willows, and wildrose mentioned elsewhere); the mowed hay meadows the color of pumpkins; the writer's own body the color of dead coral; the completion of autumn chores as the harvest moon gives way to the hunter's moon (the mountains, now empty of cattle, fill up with elk, deer, and moose hunters); then the anecdote about the resourcefulness of the injured hunting guide.

The fourth section turns to the October skies, where waves of clouds logjam in the mountains, and to the muddy roads with rain-filled potholes, and to the snow-covered mountains again, where elk are fighting and mating, and to the writer's own phallic hallucinations amidst the cornstalks (which mirror the hallucinatory dream about stud colts described in the first section). Even in the "frictional sawing" of the dried and dying stalks, the corncobs suggest regeneration.

The fifth section concludes Ehrlich's hymn to autumn: "fruition is also death . . . ripeness is a form of decay." Willows, those water-loving trees, begin to rust, and leaves are "verbs that conjugate the seasons." To confirm the spiritual force that informs the paradox of life in death, Ehrlich likens the sky to a communion wafer that she places under her tongue to strengthen herself for the winter ordeal. The worst has happened; the season rots and thus can no longer be corrupted. "Death is its purity, its sweet mud" (the third mention of this image). After filing across Wyoming "like elephants tied trunk to tail," the storms are bleeding into stillness. Everything is still, except perhaps where snow geese waddle in the grainfields; the antlers are about to fall from the elk (to sprout again); and the autumn light is going out. One year is over, but another is already gathering.

There is nothing random or self-indulgent, then, about "A Storm, the Cornfield, and Elk." As a series of narrative-descriptive sketches structured thematically around a sequence of related images, the essay has found yet another way to achieve unity, coherence, and emphasis. The sketches also move rhythmically between sky and earth. Ehrlich is continually looking up and down—up to the storm clouds and down to the trees and fields they have pummeled, up to the intense blue of the sky and down to the dry washes and grasslands that it "inks" with silence, up to the mountains and down to the valley, up to the island of rimrock where the elk mate and down to her cornfield, where she wants to lie down and look up. And, in the last paragraph, the sky is a wafer that she places under her tongue before she returns to the idea of the sweet mud.

Instead of pursuing a continuous flow of ideas as we would expect of a more conventional essay, "A Storm, the Cornfield, and Elk" finds its own unity in a sequence of related images and actions. Its method is chiefly descriptive and dramatic, but it is of a piece; it is about one thing.

Writing with Figurative Language   Most of us would concede that we are not up to the level of figurative language that seems to come so easily to Gretel Ehrlich. A cattle roundup in the mud as "a wild game of touch football played on skis," leafless willows as "pink and silver batons conducting inaudible river music," a string of storms coming across Wyoming "like elephants tied tail to trunk," electric lines looped to the ground "like dropped reins"—such comparisons simply would not occur to most of us. What, then, are we to do? If we try to force metaphors and similes, the results can be disastrous, even ludicrous: "The sun rose slowly, like a fiery fur ball coughed up uneasily onto a sky-blue carpet by a giant unseen cat," or "The horizon coughed up the morning sun much as if Atlas had lowered the world from his mighty shoulders and given it the Heimlich maneuver."

These figures of speech are deliberate parodies, but they parody something genuine: the attempt to parade our ingenuity, to impress rather than to be accurate. But at least they are consistent. In the attempt to find clever comparisons, some writers forget to visualize: "A loaded gun is a two-edged sword"; "If you go to the well once too often, you'll be burned"; "Don't beat your head against a dead horse." Other times, we might have stumbled honestly onto a useful comparison but cannot express it economically: "Her flamethrower passion ignited his spent desire, like those little paper wrappers you see on bran muffins when you leave them in the oven too long." In this case the simile is unnecessary. There is already a vivid comparison in the idea of ignited desire, and readers know what it is like when something catches on fire. And even professional writers can commit this excess. In one passage from *Women in Love*, D. H. Lawrence reports that a character's emotions "had poured to the ground and spilled out." If a liquid has been poured on the ground, it *has* spilled out.

If, afraid of such disasters, we avoid figurative language, we forfeit a valuable resource. But metaphors and similes are such vivid descriptive devices that their very conspicuousness can overpower their setting, like a moose in a canoe.

Exercise   The following is Ehrlich's opening paragraph, heavy with metaphors and similes, the former often in the verbal form ("jackknifed" instead of "folded up"). Revise the paragraph without such figures of speech, Be completely literal, but also try to construct a vivid and moving description.

Then write a brief paragraph explaining what you learned by removing the figurative language.

> [1]Last week a bank of clouds lowered itself down summer's green ladder and let loose with a storm. [2]A heavy snow can act like fists: trees are pummeled, hay- and grainfields are flattened, splayed out like deer beds; field corn, jackknifed and bleached blond by the freeze, is bedraggled by the brawl. [3]All night we heard groans and crashes of cottonwood trunks snapping. [4]"I slept under the damned kitchen table," one rancher told me. [5]"I've already had one of them trees come through my roof." [6]Along the highway electric lines were looped to the ground like dropped reins.

Using Colons and Semicolons   Like all polished writers Ehrlich has mastered the rhetoric of punctuation, elevating to an art the mechanical business of connecting and separating sentence elements. Punctuation is not simply a matter of learning conventions, of memorizing rules; it involves developing a feel for how to arrange and sequence and pace our assertions, for how to dramatize the relationship between our ideas. Ehrlich displays such a feel in "A Storm, the Cornfield, and Elk," even with those marks that so often confound the average writer, colons and semicolons.

One function of a colon is to divide one kind of two-part sentence: before the colon appears a generalization; after follows one or more explanatory or illustratative statements. A writer might punctuate such statements as separate sentences, but at the cost of weakening the relationship between them—the implied inevitability of assertion tied to support. Ehrlich illustrates several times:

> A heavy snow can act like fists: trees are pummeled, hay- and grainfields are flattened, splayed out like deer beds; field corn, jackknifed and bleached blond by the freeze, is bedraggled by the brawl.

> All through Autumn we hear a double voice: one says everything is ripe; the other says everything is dying.

> Riding for cows resembles a wild game of touch football played on skis: cows and cowboys bang into each other, or else, as the cows run back, the horse just slides.

The first example could be a miniparagraph, one with a unifying theme: A heavy snow acts like fists, pummeling trees, flattening hay- and grainfields, and leaving corn looking as if it had been in a brawl. And because the explanatory statements contain their own internal punctuation, she separates them with semicolons (otherwise, she could have used commas). She again uses semicolons in the second example, but by a different logic. There, she wishes to give more weight to the two voices of autumn: "one says everything is ripe; the other says everything is dying." The third example also uses a colon to introduce twin statements, but they are linked by a coordinating conjunction: "cows and cowboys bang into each other, or else, as the cows run back, the horse just slides."

And then she draws upon the colon to play a more familiar role, to introduce and emphasize a quotation:

> My reading brings me this thought from the mad Zen priest Ikkyu: "Remember that under the skin you fondle lie the bones, waiting to reveal themselves."

In addition to using semicolons to separate items in a series, Ehrlich also uses them in another familiar role, to connect a series of independent clauses:

> Third and fourth cuttings of hay are stacked; cattle and sheep are gathered, weaned, and shipped; yearling bulls and horse colts are sold.

Without the internal punctuation in the second clause, she could have linked the series of independent clauses with simple commas and no conjunctions:

> **Third and fourth cuttings of hay are stacked, cattle and sheep are gathered and shipped, yearling bulls and horse colts are sold.**

And, of course, she might have punctuated them as separate sentences:

> **Third and fourth cuttings of hay are stacked. Cattle and sheep are gathered, weaned, and shipped. Yearling bulls and horse colts are sold.**

Notice that by combining the three statements into a single sentence, Ehrlich emphasizes the busyness, the near simultaneity of the frenzied fall roundup.

Revision Assignments   Select one of the following strategies and revise "A Storm, the Cornfield, and Elk." Include a brief statement explaining your choice and its effect on the arrangement and presentation of material.

1. Choose several of the paragraphs from "A Storm, the Cornfield, and Elk" that are most laden with similes, metaphors, and other figurative language. Then, to the best of your ability, remove them and substitute literal equivalents. Be accurate, but also be "prosaic."

2. Throughout the essay Ehrlich narrates primarily in the present tense. Rewrite the second section in the past tense, making any other changes that might seem appropriate after you change the verbs. Then compare the two versions.

Writing Assignments

1. Compose your own lyrical, impressionistic account of a seasonal ritual, one capturing the feeling of the weather (sights, sounds, smells), and one frequently using the present tense for a sense of immediacy. Locate this ritual in a specific place, being concrete about weather, geography, vegetation, animal and human activity, and so on.

2. Gretel Ehrlich's "A Storm, the Cornfield, and Elk" and Edward Abbey's "Even the Bad Guys Wear White Hats" present two different views of ranch life. Compare and contrast the two visions, considering how each writer would view the other's (recalling that Ehrlich did read Abbey's essay and disapproved of his pugnacious attitude).

3. Like Annie Dillard's "In the Jungle," "A Storm, the Cornfield, and Elk" salutes a geographically distinctive place, one far removed from the experience of most city and town dwellers. Compare the two accounts—their themes, their language, their organization, the role of the narrators.

A Backyard Robin, Ho-Hum

PAUL GRUCHOW

Base camp: a green shelf a story above a narrow lake in the Bighorn Basin, a wild, inaccessible place bitten out of Wyoming's Big Horn Mountains. Several stunted pines sheltered us against the winds. We pitched our tent upon a carpet of pine needles. Near its door stood a small, flat rock, our dining table. To the north, the lake—shallow except along the serpentine channel of the stream running through it—was actually less a lake than a widening of the stream. Its water was ice cold and clear as air. Across the lake, another stand of pines, and then eighty towering stories of granite. To the south, three or four square yards of alpine meadow, an animal trail, another rock wall seventy-five stories high. To the east and west, waterfalls, tumbling from and leading into lakes.

On our ledge we could watch the trout emerging from the shadows of submerged rocks, gliding along the brown-green bottom, suddenly bursting upward to snatch hatching insects, invisible to us, on the surface. There is some evidence that trout, which have a rather good sense of smell, can catch the scent of their tiny prey. Perhaps they can also hear them. Trout perceive underwater sounds acutely through a series of sonar sensors along their lateral lines, and the nymphs on which they prey pop when they hatch, sometimes loudly enough that the sound is audible to human ears. The source of the popping noise is the little gas bubble that forms in the nymphal sac just prior to hatching. It serves as a balloon, propelling the nymph to the water's surface, and when it explodes there, it also helps the nymph emerge from its birth chamber.

In the pristine waters of high mountain lakes, you can see the trout as clearly as if they were swimming in an aquarium. Those feeding in the lake below our tent site, we could see, were members of a species new to us, *Salmo aguabonita*, beautiful-water trout, commonly known as golden trout. Once the species was found only in the headwaters of the South Fork of the Kern River in the Sierra Nevada, to which it was limited by high and inaccessible waterfalls. It has since been transplanted to other streams, but it is still something of a rarity, a creature of very pure, very high mountain pools and rapids. It is among the most beautiful of freshwater fishes, tropical in the brilliance of its coloring: a speckled green along its back, scarlet in its gills and along its lateral lines, splashed with brick red on its belly, which is the color of aspen leaves in autumn or—as outdoorsman Stewart Edward White, who first saw the fish in its original habitat in 1903, said—the color of "the twenty-dollar goldpiece, the same satin finish, the same gold yellow." "One would almost expect," he said, "that on cutting the flesh it would be found golden through all its substance." It darts through the water like a liquid rainbow.

We were at timberline. On the next step up the glacial staircase, thickets of dwarf willows grew, and above that only grasses, sedges, mosses, and ground-hugging forbs. In "ecological latitude" we were at the equivalent of Hudson Bay. We were soon to be forcefully reminded of this.

John, my fellow camper, had caught a pair of trout for supper and was thinking of cleaning them when a chill rain began to fall. We had just hustled into rain gear when hail came, thick as snow, marble-sized. (These measurements are, as far as I know, standard in hail country: pea-sized, marble-sized, golf-ball sized, baseball-sized.) The stones felt as hard as marbles, hurled as they were out of violent clouds and free-falling thousands of feet onto our thin-skinned bodies. One whacked against my forehead, sending tremors through my skull. "Shit!" I said, and then, as if I were still a little boy being punished for swearing, I got a good stiff smack against a bone in the back of my hand. Above the blasts of the wintry wind I would hear John cursing too as we scrambled in opposite directions toward the paltry shelter offered by the pines. There we perched like a pair of bedraggled grouse while the hailstones piled up around us. The ice storm, mercifully, did not last long, but the winds continued to gust out of the west, thick with a fine mist.

We schemed to wait the weather out, but it had more energy than we. Eventually John emerged from his tree-cave and took the trout down to the edge of the lake to clean them. I, in the meantime, hauled the tiny stove out of a soggy pack, set it up in the shelter of our dining rock, and anxiously nursed it. It sputtered and moaned in the wind but caught hold, its throbbing flame making a cheerful roar. John returned with the fillets. "It's so cold," he said, "that the lake water actually feels warm." I fried the fish in a little butter. They curled in the pan, as if they were still capable of fleeing from the heat. We ate them, every tender, succulent flake, under a steady drizzle, our backs turned to the wind while we stomped our soaked and stiffening feet to warm them. At a fish apiece we dined modestly. White reported that he and his two companions sat down, the first time they fished for golden trout, to a supper of sixty-five fish.

The rain failed to thaw the hailstones, hot chocolate failed to thaw us, and the thick, black storm clouds had imposed an early dusk. We were content to retreat to our sleeping bags. Rain pattered against the tent, which was billowing and sagging in the gale, but we were warm and cozy and free as the wind. We could not be summoned from anywhere by anybody; not another soul on Earth had any idea where to find us. Nothing demanded doing, nothing remained unattended. Our sole obligation, at that moment, was to abandon ourselves to the blustery night. We did so feeling wealthy in everything we had to spend: those dark and secure hours and the whole range of our half-awake imaginings.

In the morning the sun arrived to pay a long visit. It seemed more than fortuitous, beyond the normal course of events, a gift, like a yellow rose in the breadbox. That the mountain did not stand in the way of the sun seemed somehow a concession on its part, and the mountain never makes concessions. It is unforgiving, unyielding, not in the least considerate. It does not care whether you come or go, prosper or fail, find your way or lose it. To the mountain, it is all the same: You respect it, or wish later that you had. Either way, the mountain says. Have it as you wish. But in the end it always prevails.

The sun beamed down upon us, seeming benevolent, but the robin nest-   9
ing in the pine tree just beyond our tent door was furious at the intrusion and
voiced its opinion loudly before retreating a discreet distance to await happier developments. Our immediate and permanent departure, preferably.

The robin! Like the story someone is forever telling about bumping into   10
the mailman in a back alley in Budapest or sitting down at a table in the only
restaurant in Urubamba [Peru] and seeing the cousin who hasn't been heard
from in twenty years at the table directly opposite, deep in conversation with
the Homecoming Queen of 1952, and neither of them looking a day older. A
backyard robin, ho-hum. Bob-bob-bobbing along.

Unfair, I know. The robin has become commonplace, adapted to a virtu-   11
osic range of habitats, from coast to coast, from sea level to 12,000 feet or so
in elevation, from city streets to remote wilderness regions. But it was not always so. At the advent of European settlement the robin occurred in much
smaller numbers and in much more localized populations than it does today.
It is by its nature a creature of edges. It prefers to nest in trees, although it
will settle for almost any aboveground structure: There is a report in the bird
literature of a robin successfully nesting on the boom of a construction crane,
even though it was in regular use at the time. Yet the robin favors relatively
open country. So it once routinely avoided vast areas of the continent—the
extensive prairies of the midcontinent and the interior regions of the dense
eastern forests in particular.

Robins have suffered serious setbacks since then. In the 19th Century   12
they were profligately hunted, particularly in the South, as were meadowlarks, bobolinks, and passenger pigeons, among others. No less an authority
than John James Audubon pronounced them "fat and juicy . . . excellent eating." The toll was so heavy that, at the turn of the century, robins seemed
destined to become a rare, if not extinct, species. Not until 1913 did they and
other songbirds come under protection of the U.S. Migratory Bird Treaty
Act, and it took years to establish effective enforcement of the law. The ultimately unsuccessful war against Dutch elm disease, fought for a long time
with DDT, incidentally resulted in an extravagant slaughter, not only of robins and other birds but also of the scavengers of their carcasses. And robins
have been subjected to chemical barrages of a more localized sort: In 1972 a
single application of Azodrin to combat potato aphids in Dade County, Florida, killed 10,000 migrating robins in three days. Until 1973 blueberry growers in New Brunswick, Canada, waged aggressive battle against robins—
which happen to be prodigious harvesters of insect pests—until they were
brought up short by an equally aggressive public opinion campaign.

Still, on the whole, robins have thrived, and in the last couple of centuries   13
they have become nearly ubiquitous in North America. This has been read as
a triumph of adaptability. The most extreme statement of the case, I think, is
this one, from the book *The American Robin* by Len Eiserer:

"The Robin's many successes in extending its range over pre-Colonial   14
times offer a marked contrast to the achievements of most other native
American populations. Consider, for example, the Indian: With the coming of
white civilization, both the American Robin and the American Indian
watched the wholesale loss of a great primeval way of life. But it might
be suggested (albeit with oversimplification) that while one group

compromised, adapted, and consequently prospered, the other group resisted, clung to the old, and was largely destroyed."

This statement is inherently racist (there was a Migratory Bird Treaty 15 Act, it might be noted, but never, when it would have mattered, a Native American Protection Act) and manifests a certain self-hatred—a willingness to celebrate any circumstance in which another species is perceived as having bested humans, a dangerous and counterproductive strain of environmentalism. But beyond this, it follows a trivial and falsely comforting line of reasoning. There is, in fact, little evidence that the robin's success has been due to its adaptability. Rather, the continent itself has been altered on a large scale with a result that replicates conditions the robin favored before settlement. As the eastern forests have been cleared or thinned and the prairies plowed and domesticated, the robin's natural range has been vastly extended. The landscape, not the robin, has changed. I doubt whether this is a triumph for nature, even though it has promoted the prosperity of one species of bird. On the contrary, it is one more reason to doubt the efficacy of our management of the biosphere.

We now perceive the homogenization of urban America as a truism. The 16 pervasive influence of the mass media and the concentration of economic power have helped to create a society in which many local, or even regional, distinctions have vanished. We all watch the same television programs, read essentially the same newspapers, shop in the same national stores, live in the same houses, and subscribe, mostly, to the same middle-of-the-road politics and philosophy of life. A person crossing the country from one airport or commercial strip or housing development to the next has only the local road signs and certain peculiarities of flora—if there are palm trees in the boulevards, it can't be Ohio—as reliable visual clues to place. This monotony of physical detail has, perhaps, promoted social stability and a certain kind of economic efficiency. But we rightly wonder what strengths of culture, what resiliency, we have sacrificed in adopting such bland uniformity.

Less often remarked is the phenomenon the robin represents, the parallel 17 homogenization of the natural landscape. As we have drained the swamps and marshes, leveled the forests, farmed the prairies, and diverted the waters of the western rivers for the greening of the deserts, we have done something more pervasive than simply destroying a multitude of local habitats. Not only have we undermined the framework for biological diversity but we have—sometimes deliberately, sometimes unintentionally—substituted look-alike ecosystems for regionally distinctive ones.

In my prairie town of Worthington, Minnesota, the upland sandpipers 18 and bobolinks are mostly gone and meadowlarks become rarer every year, but I see plenty of robins and eastern bluebirds. White pelicans no longer nest there, but wood ducks do, in artificial nests. The gray wolf is extinct, but the coyote has moved east to replace it. The only elk I have ever seen at home was an escapee from a game farm, but I see white-tailed deer, a woodland animal, almost every time I go for a walk. The otter has disappeared, but there are plenty of beaver in that formerly treeless landscape. As I write, they are busy cutting down the crabapple trees in the city park near my house. I have no chance of seeing a pronghorn antelope anymore, but opossums are plentiful. Most prairie children do not now encounter any of the magnificent large mammals of their place—the grizzlies, the elk, the antelopes, the bison—until they take a trip to one of the sanctuaries of the intermountain West, to Yellowstone National Park, for example. Their own biological heritage no longer exists at home.

That heritage has so thoroughly vanished, in fact, that it no longer survives even in memory. A few years ago the biology department at the community college in my town set out to turn a vacant corner of the campus into a nature study area. The first step: A magnificent stand of native cottonwood trees were razed and replaced with Colorado blue spruces! I was furious, but I also found the whole project screamingly funny. I soon learned it was a joke I couldn't share with my neighbors. I always had to explain the punch line. "Well, you see, the cottonwood is natural here, and the blue spruce isn't, and this is a *nature* study area . . . " The prairie, I discovered, is an arcane subject in my prairie town.   19

The robin flew angrily from its pine tree next to our tent and perched nearby on a rock in the shadow of a shrubby cinquefoil bush, one of the potentillas.   20

We know the potentillas quite well, of course, in Worthington. A third of the foundation plantings and rock gardens here, I would guess, contain species of potentilla. Spruce, Douglas fir, mountain ash, cedar: These we also know well. The nurseries stock them routinely. But suppose you wanted to plant a tree or shrub native to the region. Suppose you wanted a bur oak or a basswood or a hackberry, a chokeberry or a buffalo berry. In that case, you had better think again. There is no ready commercial stock of such species. The same goes for the grasses. We have lots of grass in this former grassland: corn, Kentucky bluegrass, Bermuda grass, lovingly tended, tended to an obsession, sprayed and manicured, raked and fertilized, watered and weeded. Our little prairie lake is choking to death on the chemical residues of our zeal. A good man in Worthington is thrice married: to his wife, to his job, and to his lawn. But big bluestem, or Indian grass, or prairie dropseed? Our affection for grasses stops well short of native species. Of the 400,000 acres in our county about forty support remnants of the pre-settlement vegetation.   21

The point, though, is not that we have radically altered our world, which is old news, but that we have homogenized it. A backyard in Worthington, Minnesota, is no longer distinguishable from one in New Haven, Connecticut; Great Falls, Montana; Bend, Oregon. We plant the same trees, tend the same grasses, nurture the same flowers, play host to the same birds. Our backyards have become as regular and predictable as our McDonald's. We have industrialized nature.   22

From time to time we get some inkling of the folly of our conformity. Every boulevard in Worthington for seventy-five years was planted in American elms. And what an enchanting cityscape they made! (We have almost forgotten those graceful tall trees, arching until their crowns met high over sun-dappled streets.) Then Dutch elm disease struck, and within a decade our town was naked again, as it was in the beginning. We cut down the arching elms, hauled them to a landfill on the edge of town, burned them, dug out the stumps, and we started over. We planted maples. Do we really doubt that in another seventy-five years or so we will be battling maple disease? What is   23 it that causes us to believe so deeply and passionately that one kind of anything is sufficient?

But that is not exactly what I had in mind either. The point that lies forgotten underneath all this is that, in industrializing nature, we have squandered our claim to place.

Bruce Chatwin has recently written a provocative novel, called *Songlines*, about an encounter with the Australian aborigines. The aborigines are, of course, nomads in a land as spare and parsimonious as any upon the habited earth, and so they are obliged to be almost constantly on the move across vast stretches of desert, vast particularly if you consider that they move on foot, carrying all they possess. They come to know an area hundreds of miles down to its minutest detail, every waterhole, every patch of vegetation, every animal lair, and they never lose their way. How do they do it? They have no written language, make no notes, carry no maps. How do they memorize it all and pass the memories along? The answer is that they sing the landscape. Every landmark in the territory has its own verse, a snatch of melody, a fragment of poetry, and the sum of an aborigine's territory is the accumulation, in sequence, of its songs, its *songline*. Chatwin writes, "Richard Lee (an anthropologist at the University of Toronto) calculated that a Bushman child will be carried a distance of 4,900 miles before he begins to walk on his own. Since, during this rhythmic phase, he will be forever naming the contents of his territory, it is impossible he will not become a poet."

Chatwin's point is that we are born, like the Australian aborigines, to wander. He believes that the nomadic life is the natural way. I think he is wrong. The real meaning of his story is that even wanderers have found, sometimes with awesome vision and beauty, as in this case, how to make for themselves a place in the world. And his story means, further, that the deepest and most satisfying sense of place comes from the keenest appreciation of its manifold distinctions. When the uniqueness of a place sings to us like a melody, then we will know, at last, what it means to be at home.

But how shall a place sing to us like a melody if we have already rendered it monotonal?

We have lots of utilitarian answers to the question "Why must there be wild places?" But the most important answer is not utilitarian. It is wildly, hopelessly, unscientific. It is that except by the measure of wildness we shall never really know the nature of a place, and without a sense of place we shall never make a poem, and without a poem we shall never be fully human.

I was disappointed when I crawled from a tent into the bright sunlight of a new morning in the Bighorn Basin of the Big Horn Mountains and encountered a scolding robin whose territory had been invaded. It was not the robin itself that disappointed me, or the scolding. Both were entirely appropriate to the place and the circumstances. I was disappointed in us for making a world so full of robins that when we finally meet one in its own place, our first thought is that it must be out of place; so many robins at the expense of so many other birds; an embarrassment of robins, which is how a robin, like anything else, begins to be undervalued. It would be better for the world and for robins, I thought, if there were still places in it inhospitable to them.

At the same time, I was annoyed at myself for being disappointed. The 30
truth is, I was also disappointed in the robin, for its ordinariness. I went into
the wilderness hoping for something more exotic than an engagement with a
screaming robin.

When I visited New York for the first time, as a young man, I wanted 31
above everything else to see a Broadway play. I didn't much care what the
play was or who the players were. It was the experience of being present on
Broadway that I was after. I visited a scalper the afternoon I arrived in town.
"I want something, anything on Broadway," I said. "Tonight." I was sold a
ticket, an excellent seat, to a performance of *A Delicate Balance* by Edward Al-
bee. I no longer remember the name of the theater, but I do remember the
price of the ticket, forty-five dollars, which happened to be equal to the sum
I was then paying for a month's rent in a student hovel in Minneapolis. And I
remember how disappointed I was. Not that it wasn't an engaging play. It
was. And not that I didn't find the performance satisfying in every way. I did.
I was disappointed because the stars were Hume Cronyn and Jessica Tandy,
whom I had already seen on the stage at the Guthrie Theater in Minneapolis.
Something I had already seen: How could that be so special?

A robin, I thought? So what? 32

The robin flew back to the pine tree and stood on a branch scolding me. 33
"Dumb! Dumb!" it seemed to be saying. That, at any rate, was what I heard.

1988

Profile   Gruchow's essay opens unconventionally and even misleadingly.
It begins with the idyllic spectacle of two people enjoying the splendors of
Wyoming's unspoiled Big Horns—a stream, a clear mountain lake, plentiful
fish, sheer rock walls, an alpine meadow, pines. To many harried city dwellers the picture will suggest paradise, and as an escapist fantasy it could stand
by itself. But in opening his essay with this narrative interlude, Gruchow ig-
nores all the familiar advice: He does not identify his subject; he does not announce his intentions with a thematic statement; he does not orient his readers so that they know what to expect. In other words, he gives no clue to
where he is going.

Despite all these "failings" his opening does satisfy the first demand of a
good beginning: It makes the inquisitive reader want to keep reading (and,
presumably, it satisfies the second—it allows the writer to keep writing).
Furthermore, as we appreciate in retrospect, he has been preparing us for
what he has to say.

Gruchow opens narratively, with an anecdote, a popular choice among
contemporary writers. Experienced readers expect an essay with such an
opening to follow an *inductive* or specifics-to-general pattern, that is, one beginning with a particular incident or detail and leading to a statement of context, some kind of explanatory generalization. What makes this opening
unusual is its length: not until paragraph 16 does Gruchow reveal his argumentative purpose. First, he sets the scene: Two people are on a camping
trip in the picturesque Big Horn Mountains of Wyoming, getting away from
traffic and noise and crime, away from our overdeveloped urban landscape.
Thus, he luxuriates in details alien to city life: sheer rock walls seventy-five
stories high, tumbling waterfalls, and golden trout swimming in waters as

clear as the mountain air (though the trout have been "planted" by humans). These are the delights of unspoiled nature, and he dwells on them for nine paragraphs before introducing an intruder—not an outboard motor or a trail bike or even a hiking party, but a robin, a robin that seems out of place in what turns out to be its original habitat.

Here, finally making its appearance, is the subject announced in the title of the essay, "A Backyard Robin, Ho-Hum." And not until several paragraphs later, almost halfway through his essay, does he reveal his thesis: the homogenization of America, the industrialization of our biosphere. The leisurely narrative not only takes readers through the stages of the writer's awakening, but treats them to a vision of unhomogenized, unindustrialized America, so they will appreciate what has been lost. By the time Gruchow introduces his robins, his readers are more than ready to share his indignation.

Using Sources   Gruchow cites a number of sources, beginning with Stewart Edward White, who aptly compared the color of a golden trout to that of a twenty-dollar gold piece. But he draws upon two other sources for a different reason, to take issue with them. The common (but less bold) practice is to cite only those who agree with us. Such agreement may add to the consensus we are trying to build, but at the expense of energy and drama, creating the impression that we are writing on a safe topic, one free from the fireworks of controversy. From Gruchow we learn that the best sources are often those with whom we disagree because they lend an intensity and interest lost in pursuing unanimity. In the first case he cites Len Eiserer's *The American Robin* (paragraph 13), who mistakenly applauds the robin's alleged adaptability. Eiserer, then, is a prime supporter of the very misbelief that Gruchow wishes to correct. His second source is Bruce Chatwin's *Songlines* (paragraph 25), whose admiration for the Australian aborigines he shares but whose conclusions he disputes. Rather than expressing a nomadic impulse, as Chatwin contends, the aboriginal songlines attest that even wanderers find a way to connect with specific places, a way to remember and to create a sense of belonging. Their songlines both commemorate and celebrate the particularity of the locales they have visited, attesting to their appreciation of differences. By contrast, Americans homogenize, replicating the same scenes over and over. In consequence, we have fewer "songs."

Gruchow models one kind of essay, one whose purpose is to correct a popular misconception. For a writer facing such a task, the most fruitful sources will be those that exemplify the error in question.

Parallelism   Parallelism uses repeated structures to reinforce a relationship between ideas. In other words, it is one more device that promotes unity, coherence, and emphasis. In the following Gruchow uses parallel verb phrases in a dependent clause:

> As we have drained the swamps and
> > marshes,
> > leveled the forests,
> > farmed the prairies, and
> > diverted the waters of the western rivers for the greening of the deserts,

we have done something more pervasive than simply destroying a multitude of local habitats.

Sometimes we reinforce the parallelism even further by repeating the same word or words at the beginning of each item in a series, a device called *anaphora:*

> The robin has become commonplace,
>> adapted to a virtuosic range of habitats,
>>> from coast to coast,
>>> from sea level to 12,000 feet or so in elevation,
>>> from city streets to remote wilderness regions.

Exercise Read the following paragraph closely. To what extent does each successive sentence grow out of the previous one and prepare for the next? Specifically, what do unity, coherence, and emphasis mean *here?*

[1]We now perceive the homogenization of urban America as a truism. [2]The pervasive influence of the mass media and the concentration of economic power have helped to create a society in which many local, or even regional, distinctions have vanished. [3]We all watch the same television programs, read essentially the same newspapers, shop in the same national stores, live in the same houses, and subscribe, mostly, to the same middle-of-the-road politics and philosophy of life. [4]A person crossing the country from one airport or commercial strip or housing development to the next has only the local road signs and certain peculiarities of flora—if there are palm trees in the boulevards, it can't be Ohio—as reliable visual clues to place. [5]This monotony of physical detail has, perhaps, promoted social stability and a certain kind of economic efficiency. [6]But we rightly wonder what strengths of culture, what resiliency, we have sacrificed in adopting such blind uniformity.

Revision Assignments Select one of the following strategies and revise "A Backyard Robin, Ho-Hum." Include a brief statement explaining your choice of strategy and its effect on the arrangement and presentation of material.

1. You have submitted this essay to *Paw and Claw* magazine and the editor wants to use it. But there is a problem: It is too long. They will print the essay at no more than half its present length. Make the necessary revisions, trying to make your point as forcefully and memorably as possible (or, to save time, you may simply outline the shortened version).

2. To force a serious consideration of form and thesis, to determine what is essential and what expendable, shorten Gruchow's essay to under a thousand words. Do you throw out the entire first section, for example, or shorten passages and compose new transitions ("The sun beamed down upon us, seeming benevolent, but a nearby robin was not so good-willed. From its nesting place in the pine tree just beyond our tent door, it scolded us for our intrusion . . . ")? Your major decision is whether to cut and rearrange entire sections or to follow Gruchow's order and cut each section by three-fourths.

Writing Assignments

1. Continue Gruchow's discussion of the homogenization or industrialization of America (its "bland uniformity"). What evidence do you see of increasing disregard for the individuality of places, for geographical and regional diversity? What have "they" (we?) done to make your locale resemble everyone else's? Like Gruchow use your own experiences and observations. Be concrete.

2. Gruchow clearly believes that, in homogenizing America, we have lost more than we have gained. Take the contrary position: In planting nonregional species, we have simply multiplied our choices, extending our freedom of self-definition to the world around us. Our traditional American right to reshape our lives entails the right to reshape our setting. In other words, what is so wrong about having a Japanese or an English rather than a mission garden in San Luis Obispo?

No Wonder They Call Me a Bitch

ANN HODGMAN

I've always wondered about dog food. Is a Gaines-burger really like a ham- 1
burger? Can you fry it? Does dog food "cheese" taste like real cheese? Does
Gravy Train actually make gravy in the dog's bowl, or is that brown product
just dissolved crumbs? And exactly what *are* by-products?

Having spent the better part of a week eating dog food, I'm sorry to say 2
that I now know the answers to these questions. While my dachshund, Shortie, watched in agonies of yearning, I gagged my way through can after can of
stinky, white-flecked mush and bag after bag of stinky, fat-drenched nuggets. And now I understand exactly why Shortie's breath is so bad.

Of course, Gaines-burgers are neither mush nor nuggets. They are, 3
rather, a miracle of beauty and packaging—or at least that's what I thought
when I was little. I used to beg my mother to get them for our dogs, but she
always said they were too expensive. When I finally bought a box of cheese-
flavored Gaines-burgers—after twenty years of longing—I felt deliciously
wicked.

"Dogs love real beef," the back of the box proclaimed proudly. "That's 4
why Gaines-burgers is the only beef burger for dogs with real beef and no
meat by-products!" The copy was accurate: meat by-products did not appear
in the list of ingredients. Poultry by-products did, though—right there next
to preserved animal fat.

One Purina spokesman told me that poultry by-products consist of necks, 5
intestines, underdeveloped eggs and other "carcass remnants," but not feathers, heads, or feet. When I told him I'd been eating dog food, he said, "Oh,
you're kidding. Oh, *no!*" (I came to share his alarm when, weeks later, a second Purina spokesman said that Gaines-burgers *do* contain poultry heads and
feet—but *not* underdeveloped eggs.)

Up close my Gaines-burger didn't much resemble chopped beef. Rather, 6
it looked—and felt—like a single long, extruded piece of redness that had
been chopped into segments and formed into a patty. You could make one at
home if you had a Play-Doh Fun Factory.

I turned on the skillet. While I waited for it to heat up I pulled out a 7
shred of cheese-colored material and palpated it. Again, like Play-Doh, it was
quite malleable. I made a little cheese bird out of it; then I counted to three
and ate the bird.

There was a horrifying rush of cheddar cheese, followed immediately by 8
the dull tang of soybean flour—the main ingredient in Gaines-burgers. Next
I tried a piece of red extrusion. The main difference between the meat-fla-
vored and cheese-flavored extrusions is one of texture. The "cheese" chews
like fresh Play-Doh, whereas the "meat" chews like Play-Doh that's been
sitting out on a rug for a couple of hours.

Frying only turned the Gaines-burger black. There was no melting, no 9
sizzling, no warm meat smells. A cherished childhood illusion was gone. I

flipped the patty into the sink, where it immediately began leaking rivulets of red dye.

As alarming as the Gaines-burgers were, their soy meal began to seem like an old friend when the time came to try some *canned* dog foods. I decided to try the Cycle foods first. When I opened them, I thought about how rarely I use can openers these days, and I was suddenly visited by a long-forgotten sensation of can-opener distaste. *This* is the kind of unsavory place can openers spend their time when you're not watching! Every time you open a can of, say, Italian plum tomatoes, you infect them with invisible particles of by-product. 10

I had been expecting to see the usual homogeneous scrapple inside, but each can of Cycle was packed with smooth, round oily nuggets. As if someone at Gaines had been tipped off that a human would be tasting the stuff, the four Cycles really were different from one another. Cycle-1, for puppies, is wet and soyish. Cycle-2, for adults, glistens nastily with fat, but it's passably edible—a lot like some canned Swedish meatballs I once got in a Care package at college. Cycle-3, the "lite" one, for fatties, had no specific flavor; it just tasted like dog food. But at least it didn't make me fat. 11

Cycle-4, for senior dogs, had the smallest nuggets. Maybe old dogs can't open their mouths as wide. This kind was far sweeter than the other three Cycles—almost like baked beans. It was also the only one to contain "dried beef digest," a mysterious substance that the Purina spokesman defined as "enzymes" and my dictionary defined as "the products of digestion." 12

Next on the menu was a can of Kal Kan Pedigree with Chunky Chicken. Chunky *chicken*? There were chunks in the can, certainly—big purplish-brown chunks. I forked one chunk out (by now I was becoming more callous) and found that while it had no discernible chicken flavor, it wasn't bad except for its texture—like meat loaf with ground-up chicken bones. 13

In the world of canned dog food, a smooth consistency is a sign of low quality—lots of cereal. A lumpy, frightening, bloody, stringy horror is a sign of high quality—lots of meat. Nowhere in the world of wet dog foods was this demonstrated better than in the fanciest I tried—Kal Kan's Pedigree Select Dinners. These came not in a can but in a tiny foil packet with a picture of an imperious Yorkie. When I pulled open the container, juice spurted all over my hand, and the first chunk I speared was trailing a long gray vein. I shrieked and went inside for a plain chunk, which I was able to swallow only after taking a break to read some suddenly fascinating office equipment catalogues. Once again, though, it tasted no more alarming than, say, canned hash. 14

Still, how pleasant it was to turn to *dry* dog food! Gravy Train was the first I tried, and I'm happy to report that it really does make a "thick, rich, real beef gravy" when you mix it with water. Thick and rich, anyway. Except for a lingering rancid-fat flavor, the gravy wasn't beefy, but since it tasted primarily like tap water, it wasn't nauseating either. 15

My poor dachshund just gets plain old Purina Dog Chow, but Purina also makes a dry food called Butcher's Blend that comes in Beef, Bacon & Chicken flavor. Here we see dog food's arcane semiotics[1] at its best: a red 16

[1]The study of meaning; here, a system of symbols.

triangle with a *T* stamped into it is supposed to suggest beef; a tan curl, chicken; and a brown *S*, a piece of bacon. Only dogs understand these messages. But Butcher's Blend does have an endearing slogan: "Great Meaty Tastes—without bothering the butcher!" *You know, I wanted to buy some meat, but I just couldn't bring myself to bother the butcher . . .*

Purina O.N.E. ("Optimum Nutritional Effectiveness") is targeted at people who are unlikely ever to worry about bothering a tradesperson. "We chose chicken as a primary ingredient in Purina O.N.E. for several reasonings," the long, long essay on the back of the bag announces. Chief among these reasonings, I'd guess, is the fact that chicken appeals to people who are—you know—*like us*. Although our dogs do nothing but spend eighteen-hour days alone in the apartment, we still want them to be *premium* dogs. We want them to cut down on red meat, too. We also want dog food that comes in a bag with an attractive design, a subtle typeface, and no kitschy pictures of slobbering golden retrievers.

Besides that, we want a list of the Nutritional Benefits of our dog food— and we get it on O.N.E. One thing I especially like about this list is its constant references to a dog's "hair coat," as in "Beef tallow is good for the dog's skin and hair coat." (On the other hand, beef tallow merely provides palatability, while the dried beef digest in Cycle provides palatability *enhancement*.)

As with people food, dog snacks taste much better than dog meals. They're better looking too. Take Milk-Bone Flavor Snacks. The loving-hands-at-home prose describing each flavor is colorful; the writers practically choke on their own exuberance. Of bacon they say, "It's so good, your dog will think it's hot off the frying pan." Of liver: "The only taste your dog wants more than liver—is even more liver!" Of poultry: "All those farm fresh flavors deliciously mixed in one biscuit. Your dog will bark with delight!" And of vegetable: "Gardens of taste! Specially blended to give your dog that vegetable flavor he wants—but can rarely get!"

Well, I may be a sucker, but advertising *this* emphatic just doesn't convince me. I lined up all seven flavors of Milk-Bone Flavor snacks on the floor. Unless my dog's palate is a lot more sensitive than mine—and considering that she steals dirty diapers out of the trash and eats them, I'm loath to think it is—she doesn't detect any more difference in the seven flavors than I did when I tried them.

I much preferred Bonz, the hard-baked, bone-shaped snack stuffed with simulated marrow. I liked the bone part, that is; it tasted almost exactly like the cornmeal it was made of. The mock marrow inside was a bit more problematic: in addition to looking like the sludge that collects in the threads of my running shoes, it was bursting with tiny hairs.

I'm sure you have a few dog food questions of your own. To save us time, I've answered them in advance.

Q. *Are those little cans of Mighty Dog actually branded with the sizzling word BEEF, the way they show in the commercials?*

A. You should know by now that that kind of thing never happens.

Q. *Does chicken-flavored dog food taste like chicken-flavored cat food?*

A. To my surprise, chicken cat food was actually a little better—more chickeny. It tasted like inferior canned pâté.

Q. *Was there any dog food that you just couldn't bring yourself to try?*

A. Alas, it was a can of Mighty Dog called Prime Entree with Bone Marrow. The meat was dark, dark brown, and it was surrounded by gelatin that was almost black. I knew I would die if I tasted it, so I put it outside for the raccoons.

1989

Profile   This is one of those inspiration-driven pieces, the kind arising out of an ingenious idea that many other writers might wish they had gotten sooner (or at least ones with strong stomachs). The idea is so entertaining and its pursuit so natural that the essay seems to write itself, but this impression only testifies to how well Ann Hodgman has done her job. The easy part is getting a clever idea; the hard part is in the execution, the application, the follow-through.

Hodgman's essay is richly informational, telling us more about the taste and consistency of dog food than most of us would ever want to know. She works methodically through the major brands, trying out the different flavors, working from meaty to dry to doggie snacks, comparing what she finds with the language on the packaging. But what makes her presentation work is its tone: its humor and liveliness, the colloquial first-person narration, the quotations, the asides, the freewheeling punctuation. The interest, after all, is not simply in the subject but in the writer's willingness to play guinea pig. She is the one actually being tested (in the words of the Purina spokesman: "Oh, you're kidding! Oh *no*!").

In fact, like many good narratives, Hodgman's essay works by resolving several issues at once. The first, of course, is the dog food one. Maybe some of us hadn't gotten around to wondering actively about canine cuisine, but it does have some latent interest. But the second issue, the dog food taster's response, is the most interesting: Hodgman is not only going to tell us what the stuff was like, she is going to tell us what it was like to eat it. *Eating* dog food, then, energizes the subject of dog food. Whatever interest the subject itself possesses, it is amplified by the writer's response to it. In other words, there is a dynamic relationship between writer and subject, and this is the lesson of Hodgman's essay.

Hodgman's essay, like Jared Diamond's "What are Men Good For?" and Tristram Wyatt's "Submarine Beetles," illustrates a valuable point: Informational writing, even humorous informational writing, needn't rest on information alone. Without a context, after all, information is inert, static. And what better context than the writer's pursuit of knowledge, the process whereby she raised and answered the relevant questions? From the Pueblo people in Leslie Marmon Silko's essay and the Kiowa in N. Scott Momaday's memoir to scientific writers like June Kinoshita and Wyatt, humans have long recognized the power of stories to carry information. There are as many applications as there are stories.

Using Dashes   In formal writing, dashes appear infrequently and in a limited number of roles—to introduce a series; to set off interruptive material, concluding appositives, and dramatic conclusions; and, on rare occasions, to separate independent clauses. Because it creates a meaningful delay, the dash is an emphatic device, suggesting that it should be saved for special occasions. In informal writing, dashes often appear more frequently. Hodgman, in the same spirit that made her a dog food tester (and in imitation of the people who write advertising copy?), uses them freely. Sometimes, to create a dramatic conclusion, she inserts them where she could have easily used a comma:

> The copy was accurate: meat by-products did not appear in the list of ingredients. Poultry by-products did, though—right there next to preserved animal fat.

> This kind was far sweeter than the other three Cycles—almost like baked beans.

> I forked one chunk out (by now I was becoming more callous) and found that while it had no discernible chicken flavor, it wasn't bad except for its texture—like meat loaf with ground-up chicken bones.

Or she uses them to set off concluding appositives:

> There were chunks in the can, certainly—big, purplish-brown chunks.

> A lumpy, frightening, bloody, stringy horror is a sign of high quality—lots of meat.

> Nowhere in the world of wet dog foods was this demonstrated better than in the fanciest I tried—Kal Kan's Pedigree Select Dinners.

Or, her favorite, she uses them for dramatic interruptions:

> When I finally bought a box of cheese-flavored Gaines-burgers—after twenty years of longing—I felt deliciously wicked.

> Rather, it looked—and felt—like a single long, extruded piece of redness that had been chopped into a patty.

> Chief among these reasonings, I'd guess, is the fact that chicken appeals to people who are—you know—*like us.*

> Unless my dog's palate is a lot more sensitive than mine—and considering she steals dirty diapers out of the trash and eats them, I'm loath to think it is—she doesn't detect any more difference in the seven flavors than I did when I tried them.

In most writing, especially academic writing, dashes should be treated as special effects and used sparingly. Exploited as all-purpose punctuators, a practice perhaps acquired taking class notes, they soon lose their effectiveness and—worse—discourage learning the proper uses of the other punctuation devices.

Revision Assignments   Select one of the following strategies and revise "No Wonder They Call Me a Bitch." Include a brief statement explaining your choice of strategy and its effect on the arrangement and presentation of material.

1. Rewrite part of the essay in a dry third-person voice, presenting the simple facts about the consistency and taste of dog food, and refraining from personal judgments, humorous remarks, and playful comparisons (with Play-Doh, for example), and using no dashes, italics, or parenthetical remarks. Make the writer as invisible as possible. Inform; do not try to entertain. Be clinical.

2. You're Shortie the dachshund and your master (mistress?) has broken the first rule of good manners: She has eaten something yummy in front of you without offering to share. Tell your side of the story. In other words, try to present Hodgman's product test from the viewpoint of a very interested spectator (perhaps you get to lick out the cans, sniff some wrappers, paw at some crumbs).

Writing Assignments

1. Hodgman begins, "I've always wondered about . . . " Follow her lead and that of Sallie Tisdale in "Shoe and Tell?": Take some product you've always wondered about and look into it (competing brands of dry soup, gourmet ice cream, frozen dinners, chocolate chip cookies, coffee as served in coffee bars, candy masquerading as breakfast cereal—or other "miracles of beauty and packaging"). Resolve your questions, beginning with the doubts you have had about advertising claims. (Except for the opening statement, Hodgman's first paragraph is all questions.) Test the products; talk to company spokespeople. And present your investigations in a narrative.

2. Hodgman's satire is aimed in part at the language of dog food advertisements, language meant to glorify the product and impress the human buyer. Select another product line and examine its use of words, its attempts (using hyperbole and euphemism and attractive imagery) to glorify, prettify, and generally misrepresent the product. As Hodgman says, "the writers practically choke on their own exuberance" (after all, their product is so, well, *wonderful*).

On Seeing England for the First Time

JAMAICA KINCAID

When I saw England for the first time, I was a child in school sitting at a desk. The England I was looking at was laid out on a map gently, beautifully, delicately, a very special jewel; it lay on a bed of sky blue—the background of the map—its yellow form mysterious, because though it looked like a leg of mutton, it could not really look like anything so familiar as a leg of mutton because it was England—with shadings of pink and green, unlike any shadings of pink and green I had seen before, squiggly veins of red running in every direction. England was a special jewel all right, and only special people got to wear it. The people who got to wear England were English people. They wore it well and they wore it everywhere: in jungles, in deserts, on plains, on top of the highest mountains, on all the oceans, on all the seas, in places where they were not welcome, in places they should not have been. When my teacher had pinned this map up on the blackboard, she said, "This is England"—and she said it with authority, seriousness, and adoration, and we all sat up. It was as if she had said, "This is Jerusalem, the place you will go when you die but only if you have been good." We understood then—we were meant to understand then—that England was to be our source of myth and the source from which we got our sense of reality, our sense of what was meaningful, our sense of what was meaningless—and much about our own lives and much about the very idea of us headed the list.

At the time I was a child sitting at my desk seeing England for the first time, I was already very familiar with the greatness of it. Each morning before I left for school, I ate a breakfast of half a grapefruit, an egg, bread and butter and a slice of cheese, and a cup of cocoa; or half a grapefruit, a bowl of oat porridge, bread and butter and a slice of cheese, and a cup of cocoa. The can of cocoa was often left on the table in front of me. It had written on it the name of the company, the year the company was established, and the words "Made in England." Those words, "Made in England," were written on the box the oats came in too. They would also have been written on the box the shoes I was wearing came in; a bolt of gray linen cloth lying on the shelf of a store from which my mother had bought three yards to make the uniform that I was wearing had written along its edge those three words. The shoes I wore were made in England; so were my socks and cotton undergarments and the satin ribbons I wore tied at the end of two plaits of my hair. My father, who might have sat next to me at breakfast, was a carpenter and cabinet maker. The shoes he wore to work would have been made in England, as were his khaki shirt and trousers, his underpants and undershirt, his socks and brown felt hat. Felt was not the proper material from which a hat that was expected to provide shade from the hot sun should be made, but my father must have seen and admired a picture of an Englishman wearing such a hat in England, and this picture that he saw must have been so compelling that it caused him to wear the wrong hat for a hot climate most of his long

"On Seeing England for the First Time" by Jamaica Kincaid, *Transition* 51:32–42 (1991). Reprinted by permission of Oxford University Press.

life. And this hat—a brown felt hat—became so central to his character that it was the first thing he put on in the morning as he stepped out of bed and the last thing he took off before he stepped back into bed at night. As we sat at breakfast a car might go by. The car, a Hillman or a Zephyr, was made in England. The very idea of the meal itself, breakfast, and its substantial quality and quantity was an idea from England; we somehow knew that in England they began the day with this meal called breakfast and a proper breakfast was a big breakfast. No one I knew liked eating so much food so early in the day; it made us feel sleepy, tired. But this breakfast business was Made in England like almost everything else that surrounded us, the exceptions being the sea, the sky, and the air we breathed.

At the time I saw this map—seeing England for the first time—I did not say to myself, "Ah, so that's what it looks like," because there was no longing in me to put a shape to those three words that ran through every part of my life, no matter how small; for me to have had such a longing would have meant that I lived in a certain atmosphere, an atmosphere in which those three words were felt as a burden. But I did not live in such an atmosphere. My father's brown felt hat would develop a hole in its crown, the lining would separate from the hat itself, and six weeks before he thought that he could not be seen wearing it—he was a very vain man—he would order another hat from England. And my mother taught me to eat my food in the English way: the knife in my right hand, the fork in my left, my elbows held still close to my side, the food carefully balanced on my fork and then brought up to my mouth. When I had finally mastered it, I overheard her saying to a friend, "Did you see how nicely she can eat?" But I knew then that I enjoyed my food more when I ate it with my bare hands, and I continued to do so when she wasn't looking. And when my teacher showed us the map, she asked us to study it carefully, because no test we would ever take would be complete without this statement: "Draw a map of England."

I did not know then that the statement "Draw a map of England" was something far worse than a declaration of war, for in fact a flat-out declaration of war would have put me on alert, and again in fact, there was no need for war—I had long ago been conquered. I did not know then that this statement was part of a process that would result in my erasure, not my physical erasure, but my erasure all the same. I did not know then that this statement was meant to make me feel in awe and small whenever I heard the word "England": awe at its existence, small because I was not from it. I did not know very much of anything then—certainly not what a blessing it was that I was unable to draw a map of England correctly.

After that there were many times of seeing England for the first time. I saw England in history. I knew the names of all the kings of England. I knew the names of their children, their wives, their disappointments, their triumphs, the names of people who betrayed them, I knew the dates on which they were born and the dates they died. I knew their conquests and was made to feel glad if I figured in them; I knew their defeats. I knew the details of the year 1066 (the Battle of Hastings, the end of the reign of the Anglo-Saxon kings) before I knew the details of the year 1832 (the year slavery was abolished). It wasn't as bad as I make it sound now; it was worse. I did like so much hearing again and again how Alfred the Great, traveling in disguise, had been left to watch cakes, and because he wasn't used to this the cakes got burned, and Alfred burned his hands pulling them out of the fire, and the woman who had left him to watch the cakes screamed at him. I loved King Alfred. My grandfather was named after him; his son, my uncle, is named after King Alfred; my brother is named after King Alfred. And so there are three people in my family named after a man they have never met, a man who died over ten centuries ago. The first view I got of England then was not unlike the first view received by the person who named my grandfather.

This view, though—the naming of the kings, their deeds, their disappointments—was the vivid view, the forceful view. There were other views, subtler ones, softer, almost not there—but these were the ones that made the most lasting impression on me, these were the ones that made me really feel like nothing. "When morning touched the sky" was one phrase, for no morning touched the sky where I lived. The mornings where I lived came on abruptly, with a shock of heat and loud noises. "Evening approaches" was another, but the evenings where I lived did not approach; in fact, I had no evening—I had night and I had day and they came and went in a mechanical way: on, off; on, off. And then there were gentle mountains and low blue skies and moors over which people took walks for nothing but pleasure, when where I lived a walk was an act of labor, a burden, something only death or the automobile could relieve. And there were things that a small turn of the head could convey—entire worlds, whole lives would depend on this thing, a certain turn of the head. Everyday life could be quite tiring, more tiring than anything I was told not to do. I was told not to gossip, but they did that all the time. And they ate so much food, violating another of those rules they taught me: do not indulge in gluttony. And the foods they ate actually: if only sometime I could eat cold cuts after theater, cold cuts of lamb and mint sauce, and Yorkshire pudding and scones, and clotted cream, and sausages that came from up-country (imagine, "up-country"). And having troubling thoughts at twilight, a good time to have troubling thoughts, apparently; and servants who stole and left in the middle of a crisis, who were born with a limp or some other kind of deformity, not nourished properly in their mother's womb (that last part I figured out for myself; the point was, not to have an untrustworthy servant); and wonderful cobbled streets onto which solid front doors opened; and people whose eyes were blue and who had fair skins and who smelled only of lavender, or sometimes sweet pea or primrose. And those flowers with those names: delphiniums, foxgloves, tulips, daffodils, floribunda, peonies; in bloom, a striking display, being cut and placed in large glass bowls, crystal, decorating rooms so large twenty families the size of mine could fit in comfortably but used only for passing through. And the weather was so remarkable because the rain fell gently always, only occasionally in deep gusts, and it colored the air various shades of gray, each an appealing shade for a dress to be worn when a portrait was being painted; and when it rained at twilight, wonderful things happened: people bumped into each other unexpectedly and that would lead to all sorts of turns of events—a plot, the mere weather caused plots. I saw that people rushed: they rushed to catch trains, they rushed toward each other and away from each other; they rushed and rushed and rushed. That word: Rushed! I did not know what it was to do that. It was too hot to do that, and so I came to envy people who would rush, even though it had no meaning to me to do such a thing. But there they are again. They loved their children; their children were sent to their own rooms as a punishment, rooms larger than my entire house. They were special, everything about them said so, even their clothes; their clothes rustled, swished, soothed. The world was theirs, not mine; everything told me so.

If now as I speak of all this I give the impression of someone on the outside looking in, nose pressed up against a glass window, that is wrong. My nose was pressed up against a glass window all right, but there was an iron vise at the back of my neck forcing my head to stay in place. To avert my gaze was to fall back into something from which I had been rescued, a hole filled with nothing, and that was the word for everything about me, nothing. The reality of my life was conquests, subjugation, humiliation, enforced amnesia. I was forced to forget. Just for instance, this: I lived in a part of St. John's, Antigua,[1] called Ovals. Ovals was made up of five streets, each of them named after a famous English seaman—to be quite frank, an officially sanctioned criminal: Rodney Street (after George Rodney), Nelson Street (after Horatio Nelson), Drake Street (after Francis Drake), Hood Street, and Hawkins Street (after John Hawkins). But John Hawkins was knighted after a trip he made to Africa, opening up a new trade, the slave trade.[2] He was then entitled to wear as his crest a Negro bound with a cord. Every single person living on Hawkins Street was descended from a slave. John Hawkins's ship, the one in which he transported the people he had bought and kidnapped, was called *The Jesus*. He later became the treasurer of the Royal Navy and Rear Admiral.

Again, the reality of my life, the life I led at the time I was being shown these views of England for the first time, for the second time, for the one-hundred-millionth time, was this: the sun shone with what sometimes seemed to be a deliberate cruelty; we must have done something to deserve that. My dresses did not rustle in the evening air as I strolled to the theater (I had no evening, I had no theater; my dresses were made of a cheap cotton, the weave of which would give way after not too many washings). I got up in the morning, I did my chores (fetched water from the public pipe for my mother, swept the yard), I washed myself, I went to a woman to have my hair combed freshly every day (because before we were allowed into our classroom our teachers would inspect us, and children who had not bathed that day, or had dirt under their fingernails, or whose hair had not been combed anew that day, might not be allowed to attend class). I ate that breakfast. I walked to school. At school we gathered in an auditorium and sang a hymn, "All Things Bright and Beautiful," and looking down on us as we sang were portraits of the Queen of England and her husband; they wore jewels and medals and they smiled. I was a Brownie. At each meeting we would form a

[1]A Caribbean island east and south of Puerto Rico and the Virgin Islands. Formerly part of what was called the British West Indies, it achieved independence in 1981.

[2]Hawkins (1532–95) initiated English participation in the slave trade when he sailed to Africa's Guinea coast and robbed Portuguese slavers, smuggling the slaves to Spanish possessions in the New World.

little group around a flagpole, and after raising the Union Jack, we would say, "I promise to do my best, to do my duty to God and the Queen, to help other people every day and to obey the scouts' law."

Who were these people and why had I never seen them, I mean really seen them, in the place where they lived? I had never been to England. No one I knew had ever been to England, or I should say, no one I knew had ever been and returned to tell me about it. All the people I knew who had gone to England had stayed there. Sometimes they left behind them their small children, never to see them again. England! I had seen England's representatives. I had seen the governor general at the public grounds at a ceremony celebrating the Queen's birthday. I had seen an old princess and I had seen a young princess. They had both been extremely not beautiful, but who of us would have told them that? I had never seen England, really seen it, I had only met a representative, seen a picture, read books, memorized its history. I had never set foot, my own foot, in it. 9

The space between the idea of something and its reality is always wide and deep and dark. The longer they are kept apart—idea of thing, reality of thing—the wider the width, the deeper the depth, the thicker and darker the darkness. This space starts out empty, there is nothing in it, but it rapidly becomes filled up with obsession or desire or hatred or love—sometimes all of these things, sometimes some of these things, sometimes only one of these things. The existence of the world as I came to know it was a result of this: idea of thing over here, reality of thing way, way over there. There was Christopher Columbus, an unlikable man, an unpleasant man, a liar (and so, of course, a thief) surrounded by maps and schemes and plans, and there was the reality on the other side of that width, that depth, that darkness. He became obsessed, he became filled with desire, the hatred came later, love was never a part of it. Eventually, his idea met the longed-for reality. That the idea of something and its reality are often two completely different things is something no one ever remembers; and so when they meet and find that they are not compatible, the weaker of the two, idea or reality, dies. That idea Christopher Columbus had was more powerful than the reality he met, and so the reality he met died. 10

And so finally, when I was a grown-up woman, the mother of two children, the wife of someone, a person who resides in a powerful country that takes up more than its fair share of a continent,[3] the owner of a house with many rooms in it and of two automobiles, with the desire and will (which I very much act upon) to take from the world more than I give back to it, more than I deserve, more than I need, finally then, I saw England, the real England, not a picture, not a painting, not through a story in a book, but England, for the first time. In me, the space between the idea of it and its reality had become filled with hatred, and so when at last I saw it I wanted to take it into my hands and tear it into little pieces and then crumble it up as if it were clay, child's clay. That was impossible, and so I could only indulge in not-favorable opinions. 11

[3]Kincaid now lives in Vermont.

There were monuments everywhere; they commemorated victories, bat- 12
tles fought between them and the people who lived across the sea from
them, all vile people, fought over which of them would have dominion over
the people who looked like me. The monuments were useless to them now,
people sat on them and ate their lunch. They were like markers on an old
useless trail, like a piece of old string tied to a finger to jog the memory, like
old decoration in an old house, dirty, useless, in the way. Their skins were so
pale, it made them look so fragile, so weak, so ugly. What if I had the power
to simply banish them from their land, send boat after boatload of them on a
voyage that in fact had no destination, force them to live in a place where
the sun's presence was a constant? This would rid them of their pale com-
plexion and make them look more like me, make them look more like the
people I love and treasure and hold dear, and more like the people who occupy the near and far reaches of my imagination, my history, my geography,
and reduce them and everything they have ever known to figurines as evidence that I was in divine favor, what if all this was in my power? Could I resist it? No one ever has.

And they were rude, they were rude to each other. They didn't like each 13
other very much. They didn't like each other in the way they didn't like me,
and it occurred to me that their dislike for me was one of the few things they
agreed on.

I was on a train in England with a friend, an English woman. Before we 14
were in England she liked me very much. In England she didn't like me at
all. She didn't like the claim I said I had on England, she didn't like the
views I had of England. I didn't like England, she didn't like England, but
she didn't like me not liking it too. She said, "I want to show you my England, I want to show you the England that I know and love." I had told her
many times before that I knew England and I didn't want to love it anyway.
She no longer lived in England; it was her own country, but it had not been
kind to her, so she left. On the train, the conductor was rude to her; she
asked something, and he responded in a rude way. She became ashamed.
She was ashamed at the way he treated her; she was ashamed at the way he
behaved. "This is the new England," she said. But I liked the conductor being rude; his behavior seem quite appropriate. Earlier this had happened: we
had gone to a store to buy a shirt for my husband; it was meant to be a special
present, a special shirt to wear on special occasions. This was a store where
the Prince of Wales has his shirts made, but the shirts sold in this store are
beautiful all the same. I found a shirt I thought my husband would like and I
wanted to buy him a tie to go with it. When I couldn't decide which one to
choose, the salesman showed me a new set. He was very pleased with these,
he said, because they bore the crest of the Prince of Wales, and the Prince of
Wales had never allowed his crest to decorate an article of clothing before.
There was something in the way he said it; his tone was slavish, reverential,
awed. It made me feel angry; I wanted to hit him. I didn't do that. I said, my
husband and I hate princes, my husband would never wear anything that had
a prince's anything on it. My friend stiffened. The salesman stiffened. They
both drew themselves in, away from me. My friend told me that the prince
was a symbol of her Englishness, and I could see that I had caused offense. I
looked at her. She was an English person, the sort of English person I used to

know at home, the sort who was nobody in England but somebody when they came to live among people like me. There were many people I could have seen England with; that I was seeing it with this particular person, a person who reminded me of the people who showed me England long ago as I sat in church or at my desk, made me feel silent and afraid, for I wondered if, all these years of our friendship, I had had a friend or had been in the thrall of a racial memory.

I went to Bath—we, my friend and I, did this, but though we were to- ₁₅gether, I was no longer with her. The landscape was almost as familiar as my own hand, but I had never been in this place before, so how could that be again? And the streets of Bath were familiar, too, but I had never walked on them before. It was all those years of reading, starting with Roman Britain. Why did I have to know about Roman Britain? It was of no real use to me, a person living on a hot, drought-ridden island, and it is of no use to me now, and yet my head is filled with this nonsense, Roman Britain. In Bath, I drank tea in a room I had read about in a novel written in the eighteenth century. In this very same room, young women wearing those dresses that rustled and so on danced and flirted and sometimes disgraced themselves with young men, soldiers, sailors, who were on their way to Bristol or someplace like that, so many places like that where so many adventures, the outcome of which was not good for me, began. Bristol, England. A sentence that began "That night the ship sailed from Bristol, England" would end not so good for me. And then I was driving through the countryside in an English motorcar, on narrow winding roads, and they were so familiar, though I had never been on them before; and through little villages the names of which I somehow knew so well though I had never been there before. And the countryside did have all those hedges and hedges, fields hedged in. I was marveling at all the toil of it, all that clipping, year after year of clipping, and I wondered at the lives of the people who would have to do this, because wherever I see and feel the hands that hold up the world, I see and feel myself and all the people who look like me. And I said, "Those hedges" and my friend said that someone, a woman named Mrs. Rothchild, worried that the hedges weren't being taken care of properly; the farmers couldn't afford or find the help to keep up the hedges, and often they replaced them with wire fencing. I might have said to that, well if Mrs. Rothchild doesn't like the wire fencing, why doesn't she take care of the hedges herself, but I didn't. And then in those fields that were now hemmed in by wire fencing that a privileged woman didn't like was planted a vile yellow flowering bush that produced an oil, and my friend said that Mrs. Rothchild didn't like this either; it ruined the English country-side, it ruined the traditional look of the English countryside.

It was not at that moment that I wished every sentence, everything I ₁₆knew, that began with England would end with "and then it all died; we don't know how, it just all died." At that moment, I was thinking, who are these people who forced me to think of them all the time, who forced me to think that the world I knew was incomplete, or without substance, or did not measure up because it was not England; that I was incomplete, or without substance, and did not measure up because I was not English. Who were these people? The person sitting next to me couldn't give me a clue; no one person could. In any case, if I had said to her, I find England ugly, I hate England; the weather is like a jail sentence, the English are a very ugly people, the food in England is like a jail sentence, the hair of English people is so straight, so dead looking, the English have an unbearable smell so different from the smell of people I know, real people of course, she would have said that I was a person full of prejudice. Apart from the fact that it is I—that is, the people who look like me—who made her aware of the unpleasantness of such a thing, the idea of such a thing, prejudice, she would have been only partly right, sort of right: I may be capable of prejudice, but my prejudices have no weight to them, my prejudices have no force behind them, my prejudices remain opinions, my prejudices remain my personal opinion. And a great feeling of rage and disappointment came over me as I looked at England, my head full of personal opinions that could not have public, my public, approval. The people I come from are powerless to do evil on a grand scale.

The moment I wished every sentence, everything I knew, that began with England would end with "and then it all died, we don't know how, it just all died" was when I saw the white cliffs of Dover. I had sung hymns and recited poems that were about a longing to see the white cliffs of Dover again. At the same time I sang the hymns and recited the poems, I could not really long to see them again because I had never seen them at all, nor had anyone around me at the time. But there we were, groups of people longing for something we had never seen. And so there they were, the white cliffs, but they were not that pearly majestic thing I used to sing about, that thing that created such a feeling in these people that when they died in the place where I lived they had themselves buried facing a direction that would allow them to see the white cliffs of Dover when they were resurrected, as surely they would be. The white cliffs of Dover, when finally I saw them, were cliffs, but they were not white; you would only call them that if the word "white" meant something special to you; they were dirty and they were steep; they were so steep, the correct height from which all my views of England, starting with the map before me in my classroom and ending with the trip I had just taken, should jump and die and disappear forever.

1991

Profile   Jamaica Kincaid's essay presents multiple experiences of seeing England for the first time: on school maps, in history books and novels, on cereal and shoe boxes and, finally, on the soil of England itself, where she releases a backlog of accumulated resentment. The result is an autobiographical essay bristling with indignation, indignation for what has been done to her and hers in the name of England. As a helpless child growing up on the "drought-ridden" Caribbean island of Antigua, she suffers a life dominated by the rainy kingdom, from her school courses to her diet to her clothing. Everywhere, publicly and privately, adults present England as the measure of all things: English people are special, her own father prides himself on wearing hats from England, and in school she must learn to draw maps of England, memorize the reigns of English kings, and study the Roman occupation of Britain. Worst of all—the offense against a child she cannot forgive—she was made to feel "silent and afraid," that she was nothing, that she and her people were without value.

Like George Orwell's "Shooting an Elephant," "On Seeing England for the First Time" confronts the evils of colonialism, the arrogance and presumption of one culture usurping the territory and governance of another. But Orwell writes as one of the offending colonial occupiers. Although he testifies to his own awakening, to his recognition of the personal costs paid even by the colonialists, he still writes as an outsider. But Jamaica Kincaid writes as an insider, as one of those suffering under an "enlightened" colonial administration, giving eloquent testimony to the loss, humiliation, and—finally—hatred.

Kincaid develops her essay in two parts. In patient detail she first recounts her brainwashing at the hands of anglophile adults, including her own parents, who have accepted unquestioningly the cultural ascendancy of the English. She tells of the England-centered school curriculum, the English world she absorbs from her private reading (novels with faithless servants, lush gardens, single rooms larger than her entire house, and heroines whose clothes "rustled, swished, soothed"). As she concludes one paragraph, "The world was theirs, not mine; everything told me so." The sum total of all she learns of England is that her own life does not measure up (her cheap cotton dresses will not rustle, and she must fetch water from the public pipe like a servant).

The second part opens by discussing the dynamic of prolonged idealization. When the space "between the idea of something and its reality is always wide and deep and dark," when the two are kept apart for too long, the space eventually fills "with obsession or desire or hatred or love." For Kincaid this space between the relentless idea of England and its reality becomes filled with hatred. And because the idea of something and its reality are often so very different, their meeting must usually result in the death of one.

So, as an adult, a wife, and a mother, and to exorcise the specter of England, Kincaid finally sets foot on its soil. What she experiences there is not so much disappointment, because she expects to dislike it, but difficulty containing what her English traveling companion would call prejudice. She admits to her prejudice, seems even to embrace it, almost eager to shock her companion with her "not-favorable opinions":

> I find England ugly, I hate England; the weather is like a jail sentence, the English are a very ugly people, the food in England is like a jail sentence, the hair of English people is so straight, so dead looking, the English have an unbearable smell so different from the smell of people I know . . .

But if she will admit to her prejudice, the admission only increases her sense of helplessness. Her prejudices, after all, are only her own personal feelings (not institutional policies), and thus are impotent. The people she comes from "are powerless to do evil on a grand scale."

At the end, seeing the dirty, gray cliffs of Dover, she is left wishing that all things English would disappear and, in her manic rejection of all things English, gives testimony to just how thoroughly England has lodged itself in her consciousness.

Paragraphing   Just leafing through her essay, we can recognize one peculiarity of Kincaid's writing, her unusually long paragraphs. There are no clear
rules governing the length of paragraphs. Some, like Kincaid's, can run to a
page and a half and longer, testing the average reader's attention span.
Others, to make an emphatic point, may consist of a single sentence. For
writers and readers alike, though, they are a convenience, a way to organize
and subdivide an essay, article, or chapter. In other words, paragraphs are organizational units, often appearing in groups and usually containing formations of "thematically related" sentences. But since units often contain
subunits, paragraphs, especially longer paragraphs, may contain subdivisions
that have the potential to become paragraphs in their own right. A writer
breaks them up or keeps them intact, depending on his or her sense of effective grouping.

Consider paragraph 15, all sixteen sentences and 477 words of it. In this
one organizational unit she covers all of the following: visiting Bath, and its
familiarity to her from her reading and its importance to Roman Britain;
drinking tea in a room she had read about in an eighteenth-century novel
and where many young women had danced and disgraced themselves with
young men, some of whom were bound for Bristol, from which they sailed
on voyages that meant no good to Kincaid's ancestors; then of driving
through the familiar English countryside with its hedge rows, noting all the
maintenance they require, thinking of the people like herself who do all
such work to "hold up the world," hearing of a rich lady's campaign to save
the hedges, and learning of the "vile flowering bush" that is allegedly ruining the traditional English countryside.

What holds such a wildly wandering paragraph together? Her own memories and associations. But it could just as easily be subdivided into three or
four shorter units. The following is one possibility:

> I went to Bath—we, my friend and I, did this, but though we were together, I was
> no longer with her. The landscape was almost as familiar as my own hand, but I
> had never been in this place before, so how could that be again? And the streets
> of Bath were familiar, too, but I had never walked on them before. It was all
> those years of reading, starting with Roman Britain. Why did I have to know
> about Roman Britain? It was of no real use to me, a person living on a hot,
> drought-ridden island, and it is of no use to me now, and yet my head is filled
> with this nonsense, Roman Britain.
>
> In Bath, I drank tea in a room I had read about in a novel written in the eight-
> eenth century. In this very same room, young women wearing those dresses that
> rustled and so on danced and flirted and sometimes disgraced themselves with
> young men, soldiers, sailors, who were on their way to Bristol or someplace like
> that, so many places like that where so many adventures, the outcome of which
> was not good for me, began. Bristol, England. A sentence that began "That night
> the ship sailed from Bristol, England" would end not so good for me.
>
> And then I was driving through the countryside in an English motorcar, on
> narrow winding roads, and they were so familiar, though I had never been on
> them before; and through little villages the names of which I somehow knew so
> well though I had never been there before. And the countryside did have all
> those hedges and hedges, fields hedged in.

I was marveling at all the toil of it, the planting of the hedges to begin with and then the care of it, all that clipping, year after year of clipping, and I wondered at the lives of the people who would have to do this, because wherever I see and feel the hands that hold up the world, I see and feel myself and all the people who look like me. And I said, "Those hedges" and my friend said that someone, a woman named Mrs. Rothchild, worried that the hedges weren't being taken care of properly; the farmers couldn't afford or find the help to keep up the hedges, and often they replaced them with wire fencing. I might have said to that, well if Mrs. Rothchild doesn't like the wire fencing, why doesn't she take care of the hedges herself, but I didn't. And then in those fields that were now hemmed in by wire fencing that a privileged woman didn't like was planted a vile yellow flowering bush that produced an oil, and my friend said that Mrs. Rothchild didn't like this either; it ruined the English countryside, it ruined the traditional look of the English countryside.

Paragraphing, then, is at least partially a matter of individual taste, governed by several general considerations. One is variety. Like Kincaid we should vary the length of sentences and paragraphs alike. Too many short paragraphs and our work will seem choppy and poorly developed; too many long paragraphs and we tax the reader's patience. Paragraph breaks, after all, are also rest stops.

As groups of thematically related sentences, paragraphs should have reasonably obvious unity, helped along by repetition of key terms and continuous pronoun chains, and by clear transitions from idea to idea.

All of these issues we can address when we are revising. Most writers paragraph instinctively, then reshape and clarify and polish later. Technically, we usually do not "build" paragraphs; we remodel them.

Exercise   By most standards Kincaid's paragraph 14 is quite long. Subdivide it into two or three paragraphs, each with its own unity, coherence, and emphasis. Write a brief paragraph explaining your divisions.

The Passionate Style   Kincaid's rhetorical purpose is to express her anger and resentment at the "cultural erasure" she experienced as a helpless schoolchild. But in addition to expressing her feelings, she wants her readers to share in them, to experience her indignation. In order to accomplish this purpose, she exploits a number of devices, including name-calling ("an unlikable man, an unpleasant man," "vile people"), dismissive comparisons ("they [London monuments] were like markers on an old useless trail, like a piece of old string tied to a finger to jog one's memory, like old decorations in an old house, dirty, useless, in the way"), and vivid portrayals of her misuse at the hands of colonial administrators. Thus, we have the account of the ceaseless classroom deferral to all things English: drawing maps of England; memorizing the names of English kings, their families, their battles; learning about the Roman occupation of Britain. And we have a detailed contrast between the idealized world of English novels and the unglamorous terms of her own existence in the heat, humidity, and poverty of Antigua (instead of having a servant like the young ladies in English novels, she must fetch water for her mother from the public pipe). In a startling image she sums up her humiliation by saying that it is as if her neck had been in an iron vice, forcing her nose against a glass window on the other side of which was the English world.

But repetition is the most incessant feature of Kincaid's passionate style. In paragraph after paragraph she illustrates why Gertrude Stein preferred to call repetition *insistence*, especially in paragraph 4, where each sentence begins the same way:

> *I did not know then that the statement* "Draw a map of England" was something far worse than a declaration of war, for in fact a flat-out declaration of war would have put me on alert, and again in fact, there was no need for war—I had long ago been conquered. *I did not know then that this statement* was part of a process that would result in my erasure, not my physical erasure, but my erasure all the same. *I did not know then that this statement* was meant to make me feel in awe and small whenever I heard the word "England": awe at its existence, small because I was not from it. *I did not know* much of anything *then*—certainly not what a blessing it was that I was unable to draw a map of England correctly.

Kincaid returns repeatedly to "I did not know then," each time suggesting that she knows *now*, knows very well. By repeating key words from sentence to sentence, a writer emphasizes paragraph coherence. By repeating the first part of a sentence four consecutive times, Kincaid goes further. She insistently returns to her childhood ignorance, her childhood vulnerability. By dwelling on her ignorance, and further developing its implications in each successive statement, she relives for herself and her readers the terms of her classroom indoctrination. The reader can almost hear her voice rising with each sentence.

Used carelessly, the passionate style may relieve the writer but alienate the reader. Used carefully, it can draw the reader into the writer's emotional state, can become a vehicle for sympathy and identification.

Revision Assignments   Select one of the following strategies and revise "On Seeing England for the First Time." Include a brief statement explaining your choice and its effect on the arrangement and presentation of material.

1. Paragraphing, the grouping and linking sentences into meaningful formations, is as much an art as a science. That is, paragraphing allows generous room for individual tastes and judgments. Take either paragraph 2 or 6, both quite long by normal standards, and divide them into shorter paragraphs, making any revisions necessary to make the new divisions coherent. Then write a brief explanation of your decisions.

2. One of Kincaid's rhetorical purposes is to vent her anger and indignation at the "cultural erasure" she experienced as a school child. To communicate this indignation, she openly displays her emotions. Revise paragraph 12 so that it has a calmer, cooler, more judicious tone, a more rational appeal. Imagine a more tactful Kincaid, one writing to an English audience she does not wish to alienate. At the same time, allow her to justify her anger.

Writing Assignments

1. Have you yourself had an experience like Kincaid's; that is, have you survived an early period of intense indoctrination, then later freed yourself by achieving intellectual and emotional independence? Perhaps you were brought up to be a true and uncritical believer of some religious, political, or other philosophical system. If so, write about this experience, following loosely the structure of Kincaid's essay: Give a vivid account of your indoctrination, then describe your awakening or "recovery" and then its aftermath in new attitudes, new mental self-reliance.

2. "The space between the idea of something and its reality is always wide and deep and dark," writes Kincaid (paragraph 10):

   > The longer they are kept apart . . . the wider the width, the deeper the depth, the thicker and darker the darkness. This space starts out empty, there is nothing in it, but it rapidly becomes filled up with obsession or desire or hatred or love . . . That the idea of something and its reality are often two completely different things is something no one ever remembers; and so when they meet and find that they are not compatible, the weaker of the two, idea or reality, dies.

   Write about an occasion like the one described above, a time when an idea flourished in your imagination, became idealized and romanticized until you were "filled up with obsession or desire or hatred or love," and then confronted the reality. It might have been the idea of a person, a career, a place, an achievement, or an institution (whether a school or marriage or parenthood). Describe the idea, trying to capture your passion and enthusiasm; then describe the encounter with reality and its aftermath, your disillusionment or other revised attitudes.

3. In "Shooting an Elephant" Orwell records his discovery of how thoroughly the subjugation of another people corrupts and debases the colonial masters. In "On Seeing England for the First Time," what might Kincaid be suggesting about the effects of such subjugation *on the subjugated*? In England she is angry and uncivil, even to those trying to be kind to her, and she admits that she was full of hatred and prejudice (giving the English some of their own medicine, she finds them ugly and complains about how they smell). Is she saying that hatred and prejudice are sometimes justified, or that domination and injustice breed such feelings? Orwell would say that, in the equation of colonial domination (or any other kind of subjugation), all parties suffer, morally and psychologically. Would Kincaid agree? Would you agree? Or do you think we can take Kincaid's anger at face value and need make no apologies for her position?

Maya Art for the Record

JUNE KINOSHITA

It was in 1900 that Adela Catherine Breton first rode into the archaeological   1
camp at the great Maya temple city of Chichen Itza. Bundled up in a Victorian riding costume with her severe, girlish face protected from the Yucatan
sun by a low-brimmed hat, the 50-year-old Breton cut a striking figure. Over
the next eight years, the Englishwoman time and again braved heat, ticks
and foot-dragging bureaucrats to return to Chichen Itza to sketch and paint
the stone reliefs and colorful murals that enlivened the limestone walls of the
ruins.

Today Maya scholars are grateful for her efforts. In the 80-odd years since   2
her visits, many of the murals that Breton so painstakingly copied at Chichen
Itza and other Maya sites have been lost. The steamy Mesoamerican climate
and burning sun have exacted a heavy toll on the colors, particularly the intense, indigo-based azure known as Maya blue. Vandals and tourists have
spirited away many fragments, and the surviving paintings are prone to attack
by algae and vegetation. In many instances Breton's watercolors are the only
records of these Maya relics. Her work was donated to the Peabody Museum
at Harvard University and to the City of Bristol Museum and Art Gallery in
England, which commemorated her achievements in a special exhibit this
past winter.

Breton was not the only eccentric Victorian to explore the world armed   3
with a sketchbook, but she was unusual for her rigorous attention to color.
"The murals are packed with information carried by color," says Arthur G.
Miller, Professor of art history at the University of Maryland at College Park.

Ablaze in Color

Consider the now badly defaced battle scene on the south wall in the Upper   4
Temple of the Jaguars at Chichen Itza (A.D. 900–1100). Breton's watercolors
show the circular shields of the combatants rimmed with red or blue to indi-
cate the opposing armies. "Color is part of the cosmic view of the ancient
Meso-americans," says National Geographic Society archaeologist George E.
Stuart.

The cardinal directions, for example, are color-coded: east is painted red,   5
west black, north white, south yellow and center blue-green. "The color of
deities' costumes show directional associations," Stuart explains. "For humans, color may signify rank or where they're from. The shapes of objects
can be similar: without color it's hard to tell if something is jade or maize."
Maryland's Miller notes that "mostly we see only bare limestone. The murals
give us a glimpse of what the sculpture looked like."

Not only murals and sculpture but whole cities were "ablaze in color,"   6
says Merle Greene Robertson, director of the Pre-Columbian Art Research
Institute in San Francisco. Robertson should know. In 1973 she embarked on
a thorough survey of color at Palenque. The classic-period city, located amid

the lush rain forests at the foot of a chain of hills in northern Chiapas state, reached its apex in the reign of Pacal the Great (A.D. 615–683). It is renowned for delicate stucco reliefs and numerous hieroglyphic inscriptions.

Using a standard color chart, Robertson, whom fellow Mayanists describe affectionately as "the proverbial little old lady in tennis shoes," set out to document the vestiges of paint that once adorned the buildings and bas reliefs. According to Robertson, the walls were once painted in intense red, inside and out. Human skin was rendered in red, that of gods in blue.

When Robertson began her project, most of the painted surfaces were still clean, she recalls. But by the early 1980's they had become encrusted with "black scab," which forms when limestone reacts with acidic moisture. The unsightly encrustations obscured what little color was left. She attributes the black scab to acid rain, which she says wafts in from uncapped oil wells and smokestacks near the Gulf Coast cities of Coatzacoalcos and Carmen, 125 kilometers north of Palenque.

Robertson sounded the alarm on acid rain last year in a study for the National Geographic Society. In the famed Temple of the Inscriptions at Palenque, she reported, the black scab was "so bad that upon looking at them [the inscriptions], one seemed to be looking at a piece of flat, black sculpture." Seymour Z. Lewin, a chemist at New York University who has examined weathering patterns at several Maya sites, agrees that "the evidence is typical of the weathering produced by acid rain." But he adds that "paint suffers more from microorganisms and the leaching of salt" than from acid rain.

Robertson's survey of Palenque was nearing completion in 1982 when disaster struck: the volcano El Chichon, which had been dormant for 600 years, suddenly erupted, ejecting a dense cloud of ash and sulfuric acid droplets. The eruption dumped hundreds of tons of abrasive ash on Palenque, leaving it looking as though a freak blizzard had struck. Mary E. Miller, a Maya scholar from Yale University (no relation to Arthur Miller), says: "When the rains started, it scoured off the black goop, but it also took off the paint." Six weeks after the eruption, she recalled, "the whole site looked like it had been scrubbed with Bon Ami."

Fortunately, Robertson's records by that time were complete enough to enable her to reconstruct the original appearance of Palenque's halls in a series of vivid paintings. "I think Robertson's reconstructions are very good," Mary Miller says. "The colors seem hard, flat and excessively bright—and that's how they were."

Just as urgent as retrieving the lost color of the ruins is the task of recording the murals that still survive. Even the most celebrated of Maya paintings—the murals at Bonampak—have not yet been satisfactorily recorded, experts say. This remote, late classic site tucked away in the southeast corner of Chiapas state was first brought to the attention of the outside world by the English explorer Giles G. Healey, who was led there by local villagers in 1946.

Unwitting Obliteration

Dated to A.D. 800, the Bonampak murals cover the interiors of three stone chambers. In brilliant colors the realistic images depict a battle, its gory aftermath and the victory celebrations. At the time of Bonampak's discovery, the established view held that the classical Maya were a peaceful race who had no written history. Bonampak overturned that view and revealed the Maya for what they were: a warlike people who recorded their story in hieroglyphs. "Bonampak was a watershed in Maya studies," Mary Miller notes.

Because of their importance, the murals' precarious condition alarms   14
many scholars. "The site was shrouded in deep tropical rain forest and was kept dark and damp for 1,000 years," Mary Miller explains. "The first thing they did after the murals were found was to cut down the trees and put a galvanized tin roof over the site. This made it very hot in the day and cold at night." In the 1960's conservators injected the walls with silicone, which held the paintings up, "just as it would a woman's face," she observes. "But then the silicone flowed down, and the murals ended up being worse off." Conservators also unwittingly obliterated parts of the murals when they sealed several large cracks with cement.

Urgent Need

A few years ago the murals were cleaned. A milky layer of calcium carbonate   15
had hardened over the painted surface, and when it was removed, the underlying scenes were revealed in their full glory. Ironically, the cleaning could hasten their destruction. "The reason they survived in the first place is [that] they were behind calcium carbonate," Mary Miller says. Now that the paintings are exposed, they remain subject to gyrating temperatures, humidity and microorganisms. "It's dangerous to have revealed them without providing better protection," she fears. "I'm concerned about their future."

There is consequently an urgent need to make a modern record of the   16
Bonampak murals. Several have been made, in fact, including photographs taken in 1946 by Healey, another set by Hans Ritter and four reconstruction paintings, one a spectacularly detailed reconstruction of the first chamber. It was painted in the mid-1970's by Felipe Davalos for the Florida Museum of Natural History in Gainesville.

Yet as good as some of these reconstructions are—particularly those by   17
Davalos—none is complete, scholars say. Except for the Davalos reconstruction, "the hieroglyphs looks like spaghetti," Stuart says. "It's hard to draw that stuff. It took me a year to learn to draw in the Maya art style." Breton put it this way in a letter to her colleague Alfred M. Tozzer: "Making drawings of them [Maya art] would require not modern artistic skill, but the very different capacity of seeing them as ancient Americans did."

According to Stuart, "the Bonampak murals in their entirety have never   18
been properly photographed or drawn." That situation may soon change. Roberto Garcia Moll, director of Mexico's National Institute of Anthropology and History, has expressed interest in such a project. Mary Miller supports this move, saying that "records are more important than restorations."

New murals continue to be discovered throughout Mesoamerica. Last   19
year Mexican archaeologists dug down to a buried staircase at Cacaxtla, a ruined palace complex 100 kilometers east of Mexico City, and uncovered a pair of breathtakingly fresh-looking murals on the two walls flanking the stairs. Along with two other murals that were found in the mid-1970's at

Cacaxtla, the new find makes the group one of the most significant in Mesoamerica. The murals were created between A.D. 655 and 835 by the Olmeca-Xixalanca, a people of probable Gulf Coast origin, says Ellen T. Baird of the University of Nebraska at Lincoln. The murals are "a unique mix of Maya style and central Mexican motifs," she says.

The styles apparently became mixed, according to the late Donald Robertson of Tulane University, because the lords of Cacaxtla hired Maya artists; the artists painted in their native style but put in Highland Mexican glyphs in accordance with their patrons' wishes. Mary Miller marvels at the explicit rendering of the maize god in the newly found murals: heads of yellow maize bearing human faces poke out between green leaves on a stalk. "This is iconography for dummies," she says.

The Mexican government has built a large shelter over the entire site. Still, the murals unearthed in the mid-1970's have already faded perceptibly, observers say. Fortunately, they have been copied by a Mexican team. The newly discovered paintings at Cacaxtla were photographed this past winter under the auspices of National Geographic. These murals are in such superb condition that photographic records may be adequate, Mary Miller says. Less pristine murals may require hand copying as well. "This strikes many people as terribly old fashioned, yet the eye can see things the camera can't pick up," she notes.

Nothing Romantic

Most important is the recording of "what is extant before it fades," Arthur Miller agrees. Few people, however, are willing to expend the time and effort to make such records. He notes that his own work on the murals at Tulum, a postclassic (15th- to 16th-century) complex perched above the sea on the eastern coast of Yucatan, consumed four years. "It takes commitment, experience and painstaking effort," he says. "There's nothing very romantic about it."

Adela Breton would have sympathized. Copying murals is "very trying to brain and nerves as well as to eyes and hand," she complained to an acquaintance. Indeed, one reason the Bonampak murals have never been replicated completely may be that the artists simply ran out of steam. Davalos's efforts on the second and third rooms do not begin to compare with his reconstruction of the first room. Another artist working on a Bonampak replica in Mexico City started with the third room but appears to have flagged by the time she got to the others.

Good replicas are increasingly important because many Maya sites are vulnerable to economic development. At Tulum the walls are black from soot belched by tour buses. Tourists, who bring in much needed foreign exchange, raise the humidity inside the stone chambers and exhale plant spores, which can take root on the walls. The oil wells and smokestacks operated by Pemex, Mexico's national oil company, may be contributing to acid rain. "There's a tension between conservation and economics," Arthur Miller observes. The solution, he suggests, is to make replicas and install them in place of the originals, which would be relocated to museums.

Even with safeguards, degradation is inevitable for ancient artifacts, especially painted ones. "Once you've found them, you may as well write them
off," Stuart observes. "That's why we want to record them—for all time."

1990

Profile   "Maya Art for the Record" originally appeared in the "Science in
Pictures" section of *Scientific American*, accompanied by a dozen illustrations
of Mayan murals. Although the text supplements and arouses curiosity about
the pictures, it is able to stand by itself as an example of skillful informational writing, writing in which a wealth of material is integrated into a lively
narrative. The essential theme is the conflict between economic development and the need to protect archaeological sources, a story Kinoshita could
have told by discussing the current state of the murals, the effects of industrial pollution, tourism, and even a recent volcanic eruption. And she could
have dwelled on the irony that the murals may have suffered more from efforts to study and preserve them than from centuries of neglect. Such an account could have been handled with straight exposition.

Instead, she tells a story of discovery and reclamation, of cooperation between cultures and generations. And she tells a story not of anonymous scientists and archaeologists, but of individuals, personalities like the intrepid
middle-aged Englishwoman, Adela Catherine Breton, who began her work
in 1900, and her successors today, like Arthur G. Miller, George Stuart, Mary
E. Miller, Felipe Davalos, and—especially—Merle Greene Robertson. But,
intentionally or unintentionally, Breton struck the theme of reclamation, her
patient attention to color in her sketches and paintings saving what turns out
to have been the key to the Maya murals. "The murals are packed with information carried by color," Arthur Miller confirms, information that would
be lost if Breton had not made such a faithful record almost a century ago.
Now, other sites have been discovered, like that at Bonampak, and with the
help of Breton's sketches their murals have been deciphered and our understanding of Maya history revised. Even as weather, tourists, vandals, and industrial pollution combine to efface them, the murals continue to tell their
stories, thanks to an unlikely visitor with an appreciation for color.

"Maya Art for the Record" could have been a dry but competent summary of information, a methodical report on the factors endangering the
Maya heritage. Instead, Kinoshita brings her subject to life by humanizing it,
turning it into a story of living, speaking people (even if some must now live
and speak in their drawings and letters). Instead of limiting herself to abstractions and generalities, to statistics and anonymous authorities, she gives us
names and voices, living personalities. And in so doing, she also gives a valuable lesson in arranging and presenting information. Like John McPhee in
"In Virgin Forest," she appreciates that at the heart of every good story are
people, sometimes struggling and suffering but also often industrious, dedicated, and—in some respect—triumphant.

Using Sources   In using sources, we have three choices: to quote directly, to quote indirectly, and to paraphrase. A *direct quote*, of course, uses
quotation marks and carries the promise that it is an exact transcription of
what someone else has said or written. Such quotes are usually accompanied

by a *signal phrase* to identify the source. Whether the signal phrase appears before or after the quote depends largely on factors like continuity and emphasis: Does a writer wish to emphasize the quote or the source? Kinoshita illustrates:

> Breton was not the only eccentric Victorian to explore the world armed with a sketchbook, but she was unusual for her rigorous attention to color. "The murals are packed with information carried by color," *says Arthur G. Miller, Professor of art history at the University of Maryland at College Park.*

Postponing the signal phrase allows Kinoshita to move directly from her own statement about color to Miller's. The signal phrase here simply authenticates the quoted material.

Sometimes, to tailor a quote to fit into our own sentence or paragraph, we must add or subtract material. If an explanatory word or phrase must be added, we use brackets. Thus, explaining the difficulty of recording Maya hieroglyphics, Kinoshita quotes Breton:

> Breton put it this way in a letter to her colleague Alfred M. Tozzer: "Making the drawings of them [Maya art] would require not modern artistic skill, but the very different capacity of seeing them as ancient Americans did."

Or later, she wishes to clarify a statement by Merle Greene Robertson:

> In the famed Temple of the Inscriptions at Palenque, she reported, the black scab was "so bad that upon looking at them [the inscriptions], one seemed to be looking at a piece of flat, black sculpture."

Still later in the article, Kinoshita wishes to quote the substance of what Breton has said, but not her entire statement. Thus, she *paraphrases* (shortens and puts into her own words) the first part of the sentence, then uses Breton's exact words:

> Copying murals is "very trying to brain and nerves as well as to eyes and hand," she complained to an acquaintance.

In another passage, probably for economy, she relies entirely on paraphrase, summarizing one authority's conclusions on the blending of Maya art with another style:

> The styles apparently became mixed, according to the late Donald Robertson of Tulane University, because the lords of Cacaxtla hired Maya artists; the artists painted in their native style but put in Highland Mexican glyphs in accordance with their patrons' wishes.

Located between a direct quote and a paraphrase is an *indirect quote*, a reasonably close approximation of what someone has said or written but neither precisely quoted nor greatly abbreviated, as Kinoshita demonstrates in the following:

> "There's a tension between conservation and economics," Arthur Miller observes. *The solution*, he suggests, *is to make replicas and install them in place of the originals, which would be relocated to museums.*

When we cite authorities directly, we are transplanting sentences from someone else's paragraphs to our own. To ensure that they adapt gracefully to their new environment, we can adjust our introductory remarks, shift the location of signal phrases, add or delete words, and—if necessary—quote indirectly or paraphrase. If we do the latter, we must remain faithful to the spirit of the original. And if we do any of the three—quote directly or indirectly or even paraphrase—and do not identify our source, we are guilty of *plagiarism.*

Revision Assignments   Select one of the following strategies and revise "Maya Art for the Record." Include a brief statement explaining your choice and its effect on the arrangement and presentation of material.

1.   Write a newspaper feature story on the threat to Maya murals—the efforts of archaeologists to preserve the paintings, the effect of acid rain and other industrial pollutants, the difficulty of imitating the work of the ancient artists, and so on. Make this an informational piece, minimizing narrative and using quotations sparingly. (The personalities and adventures of specific archaeologists and artists are irrelevant.)

2.   Write a new opening for the story, one beginning with a thesis statement or introductory generalization and running for at least five or six paragraphs. Then outline how the rest of the story might go.

3.   Revise the story into a question-and-answer format. To do so, you will have to create an informed questioner and then make good use of the quotes provided by Kinoshita. Such Q & A's are often preceded by an introductory paragraph to establish a setting and orient the reader, though most of the information will emerge from the discussion.

Writing Assignment

1.   June Kinoshita reveals a dilemma that applies not only to Maya murals but to other archaeological sites as well (see Barry Lopez's "Stone Horse"). In our efforts to study and preserve, we often threaten the very things we seek to protect, once again illustrating the problems of human intervention (see John McPhee's "In Virgin Forest"). By advertising and displaying ancient sites in the hopes of attracting public support, officials often expose the sites to accelerated wear. And then there is the conflict between knowledge-seekers on the one hand and museum curators on the other (the process of unearthing and displaying often destroys information). Sometimes, the excavations that yield the greatest knowledge also detract the most from the scenic value of the site. And there is also the issue of disturbing the resting places of ancient peoples. How do we best serve our ancestors: by allowing them to rest undisturbed but sometimes behind a veil of ignorance and neglect, or by learning what we can about their achievements, even when it means dismantling some of what they created? Using "Maya Art for the Record" and "Stone Horse," plus other knowledge you may have, explore the dilemma and take a position.

Burnt Offerings

LEWIS H. LAPHAM

"If there were a Super Bowl every day, no American would ever need a sleeping pill."
—Russell Baker

The kind of people who like to name a principal cause for all the country's 1
troubles lately have appointed the scenes of crime and violence in Hollywood movies to the office held in prior years by the Soviet empire, sexual
permissiveness, godless communism, the cocaine trade, and demon rum.
The new proposition is as witless as its predecessors, but for the last four or
five months it has been all but impossible to escape. Waiting for a table in a
New York restaurant last November, I overheard a woman say that she had
seen statistics proving the correlation between the box-office receipts of *The
Last Boy Scout* and the number of murders taking place on Saturday nights in
the South Bronx. Her companion, a smiling and agreeable man in an expen-
sively tailored suit, assured her that he'd never met a movie producer who
wasn't either a professional criminal or an amateur psychopath.

Two days later, in the news from Washington, I noticed that both Janet 2
Reno, the attorney general, and Senator Paul Simon (D., Ill.) once again were
suggesting that some sort of legal constraint be placed on Hollywood's passion for savage bloodletting and continuous gunfire. Over the next several
weeks a chorus of newspaper columnists inveighed against what they called
"the culture of violence," deploring the casting of toxic images into the pure
streams of American thought, quoting like-minded sentiments expressed by
President Clinton and the American Psychological Association, citing figures
supplied by Senator Ernest E. Hollings (D., S.C.) to the effect that the nation's television syndicates present the nation's schoolchildren with 8,000
murders a year. I couldn't follow all the lines of the arguments but I think
somebody said that the country would find its way back to God if only we
could rid it of Steven Seagal and Chuck Norris, and I remember somebody
else saying that the government should impose an excise tax on Hollywood's
use of violence—like the taxes on liquor and cigarettes.

Although I can think of many objections to most of the movies in ques- 3
tion, I never know what the critics expect Hollywood to put in their place.
Within the American scheme of things, the romance of violence is as traditional as the singing of "The Star-Spangled Banner." The winning of the
American West was largely accomplished by greedy and ignorant men in
search of something for nothing, governed by their basest instincts, and
praised, in the words of John Terrell's *Land Grab*, "for courage that they
didn't possess and eulogized for moral principles utterly foreign to them."
When the James gang held up the Kansas City fair in 1872, the local newspaper described the robbery as being "so diabolically daring and utterly in contempt of fear that we are bound to admire it and revere its perpetrators."
Two days later the paper compared the gang to the knights of King Arthur's
Round Table. Michel Chevalier, an astute and observant traveler in

late-nineteenth-century America, noticed that American society had the morality of an army on the march, an opinion seconded by Albert J. Nock in his *Memoirs of a Superfluous Man*. Describing his boyhood in the 1870s, Nock remembered that it was the freebooters carrying off the heaviest sacks of spoil who "were held up in the schools, the press, and even in the pulpit, as prototypal of all that was making America great, and hence as *par excellence* the proper examples for well-ordered youth to follow."

Numerous other writers, both domestic and foreign, have made similar observations, noticing also that in most American narratives—whether of Wall Street or the Alamo—it is the violent man who proves to be the hero of the tale. If they're worth the respect of their horses, both the good guys and the bad guys show contempt for an abstraction as bloodless and chicken-hearted as due process of the law. The archetypal man on horseback (sometimes known as John Wayne or Randolph Scott, at other times taking the alias of John Rambo or Ronald Reagan) rides into the dusty, wooden town (i.e., Abilene or Ban Me Thuot or Washington D.C.) and discovers evil in even the most rudimentary attempts at civilization. The villains invariably belong to "the system," which, as every cowhand and aspiring politician knows, is corrupt. The hero appears as a god descended from a cloud, come to punish the sin of pride and scourge the wicked with a terrible vengeance. No matter what the sociopolitical map co-ordinates—*Miami Vice, The Terminator*, the James Bond and Clint Eastwood movies, *Star Wars, State of Siege*, etc.—and no matter what the outward trappings of character (as gunfighter, police detective, or renegade CIA agent), the conventional American hero casts himself as both judge and executioner, pursuing his quarry, on foot or on horseback, by helicopter or automobile, across the Siberian steppe or through the streets of downtown Detroit, proclaiming himself the enemy of the society that reared him, shrugging off the obligations to family and state as if they were the rain on his hat or the mud on his boots. All the stories take place in a moral wilderness that resembles the ruin of Sarajevo, and after the requisite number of killings, the hero departs, leaving to mortal men (i.e., to women and shopkeepers) the tedious business of burial, marriage, and settlement.

The stories haven't changed much since I first began going to the movies fifty years ago, but what has changed is the purpose to which Hollywood directs the scenes of violence. Instead of advancing the plot, the killing serves as set decoration, meant to be admired for nothing other than itself, as if the sight of a knife being driven into the villain's forehead were comparable to a gilded fire screen or an ornamental vase. The producers apparently have abandoned the hope of art or verisimilitude, and when I see Sylvester Stallone setting fire to a town in Oregon, or Mel Gibson decimating a regiment of road warriors, I attribute the dreams of Armageddon to people who have derived their notions of violent death from the study of other movies. By glorifying the acts of violence as expensive sumptuary[1] objects (bigger explosions, uglier wounds, more generous flows of blood), they somehow achieve the paradoxical effect of making them trivial. The killings play like the gag lines on television sitcoms—as novelties meant to lead into the commercial

---

[1]Sumptuary laws regulate or limit personal expenditure, especially on objects of luxury. In other words, they are meant to discourage wasteful consumption.

or conceal the fatuousness of the plot—and I suspect that their smirking, undergraduate character follows from the cynicism of the people who write the scripts and dress the sets. I watch Schwarzenegger in *Commando*, setting off explosions on an island in the Santa Barbara Channel, and I think of the screen writer and the assistant director arranging swatches of red and orange as if they were flowers or throw pillows.

The dialogue strains for a similarly decorative effect. Before remanding their antagonists to oblivion in a swarm of sharks or fusillade of dumdum bullets, James Bond and Harry Callahan pause briefly for a *bon mot* in the manner of Oscar Wilde. They domesticate the acts of violence by changing them into jokes, and the moviegoing public—safe behind popcorn boxes and fortified with Raisinets and M & M's—gladly lets go its fear of the world outside the Cineplex in gusts of grateful laughter. 6

What Russell Baker said of the midwinter Super Bowl also can be said of the midsummer bloom of action films. The semi-annual festivals of violence serve as soporifics, not as stimulants, and the critics who think otherwise, who mistake a sophomore's fantasy of suburban revenge for an incitement to urban riot, might do well to reread Shakespeare or Homer. Neither author was squeamish about the depiction of violence, but they had it in mind to describe the actual world of human character and event, not the fairy-tale land of wish and dream. 7

Maybe it's my age, but if I replay in my mind the sequence of brutal images that I remember seeing in the movies over the last twenty-odd years, I'm struck by their increasingly cartoonish character, which makes it difficult for me to take seriously the fretting of people like Senators Simon and Hollings. Were I to do so, I first would have to grant their prior assumption that the movies under review possess the force of art, that they awaken in the mind of their audiences emotions strong enough to excite action or thought. 8

But once divorced from the emotional contexts of human suffering, the scenes of violence lose both meaning and power, and it was this weakness of which I was pointedly reminded in late January when I had occasion to read passages of the *Iliad* (assigned as homework to my twelve-year-old son) on the same evening that HBO presented Eastwood in *Pale Rider*—i.e., as Achilles on the old American frontier bringing rough and divine justice to the wayward operators of a California mining camp. The distance between the two variations on the theme of vengeance is the distance between newsreel footage of the Normandy invasion and a fashion photograph promoting Bugle Boy jeans. 9

Here is Homer, in the translation by Robert Fagles, describing the death of the warrior Harpalion: 10

> But Meriones caught him in full retreat,
>   he let fly
> with a bronzed-tipped arrow, hitting his
>   right buttock
> up under the pelvic bone so the lance
>   pierced the bladder.
> He sank on the spot, hunched in his

dear companion's arms,
gasping out his life as he writhed along
  the ground
like an earthworm stretched out in
  death, blood pooling,
soaking the earth dark red . . .

Or again, on a different day in another part of the Trojan plain, Achilles   11
killing Polydorus, Hector's brother:

[Achilles] speared him square in the
  back where his war-belt clasped,
golden buckles clinching both halves
  of his breastplate—
straight on through went the point and
  out the navel,
down on his knees he dropped—
screaming shrill as the world went black
  before him—
clutched his bowels to his body, hunched and sank.

The lines evoke the emotions of terror and fear because Homer employs   12
the imagination as a means of appreciating reality rather than as a means of
escaping it. Or, as Bernard Knox puts it in his fine introduction to Fagles's
translation, "Men die in the *Iliad* in agony; they drop, screaming, to their
knees, reaching out to beloved companions, gasping their life out, clawing
the ground with their hands; they die roaring, like Asius, raging, like the
great Sarpedon, bellowing, like Hippodamus, moaning, like Polydorus."

The gunmen in the Eastwood film fall like targets in a shooting gallery.   13
We see blood spurt from their bodies, but because we never understand
them as men, never see them as anything other than symbolic manifestations
of evil dressed in matching greatcoats that could have been designed by
Ralph Lauren, we look at their deaths as clever tropes.[2] I don't think it improbable that Eastwood intended the movie as an epic metaphor. The
camera dwells lovingly on the bleak landscape of the high desert, on the de-
serted street, on the tentative wooden town lost in an immense wilderness
under an empty sky, and I imagine that he intended the figure on horseback,
identified simply as "the preacher," to stand as an emblem of righteousness.
But after all the gunmen have been punished, the town purified, and the
preacher gone over the horizon, nothing has been said that might evoke in
the audience even the slightest hint of pity or awe.

Homer can vividly imagine the desolation of death, because he so vividly   14
delights in the spring and surge of life. A surprisingly large number of lines in
the *Iliad* speak of the joys of peace, of the generations succeeding one another in a bright and rapturous dance, of young boys in "fine-spun tunics
rubbed with a gloss of oil" and young girls "crowned with a bloom of fresh
garlands." Meaning to sing not only the wrath of Achilles but also the preciousness of life that he so wantonly destroys, Homer imparts to his poem the

---

[2]Figurative use of words or images. In other words, Eastwood's victims are abstractions, not real people.

heavy sense of tragic loss, and I read his lines with fear and dread. I come across Thestor "cowering, crouched in his fine polished chariot,/crazed with fear," and I remember that as a young reporter in San Francisco I was surprised by the smell of death in furnished rooms, by the victims of automobile accidents and multiple stab wounds losing command of their bowels, sobbing like children, afraid of the dark, never coming up with a smart remark.

But when I look at Bruce Willis or Mel Gibson annihilating gargoyles, 15 nothing remains of the mess and stink of death. The omission is deliberate. Just as the smiling hosts in the NFL broadcast booths turn fastidiously away from the injured players twisted in pain on the forty-yard line, the manufacturers of synthetic murder delete the sight of human beings reduced to earthworms. Their cameras lift lightly into the air, en route to the next automobile chase or pillar of fire, and although I know that Senators Hollings and Simon like to say that the soul of the nation's youth remains trapped in the burning wreckage with the drug money and the Guatemalan hit men, I think that they underestimated the sophistication of an audience that knows the difference between what is real and what is make-believe. Each of my own children, well before they reached the age of nine, understood *Die Hard* and *Lethal Weapon 2* as video games.

If the Hollywood daydreams lately have become louder and more violent, 16 I suspect that it's because the higher quotients of public anxiety and alarm stimulate the need for stronger sedatives. Even during the excitements of the Second World War, the patients standing in line at the box office could be comforted with *Casablanca* or *The Secret Life of Walter Mitty*. It was enough to know that Humphrey Bogart had been to Europe and could tell the difference between a Nazi, a love song, and a crooked roulette table. Most members of the audience assumed that if they had been blessed with a similar degree of sophistication, they, too, could outwit Sydney Greenstreet and leave Claude Rains standing in the rain at the airport with his list of usual suspects. Neither they nor Bogart thought it necessary to carry a semi-automatic rifle or practice the art of kick-boxing. By 1950 the United States enjoyed a position of absolute supremacy in the world, and the Americans who sallied so bravely forth to the frontiers of the Cold War (in Berlin and Central America and Indochina) traveled on passports stamped with the visas of omnipotence.

I don't know how many readers will remember Danny Kaye as Walter 17 Mitty, but I think of the movie as the preamble to the James Bond films. Frankly presented as daydream (timid milquetoast falls asleep and imagines himself performing heroic feats of derring-do), the movie anticipates the urbane British intelligence agent on the grand tour of the world's leading resorts, collecting beautiful women as if they were baseball cards, knowing how to play with the most dangerous toys in the Soviet and American arsenals, warding off the evil spirit of nuclear war. But although not unacquainted with sinister plots, Bond is still skittish about the sight of blood. He carries a gun, but he seldom has a use for it, preferring instead the hand-to-hand struggles on the edge of a cliff or a knife.

By 1980 the times had changed, and most of the important protagonists in 18 the Hollywood action films had become paramilitary figures, moving furtively through always hostile terrain, heavily armed with 9mm pistols and semi-automatic rifles, sometimes with antitank weapons and grenade launchers. Unlike Bogart, Mitty, or Bond, the newly arrived soldiers of fortune were both paranoid and enraged—angry at anybody and everybody to whom they could assign the fault for the world's evil and on whom they could bestow the proofs of their disappointment. Their enemies were so many and so various—Colombian drug lords, Los Angeles street gangs, wardens of North Vietnamese prisons, Irish terrorists, etc.—that it was no longer possible to ascribe the killing to either a patriotic or an ideological motive. Clearly something had gone wrong in the world, and if the American public was becoming increasingly fearful of both its cities and its politicians, then the cinematic palliative needed to be strengthened and re-enforced. The theatergoing audience couldn't drift quietly off to sleep unless it could hear the distant sound of gunfire in the forest on the other side of the freeway, reassured as if by a lullaby that John Rambo or Harry Callahan (or Mel Gibson or Charles Bronson or Chuck Norris) was shooting down the shadows in the trees.

The television networks preach a corollary sermon, but not, as the critics would have it, in their entertainment divisions. Over the last several years, the children's hour (a.k.a. prime time) has been largely occupied by sitcoms or by police dramas that prefer the uses of sex to those of violence. It is the news programs that bring the specters from the abyss—the news programs and their "reality based" imitations set in bas-relief against the advertisements for Chanel perfume and Caribbean resorts. Like the illustrations in a fifth-grade reader, the sequence of scenes teaches the late-twentieth-century American catechism: first, at the top of the news, the admonitory row of body bags being loaded into ambulances in Brooklyn or South Miami; second, the inferno of tenement fires and burning warehouses; third, a sullen procession of criminals arraigned for robbery or murder and led away in chains. The text of the day's lesson having been thus established, the camera makes its happy return to the always smiling anchorwoman, and so—with her gracious permission—to the preview of heaven in the airline and travel advertisements. The homily is as plain as a medieval morality play or the bloodstains on Don Johnson's Armani suit—obey the law, pay your taxes, speak politely to the police officer, and you go to the Virgin Islands on the American Express card. Disobey the law, neglect your insurance payments, speak rudely to the police, and you go to Kings County Hospital in a body bag.

It is the business of the mass media to sell products—their own as well as those of their clients and sponsors—and the critics who complain about the ceaseless shows of violence miss the comparison to the cocaine trade. Whether staged as news or entertainment, synthetic violence is a drug, which, happily for its suppliers, returns a handsome profit in all the major markets. Among the urban poor (i.e., people who might be inclined to take up arms against the state), the bloody anodynes[3] check the fever of non-specific rage. Draw off the pestilent air of perceived injustice through the vents of wish and dream, and it is less likely to seek expression on a commuter train or in an election. Among the American suburban middle classes (i.e., people increasingly hard pressed to maintain their status as residents of the

19

20

[3]Something that soothes or eliminates pain.

increasingly precarious American Eden, who believe themselves surrounded by enemies of infinite number), the dreadful images confirm the impression of a world beyond the shopping mall that resembles a pitiless desert or a malevolent wilderness. Instill in such people the habit of fear, and it is more likely that their generous and charitable impulses will turn to stone.

Both states of paralysis serve the interests of the corporate media that 21
hopes for nothing better than passive compliance on the part of people shopping for the intimations of immortality. Any doubts that I may have entertained on the point were dispelled some years ago by a well-placed executive at CBS. I had asked him why the networks make so little attempt to broadcast anything other than fairy tales, and he in turn asked me if I ever looked at television.

"Not very often," I said. 22

"Of course not," he said. "Neither do I. I would hope that we have some- 23
thing better to do."

The mass audience, he said, consisted mostly of people who didn't have 24
anything better to do, who lacked either the will or the travel money to walk out their own front door. Why deprive them of their only means of escape? Why trouble them with the pain of doubt or the labor of thought? Let them feed on wishes and dreams, and they will repay the kindness by looking at more television, swelling the sum of the Nielsen ratings, contribute their pauper's mite to the general state of commercial prosperity and sociopolitical well-being.

1994

Profile   In a monthly column in *Harper's* magazine, Lewis Lapham presents his outspoken and often controversial views on American politics and society. His stance is usually that of a cranky establishment dropout, that is, someone familiar with the inner workings of Washington and pessimistic about the directions in which it is taking America. Lapham's role is to sound public alarms, to summon people from their ignorance, their indifference, and—especially—their escapism. At the same time, as an essayist and editorialist with a guaranteed monthly forum, he has a core of faithful readers, a following like that of Barbara Ehrenreich ("Talking in Couples"). Thus, without apology or justification, he is free to deliver personal opinions and make value judgments, pronouncing with a certitude that will disturb some readers. Like Edward Abbey ("Even the Bad Guys Wear White Hats") and Wendell Berry ("The Pleasures of Eating"), Lapham operates with a clear sense of right and wrong, unworried about offending those Abbey describes as "moral jellyfish" and whom he himself would see as *recreant* (disloyal, unfaithful, negligent) citizens.

In "Burnt Offerings" Lapham targets those "who like to name a principal cause for all the country's trouble" and thereby simplify and misrepresent our real problems. The reigning Cause For All Our Troubles and target for would-be censors is movie and television violence, but as Lapham points out, Americans historically have admired violence, as illustrated by the nineteenth-century romanticization of Jesse James and his gang. All that has changed is the representation of heroes and their commitment to violence. Today's movie hero, whether played by Clint Eastwood, Sylvester Stallone, or Steven Seagal, is often a paramilitary figure equipped with automatic weapons and a taste for mass destruction. In fact, if there is anything new in the depiction of screen violence, it is that it has become an end in itself. It no longer advances the plot or serves any other narrative purpose. It is merely a set decoration.

But while movie destruction is becoming increasingly sensationalized and cartoonish, it does not, Lapham argues, possess "the force of art." That is, it does not awaken in audiences "emotions strong enough to excite action or thought." Instead, its representation is so divorced from reality, from true pain and tragedy, that it serves only as distracting entertainment. Contrary to what the critics say, then, movie violence does not dispose moviegoers to real violence; instead, it diverts them from their real-world concerns. And ultimately, as anxiety about the world beyond the Cineplex grows, so does the appetite for stronger and stronger distractions. Violent movies are a sedative, not a stimulant, lulling rather than arousing their viewers.

Criticism and Satire Many readers shy instinctively from satire and other critical commentary, especially when it seems to deal too harshly with contemporary manners and morality. They reject critics suspected of being too "judgmental" (see Carol Bly) and—worse—of being too negative, too gloomy and pessimistic. They find such criticism to be "counterproductive," inviting resistance and noncooperation. Such readers look to their reading and entertainment principally for encouragement and reassurance, wanting to cling to their optimism. If they are to endure fault-finding, they want it to be immediately constructive, to hold the promise for a solution, preferably— in the words of Jonathan Swift's modest proposer in "A Modest Proposal"— a "cheap and easy" one. These are the very readers Lewis Lapham makes most uncomfortable.

On a cursory reading "Burnt Offerings" may seem to be an ill-humored tirade against the preferred entertainment of average Americans (the country is going to hell in a handbasket because not enough people are like the writer). Its judgments may seem merely to represent Lapham's personal preferences and eccentricities, his personal anger and pessimism. Like Jonathan Swift and Joan Didion, though, Lapham writes out of a center of constructive belief, one inferred without too much difficulty, and his values are shared by many of his readers. Thus, even while he devotes most of his essay to a problem, to escapism in contemporary movie and television entertainment, he implies a constructive alternative: As Homer and Shakespeare have demonstrated, rather than being a means of escaping reality, imaginative art can be a means of appreciating and understanding and confronting it. Perhaps Hollywood could learn something from their example.

And even as he is cynical about the motives of some ("The winning of the American West was largely accomplished by greedy and ignorant men in search of something for nothing, governed by their basest instincts . . . "), Lapham admires the achievements of others ("Homer can vividly imagine the desolation of death, because he so vividly delights in the spring and surge of life"). He condemns greed and ignorance (both of which can at least be alleviated), and he embraces the affirmation of life and the willingness to face reality—values most of us would endorse, at least in the abstract.

Lapham, then, does not write out of rage, frustration, and superiority. He writes out of civic concern, using humor, irony, and ridicule to spur his readers to action. Our society is ill, and his diagnosis is simple: The rank and file of Americans are not acknowledging and confronting their society's problems, but instead are taking refuge in the "soporifics" and sedatives of escapist entertainment, whether the Super Bowl or Arnold Schwarzenegger and Sylvester Stallone movies. As this and his other columns testify, Lapham would agree with the nineteenth-century educator Horace Mann: "In a republic, ignorance is a crime." In other words, the survival of a democratic society depends upon an informed citizenry, one with a healthy maintenance ethic and the courage to face problems. To be in an habitual escapist mode is to be negligent and to compound our troubles.

Exercise   The following is Lapham's twentieth paragraph with all its certitude and critical edge. Sentence by sentence, paraphrase and revise the paragraph to make it sound more tentative, less sure of itself. In other words, tone it down so that it is less aggressively assertive, less biting, less alienating to an audience of politicians and Hollywood producers.

[1]It is the business of the mass media to sell products—their own as well as those of their clients and sponsors—and the critics who complain about the ceaseless shows of violence miss the comparison to the cocaine trade. [2]Whether staged as news or entertainment, synthetic violence is a drug, which, happily for its suppliers, returns a handsome profit in all the major markets. [3]Among the urban poor (i.e., people who might be inclined to take up arms against the state), the bloody anodynes check the fever of non-specific rage. [4]Draw off the pestilent air of perceived injustice through the vents of wish and dream, and it is less likely to seek expression on a commuter train or in an election. [5]Among the American suburban middle classes (i.e., people increasingly hard pressed to maintain their status as residents of the increasingly precarious American Eden, who believe themselves surrounded by enemies of infinite number), the dreadful images confirm the impression of a world beyond the shopping mall that resembles a pitiless desert or a malevolent wilderness. [6]Instill in such a people the habit of fear, and it is more likely that their generous and charitable impulses will turn to stone.

Revision Assignments   Select one of the following strategies and revise "Burnt Offerings." Include a brief statement explaining your choice and its effect on the arrangement and presentation of material.

1. Lapham writes for a small, literate audience, one that has read Homer but one that is also familiar with monuments of popular culture, like *Pale Rider*. Revise paragraph 5 (or another paragraph of your choice) into a style more accessible to a local or even campus newspaper (you might also want to break it into several shorter paragraphs).

2. Condense Lapham's essay into about a quarter of its length, preserving the heart of his argument and supporting it as well as you can (again making it more accessible for the average reader).

Writing Assignments

1. You have your own opinion column. Reply to Lapham's argument, confirming or denying it. Do you agree that movies and TV exist primarily to supply escapist entertainment? What do you think is the cumulative effect of a heavy (if not exclusive) diet of such entertainment? Homer and Shakespeare were and still are read for entertainment as well as for enlightenment. What do you think about Lapham's assessment of violence in America?

2. Lapham's specific subject is the place of violence in American entertainment, but his larger subject is the current state of America. Read his essay carefully for both explicit statements and implicit assumptions about American society today (especially for any assumptions that you may not share). Then write a paper on "America According to Lapham."

3. In paragraph 15, Lapham argues that most young viewers can discriminate between reality and fiction, realizing that most action movies are "cartoons" and "video games." Do you agree, and if so, what effect do you think such movies have on their attitudes and sensibilities? (They do, after all, attend such movies in huge numbers, saying something about their tastes and preferences.)

4. Discuss a movie or TV program that you believe accomplishes what Lapham says of Homer and Shakespeare, that is, that "possess[es] the force of art . . . [awakening] in the mind of their audience emotions strong enough to excite action or thought," that "employs the imagination as a means of *appreciating* [my italics] reality rather than as a means of escaping it."

5. Read the last paragraph, and then compose a response. If you agree about the collective impact of television entertainment, what solution do you see? If you disagree, explain why.

6. *Pale Rider* was modeled in part on the 1953 classic western *Shane* (both are available in many video stores). Using Lapham's criteria and your own, compare the two versions. What role is played in both by violence and dialogue? Compare the respective roles of Alan Ladd and Clint Eastwood. For what qualities are they admired? How is violence depicted? What alternatives do the two films suggest to violence? Can *Shane* be said to possess "the force of art"?

The Stone Horse

BARRY LOPEZ

1

The deserts of southern California, the high, relatively cooler and wetter Mo-   1
jave and the hotter, dryer Sonoran to the south of it, carry the signatures of
many cultures. Prehistoric rock drawings in the Mojave's Coso Range, probably the greatest concentration of petroglyphs in North America, are at least
three thousand years old. Big-game hunting cultures that flourished six or
seven thousand years before that are known from broken spear tips, chop-
pers, and burins[1] left scattered along the shores of great Pleistocene lakes,
long since evaporated. Weapons and tools discovered at China Lake may be
thirty thousand years old; and worked stone from a quarry in the Calico
Mountains is, some argue, evidence that human beings were here more than
200,000 years ago.

Because of the long-term stability of such arid environments, much of   2
this prehistoric stone evidence still lies exposed on the ground, accessible to
anyone who passes by—the studious, the acquisitive, the indifferent, the
merely curious. Archaeologists do not agree on the sequence of cultural history beyond about twelve thousand years ago, but it is clear that these broken
bits of chalcedony, chert, obsidian, like the animal drawings and geometric
designs etched on walls of basalt throughout the desert, anchor the earliest
threads of human history, the first record of human endeavor here.

Western man did not enter the California desert until the end of the   3
eighteenth century, 250 years after Coronado brought his soldiers into the
Zuni pueblos in a bewildered search for the cities of Cibola. The earliest ap-
praisals of the land were cursory, hurried. People traveled *through* it, en route
to Santa Fe or the California coastal settlements. Only miners tarried. In 1823
what had been Spain's became Mexico's, and in 1848 what had been Mexico's became America's; but the bare, jagged mountains and dry lake beds,
the vast and uniform plains of creosote bush and yucca plants, remained as
obscure as the northern Sudan until the end of the nineteenth century.

Before 1940 the tangible evidence of twentieth-century man's passage   4
here consisted of very little—the hard tracery of travel corridors; the widely
scattered, relatively insignificant evidence of mining operations; and the fair
expanse of irrigated fields at the desert's periphery. In the space of a hundred years or so the wagon roads were paved, railroads were laid down, and
canals and high-tension lines were built to bring water and electricity across
the desert to Los Angeles from the Colorado River. The dark mouths of gold,
talc, and tin mines yawned from the bony flanks of desert ranges. Dust-en-
crusted chemical plants stood at work on the lonely edges of dry lake beds.
And crops of grapes, lettuce, dates, alfalfa, and cotton covered the Coachella
and Imperial valleys, north and south of the Salton Sea, and the Palo Verde
Valley along the Colorado.

[1]A tool for cutting rocks.

These developments proceeded with little or no awareness of earlier hu- 5
man occupations by cultures that preceded those of the historic Indians—the
Mojave, the Chemehuevi, the Quechan. (Extensive irrigation began actually
to change the climate of the Sonoran Desert, and human settlements, the
railroads, and farming introduced many new, successful plants into the
region.)

During World War II, the American military moved into the desert in 6
great force, to train troops and to test equipment. They found the clear
weather conducive to year-round flying, the dry air and isolation very attractive. After the war, a complex of training grounds, storage facilities, and gun-
nery and test ranges was permanently settled on more than three million
acres of military reservations. Few perceived the extent or significance of the
destruction of the aboriginal sites that took place during tank maneuvers and
bombing runs or in the laying out of highways, railroads, mining districts, and
irrigated fields. The few who intuited that something like an American Dor-
dogne Valley[2] lay exposed here were (only) amateur archaeologists; even
they reasoned that the desert was too vast for any of this to matter.

After World War II, people began moving out of the crowded Los Ange- 7
les basin into homes in Lucerne, Apple, and Antelope valleys in the western
Mojave. They emigrated as well to a stretch of resort land at the foot of
the San Jacinto Mountains that included Palm Springs, and farther out to
the old railroad and military towns like Twentynine Palms and Barstow. People also began exploring the desert, at first in military-surplus jeeps and
then with a variety of all-terrain and off-road vehicles that became available
in the 1960s. By the mid 1970s, the number of people using such vehicles
for desert recreation had increased exponentially. Most came and went in
innocent curiosity; the few who didn't wreaked a havoc all out of proportion
to their numbers. The disturbance of previously isolated archaeological sites
increased by an order of magnitude. Many sites were vandalized before
archaeologists, themselves late to the desert, had any firm grasp of the
bounds of human history in the desert. It was as though in the same moment
an Aztec library had been discovered intact various lacunae[3] had begun to
appear.

The vandalism was of three sorts: the general disturbance usually caused 8
by souvenir hunters and by the curious and the oblivious; the wholesale
stripping of a place by professional thieves for black-market sale and trade;
and outright destruction, in which vehicles were actually used to ram and
trench an area. By 1980, the Bureau of Land Management estimated that
probably 35 percent of the archaeological sites in the desert had been vandalized. The destruction at some places by rifles and shotguns, or by power
winches mounted on vehicles, was, if one cared for history, demoralizing to
behold.

In spite of public education, land closures, and stricter law enforcement 9
in recent years, the BLM estimates that, annually, about 1 percent of the archaeological record in the desert continues to be destroyed or stolen.

[2]A region in central France famous for its prehistoric cave paintings.
[3]Missing parts or gaps, especially in manuscripts.

2

A BLM archaeologist told me, with understandable reluctance, where to [10] find the intaglio.[4] I spread my Automobile Club of Southern California map of Imperial County out on his desk, and he traced the route with a pink felt-tip pen. The line crossed Interstate 8 and then turned west along the Mexican border.

"You can't drive any farther than about here," he said, marking a small X. [11] "There's boulders in the wash. You walk up past them."

On a separate piece of paper he drew a route in a smaller scale that would [12] take me up the arroyo to a certain point where I was to cross back east, to another arroyo. At its head, on higher ground just to the north, I would find the horse.

"It's tough to spot unless you know it's there. Once you pick it up . . . " [13] He shook his head slowly, in a gesture of wonder at its existence.

I waited until I held his eye. I assured him I would not tell anyone else [14] how to get there. He looked at me with stoical despair, like a man who had been robbed twice, whose belief in human beings was offered without conviction.

I did not go until the following day because I wanted to see it at dawn. I [15] ate breakfast at four A.M. in El Centro and then drove south. The route was easy to follow, though the last section of the road proved difficult, broken and drifted over with sand in some spots. I came to the barricade of boulders and parked. It was light enough by then to find my way over the ground with little trouble. The contours of the landscape were stark, without any masking vegetation. I worried only about rattlesnakes.

I traversed the stone plain as directed, but, in spite of the frankness of the [16] land, I came on the horse unawares. In the first moment of recognition I was without feeling. I recalled later being startled, and that I held my breath. It was laid out on the ground with its head to the east, three times life size. As I took in its outline I felt a growing concentration of all my senses, as though my attentiveness to the pale rose color of the morning sky and other peripheral images had now ceased to be important. I was aware that I was straining for sound in the windless air, and I felt the uneven pressure of the earth hard against my feet. The horse, outlined in a standing profile on the dark ground, was as vivid before me as a bed of tulips.

I've come upon animals suddenly before, and felt a similar tension, a pre- [17] cipitate heightening of the senses. And I have felt the inexplicable but sharply boosted intensity of a wild moment in the bush, where it is not until moments later that you discover the source of electricity—the warm remains of a grizzly kill, or the still moist tracks of a wolverine.

But this was slightly different. I felt I had stepped into an unoccupied [18] corridor. I had no familiar sense of history, the temporal structure in which to think: this horse was made by Quechan[5] people three hundred years ago. I felt instead a headlong rush of images: people hunting wild horses with spears on the Pleistocene veld of southern California; Cortes riding across the causeway into Montezuma's Tenochtitlan; a short-legged Comanche, astride

---

[4]A figure or design carved on stone or metal.

[5]Native American people of the lower Colorado River. Also called *Yuman.*

his horse like some sort of ferret, slashing through cavalry lines of young men who rode like farmers; a hoof exploding past my face one morning in a corral in Wyoming. These images had the weight and silence of stone.

When I released my breath, the images softened. My initial feeling, of facing a wild animal in a remote region, was replaced with a calm sense of antiquity. It was then that I became conscious, like an ordinary tourist, of what was before me, and thought: this horse was probably laid out by Quechan people. But when? I wondered. The first horses they saw, I knew, might have been those that came north from Mexico in 1692 with Father Eusebio Kino. But Cocopa people, I recalled, also came this far north on occasion, to fight with their neighbors, the Quechan. And *they* could have seen horses with Melchior Diaz, at the mouth of the Colorado River in the fall of 1540. So, it could be four hundred years old. (No one in fact knows.)

I still had not moved. I took my eyes off the horse for a moment to look south over the desert plain into Mexico, to look east past its head at the brightening sunrise, to situate myself. Then, finally, I brought my trailing foot slowly forward and stood erect. Sunlight was running like a thin sheet of water over the stony ground and it threw the horse into relief. It looked as though no hand had ever disturbed the stones that gave it its form.

The horse had been brought to life on ground called desert pavement, a tight, flat matrix of small cobbles blasted smooth by sand-laden winds. The uniform, monochromatic blackness of the stones, a patina of iron and magnesium oxides called desert varnish, is caused by long-term exposure to the sun. To make this type of low-relief ground glyph, or intaglio, the artist either selectively turns individual stones over to their lighter side or removes areas of stone to expose the lighter soil underneath, creating a negative image. This horse, about eighteen feet from brow to rump and eight feet from withers to hoof, had been made in the latter way, and its outline was bermed at certain points with low ridges of stone a few inches high to enhance its three-dimensional qualities. (The left side of the horse was in full profile; each leg was extended at 90 degrees to the body and fully visible, as though seen in three-quarter profile.)

I was not eager to move. The moment I did I would be back in the flow of time, the horse no longer quivering in the same way before me. I did not want to feel again the sequence of quotidian events—to be drawn off into deliberation and analysis. A human being, a four-footed animal, the open land. That was all that was present—and a "thoughtless" understanding of the very old desires bearing on this particular animal: to hunt it, to render it, to fathom it, to subjugate it, to honor it, to take it as a companion.

What finally made me move was the light. The sun now filled the shallow basin of the horse's body. The weighted line of the stone berm created the illusion of a mane and the distinctive roundness of an equine belly. The change in definition impelled me. I moved to the left, circling past its rump, to see how the light might flesh the horse out from various points of view. I circled it completely before squatting on my haunches. Ten or fifteen minutes later I chose another view. The third time I moved, to a point near the rear hooves, I spotted a stone tool at my feet. I stared at it a long while, more in awe than disbelief, before reaching out to pick it up. I turned it over in my left palm and took it between my fingers to feel its cutting edge. It is always difficult, especially with something so portable, to rechannel the desire to steal.

I spent several hours with the horse. As I changed positions and as the angle of the light continued to change I noticed a number of things. The angle at which the pastern carried the hoof away from the ankle was perfect. Also, stones had been placed within the image to suggest at precisely the right spot the left shoulder above the foreleg. The line that joined thigh and hock was similarly accurate. The muzzle alone seemed distorted—but perhaps these stones had been moved by a later hand. It was an admirably accurate representation, but not what a breeder would call perfect conformation. There was the suggestion of a bowed neck and an undershot jaw, and the tail, as full as a winter coyote's, did not appear to be precisely to scale. 24

The more I thought about it, the more I felt I was looking at an individual horse, a unique combination of generic and specific detail. It was easy to imagine one of Kino's horses as a model, or a horse that ran off from one of Coronado's columns. What kind of horses would these have been? I wondered. In the sixteenth century the most sought-after horses in Europe were Spanish, the offspring of Arabian stock and Barbary horses that the Moors brought to Iberia and bred to the older, eastern European strains brought in by the Romans. The model for this horse, I speculated, could easily have been a palomino, or a descendant of horses trained for lion hunting in North Africa. 25

A few generations ago, cowboys, cavalry quartermasters, and draymen would have taken this horse before me under consideration and not let up their scrutiny until they had its heritage fixed to their satisfaction. Today, the distinction between draft and harness horses is arcane knowledge, and no image may come to mind for a blue roan or a claybank horse. The loss of such refinement in everyday conversation leaves me unsettled. People praise the Eskimo's ability to distinguish among forty types of snow but forget the skill of others who routinely differentiate between overo and tobiano pintos. Such distinctions are made for the same reason. You have to do it to be able to talk clearly about the world. 26

For parts of two years I worked as a horse wrangler and packer in Wyoming. It is dim knowledge now; I would have to think to remember if a buckskin was a kind of dun horse. And I couldn't throw a double-diamond hitch over a set of panniers—the packer's basic tie-down—without guidance. As I squatted there in the desert, however, these more personal memories seemed tenuous in comparison with the sweep of this animal in human time. My memories had no depth. I thought of the Hittite cavalry riding against the Syrians 3,500 years ago. And the first of the Chinese emperors, Ch'in Shi Huang, buried in Shensi Province in 210 B.C. with thousands of life-size horses and soldiers, a terra-cotta guardian army. What could I know of what was in the mind of whoever made this horse? Was there some racial memory of it as an animal that had once fed the artist's ancestors and then disappeared from North America? And then returned in this strange alliance with another race of men? 27

Certainly, whoever it was, the artist had observed the animal very closely. Certainly the animal's speed had impressed him. Among the first things the Quechan would have learned from an encounter with Kino's horses was that 28 their own long distance runners—men who could run down mule deer—were no match for this animal.

From where I squatted I could look far out over the Mexican plain. Juan 29 Bautista de Anza passed this way in 1774, extending El Camino Real into Alta California from Sinaloa. He was followed by others, all of them astride the magical horse; *gente de razon*, the people of reason, coming into this country of *los primitivos*. The horse, like the stone animals of Egypt, urged these memories upon me. And as I drew them up from some forgotten corner of my mind—huge horses carved into the white chalk downs of southern England by an Iron Age people; Spanish horses rearing and wheeling in fear before alligators in Florida—the images seemed tethered before me. With this sense of proportion, a memory of my own—the morning I almost lost my face to a horse's hoof—now had somewhere to fit.

I rose up and began to walk slowly around the horse again. I had taken 30 the first long measure of it and was now looking for a way to depart, a new angle of light, a fading of the image itself before the rising sun, that would break its hold on me. As I circled, feeling both heady and serene at the encounter, I realized again how strangely vivid it was. It had been created on a barren bajada[6] between two arroyos, as nondescript a place as one could imagine. The only plant life here was a few wands of ocotillo cactus. The ground beneath my shoes was so hard it wouldn't take the print of a heavy animal even after a rain. The only sounds I heard were the voices of quail.

The archaeologist had been correct. For all its forcefulness, the horse is 31 inconspicuous. If you don't care to see it you can walk right past it. That pleases him, I think. Unmarked on this bleak shoulder of the plain, the site signals to no one; so he wants no protective fences here, no informative plaque, to act as beacons. He would rather take a chance that no motorcyclist, no aimless wanderer with a flair for violence and a depth of ignorance, will ever find his way here.

The archaeologist had given me something before I left his office that 32 now seemed peculiar—an aerial photograph of the horse. It is widely believed that an aerial view of the intaglio provides a fair and accurate depiction. It does not. In the photograph the horse looks somewhat crudely constructed; from the ground it appears far more deftly rendered. The photograph is of a single moment, and in that split second the horse seems vaguely impotent. I watched light pool in the intaglio at dawn; I imagine you could watch it withdraw at dusk and sense the same animation I did. In those prolonged moments its shape and so, too, its general character changed—noticeably. The living quality of the image, its immediacy to the eye, was brought out by the light-in-time, not, at least here, in the camera's frozen instant.

Intaglios, I thought, were never meant to be seen by gods in the sky 33 above. They were meant to be seen by people on the ground, over a long period of shifting light. This could even be true of the huge figures on the Plain of Nazca in Peru, where people could walk for the length of a day beside them. It is our own impatience that leads us to think otherwise.

---

[6]Slope (Spanish).

This process of abstraction, almost unintentional, drew me gradually   34
away from the horse. I came to a position of attention at the edge of the
sphere of its influence. With a slight bow I paid my respects to the horse, its
maker, and the history of us all, and departed.

3

A short distance away I stopped the car in the middle of the road to make a   35
few notes. I could not write down what I was thinking when I was with the
horse. It would have seemed disrespectful, and it would have required another kind of attention. So now I patiently drained my memory of the details
it had fastened itself upon. The road I'd stopped on was adjacent to the All
American Canal, the major source of water for the Imperial and Coachella
valleys. The water flowed west placidly. A disjointed flock of coots, small,
dark birds with white bills, was paddling against the current, foraging in the
rushes.

I was peripherally aware of the birds as I wrote, the only movement in the   36
desert, and of a series of sounds from a village a half-mile away. The first
sounds from this collection of ramshackle houses in a grove of cottonwoods
were the distracted dawn voices of dogs. I heard them intermingled with the
cries of a rooster. Later, the high-pitched voices of children calling out to
each other came disembodied through the dry desert air. Now, a little after
seven, I could hear someone practicing on the trumpet, the same rough
phrases played over and over. I suddenly remembered how as children we
had tried to get the rhythm of a galloping horse with hands against our
thighs, or by fluttering our tongues against the roofs of our mouths.

After the trumpet, the impatient calls of adults summoning children. Sun-   37
day morning. Wood smoke hung like a lens in the trees. The first car starts—
a cold eight-cylinder engine, of Chrysler extraction perhaps, goosed to life,
then throttled back to murmur through dual mufflers, the obbligato music of
a shade-tree mechanic. The rote bark of mongrel dogs at dawn, the jagged
outcries of men and women, an engine coming to life. Like a thousand villages from West Virginia to Guadalajara.

I finished my notes—where was I going to find a description of the horses   38
that came north with the conquistadors? Did their manes come forward
prominently over the brow, like this one's, like the forelocks of Blackfeet and
Assiniboin men in nineteenth-century paintings? I set the notes on the seat
beside me.

The road followed the canal for a while and then arced north, toward In-   39
terstate 8. It was slow driving and I fell to thinking how the desert had
changed since Anza had come through. New plants and animals—the Mac-
Dougall cottonwood, the English house sparrow, the chukar from India—
have about them now the air of the native born. Of the native species,
some—no one knows how many—are extinct. The populations of many others, especially the animals, have been sharply reduced. The idea of a desert
impoverished by agricultural poisons and varmint hunters, by off-road
vehicles and military operations, did not seem as disturbing to me, however,
as this other horror, now that I had been those hours with the horse. The
vandals, the few who crowbar rock art off the desert's walls, who dig up

graves, who punish the ground that holds intaglios, are people who devour history. Their self-centered scorn, their disrespect for ideas and images beyond their ken, create the awful atmosphere of loose ends in which totalitarianism thrives, in which the past is merely curious or wrong.

I thought about the horse sitting out there on the unprotected plain. I [40] enumerated its qualities in my mind until a sense of its vulnerability receded and it became the anchor for something else. I remembered that history, a history like this one, which ran deeper than Mexico, deeper than the Spanish, was a kind of medicine. It permitted the great breadth of human expression to reverberate, and it did not urge you to locate its apotheosis[7] in the present.

Each of us, individuals and civilizations, has been held upside down like [41] Achilles in the River Styx. The artist mixing his colors in the dim light of Altamira; an Egyptian ruler lying still now, wrapped in his byssus, stored against time in a pyramid; the faded Dorset culture of the Arctic; the Hmong and Sambaru and Walbiri of historic time; the modern nations. This great, imperfect stretch of human expression is the clarification and encouragement, the urging and the reminder, we call history. And it is inscribed everywhere in the face of the land, from the mountain passes of the Himalayas to a nameless bajada in the California desert.

Small birds rose up in the road ahead, startled, and flew off. I prayed no [42] infidel would ever find that horse.

1986

Profile Some of the essays in this collection draw primarily on the writers' personal experiences and speculations. They are the work of intelligent, sensitive people who have spent a lifetime watching, evaluating, and remembering (and, of course, trying to find the right words). If any specialized knowledge surfaces, it is likely the casual residue of their educations. "The Stone Horse" is different: It draws almost as heavily upon research as upon personal experience, upon time spent in libraries as upon time spent in the field. In fact, what Lopez models is informed opinion, informed appreciation. He brings to the stone horse a detailed familiarity with history, archaeology, and geology, as well as knowledge of local plants and animals—all necessary to put the intaglio in perspective.

Thus, Lopez can speak familiarly of chalcedony, chert, and obsidian; overo and tobiano pintos; Cortes, Coronado, Melchior Diaz, and Father Eusebio Kino; Montezuma's Tenochtitlan; an Egyptian ruler wrapped in his byssus; Hittite cavalry riding to meet the Syrians; Moors breeding Arabian and Barbary stock with the horses introduced by Romans; and the forelocks of Blackfeet and Assiniboins. His knowledge enables him to support an argument that can be made only by an informed observer. Only someone with his impressive range of information and understanding—and his sensibility—can do justice to the stone horse, can appreciate and explain its significance, can plead the case for its protection. Without such knowledge the horse is merely one more thing that is old and curious, a little crude and naive alongside modern creations like the World Trade Center and fiber optics and

---

[7]An exalted, glorified example.

laser surgery. With such knowledge the horse is a product of the same creative spirit.

But even with the requisite historical and archaeological lore, how does Lopez write for common readers without overwhelming them? How does he prevent his essay from becoming a stuffy and gratuitous display of personal erudition? The answer, as in so many other essays in this collection, is by narrative and personal presence, by using a story to carry information, a story involving the writer. Thus, after part 1—a condensed lecture on the archeology and history of the Sonoran desert, he tells the story of his visit to the stone horse. And into this story he weaves a description of his observations, historical knowledge, personal recollections, personal musings. Paragraph 19 is typical:

> When I released my breath, the images softened. My initial feeling, of facing a wild animal in a remote region, was replaced with a calm sense of antiquity. It was then that I became conscious, like an ordinary tourist, of what was before me, and thought: this horse was probably laid out by Quechan people. But when? I wondered. The first horses they saw, I knew, might have been those that came north from Mexico in 1692 with Father Eusebio Kino. But Cocopa people, I recalled, also came this far north on occasion, to fight with their neighbors, the Quechan. And *they* could have seen horses with Melchior Diaz, at the mouth of the Colorado River in the fall of 1540. So, it could be four hundred years old. (No one in fact knows.)

What happens if we remove the narrative element?

> **The site is ancient, probably laid out by the Quechan people. But when? The first horses they saw might have been those that came north from Mexico in 1692 with Father Eusebio Kino. But Cocopa people also came this far north on occasion, to fight with their neighbors, the Quechan. And they could have seen horses with Melchior Diaz, at the mouth of the Colorado River in the fall of 1540. So, it could be four hundred years old. No one in fact knows.**

Lopez is still present in this version, suggested by the conversational voice, but the information lacks a sense of immediacy. It is just information, out there, disconnected from a living, responding presence, our guide, our proxy. Gone is the effect of transitional and introductory remarks: "When I released my breath . . . My initial feeling . . . was replaced by a sense of calm antiquity. . . . It was then that I became conscious, like an ordinary tourist, of what was before me, and thought . . . The first horses they saw, I knew . . . But Cocopa people, I recalled . . . " His actions, responses, and recollections exist not for personal display, but to absorb and distribute and present information.

Put another way, Lopez is not simply a "talking head," one of those authorities we see standing in the foreground of historical sites on PBS specials. He is a caring, responding, informed individual on a pilgrimage to a personal and historical holy spot, and it is the quality of his engagement that involves us, the readers, and elevates his subject from the status of mere information, mere data. In the presence of such a living, appreciative witness, no information can remain inert or irrelevant.

Embedding Information   Again, as John McPhee reminds us, writing is not simply a matter of collecting information; it is a matter of arrangement and presentation. Successful writers do not simply gather and dispense data. They must present it both accurately and engagingly, embedding facts in a useful context, one that sequences and juxtaposes so that the facts comment on one another. Take Lopez's third paragraph:

> Western man did not enter the California desert until the end of the eighteenth century, 250 years after Coronado brought his soldiers into the Zuni pueblos in a bewildered search for the cities of Cibola. The earliest appraisals of the land were cursory, hurried. People traveled *through* it, en route to Santa Fe or the California coastal settlements. Only miners tarried. In 1823 what had been Spain's became Mexico's, and in 1848 what had been Mexico's became America's; but the bare, jagged mountains and dry lake beds, the vast and uniform plains of creosote bush and yucca plants, remained as obscure as the northern Sudan until the end of the nineteenth century.

The theme of this paragraph is Western man's tardy awareness of the California desert where the stone horse is to be found. Lopez could simply have reported that Westerners did not set eyes on the barren locale until the late 1700s, presenting information in simple chronological order. Except for miners, most simply traveled through, even while national sovereignty changed. But how would chronology embrace the description?

Let us examine the paragraph sentence by sentence:

> Western man did not enter the California desert until the end of the eighteenth century, 250 years after Coronado brought his soldiers into the Zuni pueblos in a bewildered search for the cities of Cibola.

This sentence stresses the belated discovery of the California desert: It remained unknown for two-and-a-half centuries after Coronado had visited New Mexico in search of the Seven Cities of Gold. Even after such a momentous event, 250 years went by. In addition, the description of Coronado's visit introduces the theme of cultural conflict, of an aggressive, foreign intrusion into an indigenous presence. And Coronado was looking for loot, like those people today who plunder archaeological sites.

The next three sentences stress the indifference of most early visitors, except—again—for those seeking wealth:

> The earliest appraisals of the land were cursory, hurried. People traveled *through* it, en route to Santa Fe or the California coastal settlements. Only miners tarried.

"Only miners tarried"—a curt, suggestive statement. No one else showed any appreciation for the land, for its character and history and record of human presence there. It was only a place to be gotten through, an obstacle (although, for many generations, a *home* for native peoples). And "appraisal" has a double meaning, suggesting both disinterested and mercenary evaluation. In sum, no one valued the desert, except for the mineral wealth it might hold.

Finally, we have this sentence:

> In 1823 what had been Spain's became Mexico's, and in 1848 what had been Mexico's became America's; but the bare, jagged mountains and dry lake beds,

the vast and uniform plains of creosote bush and yucca plants, remained as obscure as the northern Sudan until the end of the nineteenth century.

The semicolon separates two different kinds of information, historical events and topographical description. To appreciate the level and integration of the detail we could paraphrase the sentence this way: "While sovereignty passed from Spain to Mexico to America, the desert itself remained unknown." But Lopez phrases the transferences of control repetitively ("what had been Spain's became Mexico's, and . . . what had been Mexico's became . . . "), reminding us of the transience and illusion of human ownership. And what remains unknown? Not simply "the desert," but "the bare, jagged mountains and dry lake beds, the vast and uniform plains of creosote bush and yucca plants."

Exercise   In the following paragraph Lopez moves from narration to a discussion of local plants and animals to reflections on modern vandals. What are his transitions? How does he sequence and embed information? How does he move from one idea to the next? What is the governing idea of the paragraph? In sum, how does it achieve unity, coherence, and emphasis?

[1]The road followed the canal for a while and then arced north, toward Interstate 8. [2]It was slow driving and I fell to thinking how the desert had changed since Anza had come through. [3]New plants and animals—the MacDougall cottonwood, the English house sparrow, the chukar from India—have about them now the air of the native born. [4]Of the native species, some—no one knows how many—are extinct. [5]The populations of many others, especially the animals, have been sharply reduced. [6]The idea of a desert impoverished by agricultural poisons and varmint hunters, by off-road vehicles and military operations, did not seem as disturbing to me, however, as this other horror, now that I had been those hours with the horse. [7]The vandals, the few who crowbar rock art off the desert's walls, who dig up graves, who punish the ground that holds intaglios, are people who devour history. [8]Their self-centered scorn, their disrespect for ideas and images beyond their ken, create the awful atmosphere of loose ends in which totalitarianism thrives, in which the past is merely curious or wrong.

Revision Assignments   Select one of the following strategies and revise "The Stone Horse." Include a brief statement explaining your choice and its effect on the arrangement and presentation of material.

1. Lopez uses a first-person narrative to interweave description, information, speculations, and memories. Revise (or plunder) his essay by removing the narrative element. Forget Lopez and his visit. Writing in the third person, simply present the stone horse, identifying its location, describing it, conjecturing about its possible origins (remember that it was the Spaniards who introduced the horse to Native Americans). Make the stone horse as interesting as you can, but be informational. Do not use personal experiences and philosophizings, your own or Lopez's.

2. Paragraphs 17–24 present Lopez's actual encounter with the stone horse. Revise the paragraphs by changing the narrative point of view. Instead of the first-person *I*, describe the horse as seen in the third person by "a

visitor" (thus, "I felt I had stepped into an unoccupied corridor" might become "A visitor may feel that she has stepped into an unoccupied corridor"). Make any changes necessary consistent with the new point of view; that is, do not merely change the pronouns.

Writing Assignments

1. Lopez explores a contradiction in history: the failure of human attempts to create enduring monuments, and the undying nature of this very aspiration—both represented by the stone horse. In this case the artist's particular subject for memorialization was the horse. Nominate your own "stone horse" for a late twentieth-century artist, something noble and true whose qualities deserve to be remembered by future generations.

2. Near the end of his essay, Lopez writes the following:

   I remembered that history, a history like this one, which ran deeper than Mexico, deeper than the Spanish, was a kind of medicine. It permitted the great breadth of human expression to reverberate, and it did not urge you to locate its apotheosis [an exalted, glorified example] in the present.

   What is Lopez saying? Why is "a history like this one" like a medicine (he has just finished discussing the destructive urges of modern-day vandals)? What was the artist of the stone horse expressing? What is it about history (the kind he is discussing here) that makes the stone horse equal to more sophisticated productions of our own era?

3. In "The Stone Horse" Lopez writes about two human impulses, one exemplified by the urge to portray horses on desert slopes, the other by the urge to use off-road vehicles to "ram and trench" archaeological sites. What does each say about the other? Why is the stone horse so important to Lopez? What would it mean if humans ever stopped trying to create such figures? Or if humans ever ceased trying to destroy them?

Doing It the Hard Way

NANCY MAIRS

Not long ago, my daughter graduated from Smith College, a liberal arts college for women in Massachusetts, along with nearly seven hundred classmates. Many of the graduates were already poised to plunge into worlds of prestige and wealth, on Wall Street or Madison Avenue or Capitol Hill, glittering with the promise of a life of ease: a condo with a river view, a silver BMW convertible, summer vacations on the coast of Maine and winter vacations in Barbados. Others, deferring these rewards, planned first to attend medical school, law school, business school. And some, wavering in the face of the choices a privileged education proffers, when asked about their plans replied with comic defensiveness, "I don't know, and I don't care, so don't ask!"

Because Anne had majored in biochemistry, most people assumed that she'd go to medical school or get a Ph.D. and become a research scientist. But she's never showed a glimmer of interest in doctoring human beings, though in high school she did contemplate becoming a veterinarian and even spent a few weeks in Honduras vaccinating pigs against hog cholera. She gave some thought to training as a pharmacist, but she was heartily sick of school. Instead, she chose a course of action that surprised even those of us closest to her: she joined the Peace Corps.

Now she lives, with a tabby kitten name Nuni, in a house at one end of the village of Mfuatu in western Zaire. Nobody there speaks English, but she's picking up French and Kikongo, though when she was nursing herself through an attack of malaria recently, her attempts at explaining the use of the fever thermometer to the children who trail after her wherever she goes merely baffled everyone involved in the broken dialogue. Every morning she bathes with the other women in a nearby river, returning with enough water for the day's needs. During the day, she rides the dirt roads of her area on a Yamaha 125 motorcycle, visiting local farmers to teach them how to build ponds, stock them with tilapia, and maintain and harvest the fish to feed themselves and to sell for income. At night, by candle or kerosene lamp, she writes us letters that reflect a complicated mixture of distress and delight at her new life.

When she decided to go, her father and I were thrilled, but she encountered some resistance and even more incomprehension from some of her family and friends. Why would anyone, they wanted to know, especially a young woman as bright and promising as Anne, go off to spend two years in poverty, without even electricity or plumbing, eating a diet that has included grasshoppers and snakes, exposed to deadly diseases like yellow fever and cholera without a doctor for miles of rutted road that turns to muddy soup with every rain? What about the handsome salary, the condo, the BMW, not to mention the eligible young electrical engineer eager to make her his wife?

I'm not sure why. Anne tends to keep her own counsel, and she was too scared to talk much about her choice the summer before she left. But I don't think she was repudiating graduate school or big paychecks, or even condos and BMWs. She may well want them when she returns. They just didn't seem to be enough. I think she went in part to postpone momentous decisions about marriage and career until she knew more about herself and the world. She's always been a woman of action, not words, and the Peace Corps offered her the chance to experience the lives of others directly and help them meet their own needs, not the needs some ideologue might believe they ought to feel. But mostly, I gathered from what little she had to say, she went for the adventure, and the personal growth that carrying out difficult tasks stimulates. Materially privileged and intellectually gifted, she'd never come close to her limits, and I think she wanted to put her capacities to the test. When I hear excitement and satisfaction in the tone of her letters, I find myself thinking, "At last she's found something hard enough for her."

Most people don't have to light out for Africa in order to seek out a 6 difficult life. Indeed, some of us have difficulty plump itself right into our laps without so much as a by-your-leave. I'm going to speak in terms in having multiple sclerosis, because this incurable neurological disease is the difficulty that barged into my life uninvited. But if difficulty doesn't arrive as MS, sooner or later it arrives in some form: the lost job, the child gone wrong, the parent with Alzheimer's, the marriage truncated by death or divorce. And then we have to choose how we will respond to the "gift" of a difficult life.

Anne's adventure, and the sense I have that somehow the hardships she's 7 chosen to endure in order to have that adventure are integral to the adventure's values, have led me to reflect at length on the whole matter of "difficulty." It is, I've come to see, something of a dirty word in our society. "Take it easy," we all tell one another at the first sign of agitation. "Kick back and relax." "Don't get your liver in a quiver." A hard life isn't any fun. The good life, the media relentlessly drum into our eyes and ears, is the one that takes the least effort. We develop laborsaving devices to help achieve it, sometimes even labeling them to convey the essence of their desirability: my mother had an "Easy" washer and dryer for years, for instance. "Why do things the hard way?" we ask.

If our lives do prove difficult, troublesome, even painful, we're reluctant 8 to admit it. To experience difficulty suggests some sort of weakness, and to admit to experiencing difficulty risks accusations of whining and self-pity. In either case, we feel shame. I discovered just how pervasive this reaction is when my husband asked me what I was at work on currently.

"I'm writing about the ways people respond to a difficult life," I told him. 9

"Oh, well," George said, as though in response to a question I hadn't 10 even asked, "I don't have a difficult life." Now, this is a man who has raised three children, one of them a foster child; who has assisted a wife with multiple sclerosis for more than fifteen years; who has had two melanomas surgically removed; who holds two jobs, both teaching students who have failed in conventional settings. These are all, without question, both physically and mentally arduous undertakings. And yet the mere thought of characterizing his life as "difficult" sends him scurrying for cover.

What's wrong with "difficulty"? I want to know. I want to redeem it, as 11 both a word and a concept. I want to speak it out loud, without apology, in the same matter-of-fact tone I'd use to say, "I prefer black cats to spotted ones," or "My daughter has been known to eat grasshoppers." And then I want to figure out how I can not merely admit to having a difficult life but also use the difficulties I've acknowledged to enrich the life.

This process requires steering a tricky course between denial to starboard and masochism to port. For social reasons, as I've said, it's tempting to hide from others the fact that you're having a hard time. You want, after all, to appear independent and capable, those most valued traits of the American psyche, or at least, failing that, to be considered a trooper, a good sport. But I don't think this sort of social cover-up is as dangerous as denying your difficulty to yourself. This denial can have nasty bodily consequences for those of us with physical disabilities, as I've learned painfully. Each time I've taken a bad fall, I've been ignoring the limitations fatigue and muscular weakness place on my body. I've been treating my body as though it were some other body, an able body. But it's not. It's mine. A body in trouble. And it's my responsibility to attend to its realities and take proper care of it. I can't do that if I deny that it needs special treatment.

The emotional consequences of denial are subtler and perhaps more devastating. How many times have you been counseled by some well-meaning person, often one who's deep into denying difficulties of her own, "You think too much. You'll only make matters worse. Just ignore the problem, and it will go away"? You have a problem, however, because you are a living being, and thus the problem is inextricably entwined into your life. Ignoring the problem, then, means ignoring some essential element of your life. In some cases, it might "go away" in the sense that the portion of your life into which the problem is woven might atrophy and drop off, like a tree branch strangled by mistletoe. But do you really want a life thus mutilated?

Anyway, the difficulties created by something like MS don't even go away to that extent. Whether you ignore your body or not, you still get tired, your vision blurs, you stumble over a crack in the sidewalk, you wet yourself before you make it to the bathroom, you drop your favorite dish, the one Aunt Elsie gave you before she died, and it smashes to smithereens. The only way you can deny difficulties as mundane and relentless as these—and deny the rage and shame and sadness they produce—is through emotional anesthesia. You can shut down your feelings. But if you can no longer experience sorrow, how will you experience joy?

"Okay," you say, "you've persuaded me. I'm not going to deny I live a difficult life. I'll freely admit my problems . . . Wow, have I got problems! Oh, poor me, poor me!" Suddenly there you are, sliding over into that other danger zone I perceived in learning to use difficulty to enhance life. I called it masochism, a taste for suffering for its own sake. Now, an arduous life, well lived, may involve some suffering, but suffering is never its point. Think back to Anne. She didn't go to Zaire in order to wipe out on a rickety bridge, sending her motorcycle twenty feet straight down into the river while she sprawled, breathless and battered but otherwise intact, thank God, on the splintery boards above. That's what happened, and she bore the bruises for weeks, but that's not the reason she's in Zaire.

A great pitfall in chronic illness, which often does inflict suffering of some sort, is the temptation to focus on the suffering, even, in a way, to come to live for it. All of us have probably known at least one person—in my case it's an elderly friend with a gallbladder condition—who takes no interest in anything but her own troubles. (Actually, Edna's interest does sometimes extend to the illnesses and deaths of her acquaintances.) This is, indeed, a way of acknowledging life's difficulties, but the route's a dead end which peters out in an isolated swamp of self-pity.

I think there's an authentic alternative to either denial or masochism in response to a difficult life. You can use your hardships to augment your understanding of and appreciation for yourself and the world you dwell in. Because a difficult life is more complicated than an easy one, it offers opportunities for developing a greater range of response to experience: a true generosity of spirit. 17

One may cry harder in the clutches of a troubled existence, but one may laugh harder as well. I had almost no sense of humor at all, particularly with regard to myself, before I started really experiencing difficulties, in the form of depression and MS. I was as sour as a pickle. Now, my life seems full of merriment. Imagine me, for instance, coming home from a shopping trip one winter evening. As I enter the screened porch, Pinto, my little terrier puppy, bounces forward to greet me, throwing my precarious balance off. I spin around and fall over backward, whacking my head on the sliding glass door to the house, but a quick check (I'm getting good at those) suggests no serious damage this time. This is called a pratfall, a burlesque device used in plays and films for a surefire laugh. In keeping with this spirit, I start to giggle at the image of a woman sprawled flat on her back, helpless under the ecstatic kisses of a spotted mongrel with a comic grin who is thrilled to have someone at last get right down to his own level. The night is chilly. George isn't due home for an hour. Pinto's kisses are unpleasantly damp. "Oh Lord," I think, "if I'm too weak to get up this time, it's going to be a long night." Spurred by the cold and the kisses, I get up. 18

In addition to making me more humorous, I think the difficult life has made me more attentive. In part, this trait is self-defensive: I *have* to watch out for all kinds of potential threats—bumps and cracks, for instance, and small comic dogs lurking in doorways—that others might ignore without courting disaster. But this is only a drill for a more valuable attentiveness to the objects and people around me. I notice more details. I take more delight in them. I feel much more connected to others than I used to, more aware of their troubles, more tolerant of their shortcomings. Hardship can be terrifically humanizing. 19

The most valuable response I've developed, I think, is gratitude. I don't mean that I'm grateful for having MS. I'm not, not in the least, and I don't see why I should be. What I'm grateful for is that, in spite of having MS, I've fulfilled ambitions I never dreamed I would. When I was first diagnosed, I didn't think I'd see my children grow up, and now I have a foster son in the navy, a daughter in the Peace Corps, and a son in college. I was sure my illness would drive George and me apart, and now we've celebrated our twenty-fifth wedding anniversary. I couldn't imagine that I'd make it through graduate school, but I did—twice. I thought I'd have to give up on being a writer, but here I am, writing for my life. I might have managed all these things—maybe even managed them better—without having MS. Who 20 can tell? But through having MS, I've learned to cherish them as I don't think I could have otherwise.

In the past couple of years, my condition has deteriorated steadily. In the face of each new loss, I experience a new rush of panic and anger and sometimes despair. All the same, one morning not long ago, as I was sitting on my porch trying to marshal enough energy to stagger into the house, pull on some clothes, and drive to my studio for a day's writing, I felt, beneath the fatigue and fear of falling that were holding me back, a surge of satisfaction. Looking out at Pinto frolicking with a ball, and beyond him at the paloverde tree beside the driveway, and beyond it to the Santa Catalina Mountains, flat and bluish in the morning light, I thought, "I'm happier now, like this, than I've ever been before."

That's the joy of doing things the hard way. 22

1987

Profile　In "Doing It the Hard Way" Nancy Mairs works her own variation on the personal essay—a familiar, expressive essay drawing upon the writer's own private experiences as data. Put another way, the personal essay makes private disclosures for public consumption. Although the form may strike some as exhibitionistic and self-indulgent ("Listen while I tell about interesting and wonderful me"), it contains the implicit invitation to take our own experiences and feelings and ideas with the same seriousness, to find the same value in them. "Go forth and do likewise!" the personal essayist often seems to be saying.

Personal essays are as distinctive as the individuals who write them, similar only in their openness to almost any subject and in their willingness to pursue an idea wherever it will go. Mairs chooses to write about attitudes and their effect on the way we live our lives. More particularly, she writes about how she used the catastrophe of multiple sclerosis to expand her powers, to humanize herself, to become more attentive and understanding and generous. She could have allowed the disease simply to detract from her life, surrendering to bitterness and self-pity. Instead, she embraced the disease as a challenge, using it to augment her existence. Even as her body degenerated, her spirit and consciousness grew.

As the term suggests, personal essayists speak to us person to person, as Nancy to Liz or Jeremy or whomever, usually plunging right in without formal introductions. Thus, Mairs starts out, "Not long ago, my daughter graduated from Smith College . . . " The "my" announces the writer's presence in the essay, and "my daughter" the assumption that she and her family are pertinent to the reader. The next paragraph discloses that "Anne had majored in biochemistry." Anne, then, is her daughter's name. And so she goes, writing continually and unashamedly about her own experiences and meditations, addressing the reader like someone she might just have befriended on a plane. To maintain her tone, she uses conversational language (including contractions: *don't, you've, that's*), both the indefinite *you* ("For social reasons, as I've said, it's tempting to hide from others the fact *you*'re having a hard time") and the first-person plural, identifying the writer with the reader ("If *our* lives do prove difficult, troublesome, even painful, *we*'re reluctant to admit it"). She even addresses the reader directly (" 'Okay,' you say, 'you've persuaded me. I'm not going to deny I live a difficult life' "). In a manner of speaking, the personal essayist maintains continual eye contact with the reader.

Sequencing Information   A sentence, regardless of the kind of writing in which it appears, is a sequence of information. In effective sentences the sequence weighs almost as heavily as the information itself, especially where it affects coherence. Consider the following two sentences, Mairs' opener and a revision:

> Not long ago, my daughter graduated from Smith College, a liberal arts college for women in Massachusetts, along with nearly seven hundred classmates.

> **Not long ago, along with nearly seven hundred classmates, my daughter graduated from Smith College, a liberal arts college for women in Massachusetts.**

Given, of course, the context, why is Mairs' version preferable to the revision? One reason is that it avoids the awkward proximity of "long ago" and "along with," but the principal answer lies in the subsequent sentences:

> Not long ago, my daughter graduated from Smith College, a liberal arts college for women in Massachusetts, *along with nearly seven hundred classmates. Many of the graduates* were already poised to plunge into worlds of prestige and wealth, on Wall Street or Madison Avenue or Capitol Hill, glittering with the promise of a life of ease: a condo with a river view, a silver BMW convertible, summer vacations on the coast of Maine and winter vacations in Barbados. *Others*, deferring these rewards, planned first to attend medical school, law school, business school. And *some*, wavering in the face of the choices a privileged education proffers, when asked about their plans replied with comic defensiveness, "I don't know, and I don't care, so don't ask!"

Mairs' opener begins with her daughter, about whom she will speak for the first third of her essay, but ends with her daughter's classmates, whom she will discuss for the remainder of the paragraph. The second sentence immediately refers to these classmates, most of whom serve as contrasts to the adventurous daughter. They are "going for the gold" while Anne Mairs will choose to test herself, to find "something hard enough for her." The coherence of the paragraph grows directly out of the sequencing of the opening sentence.

Exercise   The following are some pairs of sentences from "Doing It the Hard Way." How does the sequencing of each sentence reinforce that of the other? In each case consider the effect of repositioning the italicized element.

1. *Because Anne had majored in biochemistry*, most people assumed that she'd go to medical school or get a Ph.D. and become a research scientist. But she's never showed a glimmer of interest in doctoring human beings, though in high school she did contemplate becoming a veterinarian and even spent a few weeks in Honduras vaccinating pigs against hog cholera.

2. Now she lives, with a tabby kitten named Nuni, *in a house at one end of the village of Mfuatu in western Zaire.* Nobody there speaks English, but she's picking up French and Kikongo, though when she was nursing herself through an attack of malaria recently, her attempts at explaining the use of a fever thermometer to the children who trail after her wherever she goes merely baffled everyone involved in the broken dialogue.

3. When she decided to go, her father and I were thrilled, but *she encountered some resistance and even more incomprehension from some of her family and friends.* Why would anyone, they wanted to know, especially a young woman as bright and promising as Anne, go off to spend two years in poverty, without even electricity or plumbing, eating a diet that has included grasshoppers and snakes, exposed to deadly diseases like yellow fever and cholera without a doctor for miles of rutted road that turns to muddy soup with every rain?

4. Most people don't have to light out for Africa *in order to seek out a difficult life.* Indeed, some of us have difficulty plump itself right into our laps without so much as a by-your-leave.

5. You can use your hardships to augment your understanding of and appreciation for yourself and the world you dwell in. *Because a difficult life is more complicated than an easy one,* it offers opportunities for developing a greater range of response to experience: a true generosity of spirit.

Using Quotation Marks   Most often, we use quotation marks to enclose direct quotations, someone's exact words, whether written or spoken. And the key word is *enclose*: Quotation marks come in pairs, like parentheses (something to look for when proofreading). But quotation marks have other uses—to enclose some titles and, occasionally, words used in a special sense. In "Doing It the Hard Way," Mairs uses quotation marks generously, often to include different voices in her monologue. For example, she quotes those who dispense comfortable, conventional advice:

> How many times have you been counseled by some well-meaning person, often one who's deep into denying difficulties of her own, "You think too much. You'll only make matters worse. Just ignore the problem and it will go away"?

Why is the question mark *outside* the quotation marks, not inside? Had the quotation itself been a question, the question mark would have gone inside ("And she replied, 'Do you think your problems will go away simply by ignoring them?' "). In Mairs' version the quotes are included within her own sentence, which is itself a question ("How many times have you been counseled . . . ?"). Notice, too, that she includes several complete statements inside her own sentence, complete with periods (the sentence begins with "How many times" and ends with "it will go away"?).

Mairs also uses quotation marks to give her husband a speaking part.

> "Oh well," George said, as though in response to a question I hadn't even asked, "I don't have a difficult life."

Here, Mairs interrupts her quote with a *dialogue guide* (the phrase identifying the speaker) and a descriptive remark, creating a minor sense of drama by making the reader wait for George's full response. Consider a less effective sequencing:

> **As though in response to a question I hadn't even asked, George said, "Oh, well, I don't have a difficult life."**

Notice that in quoting a statement *introduced by a dialogue guide*, we begin the quote with a capital letter and, inside the final punctuation marks, end with the appropriate terminal punctuation that fits the speaker's statement, question, or exclamation:

> **"What," George replied, "do I have a difficult life?"**

> **"Yes!" I retorted.**

But when the dialogue guide follows, the quotation ends with the appropriate terminal punctuation, inside the quotation marks:

> **"Why do things the hard way?" we ask.**

Mairs also exploits quotation marks to signal when she is using words in a special or unconventional sense. By doing so, she exercises a writer's privilege of turning familiar terms into personal coinages (though a privilege quickly worn out by overuse):

> And then we have to choose how we will respond to the "gift" of a difficult life.

> What's wrong with "difficulty"? I want to know.

Revision Assignments　　Select one of the following strategies and revise "Doing It the Hard Way." Include a brief statement explaining your choice of strategy and its effect on the arrangement and presentation of material.

1. The essay begins anecdotally with the reference to Anne's graduation, then leads into the issue, the lesson. Write a new opener for the essay, beginning with a generalization like, "Hardship can be terrifically humanizing." Then compose a rough outline for the remainder of the essay. In other words, redesign the discussion to follow a top-down, general-to-specifics form.

2. Try a startling opener, one that will shock most readers but also impel them to read on for an explanation: "I have MS and I'm grateful. I don't actually mean that I am grateful for having MS itself. I'm not, not in the least, and I don't see why I should be. But . . . " Then write the next few paragraphs.

3. Revise the essay (a familiar essay but still directed at strangers) as a letter from Mairs to her daughter. In doing so, realize that Anne will already be familiar with her mother's condition, with George and Pinto, and so on.

Writing Assignments

1. At one time or another, we have all had to face some adversity, some hardship that forced us to "do it the hard way." Explore the consequences to your behavior, character, and capacities of such an experience. Has some hardship or deprivation left you able to say, "Before *this*, I would never have been able to . . . "?

2. The opposite of difficulty is ease (comfort, freedom from pain, worry, agitation). Moralists have argued that a life of ease often breeds not only inertia but complacency, self-indulgence, and self-absorption. Can you see a time when you suffered from having it too easy, when a lack of challenges left you weak, unconscious, unappreciative, and generally unequipped to deal with hardship when it did appear? Or have you ever felt yourself at a disadvantage in competition with someone who was accustomed to overcoming difficulty?

3. According to Nancy Mairs, "Hardship *can be* [my italics] terrifically humanizing." Have you seen or experienced instances when hardship had the opposite effect, when it dehumanized? Compare cases, either two people responding differently to hardship, or one person responding differently to different crises.

In Virgin Forest

JOHN MCPHEE

In virgin forest, the ground is uneven, dimpled with pits and adjacent   1
mounds. Perfect trees rise, yes, with boles clear to fifty and sixty feet; but imperfect trees are there too—bent twigs, centuries after bending—not to mention the dead standing timber, not to mention four thousand board feet rotting as one trunk among the mayapples and the violets: a toppled hull fruited
with orange-and-cream fungi, which devour the wood, metabolize it, cause it
literally to disappear. In virgin forest, the classic symbol of virginity is a fallen
uprooted trunk decaying in a bed of herbs.

In our latitude, the primeval forest would include grapes, their free-float-   2
ing vines descending like bridge cables. Wild grapes are incapable of climbing trees. They are lifted by trees as the trees grow, and their bunches hang
from the top of the canopy. In our latitude, there is a great scarcity of virgin
forest. Cut the grapevines, make a few stumps, let your cattle in to graze, and
it's all over till the end of time. Nonetheless, we were in such a place a few
days ago, and did not have to travel far to see it. Never cut, never turned, it
was a piece of American deciduous forest in continuous evolution dating to
the tundras of mesolithic times. Some of the trees were ninety feet tall, with
redtails nesting in them, and when the hawks took off and rose above the
canopy they could see the World Trade Center.

We had made our way to Franklin Township, New Jersey, which in-   3
cludes New Brunswick and is one of the less virgin milieus in America. This
is where the megalopolis came in so fast it trapped animals between motels.
It missed, though, half a mile of primeval woods. The property, a little east of
East Millstone, was settled in 1701 by Mynheer Cornelius Van Liew and remained in one family for two hundred and fifty-four years. They cleared and
farmed most of their land but consciously decided to leave sixty-five acres
untouched. The Revolution came and went, the Civil and the World Wars,
but not until the nineteen-fifties did the family seek the counsel of a sawyer.
The big trees were ruled by white oaks, dating to the eighteenth and seventeenth centuries, and their value was expressible in carats. Being no less
frank than Dutch, the family lets its intentions be known. As often will happen in conservation crises, this brought forth a paradox of interested parties:
rod-and-gun groups, the Nature Conservancy, the Adirondack Mountain
Club, the United Daughters of the Confederacy. A tract of virgin forest is so
rare that money was raised in thirty-eight states and seven foreign countries.
But not enough. The trees were worth a good deal more. In the end, the forest was saved by, of all people, the United Brotherhood of Carpenters and
Joiners of America, whose president remarked in 1955, as he handed over the
property to Rutgers University, "What happens in the woodlands is close to
the carpenter's heart."

Named for a Brotherhood president, the tract is called Hutcheson Memo-   4
rial Forest. A brief trail makes a loop near one end. The deed limits Rutgers

to that, and Rutgers is not arguing. The university's role is to protect the periphery and to study the woods. When something attacks, Rutgers makes notes. A disease that kills American beeches is on its way from Maine. "The forest deed says basically you don't do anything about it," a biologist named Edmund Stiles explained to us. "You watch what happens." In 1981, gypsy moths tore off the canopy, and sunlight sprayed the floor. The understory thickened as shrubs and saplings responded with a flush of growth. "The canopy is now closing over again," Stiles said. "This summer, there will be a lot of death." In 1950, a hurricane left huge gaps in the canopy. "Once every three hundred years you can expect a hurricane that will knock down damned near everything," Stiles went on. "There's a real patchwork nature in an old forest, in the way it is always undergoing replacement." He stopped to admire a small white ash standing along beneath open sky. "That's going to take the canopy," he said. "It's going to go all the way. It has been released. It will fill the gap."

Forty-two years old and of middle height—wearing boots, bluejeans, a brown wool shirt—Stiles had a handsome set of muttonchops and a tumble of thick brown hair that flowed over his forehead toward inquiring blue eyes. He had been working in Hutcheson Forest for thirteen years, he told us, and had recently become director. His doctoral dissertation, at the University of Washington, was on bird communities in alder forests. More recently, he had studied the foraging strategies of insects and the symbiotic relationships of berries and migratory birds. In other words, he was a zoologist and a botanist, too. From secretive gray foxes to the last dead stick—that was what the untouched forest was about. The big oaks (red, white, and black), the shagbark hickories, sugar maples, beeches, ashes, and dogwoods—among thousands of plant and animal species—were only the trees. 5

As we talked, and moved about, tasting the odd spicebush leaf or a tendril of smilax, Stiles divided his attention and seemed not to miss a sound. "Spicebush and dogwood fruits are very high in lipids," he said. "They are taken on by birds getting ready for long migratory flights. Those are wood thrushes calling. A forest has to be at least a hundred years old to get a wood thrush. Actually, it takes about four centuries to grow a forest of this kind. The gap phenomenon is typical of old forest. There's a white-eyed vireo. Blue-winged warbler. There are cycles of openness and closedness in the canopies. Trees take advantage. Fill in the gaps. These are white-oak seedlings from a mast year. There's a nice red-bellied woodpecker." He was like Toscanini, just offstage, listening idly to his orchestra as it tuned itself up. He said he had developed a theory that out-of-season splotches of leaf color are messages to frugivorous birds—the scattered early orange among sassafras leaves of the wild strawberry, the red of the Virginia creeper when everything else is green. When fruit is ready, the special colors turn on. He heard a great crested flycatcher. He bent down to a jack-in-the-pulpit, saying that it bears bird-disseminated fruit and is pollinated by a small black fly. 6

German foresters who came to visit Hutcheson Forest have been surprised by the untidiness of the place, startled by the jumble of life and death. "These Germans are unfamiliar with stuff just lying around, with the truly virginal aspect of the forest," Stiles said. Apparently, the Germans, like almost everyone else, had a misconception of forest primeval—a picture of 7

Wotan striding through the noonday twilight, of Ludwig D. Boone shouting for *Lebensraum* among giant columns of uniform trees. "You don't find redwoods," Stiles said summarily. "You don't find Evangeline's forest. You find a more realistic forest."

You find a huge white ash that has grown up at an angle of forty-five degrees, and in a managed forest would have long ago been tagged for destruction. You find remarkably deep humus. You find a great rusty stump, maybe six feet high, and jagged where the trunk now beside it snapped off. More often, you find whole root structures tipped into the air and looking like radial engines. As you will nowhere else, you find the topography of pits and mounds. In its random lumpiness, it could be a model of glacial terrain. When a tree goes over and its roots come ripping from the ground, they bring with them a considerable mass of soil. When the tree has disappeared, the dirt remains as a mound, which turns kelly green with moss. Beside it is the pit that the roots came from. When no other trace remains of the tree, you can see by the pit and the mound the direction in which the tree fell, and guess its approximate size. If cattle graze in pit-and-mound topography, they trample and destroy it. The pits and mounds of centuries are evidence of virgin forest.

There is supporting evidence in human records and in tree rings. People from Columbia's Lamont-Doherty Geological Observatory have cored some trees in Hutcheson Forest and dated them, for example to 1699, 1678. Neighboring land was settled, and cleared for farming, in 1701. Lamont-Doherty has an ongoing project called the Eastern Network Dendrochronology Series, which has sought and catalogued virgin stands at least two hundred and fifty years old. The list is short and scattered, and the tracts are small, with the notable exceptions of Joyce Kilmer Memorial Forest, in North Carolina (thirty-eight hundred virgin acres), the cove hardwoods of Great Smoky Mountains National Park, and a large stand of hemlocks and beeches in Allegheny National Forest, in western Pennsylvania. There are three hundred virgin acres on the Wabash River in Illinois, and, in eastern Ohio, a woods of white oaks some of which were seedlings when the Pilgrims reached New England. The Ohio white oaks, like the white oaks of Hutcheson Forest, are from three to four feet in diameter. Old white oaks are found in few places, because they had a tendency to become bowsprits, barrel staves, and queen-post trusses.[1] Virgin hemlocks are comparatively common. Maine is not rich in virgin timber—some red spruce on Mt. Katahdin, some red spruce above Tunk Lake. There is a river gorge in Connecticut where trees have never been cut. Some red spruce and hemlock in the Adirondacks date to the late fifteen-hundreds, and the hemlocks of the Allegheny forest are nearly two centuries older than that. In the Shawangunk Mountains, about seventy miles northwest of our office on Forty-third Street, is the oldest known stand of pitch pine (360 years), also some white pine (370), chestnut oak (330), and eastern hemlock (500). They are up on a quartzite ridge line, though, and are very slow-growing small trees. Remnant old-growth stands tend to be in mountains, in rocky, craggy places, not in flatlands. Hutcheson Forest, in the Newark Basin—in what was once a prime piedmont area—is thus

[1]One style of framework used to support a roof.

exceptionally rare. In the region of New York City, there is nothing like it, no other clearly documented patch. In fact, it is the largest mixed-oak virgin forest left in the eastern United States.

Running through the forest is Spooky Brook, spawning ground of the 10 white sucker. Rutgers would like to control the headwaters, fearing something known as herbicide drift. Continuing population drift is no less a threat, as development fills in lingering farms. The woods are closed to visitors, except for scheduled Sunday tours. Rutgers already owns some hundred and fifty acres contiguous to the forest, and hopes, with the help of the Nature Conservancy, to get two hundred more. Manipulative research is carried out on the peripheral land, while observational research goes on in the forest, which has been described by Richard Forman, a professor at Harvard, as "probably the single most studied primeval woods on the continent." People have gone in there and emerged with more than a hundred advanced degrees, including thirty-six Ph.D.s. So many articles, papers, theses, and other research publications have come out of Hutcheson Forest that countless trees have been clear-cut elsewhere just in order to print them.

1987

Profile   John McPhee has made a reputation as a "literary journalist," someone applying imaginative techniques to informational writing. His subjects range from oranges to canoes, from New Jersey's Pine Barrens to life in rural Alaska, and from cattle branding to the disposal of used automobile tires. No one begins with a detailed knowledge of so many different subjects. One has to work them up, to educate oneself. McPhee's extraordinary range of interests testifies to the fascination that the world can hold for someone inquisitive and energetic, and he credits his readers with possessing the same qualities, treating them like fellow initiates familiar with the technical terms and the names of local plants and animals he uses for accuracy and authenticity.

McPhee does not simply collect data like an information-age pack rat and dump it in his readers' laps. For all the energy he devotes to researching his subjects, he has asserted that writing is primarily a matter of arranging and presenting information. Thus, his principal tactic is to weave his information into stories, stories about the talented and dedicated people involved in his subjects (like Edmund Stiles), and stories involving himself as direct witness and information-gatherer. In fact, like several other writers in this collection (e.g. Tristram Wyatt in "Submarine Beetles"), he often makes the information-gathering itself an organizing thread in his writing.

Nowhere is McPhee's method more apparent than in his lead-ins and transitions, in the way he introduces his subject and then moves from one detail or aspect to another. Thus, he begins "In Virgin Forest" with a definition of the term in his title, a term more familiar than understood. A virgin forest is a place "dimpled with pits and adjacent mounds" and spotted with standing dead timber and rotting logs. In other words, despite the suggestions of the term *virgin* (clean, pure), a virgin forest is a tangled clutter that is teeming with life found nowhere else.

As the first paragraph began "In virgin forest," the second begins "In our latitude" and explains that here such a forest would be bedecked with grape vines, drawn up into the canopy by the growing trees. "In our latitude," he writes a second time, "there is a great scarcity of virgin forest." Cut a few grapevines, allow in a few cattle, and the virgin forest is gone forever. "Nevertheless, we were in such a place only a few days ago, and did not have to travel far to see it." Writing for *The New Yorker*, he observes that some of the forest's trees are ninety feet tall, with redtail hawks nesting in them, "and when the hawks took off and rose above the canopy they could see the World Trade Center." As a crow (or a redtailed hawk) flies, such a rare locale is a brief flight from the largest city in America.

To explain how "we were in such a place," his third paragraph backtracks: "We had made our way to Franklin Township, New Jersey, which is one of the less virgin milieus in America." He then relates how the area grew so quickly that it hemmed in "half a mile of primeval forest," which had managed to remain in one family for 254 years. Not until the 1950s did the family think of selling the property. At that point they consulted a sawyer, someone who knew timber, and he informed them of the extent of their treasure: "The big trees were ruled by white oaks, dating to the eighteenth and seventeenth centuries, and their value was expressible in carats."

And so on. Beginning by correcting misconceptions about the meaning of *virgin* in virgin forest, the story glides naturally from one fact to the next, until it does in fact seem like *a story*, an orderly progression of related events and details waiting there all along to be discovered. To arrange and present is to embed information in a sequence of fluid relationships, to think habitually in terms of connections and transitions.

Writing for Insiders   Behind McPhee's stories are weeks and weeks of travel and interviews and research, from which he "arranges and presents," ultimately producing an integrated narrative for the pages of *The New Yorker*. Simply put, each new assignment requires McPhee to go back to school, to educate himself on a complex and demanding subject. By the time he has completed his inquiries, he has made himself an insider, able to speak knowledgeably of the necessary technicalities. Having made himself an "expert," he has two choices: to distance his readers by treating them like outsiders, defining every insider term; or to treat them as insiders, writing as if they are already largely in the know, able at least to infer from context the meaning of key terms. Most of the time, McPhee chooses the latter, giving his readers credit for sharing his range of interests.

In "In Virgin Forest," then, McPhee writes as if his readers are familiar with terms like *mesolithic, megalopolis, lipids, mast years, frugivorous, radial engines, quartzite ridge line*, and—a name that charmed McPhee—*queen-post trusses*, as well as with a range of Eastern vegetation and birds: shagbark hickories, sugar maples, spicebushes, smilax, jack-in-the pulpit, wood thrushes, white-eyed vireos, and great crested flycatchers. On the one hand, McPhee knows that most readers are flattered by being treated as well informed and broadly curious. On the other, he does not literally expect his reader to know every term and remember every detail. If they want to know a specific word or remember a specific detail, they can make a special effort. In the meantime, he has established his own credibility and treated his readers like equals. His popularity testifies to the wisdom of his approach.

Whenever possible, it is better to address our readers as knowledgeable insiders than as know-nothing outsiders, better to write over their heads than to write down to them, especially when we want their attention and their consent.

Using Quotes   McPhee has mastered the art of integrating quotes into informational articles. To begin with, he recognizes that behind every good story are interesting people, dedicated experts whose commitment dramatizes and pays tribute to the value of the subject. In "In Virgin Forest" the story rests as much upon Edmund Stiles, originally introduced simply as "a biologist," as upon the Hutcheson Memorial Forest of which he is chief guardian. So what McPhee integrates into his story is a character, a living personality who not only possesses information but also performs some of the same dramatic functions as a character in a novel. And we know this person chiefly through his language, as he discloses his knowledge and exhibits his values. The fourth paragraph is vintage McPhee:

> Named for a Brotherhood president, the tract is called Hutcheson Memorial Forest. A brief trail makes a loop near one end. The deed limits Rutgers to that, and Rutgers is not arguing. The university's role is to protect the periphery and to study the woods. When something attacks, Rutgers makes notes. A disease that kills American beeches is on its way from Maine. *"The forest deed says basically you don't do anything about it,"* a biologist named Edmund Stiles explained to us. *"You watch what happens."* In 1981, gypsy moths tore off the canopy, and sunlight sprayed the floor. The understory thickened as shrubs and saplings responded with a flush of growth. *"The canopy is now closing over again,"* Stiles said. *"This summer, there will be a lot of death."* In 1950, a hurricane left huge gaps in the canopy. *"Once every three hundred years you can expect a hurricane that will knock down damned near everything,"* Stiles went on. *"There's a real patchwork nature in an old forest, in the way it is always undergoing replacement."* He stopped to admire a small white ash standing alone beneath open sky. *"That's going to take the canopy,"* he said. *"It's going to go all the way. It has been released. It will fill the gap."*

In McPhee's hallmark fashion the introduction of Stiles is unexpected. His entry is an explanatory remark about the role of Rutgers University in protecting the forest: The University is not to intervene, regardless of what disaster threatens, "a biologist named Edmund Stiles explained to us." Then Stiles launches into the story of the 1981 gypsy moth invasion that "tore off the canopy," one such occasion when Rutgers refrained from action (no insecticide-spraying helicopters). Then Stiles goes on, like a proud parent, to point out how the forest is rebounding, as it did after the 1950 hurricane (implicitly making a point about nature's ability to heal itself without human meddling). And then he concludes by exhibiting the small white ash that will grow to the top of the canopy before it covers over again. The assertive rhythm and energy of his words reveals as much about his own passion as about its subject: "It's going to go all the way. It has been released. It will fill the gap."

Instructive is the spartan way in which McPhee words his *dialogue guides*, which, like Joan Didion's, usually follow the quote. Instead of "he boasted" or "he asserted," we get, simply, "he said." Also instructive is the way in which McPhee absorbs and presents some information without attributing it to his source. Everything after the introduction of Stiles could have been quotation—a long, unrelieved block of it. Instead, McPhee integrates Stiles' testimony into the narrative of the paragraph, sometimes summarizing in his own words what Stiles has said. (Almost certainly, it was from Stiles that McPhee learned about the 1981 gypsy moth invasion and the 1950 hurricane.) Thus, Stiles has a major speaking part at the same time that McPhee maintains control of his narrative. He is no mere traveling microphone.

Exercise Writing, John McPhee has said, consists primarily of "arranging and presenting" material, a surprising statement from a person who spends so much time *gathering* it. But in emphasizing arrangement and presentation, McPhee was distinguishing writers from investigators. The latter may be able to assemble information, but only the former can make it presentable. If anything else were true, we would have only to research our topics; our papers would then write themselves.

As we have observed elsewhere, it was not a writer who said, "You can't get there from here." Take the fourth paragraph quoted, in the previous section. It began with, "Named for a Brotherhood president, the tract is called Hutcheson Memorial Forest"; it ended with, "It will fill the gap." Despite what these two statements suggest, what falls between is not an incoherent grab bag of information but a seamlessly organized paragraph. The transition point, of course, is the seventh sentence, the quote from Stiles.

The following is the sixth paragraph, a typically long specimen with the sentences separated and enumerated for easier analysis. How does McPhee achieve not only *coherence* but also *unity* and *emphasis*?

1. As we talked, and moved about, tasting the odd spicebush leaf or a tendril of smilax, Stiles divided his attention and seemed not to miss a sound.

2. "Spicewood and dogwood fruits are very high in lipids," he said.

3. "They are taken on by birds getting ready for long migratory flights.

4. Those are wood thrushes calling.

5. A forest has to be at least a hundred years old to get a wood thrush.

6. Actually, it takes about four centuries to grow a forest of this kind.

7. The gap phenomenon is typical of old forest.

8. There's a white-eyed vireo.

9. Blue-winged warbler.

10. There are cycles of openness and closedness in the canopies.

11. Trees take advantage.

12. Fill in the gaps.

13. These are white-oak seedlings from a mast year.

14. There's a nice red-bellied woodpecker."

15. He was like Toscanini, just offstage, listening idly to his orchestra as it tuned itself up.

16. He said he had developed a theory that out-of-season splotches of leaf color are messages to frugivorous birds—the scattered early orange among sassafras leaves, the springtime red of the leaves of the wild strawberry, the red of the Virginia creeper when everything is green.

17. When fruit is ready, the special colors turn on.

18. He heard a great crested flycatcher.

19. He bent down to a jack-in-the-pulpit, saying that it bears bird-disseminated fruit and is pollinated by a small black fly.

And, finally, why does McPhee give Stiles such a long, uninterrupted speaking part in this paragraph?

Revision Assignments   Select one of the following strategies and revise "In Virgin Forest." Include a brief statement explaining your choice and its effect on the arrangement and presentation of material.

1. McPhee does not introduce himself ("we") until the middle of the second paragraph, then uses his presence only as a convenience to introduce material and render it more immediate. Revise the story as a first-person narrative: "I visited a virgin forest recently," or, "Ever since I read Longfellow's 'Hiawatha' in high school, I have harbored a curiosity about 'the forest primeval,' or virgin forests. Recently, I had an opportunity . . . "

2. At the end of paragraph 9, McPhee identifies the virgin stands of forest catalogued by Lamont-Doherty's Eastern Network Dendrochronology Series, but he does not merely give a simple, mechanical listing. He uses variety in introducing the locations, interrupting occasionally to give pertinent information about some. One of his purposes is to avoid losing the items in the list (or the forest in the trees). He treats each locale as worthy of the reader's attention. To establish the effectiveness of McPhee's technique of presentation, revise paragraph 9 into a simple, parallel listing.

Writing Assignments

1. Write an informative, insider story on some familiar subject that most people take for granted but about whose inner workings they know little (flea markets, athletic shoe stores, health clubs, bicycle shops, coffee shops, veterinary clinics, war gamers). Less important than the subject itself is an enthusiastic insider who loves to talk about it. Concentrate especially on what there is to *know*—such a person will be happy to display his or her expertise. For general guidelines look at the organization of "In Virgin Forest" and its use of quotations.

2. Using "In Virgin Forest" as a model, rearrange and re-present Barry Lopez's "The Stone Horse" after the manner of John McPhee. That is, present the information about the stone horse as if you were investigating the figure yourself, including "interviews" with Lopez (quote him the way McPhee quotes Stiles).

The Way to Rainy Mountain

N. SCOTT MOMADAY

A single knoll rises out of the plain in Oklahoma, north and west of the Wichita range. For my people, the Kiowa, it is an old landmark, and they gave it the name Rainy Mountain. The hardest weather in the world is there. Winter brings blizzards, hot tornadic winds arise in the spring, and in summer the prairie is an anvil's edge. The grass turns brittle and brown, and it cracks beneath your feet. There are green belts along the rivers and creeks, linear groves of hickory and pecan, willow and witch hazel. At a distance in July or August the steaming foliage seems almost to writhe in fire. Great green and yellow grasshoppers are everywhere in the tall grass, popping up like corn to sting the flesh, and tortoises crawl about on the red earth, going nowhere in the plenty of time. Loneliness is an aspect of the land. All things in the plain are isolate; there is no confusion of objects in the eye, but *one* hill or *one* tree or *one* man. To look upon that landscape in the early morning, with the sun at your back, is to lose the sense of proportion. Your imagination comes to life, and this, you think, is where Creation was begun.

1

I returned to Rainy Mountain in July. My grandmother had died in the spring, and I wanted to be at her grave. She had lived to be very old and at last infirm. Her only living daughter was with her when she died, and I was told that in death her face was that of a child.

2

I like to think of her as a child. When she was born, the Kiowas were living the last great moment of their history. For more than a hundred years they had controlled the open range from the Smoky Hill River to the Red, from the headwaters of the Canadian to the fork of the Arkansas and Cimarron. In alliance with the Commanches, they had ruled the whole of the Southern Plains. War was their sacred business, and they were the finest horsemen the world has ever known. But warfare for the Kiowas was pre-eminently a matter of disposition rather than of survival, and they never understood the grim, unrelenting advance of the U.S. Cavalry. When at last, divided and ill-provisioned, they were driven onto the Staked Plains in the cold rains of autumn, they fell into panic. In Palo Duro Canyon they abandoned their crucial stores to pillage and had nothing then but their lives. In order to save themselves, they surrendered to the soldiers at Fort Sill and were imprisoned in the old stone corral that now stands as a military museum. My grandmother was spared the humiliation of those high gray walls by eight or ten years, but she must have known from birth the affliction of defeat, the dark brooding of old warriors.

3

Her name was Aho, and she belonged to the last culture to evolve in North America. Her forebears came down from the high country in western Montana nearly three centuries ago. They were a mountain people, a mysterious tribe of hunters whose language has never been classified in any major group. In the late seventeenth century they began a long migration to the

4

"The Way to Rainy Mountain" by N. Scott Momaday. First published in *The Reporter*, 26 January 1967. Reprinted from *The Way to Rainy Mountain*, © 1969, The University of New Mexico Press.

south and east. It was a journey toward the dawn, and it led to a golden age. Along the way the Kiowas were befriended by the Crows, who gave them the culture and religion of the Plains. They acquired horses, and their ancient nomadic spirit was suddenly free of the ground. They acquired Tai-me, the sacred sun dance doll, from that moment the object and symbol of their worship, and so shared in the divinity of the sun. Not least, they acquired a sense of destiny, therefore courage and pride. When they entered upon the Southern Plains they had been transformed. No longer were they slaves to the simple necessity of survival; they were a lordly and dangerous society of fighters and thieves, hunters and priests of the sun. According to their origin myth, they entered the world through a hollow log. From one point of view, their migration was the fruit of an old prophecy, for indeed they emerged from a sunless world.

Though my grandmother lived out her long life in the shadow of Rainy   5
Mountain, the immense landscape of the continental interior lay like memory in her blood. She could tell of the Crows, whom she had never seen, and of the Black Hills, where she had never been. I wanted to see in reality what she had seen more perfectly in the mind's eye, and drove fifteen hundred miles to begin my pilgrimage.

A dark mist lay over the Black Hills, and the land was like iron. At the top   6
of a ridge I caught sight of Devil's Tower upthrust against the gray sky as if in the birth of time the core of the earth had broken through its crust and the motion of the world was begun. There are things in nature that engender an awful quiet in the heart of man; Devil's Tower is one of them. Two centuries ago, because of their need to explain it, the Kiowas made a legend at the base of the rock. My grandmother said:

"Eight children were there at play, seven sisters and their brother. Sud-   7
denly the boy was struck dumb; he trembled and began to run upon his hands and feet. His fingers became claws, and his body was covered with fur. There was a bear where the boy had been. The sisters were terrified; they ran, and the bear after them. They came to the stump of a great tree, and the tree spoke to them. It bade them climb upon it, and as they did so, it began to rise in the air. The bear came to kill them, but they were just beyond its reach. It reared against the tree and scored the bark all around with its claws. The seven sisters were borne into the sky, and they became the stars of the Big Dipper." From that moment, and so long as the legend lives, the Kiowas have kinsmen in the night sky. Whatever they were in the mountains, they could be no more. However tenuous their well-being, however much they had suffered and would suffer again, they had found a way out of the wilderness.

My grandmother had a reverence for the sun, a holy regard that now is all   8
but gone out of mankind. There was a wariness in her, and an ancient awe. She was a Christian in her later years, but she had come a long way about, and she never forgot her birthright. As a child she had been to the sun dances; she had taken part in that annual rite, and by it she had learned the restoration of her people in the presence of Tai-me. She was about seven when the last Kiowa sun dance was held in 1887 on the Washita River above Rainy Mountain Creek. The buffalo were gone. In order to consummate the

ancient sacrifice—to impale the head of a buffalo bull upon the Tai-me tree—a delegation of old men journeyed into Texas, there to beg and barter for an animal from the Goodnight herd. She was ten when the Kiowas came together for the last time as a living sun-dance culture. They could find no buffalo; they had to hang an old hide from the sacred tree. Before the dance could begin, a company of soldiers rode out from Fort Sill under orders to disperse the tribe. Forbidden without cause the essential act of their faith, having seen the wild herds slaughtered and left to rot upon the ground, the Kiowas backed away forever from the tree. That was July 20, 1890, at the great bend of the Washita. My grandmother was there. Without bitterness, and for as long as she lived, she bore a vision of deicide.[1]

Now that I can have her only in memory, I see my grandmother in the several postures that were peculiar to her: standing at the wood stove on a winter morning and turning meat in a great iron skillet; sitting at the south window, bent above her beadwork, and afterwards, when her vision failed, looking down for a long time into the fold of her hands; going out upon a cane, very slowly as she did when the weight of age came upon her; praying. I remember her most often at prayer. She made long, rambling prayers out of suffering and hope, having seen many things. I was never sure that I had the right to hear, so exclusive were they of all mere custom and company. The last time I saw her she prayed standing by the side of her bed at night, naked to the waist, the light of the kerosene lamp moving upon her dark skin. Her long black hair, always drawn and braided in the day, lay upon her shoulders and against her breasts like a shawl. I do not speak Kiowa, and I never understood her prayers, but there was something inherently sad in the sound, some merest hesitation upon the syllables of sorrow. She began in a high and descending pitch, exhausting her breath to silence; then again and again—and always the same intensity of effort, of something that is, and is not, like urgency in the human voice. Transported so in the dancing light among the shadows of her room, she seemed beyond the reach of time. But that was illusion; I think I knew then that I should not see her again.

Houses are like sentinels in the plain, old keepers of the weather watch. There, in a very little while, wood takes on the appearance of great age. All colors wear soon away in the wind and rain, and then the wood is burned gray and the grain appears and the nails turn red with rust. The window panes are black and opaque; you imagine there is nothing within, and indeed there are many ghosts, bones given up to the land. They stand here and there against the sky, and you approach them for a longer time than you expect. They belong in the distance; it is their domain.

Once there was a lot of sound in my grandmother's house, a lot of coming and going, feasting and talk. The summers there were full of excitement and reunion. The Kiowas are a summer people; they abide the cold and keep to themselves, but when the season turns and the land becomes warm and vital they cannot hold still; an old love of going returns upon them. The aged visitors who came to my grandmother's house when I was a child were made of lean and leather, and they bore themselves upright. They wore great black

9

10

11

[1]The murder of a god or gods.

hats and bright ample shirts that shook in the wind. They rubbed fat upon their hair and wound their braids with strips of colored cloth. Some of them painted their faces and carried the scars of old and cherished enmities. They were an old council of warlords, come to remind and be reminded of who they were. Their wives and daughters served them well. The women might indulge themselves; gossip was at once the mark and compensation of their servitude. They made loud and elaborate talk among themselves, full of jest and gesture, fright and false alarm. They went abroad in fringed and flowered shawls, bright beadwork and German silver. They were at home in the kitchen, and they prepared meals that were banquets.

There were frequent prayer meetings, and nocturnal feasts. When I was a child I played with my cousins outside, where the lamplight fell upon the ground and the singing of the old people rose up around us and carried away into the darkness. There were a lot of good things to eat, a lot of laughter and surprise. And afterwards, when the quiet returned, I lay down with my grandmother and could hear the frogs away by the river and feel the motion of the air. 12

Now there is a funeral silence in the rooms, the endless wake of some final word. The walls have closed in upon my grandmother's house. When I returned to it in mourning, I saw for the first time in my life how small it was. It was late at night, and there was a white moon, nearly full. I sat for a long time on the stone steps by the kitchen door. From there I could see out across the land; I could see the long row of trees by the creek, the low light upon the rolling plains, and the stars of the Big Dipper. Once I looked at the moon and caught sight of a strange thing. A cricket had perched upon the handrail, only a few inches away. My line of vision was such that the creature filled the moon like a fossil. It had gone there, I thought, to live and die, for there, of all places, was its small definition made whole and eternal. A warm wind rose up and purled like the longing within me. 13

The next morning, I awoke at dawn and went out on the dirt road to Rainy Mountain. It was already hot, and the grasshoppers began to fill the air. Still, it was early in the morning, and birds sang out of the shadows. The long yellow grass on the mountain shone in the bright light, and a scissortail hied above the land. There, where it ought to be, at the end of a long and legendary way, was my grandmother's grave. She had at last succeeded to that holy ground. Here and there on the dark stones were ancestral names. Looking back once, I saw the mountain and came away. 14

1967

Profile Imagine the task confronting N. Scott Momaday before he even had a title for the essay that would become "The Way to Rainy Mountain." He wanted to write about the death of an old Kiowa woman who was first of all his grandmother, someone he cherished for the hours they spent together in his childhood, for the stories she told him, for the summer banquets she hosted, for the times he watched her in her prayers. At the same time, the old Kiowa woman was one of the few surviving links to his tribal past, so her death was also a cultural and historical loss. She had been raised on tribal legends and the stories of the great migration to the plains centuries before, and she had been present at the final sun dance in 1890. As a scholar and a historian, he knows her like will never be seen again. So how does he express his grief as both a grandson and a Kiowa? How does he pay tribute to the person without reducing her to a cultural abstraction? How does he fold into one narrative the details of his pilgrimage, his personal memories of her, and—to put her loss in a historical and cultural perspective—the story of the Kiowa? And since the story of the Kiowa is also the story of their relationship to the land, how does he capture the necessary sense of the place where they found and defined themselves? And how was he to arrange and present all of this material into a little more than two thousand words?

Like his ancestors he found his inspiration in the landscape: Rainy Mountain—tribal landmark, the burial place of his grandmother, and his personal destination. The Kiowa had found their "long and legendary way" to Rainy Mountain centuries before when they migrated from the mountains to the plains; his grandmother found her way there to her final resting place; and Momaday found his way there by retracing his grandmother's final journey. Rainy Mountain, then, was both his destination and his point of departure, so there he begins his essay, radiating outward to himself and his grandmother, telling her story and that of his people, then returning. We can trace his method in the first four paragraphs by noting how he moves from Rainy Mountain to the Kiowa to himself to his grandmother to the Kiowa:

> A single knoll rises out of the plain in Oklahoma, north and west of the Wichita range. For my people, the Kiowa, it is an old landmark, and they gave it the name of Rainy Mountain. . . .

> I returned to Rainy Mountain in July. My grandmother had died in the spring . . . I was told that in death her face was that of a child. . . .

> I like to think of her as a child. When she was born, the Kiowa were living the last great moment of their history. . . .

> Her name was Aho, and she belonged to the last culture to evolve in North America. Her forebears came down from the high country in western Montana . . .

Momaday accomplished his difficult task by folding into his narrative personal recollections, topographical details, and biographical and historical information. His story is his grandmother's story is the story of the Kiowa, and back again. And the story is a sad one, finding its image in the cricket he sees on the handrail:

> My line of vision was such that the creature filled the moon like a fossil. It had gone there, I thought, to live and die, for there, of all places, was its small definition made whole and eternal.

The Kiowa seem to be sharing the fate of the cricket.

Descriptive and Narrative Verbs   Momaday's first paragraph is almost pure description—that is, it is what one person described as "literature aspiring to become painting," its purpose to represent an essentially static subject, bodies existing in space. Because the subject of description is static, the verbs in descriptive passages will be static, either the *be* verb (*is, am, are, was,* *were*), or linking verbs (*seem, become, remain,* and so on), or certain active verbs that could easily be replaced by the *be* verb. Thus, you can write that "A tree *stands* outside the classroom window," but this is a more energetic way of saying that "A tree *is* outside the classroom window" (or, perhaps more emphatically, "There is a tree outside the classroom window").

We can make a like revision of Momaday's descriptive opener: "A single knoll *rises* out of the plain in Oklahoma, north and west of the Wichita range." *Rises* is a dynamic narrative verb, transforming something inert, a knoll, into something active. With some loss he could have done without the energetic verb: "North and west of the Wichita range, on the plain in Oklahoma, there is a single knoll." This structure places the knoll in an emphatic location, but it does not activate the knoll: The knoll no longer *rises*.

For all of its descriptive character and the predominance of *be* verbs, Momaday's opening paragraph still communicates vitality, chiefly by interspersing a few active verbs and representing essentially static details in dynamic terms:

> A single knoll rises out of the plain in Oklahoma, north and west of the Wichita range. For my people, the Kiowas, it is an old landmark, and they gave it the name Rainy Mountain. The hardest weather in the world is there. Winter brings blizzards, hot tornadic winds arise in the spring, and in summer the prairie is an anvil's edge. The grass turns brittle and brown, and it cracks beneath your feet. There are green belts along the rivers and creeks, linear groves of hickory and pecan, willow and witch hazel. At a distance in July or August the steaming foliage seems almost to writhe in fire. Great green and yellow grasshoppers are everywhere in the tall grass, popping up like corn to sting the flesh, and tortoises crawl about on the red earth, going nowhere in the plenty of time. Loneliness is an aspect of the land. All things in the plain are isolate; there is no confusion of objects in the eye, but *one* hill or *one* tree or *one* man. To look upon that landscape in the early morning, with the sun at your back, is to lose the sense of proportion. Your imagination comes to life, and this, you think, is where Creation was begun.

Most of the verbs are static: "it *is* an old landmark . . . The hardest weather in the world *is* there. . . . the prairie *is* an anvil's edge. . . . The grass *turns* brittle and brown . . . There *are* green belts along the river . . . Great green and yellow grasshoppers *are* everywhere . . . Loneliness *is* an aspect of the land. . . . All things in the plain *are* isolate; there *is* no confusion of objects in the eye . . ." Into this static landscape Momaday introduces a measure of life, sometimes by avoiding static representations. Instead of "There *are* blizzards in winter and hot tornadic winds in summer," he writes, "Winter *brings* blizzards, and hot tornadic winds *arise* in the spring." And instead of simply being brittle and brown, "The grass *turns* brittle and brown, and it *cracks* beneath your feet" (a detail implied by "brittle"). By having the grass crack, Momaday animates the scene by introducing a living human presence (*you*). To this presence he adds the great green and yellow grasshoppers, "*popping up* like corn to sting the flesh," and tortoises that "*crawl* about on the red earth, *going* nowhere in the plenty of time."

And finally, there is the ultimate and culminating activity: "Your imagination comes to life, and this, you think, is where Creation was begun." Even out of a setting so barren and unpromising comes a stimulus to the human spirit.

Exercise   The following is Momaday's eighth paragraph, with the sentences separated and enumerated for convenient analysis. In studying the successive sentences, concentrate on two issues: the integration of biographical and historical information, the life of Aho and the story of the Kiowa; and coherence, the manner in which each sentence relates to previous sentences even as it serves as a bridge to the following ones. In other words, a paragraph (like a sentence) is a sequence of information. How does the sequencing work here?

1. My grandmother had a reverence for the sun, a holy regard that now is all but gone out of mankind.

2. There was a wariness in her, and an ancient awe.

3. She was a Christian in her later years, but she had come a long way about, and she never forgot her birthright.

4. As a child she had been to the sun dances; she had taken part in the annual rite, and by it she had learned the restoration of her people in the presence of Tai-me.

5. She was about seven when the last Kiowa sun dance was held in 1887 on the Washita River above Rainy Mountain Creek.

6. The buffalo were gone.

7. In order to consummate the ancient sacrifice—to impale the head of a buffalo bull upon the Tai-me tree—a delegation of old men journeyed into Texas, there to beg and barter for an animal from the Goodnight herd.

8. She was ten when the Kiowas came together for the last time as a living sun-dance culture.

9. They could find no buffalo; they had to hang an old hide from the sacred tree.

10. Before the dance could begin, a company of soldiers rode out from Fort Sill under orders to disperse the tribe.

11. Forbidden without cause the essential act of their faith, having seen the wild herds slaughtered and left to rot upon the ground, the Kiowas backed away forever from the tree.

12. That was July 20, 1890, at the great bend of the Washita.

13. My grandmother was there.

14. Without bitterness, and for as long as she lived, she bore a vision of deicide.

Revision Assignments   Select one of the following strategies and revise "The Way to Rainy Mountain." Include a brief statement explaining your choice and its effect on the arrangement and presentation of material.

1. Momaday writes movingly about the life of his grandmother, whose individual loss he feels acutely, but in her life he also sees the demise of the

Kiowa people. To appreciate how he has folded his grandmother's story into the Kiowa story, write a separate narrative of either Aho or the Kiowas, using only the information contained in Momaday's essay. Also, use a third-person narrator, someone writing from outside the story.

2. To appreciate how Momaday uses a first-person narrator to present the material about his grandmother and the Kiowa, revise the essay simply as the story of the narrator's return. Include no background information and no recollections. Simply record the events of his return, what he saw and did. At the same time, try to present a complete and coherent depiction of Rainy Mountain country.

Writing Assignments

1. Momaday recounts a pilgrimage to retrace the experiences of one ancestor, his grandmother. Describe such a pilgrimage you might take to retrace the wanderings of one of your parents or other relatives. Presumably, the person is in part a product of earlier travels. That person has responded to, either in acceptance or rejection of, such an environment, so an understanding of the place is essential to understanding the person. (That movement may have been across cities as well as oceans and continents. Personal odysseys are often measured more by psychological than by physical distance.)

2. Momaday says of his grandmother that she "had never forgot her birthright." What is your birthright? What privileged or otherwise cherished knowledge or understanding has it given you? Put another way, given your birthright, what do you know and appreciate that many others do not? Explain.

3. Each passing generation is a link with the past and with another way of life. With the passing of such people passes also the memory of those who were immediate witnesses and participants. Write an elegiac biography (one expressing sorrow for something lost) of a parent or grandparent (even if that person is still alive). Focus especially on that individual's participation in a lost way of life, whether in another land or this one. Write about what that person saw that no one will ever see again.

4. Compare and contrast the legends and beliefs of the Kiowas with that of the Pueblo people described in Leslie Marmon Silko's "Landscape, History, and the Pueblo Imagination." How, for example, are the two peoples similar in their attitudes toward the land and toward animals?

5. Structurally, in the way it exploits the first-person narrator, "The Way to Rainy Mountain" resembles Barry Lopez's "The Stone Horse." Compare and contrast how Momaday and Lopez use their narrators to arrange and present their material.

Fancydancer

JEAN NATHAN

Why the nondescript Northwestern city of Spokane was chosen as the site of the 1974 World's Fair is difficult to understand. The "attractions" are almost gone now, except for one that was there all along. Perhaps Expo 74's greatest legacy, or perhaps its only one, was to reveal a roaring stretch of the Spokane River by tearing down an inner-city rail yard that had obscured it from view for more than seventy years. 1

For centuries, the falls were a spiritual center for the Spokane, a nomadic American Indian tribe whose name means "children of the sun." The Spokane came here in the spring from their winter villages to camp in teepees by the riverbank, lured by the salmon that once ran from the Pacific up the Columbia River into this river. The tribe's first rite of spring was to fast and don beaded, feathered regalia for ceremonial dances to thank the Great Spirit for the salmon, their summer sustenance and their currency of sorts when they began to trade with the *suapi*, Spokane for "white man." 2

About a century ago, the *suapi*, in the form of the American government, sent the Spokane tribe upstream to a reservation sixty miles northwest of the city, in Wellpinit. After the Second World War, when the Indian war veterans came home to Wellpinit, they "modernized" their traditional dancing to reflect more of what they'd seen in the wider world. "Fancydancing" was the name they gave to the flashier, more improvisational version of their dance. 3

The Haleposey clan, pronounced roughly "Alepsie," was given a new name, too, but well before the Second World War. Russian fur traders who stopped by Wellpinit found the name indecipherable, and rechristened the clan "Alexie" in their ledgers. Almost every afternoon, Sherman Alexie, twenty-six, one of the youngest generation of the Haleposey descendants, returns to the sacred site of his ancestors, where he shoots hoops on the basketball courts of the Spokane Y.M.C.A. It's how he caps off a morning spent at his kitchen table doing his own version of "fancydancing," which is the name he has given to his writing. This writing-and-basketball routine has gone on for the past five years, and so far it has spawned three small-press books, a poetry fellowship from the National Endowment for the Arts, and, this past January, a six-figure, two-book contract for a short-story collection and a novel from Grove/Atlantic Press. "Salmontravelling," evoking the salmon's sometimes bloody fight upstream, hurling itself over falls and rocks to spawn, is a word one finds sprinkled through Alexie's writing. It is also a word that describes Alexie's own journey. Alexie's obstacles were the joint inheritance of poverty and alcoholism. His mother supported the family by working at the Wellpinit Trading Post or selling quilts she sewed during the long evenings when her husband was drinking. 4

Alexie shut out this world by devouring books. By the time he was in fifth grade, he'd read the entire Wellpinit school library, auto-repair manuals included. At twelve, he announced to his family that he was going to 5

Rearden High School, thirty-two miles down the road from the reservation. He started there in eighth grade.

Alexie isn't quite sure what drove him to join every possible club and be-   6
come the captain of the school's basketball team—called to his family's amusement, the Rearden Indians. Nonetheless, his overachieving gained him admittance to the Jesuit Gonzaga University, in Spokane. Gonzaga had a derailing effect on Alexie, who until that point had never tasted alcohol. There, he discovered its numbing effect, and, after his long struggle to get to college, it soothed his increasing terror about what could or should come next. Rescue was provided by his high-school girlfriend, who was going to Washington State University. Alexie transferred there with her after two years at Gonzaga. Although he continued to drink uncontrollably, he also began to write.

In 1989, from Washington State, he sent a few poems and short stories to   7
"Hanging Loose" magazine, a Brooklyn-based literary biannual he'd seen while he was hanging around the university's library. He was first published in this magazine in 1990, and later in a poetry-and-short-story collection, "The Business of Fancydancing," was published by the ancillary Hanging Loose Press.

Until 1992, Alexie had never been east of Missoula, Montana, but now   8
sixty readings have taken him, and his sense of guilt and wonder, all over America. "There were as many opportunities for me to fail as to succeed," he says. "I know a hundred other stories of people on my reservation who failed. I'm amazed that I've made it, and feel guilty because I've left some people behind. Why do doors keep swinging open at the right time?" he asks. The answer must be all that fancydancing.

His latest and longest jump shot has been onto the national literary scene.   9
Grove/Atlantic Monthly Press has made "The Lone Ranger and Tonto Fistfight in Heaven" its lead book for the fall. Alexie recently came to New York University's Loeb Student Center. He wore a special mugger's wallet he'd invented for the trip, and saw his first Broadway show. He met his agent and his publisher, but not for drinks: he won the struggle against drinking three years ago. When Indians succeed in the *suapi* world, Alexie says, "we can all hear our ancestors laughing in the trees."

1993

Profile "Fancydancing" introduces the reader to Sherman Alexie, who created a literary stir in the fall of 1993 with his collection of short stories, *The Lone Ranger and Tonto Fistfight in Heaven*. The article also gives an eye-opening lesson in arranging material. It might have used any of a dozen lead-ins, but the writer chose the World's Fair angle, how "the nondescript Northwestern city" of Spokane, Washington (this is a New Yorker speaking), drew attention by being chosen for the 1974 World's Fair. In clearing a site for the Fair, though, the city rediscovered the Spokane Falls, once spiritual center for the Spokane Indians and, for seventy years, a scenic vista obscured by a rail yard. From there the article moves to "the children of the sun," GI's returning from World War II to create "fancydancing," the way the Haleposey clan became "Alexie," and—in the middle of the fourth paragraph—to its subject, the man who fancydances on paper. One third of the article has elapsed before the reader encounters Sherman Alexie, but he now appears in a culturally significant context.

If the article had stuck purely to a chronological order, it would have begun with the Spokane traveling to their sacred site, then moved to their encounters with the Russian traders and their rechristening to Alexie, their exile to a reservation about a century ago, the World's Fair in 1974 (when Sherman Alexie was seven years old) and the rediscovery of the falls. Then the article would have addressed one particular Spokane Indian: his difficult early life, how poverty and parental alcoholism drove him to seek refuge in books, his high school career, his loss of direction at one college and his recovery at another, the beginnings of his writing career, and his current successes.

A more conventional opening might have begun immediately with the new literary sensation, Sherman Alexie, discussed his work, then filled in his background, from his ancestral origins, to his childhood amidst alcoholism and poverty, to his schooling and his struggles to start a literary career.

The writer integrates all of this material into a nearly seamless narrative, but one that finds its own logic and continuity, each detail leading into another. Consider, for example, the second paragraph: The Spokane Falls drew the Indians, who fished for salmon there and then gave thanks to the Great Spirit with ceremonial dances. The salmon were also a kind of currency for trade with the *suapi*, the white man. In the next paragraph we see how the Indian veterans of the Second World War returned and, influenced by *suapi* ways, modified their ancient ceremonial dances to create fancydancing. Folkways, history, geography, and biography all unite in one story—and in the formation of a unique talent.

Exercise   To appreciate how the article unfolds, find the connections between the following: Expo '74—the falls—"the children of the sun"—their rites—trading salmon to the *suapi*—fancydancing—the YMCA—Sherman's writing —"salmontravelling"—Sherman's early life—his schooling—his drinking—his writing—*The Lone Ranger and Tonto Fistfight in Heaven*—Sherman's success and guilt.

Arrangement and Presentation   Writing, John McPhee has said, is a matter of arranging and presenting information. Notice, he didn't say *collecting* information. If collection were all, census takers could write. And most readers do not want a load of material simply dumped in their laps. They want to find material arrayed in some significant and memorable and even artful fashion, a fashion that dramatizes its interest and importance. Only the few who write for captive audiences, like the compilers of encyclopedias and instructional manuals, can assume an inherited interest, and even they cannot afford to take it for granted.

The writer of "Fancydancer" could have treated Sherman Alexie as a generic story, this season's Native American writing sensation. Instead, the writer respected the particularity of Alexie's life. Alexie is not simply one more frustrated Native American trying to tell his people's story. He is a unique individual in a specific location with a precise personal and ethnic history. He is the Spokane Indian who shoots baskets and writes stories near the Falls where his ancestors once caught salmon, danced to their gods, and traded with Russians who gave his clan the current pronunciation of their name. He is the young man who had an alcoholic parent, devoured the local library, was all-everything in high school, had his own drinking problems in one university before transferring to another, and eventually discovered that he had a story to tell.

"Fancydancer" is revealing for the way that it slides from one topic to another, making connections so naturally that they seem to be inevitable. No competent writer ever said, "You can't get there from here." One way or another, by comparison or association or some other principle, almost any two details can be linked, and in a pattern of significance (as between Alexie's fancydancing, returning GI's, and ceremonies thanking the Great Spirit). As Susan Sontag has remarked, for a writer "nothing is irrelevant." How did the connections present themselves to the writer's imagination? One answer is that writers are full-time connectors; by instinct and training they are forever scouting for another link. But this writer found the materials for connection by respecting the uniqueness and particularity of her story, by setting aside canned ideas and preconceived forms and approaching Sherman Alexie as one of a kind—an improvising, fancydancing, salmon-travelling "child of the sun."

Punctuating Titles   In reprinting this article, we have preserved the typographical practices of *The New Yorker*, where it first appeared. Like newspapers and many periodicals, *The New Yorker* uses quotation marks to represent the titles of publications, books, movies, and so on. Thus, Sherman Alexei's short-story collection is "The Lone Ranger and Tonto Fistfight in Heaven," and his first work appeared in "Hanging Loose" magazine.

By convention in colleges and universities, papers written for English and other humanities courses adopt the format of the Modern Language Association. According to the MLA's guidelines, we italicize (or underline) the titles of books, long poems, magazines, newspapers, plays and musicals, films, works of art, radio and television programs, and any works published separately. We use quotation marks to enclose the titles of works not published separately but that appear in larger works: articles, essays, short stories, short poems, and book chapters, as well as for episodes of radio and television programs, songs, lectures, and speeches. By MLA rules, then, "Fancydancer" appeared in *The New Yorker*, announcing the publication of *The Lone Ranger and Tonto Fistfight in Heaven* and the forthcoming appearance of *Salmontravelling*.

Revision Assignments   Rearrange and re-present "Fancydancer" by using at least one of the following openers. The object is to include all the material from the original article but in a different order, to "get there from here."

1. For centuries the children of the sun would gather at the current site of Spokane Falls. There they would fast and don beaded regalia . . .

2. After the Second World War, Spokane Indian veterans returned home to their reservation at Wellpinit, where they modernized their traditional

ceremonial dancing to reflect more of what they had seen in the wider world. This flashier, more improvisational version of their dance they called "fancydancing" . . .

3. On almost any afternoon a dark-skinned twenty-six-year-old man shoots hoops at the Spokane YMCA. It's how he caps off a morning spent at his kitchen table doing his version of what he calls "fancydancing"—writing. Fancydancing is the name given by Spokane Indian veterans . . .

4. Until 1992 Sherman Alexie had never been east of Missoula, Montana. Today, sixty readings have taken him and his sense of guilt and wonder all over America . . .

5. "Salmontravelling" is a word sprinkled through the writing of Sherman Alexie. The word, translated from the language of the Spokane Indians, evokes the fish's sometimes bloody fight upstream, hurling itself over falls and rocks to spawn. Alexie, a Spokane Indian himself, likes the word because it describes his own journey. (*or,* For centuries his ancestors, "the children of the sun," left their winter villages to camp in teepees by the banks of the Spokane Falls. There they gathered to catch the salmon who had survived the run from the Pacific up the Columbia River into the Spokane . . .)

6. They called themselves "the children of the sun," the Spokane. For centuries they left their winter villages and in the spring camped in teepees at the river falls to which they gave their name. This was their spiritual center, where they performed their first rite of spring, fasting and donning beaded, feathered regalia for ceremonial dances to thank the Great Spirit for the salmon . . .

Writing Assignments

1. Compose a rave biography of yourself or of someone you admire, but one respecting the particularity of its subject and ignoring chronological order. Begin indirectly, after the manner of "Fancydancer," with some regional or ethnic or historical details, then introduce yourself and your current activity, then loop back and give some personal background, then say more about your current work.

2. Like Momaday's Kiowa grandmother in "The Way to Rainy Mountain," Sherman Alexie is a storyteller. And like Momaday, the author of "Fancydancer" is an adept arranger and presenter of information. Compare and contrast the structure of the two pieces, their themes and their methods.

The Seam of the Snail

CYNTHIA OZICK

In my Depression childhood, whenever I had a new dress, my cousin Sarah   1
would get suspicious. The nicer the dress was, and especially the more expensive it looked, the more suspicious she would get. Finally she would lift
the hem and check the seams. This was to see if the dress had been bought
or if my mother had sewed it. Sarah could always tell. My mother's sewing
had elegant outsides, but there was something catch-as-catch-can about the
insides. Sarah's sewing, by contrast, was as impeccably finished inside as out;
not one stray thread dangled.

My Uncle Jake built meticulous grandfather clocks out of rosewood; he   2
was a perfectionist, and sent to England for the clockworks. My mother built
serviceable radiator covers and a serviceable cabinet, with hinged doors, for
the pantry. She built a pair of bookcases for the living room. Once, after I was
grown and in a house of my own, she fixed the sewer pipe. She painted ceilings, and also landscapes; she reupholstered chairs. One summer she planted
a whole yard of tall corn. She thought herself capable of doing anything, and
did everything she imagined. But nothing was perfect. There was always
some clear flaw, never visible head-on. You had to look underneath, where
the seams were. The corn thrived, though not in rows. The stalks elbowed
one another like gossips in a dense little village.

"Miss Brrrrooobaker," my mother used to mock, rolling her Russian *r*'s,   3
whenever I crossed a *t* she had left uncrossed, or corrected a word she had
misspelled, or became impatient with a *v* that had tangled itself up with a *w*
in her speech. ("*Vvv*entriloquist," I would say. "*Vvv*entriloquist," she would
obediently repeat. And the next time it would come out "wiolinist.") Miss
Brubaker was my high school English teacher, and my mother invoked her
name as an emblem of raging finical obsession. "Miss Brrrrooobaker," my
mother's voice hoots at me down the years, as I go on casting and recasting
sentences in a tiny handwriting on monomaniacally[1] uniform paper. The
loops of my mother's handwriting—it was the Palmer method[2]—were as big
as soup bowls, spilling generous splashing ebullience. She could pull off, at
five minutes' notice, a satisfying dinner for ten concocted out of nothing
more than originality and panache. But the napkin would be folded a little
off center, and the spoon might be on the wrong side of the knife. She was an
optimist who ignored trifles; for her, God was not in the details but in the intent. And all these culinary and agricultural efflorescences were extracurricular, accomplished in the crevices and niches of a fourteen-hour business day.
When she scribbled out her family memoirs, in heaps of dog-eared notebooks, or on the backs of old bills, or in the margins of last year's calendar, I
would resist typing them; in the speed of the chase she often omitted words
like "the," "and," "will." The same flashing and bountiful hand fashioned

---

"The Seam of the Snail," from *Metaphor and Memory* by Cynthia Ozick. Copyright © 1989 by Cynthia Ozick.
Reprinted by permission of Alfred A. Knopf, Inc.

[1]Monomania—from two words meaning "one" and "madness": obsession or irrational preoccupation with one
thing. Thus, a monomaniac has only one interest.

[2]A method for teaching handwriting long dominant in American elementary schools.

and fired ceramic pots, and painted brilliant autumn views and vases of imaginary flowers and ferns, and decorated ordinary Woolworth platters with lavish enameled gardens. But bits of the painted petals would chip away.

Lavish: my mother was as lavish as nature. She woke early and saturated the hours with work and inventiveness, and read late into the night. She was all profusion, abundance, fabrication. Angry at her children, she would run after us whirling a cord of the electric iron, like a lasso or a whip; but she never caught us. When, in seventh grade, I was afraid of failing the Music Appreciation final exam because I could not tell the difference between "To a Wild Rose" and "Barcarole," she got the idea of sending me to school with a gauze sling rigged up on my writing arm, and an explanatory note that was purest fiction. But the sling kept slipping off. My mother gave advice like mad—she boiled over with so much passion for the predicaments of strangers that they turned into permanent cronies. She told intimate stories about people I never heard of.

Despite the gargantuan Palmer loops (or possibly because of them), I have always known that my mother's was a life of—intricately abashing word!—excellence; she was endlessly leafy and flowering. She wore red hats, and called herself a gypsy. In her girlhood she marched with the suffragettes and for Margaret Sanger[3] and called herself a Red. She made me laugh, she was so varied: like a tree on which lemons, pomegranates, and prickly pears absurdly all hang together. She had the comedy of prodigality.

My own way is a thousand times more confined. I am a pinched perfectionist, the ultimate fruition of Miss Brubaker; I attend to crabbed minutiae and am self-trammeled through taking pains. I am a kind of human snail, locked in and condemned by my own nature. The ancients believed that the moist track left by the snail as it crept was the snail's own essence, depleting its body little by little; the farther the snail toiled, the smaller it became, until it finally rubbed itself out. That is how perfectionists are. Say to us Excellence, and we will show you how we use up our substance and wear ourselves away, while making scarcely any progress at all. The fact that I am an exacting perfectionist in a narrow strait only, and nowhere else, is hardly to the point, since nothing matters to me so much as a comely and muscular sentence. It is my narrow strait, this snail's road; the track of the sentence I am writing now; and when I have eked out the wet substance, ink or blood, that is its mark, I will begin the next sentence. Only in treading out sentences am I perfectionist; but then there is nothing else I know how to do, or take much interest in. I miter every pair of abutting sentences as scrupulously as Uncle Jake fitted one strip of rosewood against another. My mother's worldly and bountiful hand has escaped me. The sentence I am writing is my cabin and my shell, compact, self-sufficient. It is the burnished horizon—a merciless planet where flawlessness is the single standard, where even the inmost seams, however hidden from a laxer eye, must meet perfection. Here "excellence" is not strewn casually from a tipped cornucopia, here disorder does not account for charm, here trifles rule like tyrants.

[3](1883–1966) A nurse who campaigned for birth control and who founded the organization that is now the Planned Parenthood Federation.

I measure my life in sentences pressed out, line by line, like the lustrous
ooze on the underside of a snail, the snail's secret open seam, its wound,
leaking attar.[4] My mother was too mettlesome to feel the force of a comma.
She scorned minutiae. She measured her life according to what poured from
the horn of plenty, which was her own seamless, ample, cascading, elastic,
susceptible, inexact heart. My narrower heart rides between the tiny twin
horns of the snail, dwindling as it goes.

And out of this thinnest thread, this ink-wet line of words, must rise a visionary fog, a mist, a smoke, forging cities, histories, sorrows, quagmires, en-
tanglements, lives of sinners, even the life of my furnace-hearted mother: so
much wilderness, waywardness, plenitude on the head of the precise and impeccable snail, between the horns. (Ah, if this could be!)

                                                                        1985

Profile   Ozick has written a comparison-contrast essay, but not one that
fits neatly into any existing format. There is nothing symmetrical or predictable about her comparison of herself with her mother, of a narrow perfectionist with a versatile and copious producer of flawed performances (illustrating
the expression "a Jack [or Jill] of all trades, master of none"). Notice the progression of the essay: the opening anecdote about the writer's flawed home-
made dresses and the disapproval of impeccable cousin Sarah—Uncle Jake
the meticulous clockmaker—her mother's prolific, "serviceable" work—
Miss Brubaker, the emblem of finical obsession—a more detailed celebration of her mother's flawed versatility—then a description of the writer's
pinched perfectionism. In the opener the writer wears a flawed garment; at
the conclusion she is eking out flawless sentences; in the middle flourishes
her mother, ironically inspiring her daughter by the very opposite style of
creativity. And the opposition is realized and celebrated in richly figurative
language, language that grows out of the subject, beginning with the seam of
a dress and ending with the "seam" of the snail.

It is not only through its use of figurative language that Ozick's comparison and contrast rises above the conventional. Whether both objects prove to
be equal or one is described at the expense of the other, most comparison
and contrasts arrive at some kind of conclusion, some kind of closure. In
"The Seam of the Snail," however, the contrast is left unresolved. Which is
"best"—the mother's or the daughter's way? When they conflict, which of
these two opposing human impulses should we cultivate? Or does the
question even have to be answered? The decision is left to the reader. Ozick's admiration for (and her envy of) her mother is almost overpowering,
yet we experience this admiration through the product of her "pinched
perfectionism."

Writing with Metaphors   To capture the difference between herself and
her mother, Ozick exploits figurative language and, especially, the metaphor. Metaphors, like similes, make connections, usually between unlike
things ("He *is* a workhorse on committees"—metaphor; "He works *like* a
horse on committees"—simile). One advantage of metaphors is that they

---

[4]An oil or perfume obtained from flowers.

allow us to discuss abstract issues in concrete, sensory terms. Thus, Ozick might have written, "My mother strove to be versatile and prolific." Instead, we have, "She measured her life according to what poured from the horn of plenty."

A further advantage of metaphors is that they are at once embracing and selective; they can bridge almost any two objects because they filter out all but a few relevant qualities. In "The Seam of the Snail" the first metaphor grows directly out of the subject itself. Having opened with the dressmaking anecdote, Ozick reels off a sampling of tasks accomplished by her mother, someone as comfortable painting ceilings as landscapes. But her work was always flawed, although "You had to look underneath, where the seams were." The seams are not literal seams but little, nit-picky, unessential details that one must strain to find. (In the time others might spend tidying up such inconsequentialities, Ozick's mother would be wrapping up another task.)

To defend herself and stigmatize contrasting behavior, Ozick's mother even coins a metaphor of her own: "Miss Brrrroooobaker." In the grip of the metaphor, Miss Brubaker, the high school English teacher who encouraged Ozick's tiny, neat handwriting (and presumably other meticulous habits), becomes a type, "an emblem of raging finical obsession." And then the handwriting itself becomes an emblem. Her mother's, a product of the Palmer method, is characterized by loops "as big as soup bowls, spilling generous splashy ebullience" (like the woman herself). While Ozick is "casting and recasting sentences in a tiny handwriting on monomaniacally uniform paper," her mother is scribbling out family memoirs "in heaps of dog-eared notebooks, or on the backs of old bills, or on the margins of last year's calendar." What better way to capture the difference between mother and daughter, the metaphor arising naturally out of careful observation and a familiarity with the subject?

In their most familiar and conspicuous form, metaphors appear in sentences after linking verbs: "*A* is *B*": "I am a kind of human snail"; "The sentence I am writing is my cabin and my shell." But metaphors often lurk more inconspicuously in other forms, in parts of speech like adjectives and verbs. Thus, the mother "was endlessly *leafy* and *flowering*." She woke early and "*saturated* the hours with work and inventiveness," and she "*boiled over* with . . . passion." As for the writer, she is "*treading out* sentences"; and "I *miter* every pair of abutting sentences as scrupulously as Uncle Jake fitted one strip of rosewood against another."

Compare "I tread out sentences" to "my sentences are a path that I walk." The first is more subtle, more suggestive, more economical; the second is self-conscious and laborious, the product of someone trying too hard to sound like a writer.

Transitions Between Paragraphs   Simply put, transitions are connections—usually words, phrases, or sentences—linking the parts of our writing. In other words, they are a principal source of *coherence*. Depending on how much the reader is challenged—literally—to *make* sense, transitions may be direct or indirect, explicit or implicit. That is, if we want to be direct and explicit, we may use an expression like *that is* to indicate that we are going to restate or otherwise explain what we have said or a word like *or* to signal that we are going to give an alternative, or we may repeat a word from previous sentences, or we may use a pronoun that refers to *it*. One way or another, such devices are open and visible indicators that our discussion is still on track.

On the other hand, writers occasionally make their transitions indirectly and implicitly, requiring the reader to make, or at least wait for, a connection. Both within and between paragraphs, Ozick uses both kinds of transitions. Consider how she moves from her first to her second paragraph:

> Sarah's sewing, by contrast, was as impeccably finished inside as out; not one stray thread dangled. ("by contrast" explicitly links this sentence to the previous one)
> My Uncle Jake built meticulous grandfather clocks out of rosewood . . .

The transition, a notional one, is obvious: The discussion is moving from one family perfectionist to another. But what about the connection between the second and third paragraphs?

> The corn thrived, though not in rows. The stalks elbowed one another like gossips in a dense little village.
> "Miss Brrrrooobaker," my mother used to mock, rolling her Russian *r*'s, whenever I crossed a *t* she had left uncrossed, or corrected a word she had misspelled . . .

The second paragraph ends with the mother's higgledy-piggledy rows of corn, another instance of her profuse but disorderly work. But the third paragraph begins abruptly with "Miss Brrrrooobaker." Who is she? What does she have to do with the subject? Then we learn of uncrossed *t*'s and misspelled words. Like Uncle Jake and Cousin Sarah, it turns out, Miss Brubaker is another meticulous worker. The reader is puzzled for a moment, the writer seeming to break the implicit agreement to stay on track, but puzzlement increases attentiveness and we are soon rewarded with an explanation.

Exercise   The following is Ozick's third paragraph, the sentences separated and enumerated for convenience. How directly or indirectly does each successive sentence relate to the former one? How, in other words, do the sentences *cohere*?

1. "Miss Brrrrooobaker," my mother used to mock, rolling her Russian *r*'s, whenever I crossed a *t* she had left uncrossed, or corrected a word she had misspelled, or became impatient with a *v* that had tangled itself up with a *w* in her speech.

2. ("*Vvv*entriloquist," I would say. "*Vvv*entriloquist," she would obediently repeat. And the next time it would come out "wiolinist.")

3. Miss Brubaker was my high school English teacher, and my mother invoked her name as an emblem of raging finical obsession.

4. "Miss Brrrrooobaker," my mother's voice hoots at me down the years, as I go on casting and recasting sentences in a tiny handwriting on monomaniacally uniform paper.

5. The loops of my mother's handwriting—it was the Palmer method—were as big as soup bowls, spilling generous splashy ebullience.

6. She could pull off, at five minutes' notice, a satisfying dinner for ten concocted out of nothing more than originality and panache.

7. But the napkin would be folded a little off center, and the spoon might be on the wrong side of the knife.

8. She was an optimist who ignored trifles; for her, God was not in the details but in the intent.

9. And all these culinary and agricultural efflorescences were extracurricular, accomplished in the crevices and niches of a fourteen-hour business day.

10. When she scribbled out her family memoirs, in heaps of dog-eared notebooks, or on the backs of old bills, or in the margins of last year's calendar, I would resist typing them; in the speed of the chase she often omitted words like "the," "and," "will."

11. The same flashing and bountiful hand fashioned and fired ceramic pots, and painted brilliant autumn views and vases of imaginary flowers and ferns, and decorated ordinary Woolworth platters with lavish enameled gardens.

12. But bits of painted petals would chip away.

Using Dashes and Parentheses   *Dashes* serve a variety of functions—to introduce a series; to set off interruptive material, concluding appositives, and dramatic conclusions; and (on rare occasions) to separate independent clauses. Used with restraint, dashes are dramatic and effective. Used too frequently as all-purpose punctuators (a habit formed by taking notes in class?), they soon lose their power. In keeping with her informal, familiar tone, Ozick uses the dash for a variety of purposes:

> The loops of my mother's handwriting—it was the Palmer method—were as big as soup bowls, spilling generous splashy ebullience. (to set off interruptive explanatory material)

> My mother gave advice like mad—she boiled over with so much passion for the predicaments of strangers that they turned into permanent cronies. (to link independent clause)

> Despite the gargantuan Palmer loops (or possibly because of them), I have always known that my mother's was a life of—intricately abashing word!—excellence: insofar as excellence means ripe generosity. (to set off an exclamation)

> It is the burnished horizon—a merciless planet where flawlessness is the single standard, where even the inmost seams, however hidden from a laxer eye, must meet perfection. (to introduce a concluding appositive)

Parentheses are enclosure marks always appearing in pairs (something to remember in proofreading). They usually serve to include additional or casual information that digresses from the main structure of a sentence or paragraph (it is "unessential" but relevant). In other words, the parenthesis enables a writer to relax (or perhaps extend) the normal boundaries of coherence. Parentheses, like dashes, should be used sparingly, as Ozick does.

> ... or became impatient with a *v* that had tangled itself up with a *w* in her speech. ("*Vvv*entriloquist," I would say. "*Vvv*entriloquist," she would obediently repeat. And the next time it would come out "wiolinist.") (three sentences: a pause to dramatize her attempts to coach her mother)

> Despite the gargantuan Palmer loops (or possibly because of them), I have always known that my mother's was a life of—intricately abashing word!—excellence ... (an alternative, one the writer does not wish to pursue)

> And out of this thinnest thread, this ink-wet line of words, must rise a visionary fog, a mist, a smoke, forging cities, histories, sorrows, quagmires, entanglements, lives of sinners, even the life of my furnace-hearted mother: so much wilderness, waywardness, plenitude on the head of the precise and impeccable snail, between the horns. (Ah, if this could be!) (an exclamatory conclusion)

Revision Assignment   The following is Ozick's paragraph 6 with all the more obvious metaphors and other figurative expressions italicized (excluding current "abstract" words that were once metaphors, like *confine*, originally meaning "to keep within borders"). To explore the advantages of such language, and to appreciate how difficult it is to write without it, convert all the italicized terms into their literal, abstract equivalents.

> My own way is a thousand times more confined. I am a *pinched* perfectionist, the ultimate *fruition* of Miss Brubaker. I attend to *crabbed* minutiae and am *self-trammeled through taking pains*. I am *a kind of human snail*, locked in and condemned by my own nature. The ancients believed that the moist track left by the snail as it crept was the snail's own essence, depleting its body little by little; the farther the snail toiled, the smaller it became, until it finally rubbed itself out. That is how perfectionists are. Say to us Excellence, and we will show you how we use up our substance and wear ourselves away, while scarcely making any progress at all. The fact that I am an exacting perfectionist *in a narrow strait only*, and nowhere else, is hardly to the point, since nothing matters to me so much as *a comely and muscular* sentence. It is *my narrow strait, this snail's road; the track* of the sentence I am writing now; and when I have eked out the *wet substance, ink or blood*, that is its mark, I will begin the next sentence. Only in *treading out* sentences am I a perfectionist; but then there is nothing else I know how to do, or take much interest in. I *miter* every pair of *abutting* sentences as scrupulously as Uncle Jake fitted one strip of rosewood against another. My mother's *worldly and bountiful hand* has *escaped* me. The sentence I am writing is *my cabin and my shell*, compact, self-sufficient. It is the *burnished horizon—a merciless planet where flawlessness is the single standard, where even the inmost seams, however hidden from a laxer eye, must meet perfection*. Here "excellence" *is not strewn casually from a tipped cornucopia*, here disorder does not account for charm, here trifles *rule like tyrants*.

Writing Assignments

1. Drawing upon your own experiences and observations, explore the pros and cons of being versatile and prolific versus being painstakingly

perfectionist. Is there one particular occasion or activity in which you are conspicuously one or the other? Or do you see yourself as a good balance of the two?

2. Consciously or unconsciously, we become like or unlike those around us, borrowing or avoiding traits and habits. At the very least, it is difficult to develop a perception of ourselves without using others as points of reference. Following Ozick's example (but not imitating her step by step), compare yourself to someone (or some others) in your life.

3. Ozick suggests but does not directly address a conflict, an internal one. On the one hand, she deeply admires her mother, is in awe of her energy and versatility and productivity; on the other, she confesses that she is nothing like her mother. Ozick must admit to herself that, in some vital essentials, she is almost the total opposite of the person she admires most in life. How do you see this conflict in the essay? And what resolutions do you find, if any?

The Descent of the Dog

DAVID QUAMMEN

Let's begin slowly, with a relatively safe statement: Not all dogs are bad.   1

We Americans live today amid a plague of domestic dogs, a ridiculous and   2
outrageous proliferation of the species, true, but not every one of those animals is damnable beyond redemption. Not every one has had its soul twisted
by misery and neglect, spending long days chained or fenced within a tiny
yard and taking its revenge by barking at the neighbors. Not every one is ill-
trained, intermittently hysterical, half insane from sensory deprivation. Not
every one is indulged to prowl free, defecating on other folks' lawns and reorganizing other folks' garbage, playfully snapping the necks of other folks'
cats. A few dogs, worthy beasts, help blind people to cross streets. Several reportedly perform ranch chores. Dozens of canines in the U.S. alone fulfill a
useful service as the quiet, well-behaved pets of old people and shut-ins.
The rest, unfortunately, are as we know them. But dogs are a sensitive subject; some dog owners, like some tobacco smokers and most members of the
Ku Klux Klan, tend to be passionately defensive about what they are pleased
to think of as their own rights. Consequently you find two diametrically opposed and equally extremist points of view: on the one hand, that all dogs are
irredeemably noxious and should be banished, at least from our cities and
suburbs, by enlightened legislation; and on the other hand, that some dogs
are okay, at least some of the time. My own view is a moderate one that falls
about halfway between these two.

Brothers and sisters, as the Lord is my witness: We got too many dogs.   3

A reliable estimate puts the total U.S. dog population at about sixty mil-   4
lion, and that figure has risen by ten million over the past decade. Roughly
five million are unclaimed strays held in animal shelters, awaiting adoption or
execution, but meanwhile pet dogs are still breeding away. As I write this
sentence there are six lunatic barkers within earshot (and one charming old
mongrel with sad friendly eyes, next door, who maintains a monk-like silence). That's just too many. The situation is crazy. The dogs of America
are—individually and demographically—out of control.

Of course we also have too many cats. Let no smug feliphile[1] deny that.   5
But there are a couple of important differences. First, cats are generally far
quieter and less intrusive. They just don't have the vocal equipment, the
heft, or the territorial instincts to assert themselves as conspicuously as dogs
do. Second, when a human society has too many cats, it is mainly the cats
who suffer. People drown them. Set them on fire for kicks. Hang them, in
cute little nooses. Club them to death and toss the carcasses into the trash.
Thereby achieving some sort of sorry equilibrium. It's less trouble that way,
evidently, than exercising a modicum of foresight to get the females spayed
and the males neutered. When a society has too many dogs, however, people
and dogs both suffer. The extras (aside from those strays who end up in animal shelters) are not killed, but instead are given away or sold cheaply to

[1]Feliphile—cat lover (Latin *feles*, cat; Greek *-phile*, one who loves).

persons who have no idea what a dog needs in terms of training and attention and sheer physical space, and who are not in a position to supply those things if they did know. Result: miserable, desperate dogs who share out that misery generously to the humans all around them.

It wasn't always this bad. Dogs come from a noble lineage, a lineage full of intelligence and good character—they are closely related to wolves, after all. Many paleontologists even think that domestic dogs are directly derived from a small Asian subspecies known as *Canis lupes pallipes*, the Indian wolf. But the descent of the species *Canis familiaris* (to which all domestic breeds belong) is like a parable on the subject of bad company. They began losing their dignity about 10,000 years ago, when they first cozied up to humanity—the greased chute to degradation. We adopted them, we tamed them, we began breeding them selectively to our own sick tastes and mad purposes; we gave them squashed faces and curly tails and sawed-off legs, brain damage and hip dysplasia[2] and hemophilia, permanent psychological infantilism; we generally brought out the worst in them. Among other particulars, we perfected the bark.

How did such sadomasochism ever start? Some people cherish a romantic belief that, in its earliest form, the dog-and-man association was a hunting partnership. According to this notion, our hunter-gatherer ancestors of the middle Stone Age reached an implicit understanding with certain canines to cooperate in the chase: The dogs were faster and better armed, the humans were smarter and more devious, both groups were social communicators, and the meat could be shared. But it's a fairy tale. No basis whatsoever in evidence. Reputable archaeologists guess, instead, that the dog's first role in civilization was to eat garbage.

Wild dogs were welcomed as scavengers, it seems, to the fringes of those nomad camps. The dogs cleaned up what would otherwise stink and draw flies. When a camp was moved they tagged along as walking garbage Disposalls. Tolerated, at a distance. Eventually they became familiar and permanent. Hunting and shepherding and sled-pulling and being coddled as pets all came later—not to mention their role as watchdogs.

For this last function they were outfitted with a new sort of voice. It was a voice lacking all modulation and felicity, but which carried and penetrated exceptionally well, with its sharp pulses of energy confined within an unwavering range of frequencies, its cough-like bursts of pure graceless noise—a voice offering the same musical quality as the sound of a pouting child whacking away at a cinder block with a cheap meat cleaver. The canine bark: one of mankind's first acts of genetic planning, and an enduring monument to our own fearful territoriality. Like the spear and loin cloth, it might well have been useful in its day.

But some people claim even today that their yappy little curs function as watchdogs—though it's a mystery to me why anyone would be foolish enough to rely on a warning system that delivers twenty false alarms every day. My own theory is that those "watchdog" people value their poodles and their scotties not for warning but as personal surrogates, less inhibited and more articulate than themselves, and take vicarious emotional satisfaction as

[2]Abnormal development (Greek *dys-*, abnormal, bad; *-plasia*, growth, development).

the dogs deliver that shrill and mindlessly angry message to the outside world.

Wolves generally don't bark. Wolves howl melodically. Coyotes seldom bark. They yodel and yelp. From the Congo jungle comes an ancient domestic dog breed known as the basenji that also, bless its very soul, almost never barks. Basenjis were highly valued for their discretion by the Pygmies, who used them for hunting antelopes in the Ituri forest. So quiet were these basenjis, in fact, that sometimes the human handler fitted one with a collar from which hung a gourd rattle, just so he could keep track of where the dog was. No one knows why basenjis originally fell silent, or retained the ancestral barklessness, but one very plausible reason would be that they were terrier-sized animals living among leopards, and therefore learned quickly the value of inconspicuousness. All honor to the good sense of the basenji. Unfortunately, most dog breeds did not evolve in the presence of leopards.

They evolved in the presence of humans, who are selectively deaf. It is a scientifically demonstrable fact that many people do not even hear the noise of their own dog. Generally that's because they tie the dog up in a backyard and go off to work downtown, leaving their pet to bark tirelessly at passing children and other dogs and the free-lance writer across the alley.

Why does a dog bark at all? One scientist who has spent the past twenty years studying dog behavior and origins, Michael W. Fox, says that "dogs may bark during greeting, play-soliciting, threat, defense, care-soliciting, distress, contact-seeking, or during group vocalizations. Barks may be simple or complex, e.g., growl-barks, repeated barks with howl-like endings and yelp-barks. This contextual variety indicates that the sound itself may not always convey specific information but rather attracts the attention of the receiver." In other words, they bark for every damn reason you can imagine, and sometimes for no reason, other than boredom. (And boredom is liable to be a large factor in the life of even a modestly bright animal left captive in a yard.) As far as attracting the attention of the receiver—there is no doubting the bark's effectiveness for that. I can vividly recall one occasion, for instance, when a pair of toy terriers had solicited my attention with such success that at 3 A.M. I got up, put on pants and shoes, walked down two flights of stairs, and crossed a street in order to throw three garbage cans over a fence at them. Like the dogs, I was seeking contact.

But of course fairness (and, even more so, my desire for continued matrimonial amity) requires me to note that not all breeds of domestic dog are equally loathsome. Golden retrievers seem to have a fair measure of charm and mental health. Toy poodles are at the other extreme, obviously. Malamutes and Siberian huskies are wonderfully handsome and tend to have a fine quiet poise about them, probably in direct correlation with the closeness of their relationship to the original wolf. Basenjis, as we've seen, should be a role model for all. And cocker spaniels are paragons of hysteria: According to one set of studies, cockers started barking with less provocation, and continued barking with more persistence, than all other breeds tested. Take a cocker spaniel at eleven weeks old, lock it behind chain link on a small patch of grass, and you have a barking machine unequaled throughout nature. One cocker in those studies set a record of infamy by barking 907 times in a ten-minute period. Interestingly, the same researcher also found from autopsy

11

12

13

14

data a trend among cocker spaniels for hydrocephaly.[3] All of which may or may not be consequent from mankind's having bred cockers towards a steeply angled forehead.

Why do dogs bark so much more—and so much more randomly, stupidly—than their wolfish ancestors? Michael Fox says: "The outstanding features of the domestic dog—barking—may be attributed to artificial selection." We humans are responsible. But that still leaves open the question of whether we produced this excessive barkishness by liberating a trait that was suppressed in wild canines, or by accentuating a trait that was otherwise barely present—by protecting the domestic dog from those leopards, or by choosing the mouthiest dogs of each generation as our favored breeders. And that question can't be settled in isolation from the matter, also still in doubt, of the domestic dog's direct ancestry. Fox tells us: "The origin(s) of the dog therefore still remains an enigma although one might conclude on the basis of this study that if the wolf were the sole progenitor of the dog, then dogs would howl more and bark much less than they do." 15

So maybe it wasn't the Indian wolf after all. Maybe that immediate ancestor to our domestic dogs was the jackal (with those elegantly wolf-like huskies and Malamutes reflecting some later cross-breeding back with real wolves). Maybe it was an earlier version of the Australian dingo. Maybe it was a missing link between dingo or jackal. Or possibly (and I offer this only as an hypothesis, understand) it was a cross between the hyena and the duck. 16

Hyenas have a certain dog-like majesty. The duck and the poodle have a similar sort of gait. And ducks are known to eat garbage. Furthermore, come to think of it, the quack is not so different from the bark. And don't I vaguely recall an etymological tie, in the old Anglo-Saxon, between the very words for the two animals: a common origin in the form *dok*?[4] It's just a thought. 17

Anyway, from wherever they come, here they are. Sixty million *Canis familiaris*: as many dogs, now, as we once had bison. That's a very sobering little gauge, in itself, of the degradation of America. Man's best friend, don't you know—at least so we are endlessly told. *The dog is man's best woof woof woof.* But with friends like that, says I, who needs enemies? Bah, humbug. 18

1985

Profile   Approaching his subject with humor and even a measure of self-ridicule ("Bah, humbug"), Quammen builds a controversial case against dog ownership, at least in the city. He opens ironically, masking an attack as a defense, pretending that the "badness" of dogs is generally recognized, and resorting to elevated language that seems too dignified for his subject ("a plague of domestic dogs," "a ridiculous and outrageous proliferation of the species," "damnable beyond redemption"). Such language is usually reserved for warnings about Threats to Life As We Know It, not for gripes about the barking of the dog next door. But far from undermining his credibility, suggesting a lack of perspective, this self-conscious exaggeration prepares Quammen's audience for the unthinkable. Of arguers who take

---

[3]Accumulation of liquid on the brain causing an enlargement of the skull (Greek *hydro-*, water; *-cephal*, brain).
[4]This is, of course (and unfortunately), a joke.

themselves too seriously, we are suspicious; of those who are willing to make a little fun of themselves, we are more tolerant.

Beneath the humor and exaggeration, though, and Quammen's exasperation with backyard barkers, lurks a serious argument about the abuse of animals and the need for more responsible pet ownership. Quammen plainly finds dogs annoying, believes that there are too many of them in the city, and would probably favor legislation limiting their ownership (when dogs are outlawed, only outlaws will have dogs?). But he does not blame the animals. The fault lies with too many owners ignorant of the nature and needs of their pets, and with humans in general, who have bred the dog for its bark ("its sharp pulses of energy confined within an unwavering range of frequency, its cough-like bursts of pure graceless noise").

One indication of his seriousness is the extensive information on canine ancestry, supported by citation of authorities and studies. His essay originally appeared in a commercial magazine (*Outside*), the kind of publication that avoids the scholarly paraphernalia of bibliographies and footnotes, but when he published the piece in a later collection, *The Flight of the Iguana* (1988), Quammen included an eleven-item list of "partial sources" that he had used in its preparation. Had he been writing a humor piece, enjoying the fun of baiting dog owners, so much information on canine origins would have been unwarranted, even distracting.

Persuading with Humor   Writers and speakers use humor because it entertains, encouraging the goodwill of their audiences. But it can also be too entertaining, becoming an end in itself, as in those clever commercials we remember even after we've forgotten the product. Or worse, humor can be like those monologues by late-night talk show hosts in which the day's news is reduced to a series of one-liners. This brand of humor may provide relief, something to which we all feel entitled, but it also trivializes, inviting us to scan the day's events not for information or understanding, but for joke material (Can we beat Jay or Dave to the punch line?). For this reason many writers harbor a suspicion of humor, at least when addressing serious issues. They have observed that we often use humor to deflect attention away from serious and therefore threatening issues (threatening to our peace of mind, if nothing else).

And humor carries another risk, especially when it involves irony: the risk that some people will not understand. But if some miss the point, others will grasp it all the more strongly. And in the process they are likely to be more receptive. It is flattering to get a joke we suspect others are missing, to feel that we are among the clever few addressed by the writer, to feel that we are insiders. The writer who has made us feel so good about ourselves has gone a long way toward winning our consent.

And humor enjoys yet another advantage: It allows the writer to escape conventionality and stereotypic thinking. In "The Descent of the Dog," for example, Quammen addresses a delicate subject, the family dog, for whom many harbor an almost indiscriminate approval. Dogs guard our homes, they play with our children, they are always happy to see us. For many, dogs are a closed subject, so how does a writer impel us to reevaluate the role of Fido? Quammen does it by turning our normal assumptions upside down—"Let's begin slowly, with a relatively safe statement: Not all dogs are bad." In one sentence he replaces our standard perspective, inviting us to think about dogs as universally recognized pests. He has shifted the argumentative burden to those who approve of dogs. Then, having created a rhetorical world where normal values are reversed and, by a strange logic, Quammen has become the dog's best friend, he can address his subject without the burden of standard assumptions. In such a context, an indictment of canines becomes at least thinkable.

As illustrated by Quammen and by Jonathan Swift (in "A Modest Proposal"), the best humor is serious. It disposes readers in favor of the writer and prepares them to entertain unconventional perspectives, perspectives from which creative solutions can arise. Most important, it leads writers and readers alike toward and not away from reality, toward and not away from their problems.

Sentence Variety   The standard English sentence follows a subject-verb-complement order (like this one). This order is simple and effective. It enables the writer to present information clearly and directly. It gives the reader few difficulties. It is the sentence we use most often. Used exclusively, though, without variety in structure and length, it can become predictable and monotonous (like the first five sentences of this paragraph); and, worse, it can make the writer appear simple-minded. How do writers avoid such monotony in their writing? Consider Quammen's paragraph 11:

> [1]Wolves generally don't bark. [2]Wolves howl melodically. [3]Coyotes seldom bark. [4]They yodel and yelp. [5]From the Congo jungle comes an ancient domestic dog breed known as the basenji that also, bless its very soul, almost never barks. [6]Basenjis were highly valued for their discretion by the Pygmies, who used them for hunting antelopes in the Ituri forest. [7]So quiet were these basenjis, in fact, that sometimes the human handler fitted one with a collar from which hung a gourd rattle, just so he could keep track of where the dog was. [8]No one knows why basenjis originally fell silent, or retained the ancestral barklessness, but one very plausible reason would be that they were terrier-sized animals living among leopards, and therefore learned quickly the value of inconspicuousness. [9]All honor to the good sense of the basenji. [10]Unfortunately, most dog breeds did not evolve in the presence of leopards.

Quammen's first four sentences are brief, emphatic, and structurally similar, all simple independent clauses exploiting the usual subject-verb order. Nevertheless, they alternate thematically, following a they-don't-do-this-they-do-that pattern ("Wolves generally don't bark. Wolves howl melodically"). Then sentence 5 escapes the structural rut, not only being longer but using inversion (verb before subject) and including an exclamation and a dependent clause ("From the Congo jungle comes an ancient domestic dog breed known as the basenji that also, *bless its very soul*, almost never barks"). But despite its greater length and structural differences, this sentence clearly coheres with its predecessors ("Wolves generally don't bark. . . . Coyotes seldom bark. . . . *an ancient domestic dog breed . . . that . . . never barks*"). Sentence 6 employs yet another structure, the passive voice ("Basenjis *were highly valued* for their discretion by the Pygmies . . ."), and concludes with a dependent clause ("who used them for hunting . . .").

Sentence 7 again exploits inversion, not "These basenjis were, in fact, so quiet that . . ." but "So quiet were these basenjis, in fact, that . . ." And like its immediate predecessor, this sentence also concludes with a dependent clause, but one more complex ("just so he could keep track of *where the dog was*"). Sentence 8 again changes direction, thematically and structurally. Thematically, it shifts from information to conjecture ("No one knows why basenjis originally fell silent . . ."), offering a tentative explanation for their "discretion." Perhaps because of its more complicated function, it contains two independent clauses ("No one knows . . . one very plausible reason would be that . . ."). Sentence 9 is another exclamation, an invocation to the gods ("All honor to the good sense of the basenji"). Then, signaling the end of this unit of his discussion, Quammen introduces his final sentence with an adverb, expressing his devout wish that all dogs were as silent as basenjis ("Unfortunately, most dog breeds did not evolve in the presence of leopards").

In revising our own work, then, we must be alert to the presence of too many consecutive Dick-and-Jane sentences ("Look, Dick, see Spot run. Run, Spot, run!"). Such a problem surfaces when we compose sentences one at a time instead of in relation to one another. One solution is to think of each successive sentence as an extension of the previous one, having a clear thematic or structural relationship (the term for this relationship is *continuity*). Read Quammen's eleventh paragraph one more time, focusing on the relationship of each sentence to its predecessor.

Sentence Types   One way we classify sentences is by purpose, by whether they make a statement, ask a question, or give an order. Each also expects a certain response from the reader or listener. Sentences that make statements are *declarative* (from a Latin word meaning "to make clear"), like this one, and they ask the reader to accept them as true. Far and away most sentences, as typified by Quammen's essay, are of this kind. They are punctuated with a period.

Sentences that ask questions are *interrogative* (from a Latin word meaning "to ask"), and they usually expect the reader to respond with information or at least to think about something. They are punctuated with a question mark.

How did such sadomasochism ever start?

Why does a dog bark at all?

Why do dogs bark so much more—and so much more randomly, stupidly—than their wolfish ancestors?

And sentences that give orders or make requests are *imperative* (from a Latin word meaning "to command"). Imperatives have an unstated or understood *you* as a subject and are usually punctuated with a period.

Let no smug feliphile deny that.

All honor to the good sense of the basenji.

Both interrogatives and imperatives appear much more frequently in speech, but both are useful to writers. As Quammen illustrates, for example, both provide relief from the monotony of continuous declarative sentences, which invite the reader to be a simple information-receiver. In a text, questions, even those that will be answered by the writer, ask the reader to think more actively about the subject. In a similar fashion imperatives, with *you* as a silent subject, address the reader, asking for some kind of action, if only a hypothetical one. To this extent, it lessens the distance between the writer and reader, like the indefinite *you*, which Quammen also uses freely.

Consistent with his lively colloquial tone and his humor, Quamen uses all three kinds of sentences, in addition to direct address (*"Brothers and sisters,* as the Lord is my witness: We got too many dogs"), the indefinite *you*, and intentional fragments. The result is a text that is lively and varied, encouraging the reader to be alert and involved.

Revision Assignments   Select one of the following strategies and revise "The Descent of the Dog." Include a brief statement explaining your choice and its effect on the arrangement and presentation of material.

1. Removing the sarcasm and the exaggeration, revise this complaint against dogs into a calm, rational case. (You might even argue from the standpoint of a dog lover whose chief motive is canine welfare.)

2. In building his case against dogs, Quammen presents a good deal of scientific and historical information about his subject. Without attacking or defending dogs, write a simple informational article aimed at a general audience: "What You Don't Know About Dogs."

Writing Assignments

1. Quammen assumes the role of a maverick, perversely addressing "a sensitive subject" in a manner calculated to offend many while setting others to thinking. His prime audience seems to be those who are at least latently sympathetic, those waiting for someone like Quammen to come along. Address another sensitive subject, some area where Americans (or Canadians or someone else) "tend to be passionately defensive about what they are pleased to think of as their own rights." Perhaps you think some people should not be allowed to have children, or to go to college, or to own word processors, or to talk to the opposite sex, or to pick out their own clothes. Be ironic, be irreverent, but also try to be convincing (or at least to advance a serious point).

2. Compose a dog's defense to Quammen's attack. Using your best canine logic, incorporate and respond to as much of Quammen's material as possible. Perhaps your thesis is that there are too many humans, ruining the world for dogs. Maybe you want to say that the world is going to the humans (in the old days people left garbage conveniently lying around, but now they seal it in metal garbage cans and dumpsters). And is a man truly a dog's best friend?

3. There are some revealing parallels between Swift's "A Modest Proposal" and Quammen's "The Descent of the Dog." Swift makes a "modest"

proposal that is outrageous, and Quammen opens with "a relatively safe statement" that is anything but safe. Each also plays on the multiple meanings of a word in his title (*modest*—"reasonable" and "humble," and *descent*—"ancestry" and "decline"). Compare and contrast the uses of humor and indirection in the two essays.

Landscape, History, and the Pueblo Imagination

LESLIE MARMON SILKO

From a High Arid Plateau in New Mexico

You see that after a thing is dead, it dries up. It might take weeks or years, 1
but eventually if you touch the thing, it crumbles under your fingers. It goes
back to dust. The soul of the thing has long since departed. With the plants
and wild game the soul may have already been borne back into bones and
blood or thick green stalk and leaves. Nothing is wasted. What cannot be
eaten by people or in some way used must then be left where other living
creatures may benefit. What domestic animals or wild scavengers can't eat
will be fed to the plants. The plants feed on the dust of these few remains.

The ancient Pueblo people buried the dead in vacant rooms or partially 2
collapsed rooms adjacent to the main living quarters. Sand and clay used to
construct the roof make layers many inches deep once the roof has collapsed.
The layers of sand and clay make for easy grave-digging. The vacant room
fills with the cast-off objects and debris. When a vacant room has filled deep
enough, a shallow but adequate grave can be scooped in a far corner. Archaeologists have remarked over formal burials complete with elaborate funerary
objects excavated in trash middens of abandoned rooms. But the rocks and
adobe mortar of collapsed walls were valued by the ancient people. Because
each rock had been carefully selected for size and shape, then chiseled to an
even face. Even the pink clay adobe melting with each rainstorm had to be
prayed over, then dug and carried some distance. Corn cobs and husks, the
rinds and stalks and animal bones were not regarded by the ancient people as
filth or garbage. The remains were merely resting at a midpoint in their journey back to dust. Human remains are not so different. They should rest with
the bones and rinds where they all may benefit living creatures—small rodents and insects—until their return is completed. The remains of things—
animals and plants, the clay and the stones—were treated with respect. Because for the ancient people all these things had spirit and being.

The antelope merely consents to return home with the hunter. All phases 3
of the hunt are conducted with love. The love the hunter and the people
have for the Antelope People. And the love of the antelope who agree to give
up their meat and blood so that human beings will not starve. Waste of meat
or even the thoughtless handling of bones cooked bare will offend the antelope spirits. Next year the hunters will vainly search the dry plains for antelope. Thus it is necessary to return carefully the bones and hair, and the
stalks and leaves to the earth who first created them. The spirits remain close
by. They do not leave us.

The dead become dust, and in this becoming they are once more joined 4
with the Mother. The ancient Pueblo people called the earth the Mother
Creator of all things in this world. Her sister, the Corn Mother, occasionally

merges with her because all succulent green life rises out of the depths of the earth.

Rocks and clay are part of the Mother. They emerge in various forms, but at some time before, they were smaller particles or great boulders. At a later time they may again become what they once were. Dust. 5

A rock shares this fate with us and with animals and plants as well. A rock has being or spirit, although we do not understand it. The spirit may differ from the spirit we know in animals or plants or in ourselves. In the end we all originate from the depths of the earth. Perhaps this is how all beings share in the spirit of the Creator. We do not know. 6

From the Emergence Place

Pueblo potters, the creators of petroglyphs[1] and oral narratives, never conceived of removing themselves from the earth and the sky. So long as the human consciousness remains *within* the hills, canyons, cliffs, and the plants, clouds, and sky, the term *landscape*, as it has entered the English language, is misleading. "A portion of territory the eye can comprehend in a single view" does not correctly describe the relationship between the human being and his or her surroundings. This assumes the viewer is somehow *outside* or *separate from* the territory he or she surveys. Viewers are as much a part of the landscape as the boulders they stand on. There is no high mesa edge or mountain peak where one can stand and not immediately be part of all that surrounds. Human identity is linked with all the elements of Creation through the clan: you might belong to the Sun Clan or the Lizard Clan or the Corn Clan or the Clay Clan.[*] Standing deep within the natural world, the ancient Pueblo understood the thing as it was—the squash blossom, grasshopper, or rabbit itself could never be created by the human hand. Ancient Pueblos took the modest view that the thing itself (the landscape) could not be improved upon. The ancients did not presume to tamper with what had already been created. Thus *realism*, as we now recognize it in painting and sculpture, did not catch the imaginations of Pueblo people until recently. 7

The squash blossom itself is *one thing*: itself. So the ancient Pueblo potter abstracted what she saw to be the key elements of the squash blossom—the four symmetrical petals, with four symmetrical stamens in the center. These key elements, while suggesting the squash flower, also link it with the four cardinal directions. By representing only its intrinsic form, the squash flower is released from a limited meaning or restricted identity. Even in the most sophisticated abstract form, a squash flower or a cloud or a lightning bolt became intricately connected with a complex system of relationships which the ancient Pueblo people maintained with each other, and with the populous natural world they lived within. A bolt of lightning is itself, but at the same time it may mean much more. It may be a messenger of good fortune when summer rains are needed. It may deliver death, perhaps the result of manipulations by the Gunnadeyahs, destructive necromancers. Lightning may strike 8

---

[*]Clan—*a social unit composed of families sharing common ancestors who trace their lineage back to the Emergence where their ancestors allied themselves with certain plants or animals or elements.*

[1]A carving or drawing on a rock.

down an evil-doer. Or lightning may strike a person of good will. If the person survives, lightning endows him or her with heightened powers.

Pictographs and petroglyphs of constellations or elk or antelope draw   9
their magic in part from the process wherein the focus of all prayer and concentration is upon the thing itself, which, in its turn, guides the hunter's hand. Connection with the spirit dimensions requires a figure or form which is all-inclusive. A "lifelike" rendering of an elk is too restrictive. Only the elk *is* itself. A *realistic* rendering of an elk would be only one particular elk anyway. The purpose of the hunt rituals and magic is to make contact with *all* the spirits of the Elk.

The land, the sky, and all that is within them—the landscape—includes   10
human beings. Interrelationships in the Pueblo landscape are complex and fragile. The unpredictability of the weather, the aridity and harshness of much of the terrain in the high plateau country explain in large part the relentless attention the ancient Pueblo people gave the sky and the earth around them. Survival depended upon harmony and cooperation not only among human beings, but among all things—the animate and the less animate, since rocks and mountains were known to move, to travel occasionally.

The ancient Pueblos believed the Earth and the Sky were sisters (or sister and brother in the post-Christian version). As long as good family relations are maintained, then the Sky will continue to bless her sister, the Earth,   11
with rain, and the Earth's children will continue to survive. But the old stories recall incidents in which troublesome spirits or beings threaten the earth. In one story, a malicious ka'tsina, called the Gambler, seizes the Shiwana, or Rainclouds, the Sun's beloved children.* The Shiwana are snared in magical power late one afternoon on a high mountain top. The Gambler takes the Rainclouds to his mountain stronghold where he locks them in the north room of his house. What was his idea? The Shiwana were beyond value. They brought life to all things on earth. The Gambler wanted a big stake to wager in his games of chance. But such greed, even on the part of only one being, had the effect of threatening the survival of all life on earth. Sun Youth, aided by old Grandmother Spider, outsmarts the Gambler and the rigged game, and the Rainclouds are set free. The drought ends, and once more life thrives on earth.

Through the Stories We Hear
Who We Are

All summer the people watch the west horizon, scanning the sky from south   12
to north for rain clouds. Corn must have moisture at the time the tassels form. Otherwise pollination will be incomplete, and the ears will be stunted and shriveled. An inadequate harvest may bring disaster. Stories told at Hopi, Zuni, and at Acoma and Laguna describe drought and starvation as recently as 1900. Precipitation in west-central New Mexico averages fourteen inches annually. The western pueblos are located at altitudes over 5,600 feet above sea level, where winter temperatures at night fall below freezing. Yet evidence of their presence in the high desert plateau country goes back ten

---

*Ka'tsina—*Ka'tsinas are spirit beings who roam the earth and who inhabit kachina masks worn in Pueblo ceremonial dances.*

thousand years. The ancient Pueblo people not only survived in this environment, but many years they thrived. In A.D. 1100 the people at Chaco Canyon had built cities with apartment buildings five stories high. Their sophistication as sky-watchers was surpassed only by Mayan and Inca astronomers. Yet this vast complex of knowledge and belief, amassed for thousands of years, was never recorded in writing.

Instead, the ancient Pueblo people depended upon collective memory 13
through successive generations to maintain and transmit an entire culture, a world view complete with proven strategies for survival. The oral narrative, or "story," became the medium in which the complex of Pueblo knowledge and belief was maintained. Whatever the event or the subject, the ancient people perceived the world and themselves within that world as part of an ancient continuous story composed of innumerable bundles of other stories.

The ancient Pueblo vision of the world was inclusive. The impulse was 14
to leave nothing out. Pueblo oral tradition necessarily embraced all levels of human experience. Otherwise, the collective knowledge and beliefs comprising ancient Pueblo culture would have been incomplete. Thus stories about the Creation and Emergence of human beings and animals into this World continue to be retold each year for four days and four nights during the winter solstice. The "humma-hah" stories related events from the time long ago when human beings were still able to communicate with animals and other human beings. But, beyond these two preceding categories, the Pueblo oral tradition knew no boundaries. Accounts of the appearance of the first Europeans in Pueblo country or of the tragic encounters between Pueblo people and Apache raiders were no more and no less important than stories about the biggest mule deer ever taken or adulterous couples surprised in cornfields and chicken coops. Whatever happened, the ancient people instinctively sorted events and details into a loose narrative structure. Everything became a story.

Traditionally everyone, from the youngest child to the oldest person, was 15
expected to listen and to be able to recall or tell a portion, if only a small detail, from a narrative account or story. Thus the remembering and retelling were a communal process. Even if a key figure, an elder who knew much more than others, were to die unexpectedly, the system would remain intact. Through the efforts of a great many people, the community was able to piece together valuable accounts and crucial information that might otherwise have died with an individual.

Communal storytelling was a self-correcting process in which listeners 16
were encouraged to speak up if they noted an important fact or detail omitted. The people were happy to listen to two or three different versions of the same event or the same humma-hah story. Even conflicting versions of an incident were welcomed for the entertainment they provided. Defenders of each version might joke and tease one another, but seldom were there any direct confrontations. Implicit in the Pueblo oral tradition was the awareness that loyalties, grudges, and kinship must always influence the narrator's choices as she emphasizes to listeners this is the way *she* has always heard the story told. The ancient Pueblo people sought a communal truth, not an absolute. For them this truth lived somewhere within the web of differing

versions, disputes over minor points, outright contradictions tangling with old feuds and village rivalries.

A dinner-table conversation, recalling a deer hunt forty years ago when the largest mule deer ever was taken, inevitably stimulates similar memories in listeners. But hunting stories were not merely after-dinner entertainment. These accounts contained information of critical importance about behavior and migration patterns of mule deer. Hunting stories carefully described key landmarks and locations of fresh water. Thus a deer-hunt story might also serve as a "map." Lost travelers, and lost pinon-nut gatherers, have been saved by sighting a rock formation they recognize only because they once heard a hunting story describing this rock formation. 17

The importance of cliff formations and water holes does not end with hunting stories. As offspring of the Mother Earth, the ancient Pueblo people could not conceive of themselves within a specific landscape. Location, or "place," nearly always plays a central role in the Pueblo oral narratives. Indeed, stories are most frequently recalled as people are passing by a specific geographical feature or the exact place where a story takes place. The precise date of the incident often is less important than the place or location of the happening. "Long, long ago," "a long time ago," "not too long ago," and "recently" are usually how stores are classified in terms of time. But the places where the stories occur are precisely located, and prominent geographical details recalled, even if the landscape is well-known to listeners. Often because the turning point in the narrative involved a peculiarity or special quality of a rock or tree or plant found only at that place. Thus, in the case of many of the Pueblo narratives, it is impossible to determine which came first: the incident or the geographic feature which begs to be brought alive in a story that features some unusual aspect of this location. 18

There is a giant sandstone boulder about a mile north of Old Laguna, on the road to Paguate. It is ten feet tall and twenty feet in circumference. When I was a child, and we would pass this boulder driving to Paguate village, someone usually made reference to the story about Kochininako, Yellow Woman, and the Estrucuyo, a monstrous giant who nearly ate her. The Twin Hero Brothers save Kochininako, who had been out hunting rabbits to take home to feed her mother and sisters. The Hero Brothers had heard her cries just in time. The Estrucuyo had cornered her in a cave too small to fit its monstrous head. Kochininako had already thrown to the Estrucuyo all her rabbits, as well as her moccasins and most of her clothing. Still the creature had not been satisfied. After killing the Estrucuyo with their bows and arrows, the Twin Hero Brothers slit open the Estruyuco and cut out its heart. They threw the heart as far as they could. The monster's heart landed there, beside the old trail to Paguate village, where the sandstone boulder rests now. 19

It may be argued that the existence of the boulder precipitated the creation of a story to explain it. But sandstone boulders and sandstone formations of strange shapes abound in the Laguna Pueblo area. Yet most of them do not have stories. Often the crucial element in a narrative is the terrain—some specific detail of the setting. 20

A high dark mesa rises dramatically from a grassy plain fifteen miles southeast of Laguna, in an area known as Swanee. On the grassy plain one 21 hundred and forty years ago, my great-grandmother's uncle and his brother-in-law were grazing their herd of sheep. Because visibility on the plain extends for over twenty miles, it wasn't until the two sheepherders came near the high dark mesa that the Apaches were able to stalk them. Using the mesa to obscure their approach, the raiders swept around from both ends of the mesa. My great-grandmother's relatives were killed, and the herd lost. The high dark mesa played a critical role: the mesa had compromised the safety which the openness of the plains had seemed to assure. Pueblo and Apache alike relied upon the terrain, the very earth herself, to give them protection and aid. Human activities or needs were maneuvered to fit the existing surroundings and conditions. I imagine the last afternoon of my distant ancestors as warm and sunny for late September. They might have been traveling slowly, bringing the sheep closer to Laguna in preparation for the approach of colder weather. The grass was tall and only beginning to change from green to a yellow which matched the late-afternoon sun shining off it. There might have been comfort in the warmth and the sight of the sheep fattening on good pasture which lulled my ancestors into their fatal inattention. They might have had a rifle whereas the Apaches had only bows and arrows. But there would have been four or five Apache raiders, and the surprise attack would have canceled any advantage the rifles gave them.

Survival in any landscape comes down to making the best use of all available resources. On that particular September afternoon, the raiders made better use of the Swanee terrain than my poor ancestors did. Thus the high dark mesa and the story of the two lost Laguna herders became inextricably linked. The memory of them and their story resides in part with the high black mesa. For as long as the mesa stands, people within the family and clan will be reminded of the story of that afternoon long ago. Thus the continuity and accuracy of the oral narratives are reinforced by the landscape—and the Pueblo interpretation of that landscape is *maintained*.

The Migration Story:
An Interior Journey

The Laguna Pueblo migration stories refer to specific places—mesas, springs, or cottonwood trees—not only locations which can be visited still, but also locations which lie directly on the state highway route linking Paguate village with Laguna village. In traveling this road as a child with older Laguna people I first heard a few of the stories from that much larger body of stories linked with the Emergence and Migration.* It may be coincidental that Laguna people continue to follow the same route which, according to the Migration story, the ancestors followed south from the Emergence Place. It may be that the route is merely the shortest and best route for car, horse, or foot traffic between Laguna and Paguate villages. But if the stories about boulders, springs, and hills are actually remnants from a ritual that retraces the creation and emergence of the Laguna Pueblo people as a culture,

*The Emergence—*All human beings, animals, and life which had been created emerged from the four worlds below when the earth became habitable.*
The Migration—*The Pueblo people emerged into the Fifth World, but they had already been warned they would have to travel and search before they found the place they were meant to live.*

as the people they became, then continued use of that route creates a unique relationship between the ritual-mythic world and the actual, everyday world. A journey from Paguate to Laguna down the long incline of Paguate Hill retraces the original journey from the Emergence Place, which is located slightly north of the Paguate village. Thus the landscape between Paguate and Laguna takes on a deeper significance: the landscape resonates the spiritual or mythic dimension of the Pueblo world even today.

Although each Pueblo culture designates a specific Emergence Place— usually a small natural spring edged with mossy sandstone and full of cattails and wild watercress—it is clear that they do not agree on any single location or natural spring as the one and only true Emergence Place. Each Pueblo group recounts its own stories about Creation, Emergence, and Migration, although they all believe that all human beings, with all the animals and plants, emerged at the same place and at the same time.* 24

Natural springs are crucial sources of water for all life in the desert plateau country. So the small spring near Paguate village is literally the source and continuance of life for the people in the area. The spring also functions on a spiritual level, recalling the original Emergence Place and linking the people and the spring water to all other people and to that moment when the Pueblo people became aware of themselves as they are even now. The Emergence was an emergence into a precise cultural identity. Thus the Pueblo stories about the Emergence and Migration are not to be taken as literally as the anthropologists might wish. Prominent geographical features and landmarks which are mentioned in the narratives exist for ritual purposes, not because the Laguna people actually journeyed south for hundreds of years from Chaco Canyon or Mesa Verde, as the achaeologists say, or eight miles from the site of the natural springs at Paguate to the sandstone hilltop at Laguna. 25

The eight miles, marked with boulders, mesas, springs, and river crossings, are actually a ritual circuit or path which marks the interior journey the Laguna people made: a journey of awareness and imagination in which they emerged from being within the earth and from everything in earth to the culture and people they became, differentiating themselves for the first time from all that had surrounded them, always aware that interior distances cannot be reckoned in physical miles or in calendar years. 26

The narratives linked with prominent features of the landscape between Paguate and Laguna delineate the complexities of the relationship which human beings must maintain with the surrounding natural world if they hope to survive in this place. Thus the journey was an interior process of the imagination, a growing awareness that being human is somehow different from all other life—animal, plant, and inanimate. Yet we are all from the same source: the awareness never deteriorated into Cartesian duality,[2] cutting off the human from the natural world. 27

*Creation—Tse'itsi'nako, Thought Woman, the Spider, thought about it, and everything she thought came into being. First she thought of three sisters for herself, and they helped her think of the rest of the Universe, including the Fifth World and the four worlds below. The Fifth World is the world we are living in today. There are four previous worlds below this world.

[2]Cartesian duality—from René Descartes (1596–1650), a French philosopher whose rational system separated the viewer from the thing viewed (in contrast to the Pueblo way).

The people found the opening into the Fifth World too small to allow 28
them or any of the animals to escape. They had sent a fly out through the
small hole to tell them if it was the world which the Mother Creator had
promised. It was, but there was the problem of getting out. The antelope
tried to butt the opening to enlarge it, but the antelope enlarged it only a little. It was necessary for the badger with her long claws to assist the antelope,
and at last the opening was enlarged enough so that all the people and animals were able to emerge up into the Fifth World. The human beings could
not have emerged without the aid of antelope and badger. The human beings depended upon the aid and charity of the animals. Only through inter-
dependence could the human beings survive. Families belonged to clans,
and it was by clan that the human being joined with the animal and plant
world. Life on the high arid plateau became viable when the human beings
were able to imagine themselves as sisters and landscape they found themselves in, could they *emerge*. Only at the moment the requisite balance between human and *other* was realized could the Pueblo people become a culture, a distinct group whose population and survival remained stable despite
the vicissitudes of climate and terrain.

Landscape thus has similarities with dreams. Both have the power to 29
seize terrifying feelings and deep instincts and translate them into images—
visual, aural, tactile—into the concrete where human beings may more read-
ily confront and channel the terrifying instincts or powerful emotions into
rituals and narratives which reassure the individual while reaffirming cherished values of the group. The identity of the individual as a part of the
group and the greater Whole is strengthened, and the terror of facing the
world alone is extinguished.

Even now, the people at Laguna Pueblo spend the greater portion of so- 30
cial occasions recounting recent incidents or events which have occurred in
the Laguna area. Nearly always, the discussion will precipitate the retelling
of older stories about similar incidents or other stories connected with a specific place. The stories often contain disturbing or provocative material, but
are nonetheless told in the presence of children and women. The effect of
these inter-family or inter-clan exchanges is the reassurance for each person
that she or he will never be separated or apart from the clan, no matter what
might happen. Neither the worst blunders or disasters nor the greatest financial prosperity and joy will ever be permitted to isolate anyone from the rest
of the group. In the ancient times, cohesivness was all that stood between extinction and survival, and, while the individual certainly was recognized, it
was always as an individual simultaneously bonded to family and clan by a
complex bundle of custom and ritual. You are never the first to suffer a grave
loss or profound humiliation. You are never the first, and you understand that
you will probably not be the last to commit or be victimized by a repugnant
act. Your family and clan are able to go on at length about others now passed
on, others older or more experienced than you who have suffered similar
losses.

The wide deep arroyo near the Kings Bar (located across the reservation 31
borderline) has over the years claimed many vehicles. A few years ago, when
a Viet Nam veteran's new red Volkswagen rolled backwards into the arroyo
while he was inside buying a six-pack of beer, the story of his loss joined the

lively and large collection of stories already connected with the big arroyo. I do not know whether the Viet Nam veteran was consoled when he was told the stories about the other cars claimed by the ravenous arroyo. All his savings of combat pay had gone for the red Volkswagen. But this man could not have felt any worse than the man who, some years before, had left his children and mother-in-law in his station wagon with the engine running. When he came out of the liquor store his station wagon was gone. He found it and its passengers upside down in the big arroyo. Broken bones, cuts and bruises, and a total wreck of the car. The big arroyo has a wide mouth. Its existence needs no explanation. People in the area regard the arroyo much as they might regard a living being, which has a certain character and personality. I seldom drive past that wide deep arroyo without feeling a familiarity with and even a strange affection for this arroyo. Because as treacherous as it may be, the arroyo maintains a strong connection between human beings and the earth. The arroyo demands from us the caution and attention that constitute respect. It is this sort of respect the old believers have in mind when they tell us we must respect and love the earth.

Hopi Pueblo elders have said that the austere and, to some eyes, barren plains and hills surrounding these mesa-top villages actually help to nurture the spirituality of the Hopi *way*. The Hopi elders say the Hopi people might have settled in locations far more lush where daily life would not have been so grueling. But there on the high silent sandstone mesas that overlook the sandy arid expanses stretching to all horizons, the Hopi elders say the Hopi people must "live by their prayers" if they are to survive. The Hopi way cherishes the intangible: the riches realized from interaction and interrelationships with all beings above all else. Great abundance of material things, even food, the Hopi elders believe, tend to lure human attention away from what is most valuable and important. The views of the Hopi elders are not much different from those elders in all the Pueblos. 32

The bare vastness of the Hopi landscape emphasizes the visual impact of every plant, every rock, every arroyo. Nothing is overlooked or taken for granted. Each ant, each lizard, each lark is imbued with great value simply because the creature is there, simply because the creature is alive in a place where any life at all is precious. Stand on the mesa edge at Walpai and look west over the bare distances toward the pale blue outlines of the San Francisco peaks where the ka'tsina spirits reside. So little lies between you and the sky. So little lies between you and the earth. One look and you know that simply to survive is a great triumph, that every possible resource is needed, every possible ally—even the most humble insect or reptile. You realize you will be speaking with all of them if you intend to last out the year. Thus it is that the Hopi elders are grateful to the landscape for aiding them in their quest as spiritual people. 33

1986

Profile Having grown up on the Laguna Pueblo Reservation in New Mexico, Leslie Marmon Silko writes about the Pueblo experience as an insider, but also as one who received a mainstream American education (she graduated summa cum laude from the University of New Mexico with a major in English). Familiar with both Pueblo and non-Pueblo ways, she has a frame of reference, a grounding in two cultures that define one another by contrast. Nevertheless, she does not institute a debate, does not present one way of life at the expense of another, though readers may have to resist drawing their own comparisons of the Pueblo way with contemporary American life. Instead, in a deliberate and economical fashion, she presents the Pueblo vision, respecting its consistency and beauty but also respecting her readers, most of whom are not Pueblo.

Quite fittingly, then, she positions herself between her Pueblo subjects and her non-Pueblo readers: The first word of her essay is "you." It is the *you* that hovers between the indefinite pronoun (like *one*) and the personal pronoun (you, the person I am speaking to). It is the *you* that draws the reader into the circle, blurring the separation of speaker and listener: "*You* see that after a thing is dead, it dries up. It might take weeks or years, but eventually if *you* touch the thing, it crumbles under *your* fingers." Whether you are Pueblo or Bostonian, the same thing happens.

The reader-embracing *you* all but disappears until the end of the essay. Until then, the focus is on the Pueblo people and on the narrator's own first-person experiences. In the final paragraph "you" appears more strongly than ever before:

> Stand on the mesa edge at Walpai and look west over the bare distances toward the pale blue outlines of the San Francisco peaks where the ka'tsina spirits reside. So little lies between *you* and the sky. So little lies between *you* and the earth. One look and *you* know that simply to survive is a great triumph, that every possible resource is needed, every possible ally—even the most humble insect or reptile. *You* realize *you* will be speaking with all of them if *you* intend to last out the year. Thus it is that the Hopi elders are grateful to the landscape for aiding them in their quest as a spiritual people.

"[You] Stand on the mesa edge at Walpai . . ." Silko has written earlier in the essay that the English meaning of *landscape* misleads, suggesting someone "somehow *outside* or *separate from* the territory he or she surveys. [But] Viewers are as much a part of the landscape as the boulders they stand on." And in the passage above Silko employs *you* to make the same thing true of readers, placing them inside the essay, inside the scene, sharing the Hopi vision.

Silko could have opened a debate—and perhaps her essay does make it easy for us to think about the downside of our more materialistic mainstream culture—but instead she focuses affirmatively and single-mindedly on the wholeness of the Pueblo way. It is complete and consistent and true to itself and should be seen as such, not as a thing that can be known only by what it is not. She draws the reader fully and undistractedly into the Pueblo vision in all its integrity.

Exercise The following is Silko's fourteenth paragraph, with the sentences separated and enumerated for convenience. How directly or indirectly does each successive sentence relate to the preceding one? How, in other words, does the paragraph cohere?

1. The ancient Pueblo vision of the world was inclusive.

2. The impulse was to leave nothing out.

3. Pueblo oral tradition necessarily embraced all levels of human experience.

4. Otherwise, the collective knowledge and beliefs comprising ancient Pueblo culture would have been incomplete.

5. Thus stories about the Creation and Emergence of human beings and animals into this World continue to be retold each year for four days and four nights during the winter solstice.

6. The "humma-hah" stories related events from the time long ago when human beings were still able to communicate with animals and other human beings.

7. But, beyond these two preceding categories, the Pueblo oral tradition knew no boundaries.

8. Accounts of the appearance of the first Europeans in Pueblo country or of the tragic encounters between Pueblo people and Apache raiders were no more or less important than stories about the biggest mule deer ever taken or adulterous couples surprised in cornfields and chicken coops.

9. Whatever happened, the ancient people instinctively sorted events and details into a loose narrative structure.

10. Everything became a story.

Using Fragments   A standard English sentence is a sequence of phrases that contains at least one subject and predicate in an independent clause, that is, a clause that is not a part of another structure. When we punctuate a sentence component as a sentence (with a capital letter and terminal punctuation—a period, question or quotation mark, or exclamation point), we have what English teachers are paid to identify in margins as a "frag!"—a fragment. The usual remedy is to repunctuate the item into an adjoining sentence.

In spite of disapproving English teachers, modern writers are using more and more fragments—sentence parts punctuated as separate statements. They do so for two reasons. One is that they want the "fragment" to enjoy some of the force of an independent statement, some of the emphasis that derives from existing between a capital letter and, usually, a period. They also do it in the comfortable realization that the basic unit of written composition is the paragraph. Just as a sentence is not a word list, each one to be read on its own as if it had no relationship to the others, so a paragraph is not a mere list of sentences. A paragraph is a formation of sentences, and in a formation each unit functions in relationship both to other units and to the whole. In a paragraph, then, a "fragment" is not what its name suggests— detached, isolated. It exists in a clear structural and notional relationship with surrounding sentences, one that is often closer than that between conventional sentences (many complete sentences can be extracted and make some kind of sense on their own; alone, a fragment is all but meaningless). Take one example from Silko:

The remains of things—animals and plants, the clay and the stones—were treated with respect. *Because for the ancient people all these things had spirit and being.*

She could have made her second statement grammatically "complete": "The reason was that for the ancient people all these things had spirit and being." This statement has a clear logical bearing on the previous statement, but because it is "complete"—not *structurally* dependent on another—it is in some ways less *coherent*. Furthermore, the revision gives less of a participant role to the reader. Intentional fragments draw on the reader's expectations that all the sentences in a paragraph form a coherent whole, are thematically related. When a fragment appears, the reader *makes* sense by relating it to sentences immediately preceding or following. Fragments, then, increase the reader's involvement.

Fragments are especially apt for Silko, who writes out of an oral tradition that presupposes attentive listeners, listeners with a license to break in when a fact has been left out. And if listeners can break in when a fact has been omitted, readers can supply a grammatical connection. Compare the following versions:

All phases of the hunt are conducted with love. *The love the hunter and the people have for the Antelope People. And the love of the antelope who agree to give their meat and blood so that human beings will not starve.*

All phases of the hunt are conducted with love, the love the hunter and the people have for the Antelope People, and the love of the antelope who agree to give their meat and blood so that human beings will not starve.

All phases of the hunt are conducted with the love the hunter and the people have for the Antelope People, and the love of the antelope who agree to give their meat and blood so that human beings will not starve.

The contrast between the first and second versions parallels that between the second and third: The first is more emphatic than the second, the second more emphatic than the third. The notion that hunter and victim are bound by love is a startling one. It is something not merely to remark; it is a thing to underscore, to contemplate. By using fragments, Silko achieves an emphasis unavailable from any other structural or punctuation device. Because the effect is so strong, even startling, she uses fragments in only a few cases. Such emphatic gestures soon wear out from overuse.

Revision Assignments   Select one of the following strategies and revise a section of "Landscape, History, and the Pueblo Imagination." Include a brief statement explaining your choice and its effect on the arrangement and presentation of material.

1. According to Silko, the Pueblo people use stories to carry information, but she relies primarily on exposition to present the Pueblo way. Using a story to carry information, use a first-person narrative (an *I* story) to present the contents of the third section, "Through the Stories We Hear Who We Are." To do so, you will have to add, subtract, rearrange, and substitute.

2. Silko refrains from establishing any explicit tensions or conflicts between Pueblo and non-Pueblo ways, particularly contemporary American ways. She simply presents the Pueblo way in all its beauty and consistency. Assume a more combative stance. Select one passage out of the essay (or several consecutive paragraphs, or several related paragraphs taken from different sections), then draw an explicit comparison and contrast between the Pueblo and non-Pueblo way, showing the disadvantages of the latter. In other words, how might late twentieth-century urban Americans profit from being more like the Pueblo? And how, practically, might they do it?

Writing Assignments

1. "Nothing is wasted," writes Silko of the Pueblo vision of life. "Corn cobs and husks, the rinds and stalks and animal bones were not regarded by the ancient people as garbage." Compare this attitude with our modern disposable society. How does our seeming attitude toward waste and castoffs help us understand the ancient Pueblo way? And what does our attitude about waste and disposability reveal about us?

2. Spend one day or one weekend trying to show the Pueblo respect and appreciation for other being—mineral, vegetable, animal, human ("Because for the ancient people all these things had spirit and being"). What you must use, use carefully. Waste nothing. Show no disrespect. Then write a paper on your experience, describing what you did and what you learned.

3. Silko explains that the English word *landscape* suggests an apartness, a separation of viewer and viewed, that conflicts with the Pueblo notion of the relationship between human beings and their relationship to their surroundings. Write about your (our) relationship with the urban (or rural) landscape. How would we live in our cities and suburbs if we shared the Pueblo sense of connectedness with our surroundings?

4. As Silko explains, the Pueblo people had no written language so all events were turned into stories that, in turn, everyone from the youngest to the oldest person was expected to hear and then learn, at least in part. All members of the culture, then, participated actively in preserving its record, its values, its memory. Each person was a living repository, a walking library. By contrast, in our literate culture our past and our lore are stored in books, books that are consulted by a relative few, books that are usually the work of specialists who have monopolized a small area of learning and who are often jealous of competition.

   Discuss some of the relative advantages and disadvantages of the two systems. What are some of the trade-offs we have made to have such exhaustive libraries of information and thought? What do we lose, for example, by having so much on paper and computer chips instead of in our minds and on our tongues? On the other hand, if the Pueblo people were all hearing and learning the same stories, if there was so much effort to find and preserve a communal truth, wasn't there a nearly irresistable pressure to conform to existing patterns (if a storyteller made a mistake, listeners were encouraged to speak up)? What happens when "proven strategies for survival" become obsolete? (See Jared Diamond's "What are Men Good For?") What happens to the ethic of change and innovation that contemporary American culture prizes so much?

5. One group of Pueblo people, the Hopi, believe that "Great abundance of material things, even food . . . tend to lure human attention away from what is most valuable and important." This belief is by no means unique to the Hopi; many religious and moral systems have condemned materialism. And this is not the only Pueblo value shared by other religions and cultures. Write a paper exploring similarities between the Pueblo way and the teachings of another religion or culture with which you may be familiar.

6. Reread the last paragraph of the essay. It is probably safe to say that the landscape there described is the very opposite of the one we know in the city and suburbs. Most of us inhabit a landscape that encourages us to overlook and take for granted, where life is too plentiful and varied to seem miraculous. If anything, other living beings often seem to be less allies than obstacles or competitors (for space, if for nothing else). In sum, ours is often not a landscape for which we are grateful. Write an essay in which you take a Hopi or a non-Hopi view of your landscape.

A Modest Proposal

For Preventing the Children of Poor People in Ireland, from being a Burden to
their Parents or Country; and for making them beneficial to the Public

JONATHAN SWIFT

It is a melancholy object to those who walk through this great town or travel   1
in the country, when they see the streets, the roads, and cabin doors,
crowded with beggars of the female sex, followed by three, four, or six children, all in rags and importuning every passenger for an alms. These mothers, instead of being able to work for their honest livelihood, are forced to
employ all their time in strolling to beg sustenance for their helpless infants,
who, as they grow up, either turn thieves for want of work, or leave their dear
native country to fight for the Pretender[1] in Spain, or sell themselves to the
Barbadoes.[2]

I think it is agreed by all parties that this prodigious number of children   2
in the arms, or on the backs, or at the heels of their mothers, and frequently
of their fathers, is in the present deplorable state of the kingdom a very great
additional grievance; and, therefore, whoever could find out a fair, cheap, and
easy method of making these children sound and useful members of the
commonwealth would deserve so well of the public as to have his statue set
up for a preserver of the nation.

But my intention is very far from being confined to provide only for the   3
children of professed beggars: it is of a much greater extent, and shall take in
the whole number of infants at a certain age who are born of parents, in effect as little able to support them as those who demand our charity in the
streets.

As to my own part, having turned my thoughts for many years upon this   4
important subject, and maturely weighed the several schemes of other pro-
jectors, I have always found them grossly mistaken in their computation. It is
true a child, just dropped from its dam, may be supported by her milk for a
solar year with little other nourishment; at most not above the value of two
shillings, which the mother may certainly get, or the value in scraps, by her
lawful occupation of begging; and, it is exactly at one year old that I propose
to provide for them in such a manner as, instead of being a charge upon their
parents, or the parish, or wanting food and raiment for the rest of their lives,
they shall, on the contrary, contribute to the feeding, and partly to the clothing, of many thousands.

There is likewise another great advantage in my scheme, that it will pre-   5
vent those voluntary abortions, and that horrid practice of women murdering
their bastard children, alas! too frequent among us, sacrificing the poor innocent babes, I doubt, more to avoid the expense than the shame, which would
move tears and pity in the most savage and inhuman breast.

The number of souls in Ireland being usually reckoned one million and a   6
half, of these I calculate there may be about two hundred thousand couples

---

[1] The claimant to the throne, James Stuart, whose father was deposed in the "Bloodless Revolution" of 1688.

[2] That is, as a bondservant, someone who works without wages, usually for a period of seven years.

whose wives are breeders, from which number I subtract thirty thousand couples who are able to maintain their own children (although I apprehend there cannot be so many under the present distresses of the kingdom); but this being granted, there will remain an hundred and seventy thousand breeders. I again subtract fifty thousand, for those women who miscarry or whose children die by accident or disease within the year. There only remain an hundred and twenty thousand children of poor parents annually born: the question therefore is, how this number shall be reared and provided for, which, as I have already said, under the present situation of affairs, is utterly impossible by all the methods hitherto proposed. For we can neither employ them in handicraft or agriculture; we neither build houses (I mean in the country) nor cultivate land; they can very seldom pick up a livelihood by stealing until they arrive at six years old, except where they are of towardly parts, although, I confess, they learn the rudiments much earlier, during which time they can, however, be properly looked upon only as probationers—as I have been informed by a principal gentleman in the County of Cavan, who protested to me that he never knew above one or two instances under the age of six, even in a part of the kingdom so renowned for the quickest proficiency in the art.

I am assured by our merchants that a boy or a girl before twelve years old $\quad$ 7 is no saleable commodity; and even when they come to this age, they will not yield above three pounds, or three pounds and a half crown at most, on the exchange, which cannot turn to account either to the parents or the kingdom, the charge of nutriment and rags having been at least four times that value.

I shall now therefore humbly propose my own thoughts, which I hope $\quad$ 8 will not be liable to the least objection.

I have been assured by a very knowing American of my acquaintance in $\quad$ 9 London that a young healthy child, well nursed, is at a year old a most delicious, nourishing, and wholesome food, whether stewed, roasted, baked, or boiled, and, I make no doubt, that it will equally serve in a fricassee or a ragout.

I do therefore humbly offer it to public consideration that of the hundred $\quad$ 10 and twenty thousand children already computed, twenty thousand may be reserved for breed, whereof only one fourth part to be males, which is more than we allow to sheep, black cattle, or swine; and my reason is that these children are seldom the fruits of marriage, a circumstance not much regarded by our savages; therefore, one male will be sufficient to serve four females.[3] That the remaining hundred thousand may, at a year old, be offered in sale to the persons of quality and fortune through the kingdom, always advising the mother to let them suck plentifully in the last month so as to render them plump and fat for a good table. A child will make two dishes at an entertainment for friends; and when the family dines alone, the fore or hind quarter will make a reasonable dish, and seasoned with a little pepper or salt will be very good boiled on the fourth day, especially in winter.

I have reckoned upon a medium that a child just born will weigh twelve $\quad$ 11 pounds, and in a solar year, if tolerably nursed, will increase to twenty-eight pounds.

---

[3]A rudimentary blunder for someone representing himself as an economist! If only one fourth reserved for breed are males, then one male "will be sufficient to serve" *three* females.

I grant this food will be somewhat dear, and therefore very proper for landlords who, as they have already devoured most of the parents, seem to have the best title to the children.

Infant's flesh will be in season throughout the year, but more plentiful in March, and a little before and after; for we are told by a grave author, an eminent French physician, that fish being a prolific diet, there are more children born in Roman Catholic countries about nine months after Lent, than at any other season. Therefore, reckoning a year after Lent, the markets will be more glutted than usual, because the number of Popish infants is, at least, three to one in this kingdom; and therefore it will have one other collateral advantage, by lessening the number of papists among us.

I have already computed the charge of nursing a beggar's child (in which list I reckon all cottagers, laborers, and four fifths of the farmers) to be about two shillings per annum, rags included; and I believe no gentleman would repine to give ten shillings for the carcass of a good fat child, which, as I have said, will make four dishes of excellent nutritive meat when he has only some particular friend or his own family to dine with him. Thus the squire will learn to be a good landlord and grow popular among his tenants; the mother will have eight shillings net profit and be fit for work until she produces another child.

Those who are more thrifty (as I must confess the times require) may flay the carcass, the skin of which, artificially dressed, will make admirable gloves for ladies, and summer boots for fine gentlemen.

As to our city of Dublin, shambles[4] may be appointed for this purpose in the most convenient parts of it; and butchers we may be assured will not be wanted, although I rather recommend buying the children alive and dressing them hot from the knife, as we do roasting pigs.

A very worthy person, a true lover of his country, and whose virtues I highly esteem, was lately pleased, in discoursing on this matter, to offer a refinement upon my scheme. He said that, many gentlemen of this kingdom having of late destroyed their deer, he conceived that the want of venison might be well supplied by the bodies of young lads and maidens not exceeding fourteen years of age, nor under twelve, so great a number of both sexes in every county being now ready to starve for want of work or service, and these to be disposed of by their parents, if alive, or otherwise by their nearest relations. But with due deference to so excellent a friend and so deserving a patriot, I cannot be altogether in his sentiments. For as to the males, my American acquaintance assured me from frequent experience that their flesh was generally tough and lean, like that of our school-boys, by continual exercise, and their taste disagreeable, and to fatten them would not answer the charge. Then, as to the females, it would, I think, with humble submission, be a loss to the public because they soon would become breeders themselves; and besides it is not improbable that some scrupulous people might be apt to censure such a practice (although very unjustly) as a little bordering upon cruelty, which, I confess, has always been with me the strongest objection against any project, how well soever intended.

12

13

14

15

16

17

---

[4]Butcher shops.

But in order to justify my friend, he confessed that this expedient was put [18] into his head by the famous Psalmanazar,[5] a native of the Island Formosa, who came from thence to London above twenty years ago, and in conversation told my friend that, in his country when any young person happened to be put to death, the executioner sold the carcass to persons of quality as a prime dainty; and that in his time the body of a plump girl of fifteen, who was crucified for an attempt to poison the emperor, was sold to his Imperial Majesty's prime minister of state and other great mandarins of the court, in joints from the gibbet, at four hundred crowns. Neither indeed can I deny that if the same use were made of several plump young girls in this town who, without one single groat to their fortunes, cannot stir abroad without a chair, and appear at the playhouse and assemblies in foreign fineries, which they never will pay for, the kingdom would not be the worse.

Some persons of a desponding spirit are in great concern about that vast [19] number of poor people who are aged, diseased, or maimed; and I have been desired to employ my thoughts what course may be taken to ease the nation of so grievous an encumbrance. But I am not in the least pain upon that matter because it is very well known that they are every day dying and rotting, by cold and famine and filth and vermin, as fast as can be reasonably expected. And as to the younger laborers, they are now in almost as hopeful a condition: they cannot work and consequently pine away for want of nourishment, to a degree that, if at any time they are accidentally hired to common labor, they have not strength to perform it; and thus the country, and themselves, are in a fair way of being soon delivered from the evils to come.

I have too long digressed, and therefore shall return to my subject. I think [20] the advantages by the proposal which I have made are obvious and many, as well as of the highest importance.

For, first, as I have already observed, it would greatly lessen the number [21] of papists, with whom we are yearly overrun, being the principal breeders of the nation as well as our most dangerous enemies, and who stay at home on purpose with a design to deliver the kingdom to the Pretender, hoping to take advantage by the absence of so many good Protestants, who have chosen rather to leave their country than stay at home and pay tithes against their conscience to an idolatrous Episcopal curate.[6]

Secondly, the poor tenants will have something valuable of their own [22] which, by law, may be made liable to distress and help to pay their landlord's rent, their corn and cattle being already seized and money a thing unknown.

Thirdly, whereas the maintenance of an hundred thousand children, from [23] two years old and upwards, cannot be computed at less than ten shillings apiece per annum, the nation's stock will be thereby increased fifty thousand pounds per annum, besides the profit of a new dish introduced to the tables of all gentlemen of fortune in the kingdom who have any refinement in taste;

---

[5]George Psalmanazar, an imposter who represented himself as the author of *An Historical and Geographical Description of Formosa* (London, 1704), a kind of travel book widely popular in early eighteenth-century Britain. Recognized as a fraud at the time Swift was writing his "Modest Proposal."

[6]Most of the large landowners in Ireland were Protestant (although three-quarters of the population was Roman Catholic). To escape paying taxes to the Anglican Church (the Church of England), many lived abroad, where they spent the income they extracted from Ireland.

and the money will circulate among ourselves, the goods being entirely of our own growth and manufacture.

Fourthly, the constant breeders, besides the gain of eight shillings sterling per annum, by the sale of their children, will be rid of the charge of maintaining them after the first year. 24

Fifthly, this food would likewise bring great custom to taverns, where the vintners will certainly be so prudent as to procure the best recipes for dressing it to perfection, and consequently have their houses frequented by all the fine gentlemen who justly value themselves upon their knowledge of good eating; and a skillful cook who understands how to oblige his guests will contrive to make it as expensive as they please. 25

Sixthly, this would be a great inducement to marriage, which all wise nations have either encouraged by rewards, or enforced by laws and penalties. It would increase the care and tenderness of mothers towards their children, when they were sure of a settlement for life to the poor babes provided in some sort by the public to their annual profit instead of expense. We should soon see an honest emulation among the married women which of them could bring the fattest child to the market. Men would become as fond of their wives during the time of their pregnancy as they are now of their mares in foal, their cows in calf, or sows when they are ready to farrow, nor offer to beat or kick them (as it is too frequent a practice) for fear of a miscarriage. 26

Many other advantages might be enumerated. For instance, the addition of some thousand carcasses in our exportation of barreled beef, the propagation of swine's flesh, and improvement in the art of making good bacon, so much wanted among us by the great destruction of pigs, too frequent at our tables, which are no way comparable in taste or magnificence to a well-grown fat yearling child, which, roasted whole, will make a considerable figure at a lord mayor's feast, or any other public entertainment. But this and many others I omit, being studious of brevity. 27

Supposing that one thousand families in this city would be constant customers for infant's flesh, besides others who might have it at merry meetings, particularly weddings and christenings, I compute that Dublin would take off, annually, about twenty thousand carcasses, and the rest of the kingdom (where probably they will be sold somewhat cheaper) the remaining eighty thousand. 28

I can think of no one objection that will possibly be raised against this proposal, unless it should be urged that the number of people will be thereby much lessened in the kingdom. This I freely own, and it was indeed one principal design in offering it to the world. I desire the reader will observe that I calculate my remedy for this one individual kingdom of Ireland and for no other that ever was, is, or I think ever can be upon Earth. Therefore, let no man talk to me of other expedients[7]: of taxing our absentees at five shillings a pound; of using neither clothes nor household furniture except what is of our own growth and manufacture; of utterly rejecting the materials and instruments that promote foreign luxury; of curing the expensiveness of pride, vanity, idleness, and gaming in our women; of introducing a vein of 29

---

[7]Swift's actual, non tongue-in-cheek solutions, which he had proposed in earlier nonsatiric and largely ineffectual tracts.

parsimony, prudence, and temperance; of learning to love our country, wherein we differ even from Laplanders and the inhabitants of Topinamboo; of quitting our animosities and factions, nor act any longer like the Jews,[8] who were murdering one another at the very moment their city was taken; of being a little cautious not to sell our country and consciences for nothing; of teaching landlords to have, at least, one degree of mercy towards their tenants. Lastly, of putting a spirit of honesty, industry, and skill into our shopkeepers who, if a resolution could now be taken to buy only our native goods, would immediately unite to cheat and exact upon us in the price, the measure, and the goodness, nor could ever yet be brought to make one fair proposal of just dealing, though often and earnestly invited to it.

Therefore, I repeat, let no man talk to me of these and the like expedients till he has, at least, a glimpse of hope that there will ever be some hearty and sincere attempt to put them in practice. 30

But, as to myself, having been wearied out for many years with offering vain, idle, visionary thoughts, and at length utterly despairing of success, I fortunately fell upon this proposal which, as it is wholly new, so it has something solid and real, of no expense and little trouble, full in our own power, and whereby we can incur no danger in disobliging England; for this kind of commodity will not bear exportation, the flesh being of too tender a consistence to admit to a long continuance in salt, although, perhaps, I could name a country which would be glad to eat up our whole nation without it. 31

After all, I am not so violently bent upon my own opinion as to reject any offer proposed by wise men which shall be found equally innocent, cheap, easy, and effectual. But before something of that kind shall be advanced in contradiction to my scheme, and offering a better, I desire the author, or authors, will be pleased maturely to consider two points. First, as things now stand, how they will be able to find food and raiment for a hundred thousand useless mouths and backs? And secondly, there being a round million of creatures in human figure throughout this kingdom whose whole subsistence, put into a common stock, would leave them in debt two millions of pounds sterling; adding those who are beggars by profession to the bulk of farmers, cottagers, and laborers, with their wives and children, who are beggars in effect, I desire those politicians who dislike my overture, and may perhaps be so bold to attempt an answer, that they will first ask the parents of these mortals whether they would not, at this day, think it a greater happiness to have been sold for food at a year old, in the manner I prescribe, and thereby have avoided such a perpetual scene of misfortune as they have since gone through by the oppression of landlords, the impossibility of paying rent without money or trade, the want of common sustenance, with neither house nor clothes to cover them from the inclemencies of weather, and the most inevitable prospect of entailing the like or greater miseries upon their breed forever. 32

I profess, in the sincerity of my heart, that I have not the least personal interest in endeavoring to promote this necessary work, having no other motive than the public good of my country by advancing our trade, providing for 33

---

[8]Even as Jerusalem was falling to a Roman siege in A.D. 70, factions within the city were quarreling among themselves.

infants, relieving the poor, and giving some pleasure to the rich. I have no children by which I can propose to get a single penny, the youngest being nine years old and my wife past child-bearing.

1729

Profile   First-time readers often struggle with "A Modest Proposal," initially confused by Swift's use of two voices, two personalities, one speaking from behind and through the other. The voice in the foreground is that of a fictional creation (or a *persona*), the modest proposer offering a "fair, cheap, and easy" solution to a complex and catastrophic problem: early eighteenth-century Ireland's crushing poverty. Although claiming to act in the public interest, the proposer is a self-promoting materialist driven only by greed and the demands of his own ego (thus, his favorite word seems to be *I*). In contradiction to the proposer is a second voice, that of Swift himself, appalled at the moral and economic assumptions driving national policies, appalled at the indifference of his fellow citizens.

Swift created the "modest" proposer out of exasperation. Having fruitlessly offered serious and straightforward proposals for addressing Ireland's economic dilemma, a series of reforms that the Irish themselves could enact to alleviate the effects of English oppression, he resorted to a shock tactic. If conventional argument had proved futile, then he would create a voice and a personality to embody the worst values of his day, then speak ironically through this voice. By doing so, he hoped to startle his audience, the literate middle and upper classes of Ireland, out of their apathy and into civic-minded action. Eating infants' flesh might at first seem extreme, but it was only an extension of the policies they were tolerating. In a manner of speaking, if only by neglect and indifference, his readers were already devouring the poor, and the results were no less terrible than what the proposer suggests—humans sentenced to lifetimes of misery and hopelessness.

One way to approach "A Modest Proposal," however, is to take the modest proposer at face value for a moment. What is he like? What kind of a human being is addressing the reader? There are numerous clues in his language and his method of argumentation. Take the opening sentence:

> It is a melancholy object to those who walk through this great town or travel in the country, when they see the streets, the roads, and cabin doors crowded with beggars of the female sex, followed by three, four, or six children, all in rags, and importuning every passenger for an alms.

The first thing we notice is the proposer's style, his formality and wordiness and cluttered detail ("beggars of the female sex, followed by three, four, or six children" could easily be "poor women and their children"). And what about the very phrasing of his opening sentence? Imagine a writer using the following statements to address a contemporary American problem:

> The homeless have become a familiar sight on the streets of major American cities.

> People can no longer take a walk in major American cities without being disturbed by the presence of homeless people.

The first version raises the problem of homelessness in America; the second, the inconvenience of the homeless to those using the streets. In the second sentence one class of humanity has simply become an unpleasant feature in the urban landscape—objects of resentment, pests.

Read quickly, the modest proposer's statement might seem to resemble the first version, to remark on the dimensions of Ireland's poverty. Read more carefully, though, it bears a closer resemblance to the second, a complaint about trying to take walks within sight of all those bothersome poor people (in the third paragraph he refers again to "those who demand our charity in the streets"). It asks the reader's compassion not for the poor but for those who will later be identified as "people of quality": "It is a melancholy object to those who walk through this great town or travel in the country, when they see . . ." The first sentence, then, suggests where the proposer's true sympathies lie, with his economic class, with his potential customers. And, as the saying goes, he never looks back. The tone he sets in the first sentence is the tone that prevails throughout the entire essay.

In his egotism the modest proposer seems glibly confident of his persuasive powers. From the first paragraph we can see his transparent attempts to represent self-interest as public-spiritedness, and from the first we can see him undermining his credibility, unintentionally exposing not only his greed and his inability to grasp either family or civic values but also his ineptitude. Thus, he attempts to demonstrate his sympathy by painting a tear-wrenching picture of poor mothers "forced to employ all their time strolling to beg sustenance for their helpless infants." "Helpless infants" suggests concern, but the term is overobvious: All infants are helpless (and later he will be referring to many of these "poor innocent babes" as "bastard children" and their parents as "savages").

And the use of "strolling" suggests a further inability to empathize with the poor. "To stroll" is to walk in a casual and leisurely manner, the privilege of the affluent, not the destitute. And consistent with this inappropriate use of language, the proposer later reduces poor women and their babies to livestock, the women becoming "breeders" and a newborn infant being "just dropped from its dam." Thus, we are hardly surprised that he can describe killing and eating teenagers as merely "a little bordering on cruelty."

The modest proposer discredits himself and his mentality in other ways, even as he methodically lays out the terms of his proposal. To begin with, we notice that he has no grasp of normal human priorities. According to his figures, eighty-five percent of the Irish are poverty stricken, yet "in the present deplorable state of the kingdom" this is only "a very great additional grievance." Beside what problems could such a calamity be merely another "grievance" (something to gripe about)? In fact, what is a kingdom or nation if it is not its people? And what sense of perspective can someone possess who, later in the essay, proposes serving "infant's flesh" at weddings and christenings?

The proposer further discredits himself by his circle of acquaintances. In attempting to establish his expertise, he cites personal contacts with a gentlemen from the County of Cavan who is suspiciously familiar with child criminals, a merchant who knows the market value of twelve-year-olds, and an American who can vouch for the flavor of human flesh, both of infants and of twelve-year-olds. In addition, he invokes the authority of the fraud Psalmanazar and an expert on Catholic breeding habits ("a grave author, an eminent French physician") who is in fact the comic writer Rabelais.

"A Modest Proposal," then, addresses the perennial question: Does the economy exist to feed people, or do people exist to feed the economy? The speaker represents those who take the latter view, those who view society as simply a context in which to do business, and humans in purely material terms, as mere producers and consumers, creatures devoid of emotional, intellectual, aesthetic, and spiritual needs. In such a scheme, economic utility becomes the sole measure of human worth. If humans cannot be producers and consumers, they can—by assuming the status of livestock—be products. Such a belief implicitly underwrote both national policy and private conduct, Swift implies, and such a belief leads to virtual if not literal cannibalism. We will either be one another's keepers or become predators (and, both practically and morally, Swift did not see a great difference between being predators and tolerating them).

Sequencing Information　Most of us would not break bad news the following way: "Your mother broke her best lamp when she suffered her heart attack." A sentence is a sequence of information, more precisely, an arrangement and distribution that indicates the relative importance of its contents, and the sequencing here indicates that the lamp is more important than mother. Granted, the sentence is of the *this*-happened-*then* type ("He was born on the Fourth of July"), the final position containing the central piece of news—when the event happened. But in this case the news of the heart attack overwhelms the first part of the sentence. Mother's heart attack deserves to be the central disclosure of the sentence, not a qualifier (however important) of an earlier disclosure. Mother's attack is much more than a *when* idea. In other words, the most important piece of information appears in an anticlimactic position, the location saying one thing about its importance, the content another.

We would have serious doubts about the values, perhaps even the sanity, of a person who would announce a catastrophe so casually, yet Swift's modest proposer repeatedly does something similar, typically including his most striking revelations in asides, afterthoughts, and throwaway remarks. Consider his second sentence:

> These mothers, instead of being able to work for their honest livelihood, are forced to employ all their time in strolling to beg sustenance for their helpless infants, *who, as they grow up, either turn thieves for want of work, or leave their dear native country to fight for the pretender in Spain, or sell themselves to the Barbadoes.*

Structurally, the principal news concerns the mothers: They are prevented by their children from seeking gainful employment. Then, casually, in what grammarians call a nonrestrictive or unessential modifier (a structure usually reserved for secondary or expendable news), trails an even more staggering disclosure: The children will be so desperate in adulthood that they must choose between becoming criminals, mercenary soldiers, or bond-servants.

Which is the most telling commentary on national poverty, the inability of mothers to hold jobs, or the necessity of their adult children embracing crime, war, or virtual slavery? The proposer doesn't seem to know.

Throughout "A Modest Proposal" this pattern continues, the most telling and startling information appearing in inconspicuous locations, signaling the proposer's inability to make the most basic discriminations. Consider the following comment made in passing:

> The number of souls in this kingdom being usually reckoned one million and a half, of these I calculate there may be about two hundred thousand couples whose wives are breeders, from which number I subtract thirty thousand couples who are able to maintain their own children *although I apprehend there cannot be so many, under the present distress of the kingdom* . . .

In the midst of explaining his "computations," the proposer nonchalantly questions whether even fifteen percent of Irish couples can support their children. Structurally, the placement signals that this opinion is merely a digression from the writer's more important business, but it contains one of the most staggering revelations in the entire essay: It is unlikely that even three couples in twenty can provide for their children.

The proposer makes similar use of a parenthesis later in his argument:

> I have already computed the charge of nursing a beggar's child (*in which list I reckon all cottagers, laborers, and four-fifths of the farmers*) to be about two schillings per annum, rags included; and I believe no gentleman would repine to give ten schillings for the carcass of a good fat child . . .

Again, so involved in his figuring that he cannot see the forest for the trees, or the human beings for the profits, the proposer confesses that even most of his society's employed people qualify as beggars. There is no hope even for those who can find jobs.

Such inappropriate sequencing undermines the moral authority of the proposer, the exemplar of the mentality that has worsened the misery of Ireland. For all of his claims to concerned citizenship, he is merely an opportunist, one more person seeking to prosper while his neighbors perish. But the proposer's digressions, his dispensable asides, serve a larger purpose: They allow Swift to reveal the magnitude of the problem, something perhaps not appreciated by many of his readers. To persuade his audience, he must inform them. To move them to action, he must shock them out of their apathy. And having been awakened, his readers can reconsider whether they wish—through their inaction—to empower the modest proposers of the world.

Structuring Solution Essays   Educated eighteenth-century readers would have recognized immediately "A Modest Proposal" as a textbook example of deliberative argumentation, that is, of a kind of presentation dating back to ancient Greece and Rome whose purpose was to argue a course of future action, usually in response to a public problem. According to most ancient rhetoricians, such a speech should have five major parts: introduction, narration, proof, refutation, and conclusion. In addition, some allowed for an optional sixth part, a loophole to cover exceptions—a digression.

The introduction (paragraphs 1–7) establishes the credentials of the speaker (his good sense, goodwill, and honesty), introduces the subject, and disposes the audience for the solution to follow. In "A Modest Proposal" the speaker attempts to accomplish all of this in a single stroke. By giving a tear-jerking description of the plight of Ireland, he dramatizes his compassion while establishing a need for the solution he has to offer. His next step is to brag about the additional advantages of the proposal that he is about to make (whetting his readers' appetites for his product). Then he lays out the numbers, giving the size of the population, the numerous "breeders," and the scant handful who can support themselves. And as a concluding stroke he cites authorities on the wastefulness of keeping children alive until they are twelve years old.

The purpose of the narration (paragraphs 8–16) is to set forth the facts of the situation. The proposer's narration explains the terms of the proposal, its circumstances and application. Thus, the proposer introduces the idea of a new dish ("infant's flesh"), then methodically goes about crunching the numbers and projecting profits, all the while asserting the ease with which his plan can be implemented.

In the next section (paragraphs 17–19), before getting to the main business of his argument, the proof, the proposer exercises his option to digress, which some classical rhetoricians allowed in the interests of making deliberative speeches less rigid, less mechanical. In this case the proposer offers a refinement suggested by a well-meaning friend—the consumption of twelve- to fourteen-year-olds—and then dismisses it on the basis of economic impracticality (at that age they are about to become breeders). To prepare for this proof, he next cites a historical precedent, though a false one, the alleged Formosan practice of eating the bodies of executed criminals.

In the next section (paragraphs 20–28) the proposer gets to his proof, the persuasive heart of a deliberative discourse. Here he gives six reasons his solution should be accepted: the lessening of Catholics, the production of something else that landlords will be able to seize from their tenants, the increase in national wealth (not to mention an addition to the national cuisine), the freeing of poor women from raising children over the age of one, the introduction of a popular new tavern dish, and an encouragement to marriage (contradicting his earlier proposal to have one male to every three female breeders).

Following the proof, the support of one's proposal, is the refutation (paragraphs 29–30) of anticipated objections and the demonstration of the arguer's open-mindedness, his ability to entertain and evaluate contrary opinions. In this instance, the modest proposer dismisses a series of less drastic counterproposals, all of which Swift had made earlier, on the grounds that they will never be adopted (each proposal had summoned the Irish to some kind of public-spirited behavior).

And then comes the conclusion (paragraphs 31–33), where the speaker makes a final pitch, reaffirming his credentials one more time and perhaps disclosing one final argument on behalf of the proposal. Thus, the proposer reminds his audience of the hopelessness of the situation and makes a last pitch at eliminating objections: Ask the poor if they would not rather have been put out of their misery at the age of one. In other words, the "modest" proposal is actually an act of mercy.

As a final bit of irony, the proposer disavows any hope of profiting from his scheme. After all, his own children are too old and his wife "past child-bearing."

In outlining the preferred form for a deliberative or solution speech, the Greek rhetoricians were not laying down rules but merely describing a practice that had evolved out of trial and error. Even without their example, many later speakers and writers would have arrived at a similar plan: Present the problem, propose a solution, support the solution, dispense with possible objections, then conclude with a few final supporting remarks. The structure makes as much sense as the notion that an effective persuader must first gain the audience's trust.

Revision Assignments   Select one of the following strategies and revise "A Modest Proposal." Include a brief statement explaining your choice and its effect on the arrangement and presentation of material.

1. In "A Modest Proposal" Jonathan Swift has created as his imaginary spokesman a self-impressed windbag who, among other things, imagines that he has a way with words, that he is impressing his readers with his verbal powers. The effect is heightened by the relative formality of eighteenth-century literary expression (compared to today's journalistic standard). Revise the first six paragraphs by simplifying them, by rephrasing them more directly and economically. Notice what happens to the character of the proposer.

2. In his modest proposer Swift has created a transparent fraud. Revise the first six paragraphs with a competent proposer, one not unintentionally self-indicting.

3. Swift wrote a series of non-ironic proposals setting forth serious solutions to Ireland's problems (set forth in paragraph 29). Remove the modest proposer and rewrite the opening to introduce Swift's real proposals. Your principal goal will be to reveal the magnitude of the problem.

Writing Assignments

1. Imagine that there is no persona, no Jonathan Swift standing behind the speaker in "A Modest Proposal." Forget satire, forget irony, and imagine that this proposer is a genuine person. Write a paper analyzing his personality and values.

2. Buried in Swift's essay, often relegated to throwaway remarks at the end of sentences, is a wealth of information about the state of poverty in his contemporary Ireland. Using "A Modest Proposal" as your sole source, write a paper on this subject.

3. Write your own modest proposal, using an alleged solution to define the nature of a problem. Be ironical. Enjoy creating words and arguments for an attitude you solidly dislike. (In one response to this assignment, a student proposed solving commuter gridlock in California by paving the entire state, making the point that—in the name of making it easier to get

to places—we are destroying the places where we want to go.) Remember one of Swift's clinchers: What the speaker is modestly proposing is merciful and enlightened compared to the current policies, or at least no more absurd.

4. "The more things change, the more they remain the same." Read through "A Modest Proposal" carefully, looking for attitudes and customs that are as alive today as they were in the 1720s. Then write a paper discussing these contemporary manifestations of the issues and assumptions addressed in Swift's essay.

Mother Tongue

AMY TAN

I am not a scholar of English or literature. I cannot give you much more than personal opinions on the English language and its variations in this country or others.

I am a writer. And by that definition, I am someone who has always loved language. I am fascinated by language in daily life. I spend a great deal of my time thinking about the power of language—the way it can evoke an emotion, a visual image, a complex idea, or a simple truth. Language is the tool of my trade. And I use them all—all the Englishes I grew up with.

Recently, I was made keenly aware of the different Englishes I do use. I was giving a talk to a large group of people, the same talk I had already given to half a dozen other groups. The nature of the talk was about my writing, my life, and my book, *The Joy Luck Club*. The talk was going along well enough, until I remembered one major difference that made the whole talk sound wrong. My mother was in the room. And it was perhaps the first time she had heard me give a lengthy speech—using the kind of English I have never used with her. I was saying things like, "The intersection of memory upon imagination" and "There is an aspect of my fiction that relates to thus-and-thus"—a speech filled with carefully wrought grammatical phrases, burdened, it suddenly seemed to me, with nominalized forms,[1] past perfect tenses,[2] conditional phrases,[3] all the forms of standard English that I had learned in school and through books, the forms of English I did not use at home with my mother.

Just last week, I was walking down the street with my mother, and I again found myself conscious of the English I was using, the English I do use with her. We were talking about the price of new and used furniture and I heard myself saying this: "Not waste money that way." My husband was with us as well, and he didn't notice any switch in my English. And then I realized why. It's because over the twenty years we've been together I've often used that same kind of English with him, and sometimes he even uses it with me. It has become our language of intimacy, a different sort of English that relates to family talk, the language I grew up with.

So you'll have some idea of what this family talk I heard sounds like, I'll quote what my mother said during a recent conversation which I videotaped and then transcribed. During this conversation, my mother was talking about a political gangster in Shanghai who had the same last name as her family's, Du, and how the gangster in his early years wanted to be adopted by her family, which was rich by comparison. Later, the gangster became more

---

[1]Nominalized form—one in which nouns rather than verbs carry the principal meaning, usually considered to sound more formal: *presents a transcription of* vs. *transcribes*, *make the assumption* vs. *assume*.

[2]Perfect tenses—formed with the helping verb *have* to express actions completed relative to the time of reference: "by this afternoon she *will have transcribed* all of her mother's speech" (future perfect).

[3]Conditional phrases—probably subordinate clauses of condition (stating the circumstances under which the statement of the main clause will be true: "*If I were you*, I would run, not walk, to the nearest doctor."

powerful, far richer than my mother's family, and one day showed up at my mother's wedding to pay his respects. Here's what she said in part:

"Du Yusong having business like fruit stand. Like off the street kind. He is Du like Du Zong—but not Tsung-ming Island people. The local people call putong, the river east side, he belong to that side local people. That man want to ask Du Zong father take him in like become own family. Du Zong father wasn't look down on him, but didn't take seriously, until that man big like become a mafia. Now important person, very hard to inviting him. Chinese way, came only to show respect, don't stay for dinner. Respect for making big celebration, he shows up. Mean gives lot of respect. Chinese custom. Chinese social life that way. If too important won't have to stay too long. He come to my wedding. I didn't see, I heard it. I gone to boy's side, they have YMCA dinner. Chinese age I was nineteen." 6

You should know that my mother's expressive command of English belies how much she actually understands. She reads the *Forbes* report, listens to *Wall Street Week*, converses daily with her stockbroker, reads all of Shirley MacLaine's books with ease—all kinds of things I can't begin to understand. Yet some of my friends tell me they understand 50 percent of what my mother says. Some say they understand 80 to 90 percent. Some say they understand none of it, as if she were speaking pure Chinese. But to me, my mother's English is perfectly clear, perfectly natural. It's my mother tongue. Her language, as I hear it, is vivid, direct, full of observation and imagery. That was the language that helped shape the way I saw things, expressed things, made sense of the world. 7

Lately, I've been giving more thought to the kind of English my mother speaks. Like others, I have described it to people as "broken" or "fractured" English. But I wince when I say that. It has always bothered me that I can think of no way to describe it other than "broken," as if it were damaged and needed to be fixed, as if it lacked a certain wholeness and soundness. I've heard other terms used, "limited English," for example. But they seem just as bad, as if everything is limited, including people's perceptions of the limited English speaker. 8

I know this for a fact, because when I was growing up, my mother's "limited" English limited *my* perception of her. I was ashamed of her English. I believed that her English reflected the quality of what she had to say. That is, because she expressed them imperfectly her thoughts were imperfect. And I had plenty of empirical evidence to support me: the fact that people in department stores, at banks, and at restaurants did not take her seriously, did not give her good service, pretended not to understand her, or even acted as if they did not hear her. 9

My mother has long realized the limitations of her English as well. When I was fifteen, she used to have me call people on the phone to pretend I was she. In this guise, I was forced to ask for information or even to complain and yell at people who had been rude to her. One time it was a call to her stockbroker in New York. She had cashed out her small portfolio and it just so happened we were going to go to New York the next week, our very first trip outside California. I had to get on the phone and say in an adolescent voice that was not very convincing, "This is Mrs. Tan." 10

And my mother was standing in the back whispering loudly, "Why he don't send me check, already two weeks late. So mad he lie to me, losing me money."

And then I said in perfect English, "Yes, I'm getting rather concerned. You had agreed to send the check two weeks ago, but it hasn't arrived."

Then she began to talk more loudly. "What he want, I come to New York tell him front of his boss, you cheating me?" And I was trying to calm her down, make her be quiet, while telling the stockbroker, "I can't tolerate any more excuses. If I don't receive the check immediately, I am going to have to speak to your manager when I'm in New York next week." And sure enough, the following week there we were in front of this astonished stockbroker, and I was sitting there red-faced and quiet, and my mother, the real Mrs. Tan, was shouting at his boss in her impeccable broken English.

We used a similar routine just five days ago, for a situation that was far less humorous. My mother had gone to the hospital for an appointment, to find out about a benign brain tumor a CAT scan had revealed a month ago. She said she had spoken very good English, her best English, no mistakes. Still, she said, the hospital did not apologize when they said they had lost the CAT scan and she had come for nothing. She said they did not seem to have any sympathy when she told them she was anxious to know the exact diagnosis, since her husband and son had both died of brain tumors. She said they would not give her any more information until the next time and she would have to make another appointment for that. So she said she would not leave until the doctor called her daughter. She wouldn't budge. And when the doctor finally called her daughter, me, who spoke in perfect English—lo and behold—we had assurances the CAT scan would be found, promises that a conference call on Monday would be held, and apologies for any suffering my mother had gone through for a most regrettable mistake.

I think my mother's English almost had an effect of limiting my possibilities in life as well. Sociologists and linguists probably will tell you that a person's developing language skills are more influenced by peers. But I do think that the language spoken in the family, especially in immigrant families which are more insular, plays a large role in shaping the language of the child. And I believe that it affected my results on achievement tests, IQ tests, and the SAT. While my English skills were never judged as poor, compared to math, English could not be considered my strong suit. In grade school I did moderately well, getting perhaps B's, sometimes B pluses, in English and scoring perhaps in the sixtieth or seventieth percentile on achievement tests. But those scores were not good enough to override the opinion that my true abilities lay in math and science, because in those areas I achieved A's and scored in the ninetieth percentile or higher.

This was understandable. Math is precise; there is only one correct answer. Whereas, for me at least, the answers on English tests were always a judgment call, a matter of opinion and personal experience. Those tests were constructed around items like fill-in-the-blank sentence completion, such as, "Even though Tom was _____, Mary thought he was _____." And the correct answer always seemed to be the most bland combination of thoughts, for example, "Even though Tom was shy, Mary thought he was charming," with the grammatical structure "even though" limiting the correct answer to some sort of semantic opposites, so you couldn't get answers like, "Even though Tom was foolish, Mary thought he was ridiculous." Well, according to my mother, there were very few limitations as to what Tom could have been and what Mary might have thought of him. So I never did well on tests like that.

The same was true with word analogies, pairs of words in which you were supposed to find some sort of logical, semantic relationship—for example, "*sunset* is to *nightfall* as _____ is to _____." And here you would be presented with a list of four possible pairs, one of which showed the same kind of relationship: *red* is to *stoplight, bus* is to *arrival, chills* is to *fever, yawn* is to *boring.* Well, I could never think that way. I knew what the tests were asking, but I could not block out of my mind the images already created by the first pair, "*sunset* is to *nightfall*"—and I would see a burst of colors against a darkening sky, the moon rising, the lowering of a curtain of stars. And all the other pairs of words—red, bus, stoplight, boring—just threw up a mass of confusing images, making it impossible for me to sort out something as logical as saying: "A sunset precedes nightfall" is the same as "a chill precedes a fever." The only way I would have gotten that answer right would have been to imagine an associative situation, for example, my being disobedient and staying out past sunset, catching a chill at night, which turns into feverish pneumonia as punishment, which indeed did happen to me.

I have been thinking about all this lately, about my mother's English, about achievement tests. Because lately I've been asked, as a writer, why there are not more Asian Americans represented in American literature. Why are there few Asian Americans enrolled in creative writing programs? Why do so many Chinese students go into engineering? Well, these are broad sociological questions I can't begin to answer. But I have noticed in surveys—in fact, just last week—that Asian students, as a whole, always do significantly better on math achievement tests than in English. And this makes me think that there are other Asian-American students whose English spoken in the home might also be described as "broken" or "limited." And perhaps they also have teachers who are steering them away from writing and into math and science, which is what happened to me.

Fortunately, I happen to be rebellious in nature and enjoy the challenge of disproving assumptions made about me. I became an English major my first year in college, after being enrolled as pre-med. I started writing nonfiction as a freelancer the week after I was told by my former boss that writing was my worst skill and I should hone my talents toward account management.

But it wasn't until 1985 that I finally began to write fiction. And at first I wrote using what I thought to be wittily crafted sentences, sentences that would finally prove I had mastery over the English language. Here's an example from the first draft of a story that later made its way into *The Joy Luck Club*, but without this line: "That was my mental quandary in its nascent state." A terrible line, which I can barely pronounce.

Fortunately, for reasons I won't get into today, I later decided I should envision a reader for the stories I would write. And the reader I decided upon was my mother, because these were stories about mothers. So with this reader in mind—and in fact she did read my early drafts—I began to write stories using all the Englishes I grew up with: the English I spoke to my mother, which for lack of a better term might be described as "simple"; the English she used with me, which for lack of a better term might be described as "broken"; my translation of her Chinese, which could certainly be described as "watered down"; and what I imagined to be her translation of her Chinese if she could speak in perfect English, her internal language, and for that I sought to preserve the essence, but not either an English or a Chinese structure. I wanted to capture what language ability tests can never reveal: her intent, her passion, her imagery, the rhythms of her speech and the nature of her thoughts.

Apart from what any critic had to say about my writing, I knew I had succeeded where it counted when my mother finished reading my book and gave me her verdict: "So easy to read."

22

1990

Profile   In "Mother Tongue" Amy Tan writes about an experience more commonplace than many readers might at first recognize, the experience of having several Englishes, several dialects of the language we speak. In Tan's case the experience is simply more pronounced because her Englishes extend from that taught in school to the "broken" English of her Chinese-speaking mother. But even those of us who have English as our first and perhaps only language speak several variations, using one version here, lapsing into another there, from the formal speech of school or workplace to a slangy, colloquial speech outside. Instinctively, we recognize that the language of one setting is not suitable to another, sliding in and out of our respective dialects so we can fit in.

We may also have relatives and acquaintances who speak their own distinctive versions of the language, perhaps laden with pet expressions, or non-standard phraseologies, or terms they have borrowed from songs or their reading or even originated themselves. In any event, by their language we know them. Through their words they define themselves, their distinctive passions, personalities, ways of seeing. Nowhere is their uniqueness more visible than in their words, and we can summon up vivid memories of them by repeating a favorite expression. Words, after all, are the principal way we connect with others; they are the principal currency of our relationships. We do not exchange the same language with our mother that we do with our best friend or with someone we dislike. In fact, if we ever speak "generically," it is with those we wish to keep at a distance. We do not have to be professional writers for language to be crucial in our lives. One way or another, it is the tool of all our trades.

In "Mother Tongue" Amy Tan puts her own personal stamp on a common subject for writers—the rediscovery of the familiar, of something taken for granted. After an expository opening ("I am not a scholar of English or literature"), she tells of her awakening—the public talk she had given in the presence of her mother, then follows with an anecdote about her mother, gives a deliberate transcription of her mother's speech, and concludes the first section by explaining that her mother, in spite of speaking "impeccable broken English," can understand sophisticated written English (like the rest of us, her passive knowledge of language—the words and structures she recognizes—far outstrips her active knowledge—those she uses).

In the middle section Tan concentrates on the "bad" news, on all the difficulties she has experienced with her mother's limited English, from personal misunderstandings ("my mother's 'limited' English limited *my* perception of her") to troubled business and financial and medical transactions. Tan finishes this section by tracing how she herself was seemingly victimized by her mother's English ("I think my mother's English almost had an effect on limiting my possibilities in life as well"). Early in school, Tan scored lower on language than on math tests, a discouraging beginning for someone who was to discover a vocation as a writer. At this point the reader expects to hear how Tan went on to become a writer *in spite of* her mother.

In the third section, though, Tan reverses directions. She continues to think about her mother's English, about achievement tests, and about her own resistance to being limited by stereotypic assumptions about the verbal talents of Asian-Americans, but then she discloses the ironic breakthrough that made possible her best-selling novel, *The Joy Luck Club*. After struggling with her writing, she decided to imagine a specific reader for her stories, and she chose her mother. With her mother in mind, she drew on all her Englishes, but always writing so that her mother could understand. In consequence, millions of readers could also understand, and Tan discovers for herself that what she had always regarded as a problem, her mother's limited English, had in fact been a blessing.

To summarize, Tan's essay pursues a familiar story line: the description of a problem, exploratory but misleading explanations, then a triumphant resolution. This "plot" works as well in expository essays as in detective stories.

Writing with Appositives   An *appositive* (a term meaning "placed next to") is a word or phrase renaming or redefining another word or phrase—like the parenthetical phrase in this sentence. Although most parts of speech can have appositives, they appear most frequently as nouns. Whether short or long, alone or in a series, they are convenient, structurally simple devices that allow writers to achieve both economy and elaboration. Amy Tan uses them frequently and for a variety of effects, as we can tell by comparing the originals below with the following revisions:

> I spend a great deal of my time thinking about the power of language—the way it can evoke an emotion, a visual image, a complex idea, or a simple truth.

> **I spend a great deal of my time thinking about the way language can evoke an emotion, a visual image, a complex idea, or a simple truth.**

The revision lists the powers of language, immediately, without any fanfare or any attempt to make the reader more curious, more attentive. Tan, however, uses suspense to enhance emphasis, beginning with an umbrella term ("powers of language"), then a dash to announce the arrival of an illustration or definition, in this case several: Language has the power to evoke emotions, visual images, complex ideas, and simple truths. The pairing also teaches another important lesson: Shorter is not always better. Sometimes the extra words more than pay their freight.

The next example follows some of the same logic but with several differences:

> And I had plenty of empirical evidence to support me: the fact that people in department stores, at banks, and at restaurants did not take her seriously, did not give her good service, pretended not to understand her, or even acted as if they did not hear her.

> **"And to support me I had the fact that people in department stores, at banks, and at restaurants did not give her good service, pretended not to understand her, or even acted as if they did not hear her."**

Again Tan begins with a broad term that she will define by being more concrete, "plenty of empirical evidence." And what is this evidence? "The fact that . . ." In this case, though, Tan opens with an appositive, one that she in turn illustrates with an appositive series. She has evidence. The evidence is "that people in department stores, at banks, and at restaurants did not take her [mother] seriously." And how did they not take her seriously? To answer, Tan follows with a series of verb phrases acting as appositives. They "did not give her good service, pretended not to understand her, or even acted as if they did not hear her." By contrast, the revision drops the first umbrella term ("empirical evidence"), weakening the climactic effect of accumulating appositives.

In the next example Tan uses an appositive to create emphasis, adding an important afterthought:

> I was giving a talk to a large group of people, the same talk I had given to half a dozen other groups.

> **I was giving a large group of people a talk I had already given a half dozen times.**

In Tan's version the additional modification breaks the message into two parts: she was giving a talk, a talk she had already given. The revision has one message: She was giving a talk that she had given before. By repeating and modifying "talk," Tan sends a stronger signal that the circumstances of this talk will be different from the others (otherwise, why call so much attention to them?). By postponing a vital piece of information until the climactic final position, she can emphasize that she had given the talk before without being embarrassed or self-conscious. Why? Because her mother had not been present. The revised version, without any appositive, sends the same message, but much more faintly.

In the next example Tan again creates a momentary tension by withholding her principal piece of news:

> I have been thinking about all this lately, about my mother's English, about achievement tests.

> **I have been thinking about all this lately, my mother's English and achievement tests.**

> **I have been thinking lately about my mother's English and achievement tests.**

This time she arouses momentary curiosity by being deliberately vague. She has been thinking lately "about all this." "This" is a coherence device in the best sense of the term: It points in both directions—back to what she has been discussing and forward to what is to come. She has been thinking "about all this, about [her] mother's English, about achievement exams." And the emphasis created by waiting is enhanced by the repetition of "about." The second revision leaves the original barren of any emphasis.

Throughout the essay Tan refers to "the Englishes [she] grew up with." After first viewing them as sources of confusion, as reasons she had done poorly on language achievement tests, she has the triumphant realization that she can use all of them to write her novel. Appropriately, the longest sentence in her essay enumerates these Englishes in an appositive series:

> So with this reader in mind—and in fact she did read my early drafts—I began to write stories using all the Englishes I grew up with: the English I spoke to my mother, which for lack of a better term might be described as "simple"; the English she used with me, which for lack of a better term might be described as "broken"; my translation of her Chinese, which could certainly be described as "watered down"; and what I imagined to be her translation of her Chinese if she could speak in perfect English, her internal language, and for that I sought to preserve the essence, neither an English nor a Chinese structure.

And in the next sentence she uses yet another appositive series to justify her uses of so many Englishes:

> I wanted to capture what language ability tests can never reveal: her intent, her passion, her imagery, the rhythms of her speech and the nature of her thoughts.

> **I wanted to capture her intent, her passion, her imagery, the rhythms of her speech and the nature of her thoughts.**

> **I wanted to capture her intent, her passion, her imagery, the rhythms of her speech and the nature of her thoughts—what language ability tests can never reveal.**

She wanted to capture "what language ability tests can never reveal." Most readers will sense a heightened curiosity to know what this is, what such tests can't reveal. Then, in the climactic final position, Tan tells us: "her intent, her imagery, the rhythms of her speech and the nature of her thoughts." Her immediate alternative was to reverse the order, putting the list before the umbrella term ("what language ability tests can never reveal"), as the second revision demonstrates. This version reads more like a criticism of language tests than a celebration of the qualities of her mother revealed by the different Englishes.

There is much more we can do with appositives, then, than say "My son the doctor will be late for dinner."

Revision Assignments　Select one of the following strategies and revise "Mother Tongue." Include a brief statement explaining our choice of strategy and its effect on the arrangement and presentation of material.

1. In paragraph 6 Amy Tan transcribes her mother's speech, her "broken" English. Translate her speech into standard English, and then compare. What does the translation reveal of "her intent, her passion, her imagery, the rhythms of her speech and the nature of her thoughts"?

2. Revise the opening of "Mother Tongue," beginning narratively with the event that raised Tan's consciousness of her different Englishes. For the new opening to be effective, what must you add, subtract, rearrange, and substitute? Rewrite at least the first six paragraphs.

Writing Assignments

1. Write about the Englishes that you have grown up with. In case you think you have grown up with only one, answer this: Do you use the same language with your teachers that you do with your parents, your friends, your coworkers? What do you feel you can express in one English that you cannot in another? Does your family have its own special talk? Do you have a special language of intimacy or formality? How do you speak when you wish to signal goodwill or respect? Have you mastered a professional or technical language at school or at work?

2. As a writer Amy Tan admits, "I spend a great deal of my time thinking about the power of language—the way it can evoke an emotion, a visual image, a complex idea, or a simple truth." Drawing upon your own experience, write about a difficulty that was created by the wrong words or resolved by the right ones. Explain the circumstances, describe the conflict, then present a resolution (whether an immediate practical remedy or a subsequent increase in your understanding).

3. Write about a family member or acquaintance who speaks a distinctive brand of English, that is, someone who has placed his or her personal stamp on the language. If this distinctiveness includes delivery, describe that, too. Then discuss its assets and liabilities.

4. Amy Tan suggests that she ultimately became a writer *because of*, not *in spite of*, growing up in a household with "broken" English. In other words, she came to appreciate that growing up in a "second language" home has its advantages. Being exposed to greater variations in language, she became more sensitized to the power of words, to the choices and nuances available. If you have grown up in such a home (with different Englishes or with another language entirely), discuss the effects it has had on your grasp and appreciation of language.

5. "And I use them all—all the Englishes I grew up with," says Amy Tan. In your own writing, especially for school, what Englishes do you use? Are you comfortable writing in "schoolese"? Do you ever feel you are limiting yourself by being restricted to "formal edited English"? Do you ever pepper your writing with words and phrases from your everyday speech, or wish you could?

The Tucson Zoo

LEWIS THOMAS

Science gets most of its information by the process of reductionism, explor- 1
ing the details, then the details of the details, until all the smallest bits of the
structure, or the smallest parts of the mechanism, are laid out for counting
and scrutiny. Only when this is done can the investigation be extended to
encompass the whole organism or the entire system. So we say.

Sometimes it seems that we take a loss, working this way. Much of to- 2
day's public anxiety about science is the apprehension that we may forever
be overlooking the whole by an endless, obsessive preoccupation with the
parts. I had a brief, personal experience of this misgiving one afternoon in
Tucson, where I had time on my hands and visited the zoo, just outside the
city. The designers there have cut a deep pathway between two small artificial ponds, walled by clear glass, so when you stand in the center of the path
you can look into the depths of each pool, and at the same time you can regard the surface. In one pool, on the right side of the path, is a family of otters; on the other side, a family of beavers. Within just a few feet from your
face, on either side, beavers and otters are at play, underwater and on the surface, swimming toward your face and then away, more filled with life than
any creatures I have ever seen before, in all my days. Except for the glass,
you could reach across and touch them.

I was transfixed. As I now recall it, there was only one sensation in my 3
head: pure elation mixed with amazement at such perfection. Swept off my
feet, I floated from one side to the other, swiveling my brain, staring as-
tounded at the beavers, then at the otters. I could hear shouts across my cor-
pus callosum,[1] from one hemisphere to the other. I remember thinking, with
what was left in charge of my consciousness, that I wanted no part of the science of beavers and otters; I wanted never to know how they performed their
marvels; I wished for no news about the physiology of their breathing, the co-
ordination of their muscles, their vision, their endocrine systems, their diges-
tive tracts. I hoped never to have to think of them as collections of cells. All I
asked for was the full hairy complexity, then in front of my eyes, of whole,
intact beavers and otters in motion.

It lasted, I regret to say, for only a few minutes, and then I was back in 4
the late twentieth century, reductionist as ever, wondering about the details
by force of habit, but not, this time, the details of otters and beavers. Instead,
me. Something worth remembering had happened in my mind. I was certain
of that; I would have put it somewhere in the brain stem; maybe this was my
limbic system[2] at work. I became a behavioral scientist, an experimental psy-
chologist, an ethnologist, and in the instant I lost all the wonder and the
sense of being overwhelmed. I was flattened.

---

[1]The bridge of nervous tissue connecting the left and right hemispheres of the human brain, allowing communication between the two.

[2]A system of deep brain structures common to mammals and involved in the power of scent as well as emotion, motivation, behavior, and certain autonomic functions (see note 5).

But I came away from the zoo with something, a piece of news about my- 5
self: I am coded, somehow, for otters and beavers. I exhibit instinctive behavior in their presence, when they are displayed close at hand behind glass,
simultaneously below water and at the surface. I have receptors for this display. Beavers and otters possess a "releaser" for me, in the terminology of
ethology,[3] and the releasing was my experience. What was released? Behavior. What behavior? Standing, swiveling flabbergasted, feeling exultation and
a rush of friendship. I could not, as the result of the transaction, tell you anything more about beavers and otters than you already know. I learned nothing new about them. Only about me, and I suspect also about you, maybe
about human beings at large: we are endowed with genes which code out our
reaction to beavers and otters, maybe our reaction to each other as well. We
are stamped with stereotyped, unalterable patterns of response, ready to be
released. And the behavior released in us, by such confrontations, is, essentially, a surprised affection. It is compulsory behavior and we can avoid it
only by straining with the full power of our conscious minds, making up conscious excuses all the way. Left to ourselves, mechanistic[4] and autonomic,[5]
we hanker for friends.

Everyone says, stay away from ants. They have no lessons for us; they are 6
crazy little instruments, inhuman, capable of controlling themselves, lacking
manners, lacking souls. When they are massed together, all touching, exchanging bits of information held in their jaws like memoranda, they become
a single animal. Look out for that. It is debasement, a loss of individuality, a
violation of human nature, an unnatural act.

Sometimes people argue this point of view seriously and with deep 7
thought. Be individuals, solitary and selfish, is the message. Altruism, a jargon word for what used to be called love, is worse than weakness, it is a sin, a
violation of nature. Be separate. Do not be a social animal. But this is a hard
argument to make convincingly when you have to depend on language to
make it. You have to print up leaflets or publish books and get them bought
and sent around, you have to turn up on television and catch the attention of
millions of other human beings all at once, and then you have to say to all of
them, all at once, all collected and paying attention: be solitary; do not depend on each other. You can't do this and keep a straight face.

Maybe altruism is our most primitive attribute, out of reach, beyond our 8
control. Or perhaps it is immediately at hand, waiting to be released, dis-
guised now, in our kind of civilization, as affection or friendship or attach-
ment. I don't see why it should be unreasonable for all human beings to have
strands of DNA coiled up in chromosomes, coding out instincts for usefulness and helpfulness. Usefulness may turn out to be the hardest test of fit-
ness for survival, more important than aggression, more effective, in the long
run, than grabbiness. If this is the sort of information biological science holds
for the future, applying to us as well as to ants, then I am all for science.

---

[3]The scientific study of animal behavior, especially in a natural environment, so a "releaser" would be something that stimulates an involuntary response.

[4]Mechanistic—behavior as determined by physical and biological causes.

[5]Autonomic—the autonomic nervous system automatically controls the motor functions of the heart, lungs, intestines, glands, and other internal organs.

One thing I'd like to know most of all: When those ants have made the 9
Hill, and are all there, touching and exchanging, and the whole mass begins
to behave like a single huge creature, and *thinks*, what on earth is that
thought? And while you're at it, I'd like to know a second thing: When it
happens, does any single ant know about it? Does his hair stand on end?

1974

Profile   Lewis Thomas (1913–1993) was a physician and scientist who
gained fame with a series of brief articles he began writing in 1971 for *The
New England Journal of Medicine*. The articles on medicine and research, originally directed at specialists, soon developed into less formal essays that at-
tracted a much wider audience, thanks to the grace and wit and warmth of
Thomas' voice. This voice was not that of a strict scientist—formal, authoriti-
tive, aloof, succumbing entirely to "reductionism." Instead, mixing scientific
with colloquial language, technical knowledge with wisdom and common
sense, it expressed as much wonder at the miracles of gene-splicing as at the
antics of otters and beavers frolicking in a desert zoo.

"The Tucson Zoo" is instructive because it reflects the method that Lewis followed to produce his informal, conversational essays. As he explained
in a memoir, he once attempted to work from outlines, organizing his
thoughts, committing himself to a plan, before beginning to write. The results he found to be too stiff, too orderly in the mechanical sense, something
he could not stand to reread. Ultimately, he found he was more comfortable
writing directly, beginning with a thought and pursuing it, immersing himself in an idea and letting it find its own direction. Later, he revised and revised, as witnessed by the economy and coherence of his sentences and
paragraphs.

"The Tucson Zoo," then, is an informal essay, an example of a meditation, someone enjoying mental play, taking delight in speculation, connecting previous ideas and random bits of information into fresh understandings.
To pursue his thoughts, Lewis puts his personal stamp on a conventional
opening strategy: the presentation of an existing theory or practice, then an
exploration of its inadequacy, its inability to account for a significant
phenomenon.

Technical vs. Familiar Language   Lewis Thomas writes for a thoughtful audience, one composed of specialists and nonspecialists alike. Or, rather
than "writes for," perhaps we should say "speaks to," because his delivery is
often so conversational, so colloquial. Even attentive nonscientists can follow much of his thinking, and not because he is being superficial. They can
follow because he uses technical language only when accuracy demands it,
when there is no familiar term. Otherwise, he does not seek to impress by
his rarefied vocabulary. He is struggling to present his ideas to their best advantage, not to make himself appear more intelligent than his readers.

Someone has remarked that the advantage of writing is that it enables us
to make ourselves appear more intelligent than we really are. Perhaps so, but
it is best not to push such an appearance too far. By resorting at every opportunity to the longest word, the most arcane or specialized term, the most
highfalutin language, we are more likely to appear foolish, or at least

pompous, self-impressed, unapproachable. And certainly our ideas are going to be less accessible. People read Lewis Thomas for pleasure, and get a mental workout as they strain to digest and apply scientific ideas about DNA and ethology and the autonomic nervous system. There are no everyday words for these; otherwise, he avoids jargon, which is language designed to impress rather than to communicate (thus, in hospitals they call newborns *neonates*, a term confected from two Latin words meaning . . . "new born"). Thomas is living proof that we can discuss technical subjects and complex ideas without resorting to jargon and other gratuitously polysyllabic phraseology.

Exercise   The following is Thomas's second paragraph, with the sentences separated and enumerated for easier analysis. How does Thomas achieve coherence in the paragraph? What ideas, structures, or words in each sentence relate to previous or following sentences? Your object is not to yield to an "obsessive preoccupation with the parts," but to use the parts to appreciate "the full hairy complexity" of the paragraph.

1. Sometimes it seems that we take a loss, working this way.

2. Much of today's public anxiety about science is the apprehension that we may forever be overlooking the whole by an endless, obsessive preoccupation with the parts.

3. I had a brief, personal experience of this misgiving one afternoon in Tucson, where I had time on my hands and visited the zoo, just outside the city.

4. The designers there have cut a deep pathway between two small artificial ponds, walled by clear glass, so when you stand in the center of the path you can look into the depths of each pool, and at the same time you can regard the surface.

5. In one pool, on the right side of the path, is a family of otters; on the other side, a family of beavers.

6. Within just a few feet from your face, on either side, beavers and otters are at play, underwater and on the surface, swimming toward your face and then away, more filled with life than any creatures I have ever seen before, in all my days.

7. Except for the glass, you could reach across and touch them.

Revision Assignments   Select one of the following strategies and revise "The Tucson Zoo." Include a brief statement explaining your choice and its effect on the arrangement and presentation of material.

1. Thomas opens his essay in the classic fashion, with a generalization. He wishes to establish a theoretical context for his experience at the zoo. Rewrite the first three or four paragraphs of the essay with a narrative opening, using the otter incident to introduce the ideas, instead of vice versa. In other words, arrange and present the material in a manner closer to that of Orwell's "Shooting an Elephant" or Alice Walker's "Am I Blue?"

2. "The Tucson Zoo" is a familiar essay, one in which an "I" speaker explores a subject in an informal and colloquial manner. Revise the essay to

be more formal and authoritative, removing the first-person pronouns and other expressions of the essayist's subjectivity (this is the form that Thomas originally tried to use and then abandoned).

Writing Assignments

1. We are social animals, says Lewis Thomas. Explore this idea, based on your own observations and experiences. What satisfactions do we experience from interacting with others? What frustrates socially harmonious behavior? How do you explain so much sociopathic or antisocial behavior in contemporary society? And to what extent do our schools succeed or fail to educate us as social beings? Again, use your own experiences and observations as a resource, giving concrete examples to support your generalizations.

2. In the broadest terms Thomas is writing about a common phenomenon, one that affirms our basic connectedness with other life: By attending closely and sympathetically to other beings, he learns something important about himself. To know others, "nonhuman" as well as "human animals" (as Alice Walker put it), is to know ourselves. In this case Thomas learns by the quality of his response to the otters and beavers. Write about a time you found yourself responding acutely and unexpectedly to another being, one presumably quite unrelated to you.

3. Thomas raises the issue of individualism and "altruism" (which he calls a jargon word for love but that means, more precisely, generosity, unselfishness, a willingness and even eagerness to do good for others). But as he writes elsewhere (in *The Fragile Species*), we humans are a mixture of impulses. Thus, we are coded for both selfishness and unselfishness, self-assertion and cooperation—conditioned and modified, of course, by upbringing and experience. Drawing upon your own observations, explore this idea of mixed impulses and its relationship to our upbringing.

4. Compare Thomas' "The Tucson Zoo" with Carol Bly's "A Mongoose Is Missing," Annie Dillard's "In the Jungle," or Alice Walker's "Am I Blue?" Where do they agree? To what extent do the discussions complement one another in their perception of human traits, of what "comes naturally" for human beings? In what respect are their concerns different?

Shoe and Tell?

SALLIE TISDALE

I live in Portland, Oregon, where Nike has its corporate headquarters and 1
where the first Niketown store was built, but for the last several years I've
worn Reeboks. This winter my Reeboks began to give out. It was time to
look for new shoes. I started browsing, picking up one spanking clean, aero-
dynamically designed sneaker after the other and reading the small labels
hidden inside: "Made in China." "Made in Korea." "Made in Indonesia."
"Made in Thailand." A few years ago Nike's overseas labor practices were
publicized, and the small scandal that followed made it clear that the foreign
operations of a number of U.S. shoe companies left a lot to be desired. My
Reeboks were made in Korea, and I promised myself that my next pair of
athletic shoes would be made in America.

I asked clerks about American-made shoes. The ones who weren't bewil- 2
dered by my request told me there's no such thing as an American-made
court shoe, unless you count Chuck Taylors. So I called Nike, and made my
way through voice-mail until I reached a customer-service representative.
When I told him my problem, he replied that the company was "still manufacturing in Indonesia and a lot of other countries over in that area."

"Do you know if any of those factories are unionized?" I asked. There 3
was a short silence.

"I don't know if they *have* unions in Indonesia," he finally said. 4

"Well, are Nike's domestic employees unionized?" 5

But he'd grown impatient by then. "We're all management here," he an- 6
swered. "We don't *need* unions."

I called the headquarters for L.A. Gear in Santa Monica. "I want to talk to 7
someone about how your shoes are manufactured," I told the young woman
in customer service. "Are they made in the United States?"

"Made in the U.S.?" she seemed taken aback. Their shoes were made in 8
Brazil and Asia, she said.

When I called Reebok, I identified myself as a journalist, and this time I 9
was transferred to Corporate Public Relations. "All of our shoes are manufactured outside the United States," a woman told me. I asked her which countries, but she didn't know. She did, however, send me Reebok's Human
Rights Standards brochure. Artfully designed, done up in red, white and
blue, it uses phrases like "appropriate in light of national practices and conditions" to define acceptable wages and working schedules. It took me several
more calls to find out the countries in which Reebok manufactured appropriately: China, Thailand, Indonesia, Korea and the Philippines.

Bill Krenn, a public relations manager for K-Swiss shoes, returned my call 10
but stopped me before I could finish my questions. "We do not talk about
our manufacturing," he said. "All I can tell you is that we manufacture
off-shore."

Saucony does manufacture some shoes domestically; the company was, in 11
fact, frequently suggested to me by shoe clerks. But when I called Saucony

and identified myself as a journalist, no one would answer questions unless they were submitted in writing.

I went back to stores and looked at labels—in Filas, Adidas, Avias, Etonics. China, Korea, Indonesia, the Philippines. By now, my Reeboks had a hole in them. 12

Most shoe workers in Southeast Asia are teenagers and young women. They work fifteen- to sixteen-hour days doing endless piecework. (Even Reebok's space-age brochure mentions sixty-hour work weeks as normal.) Many of these women live away from their families in barracks; in some cases, they are virtual prisoners, forbidden to leave the factory compound without a pass. The minimum wage in Indonesia is now $1.80 per day. And it's not always enforced. 13

Jeff Ballinger, a labor lawyer specializing in Asian issues, told me that even Indonesia's minimum wage at 60 hours a week fails to meet the local poverty level. He pointed out that Bata, which makes a variety of cheap shoes largely for the Asian market, pays its workers $3.90 per day—quite a bit more than companies producing for the American market. 14

The woman I spoke with at Reebok hadn't known how much Asian workers making Reeboks were paid. "We don't own the manufacturing plants," she said—a common practice. According to Jeff Fielder of the AFL-CIO, much of this kind of manufacturing is now done through third parties. American companies contract with Asian entrepreneurs, often South Korean, who buy and run the factories producing shoes for the American market. Fielder calls this "exploitation by proxy." 15

And then I called Nike one more time, as a journalist. I spoke with Keith Peters, the director of public relations. Our conversation was peppered with Peters' long silences. He told me that it wasn't "economically viable" for Nike to make its shoes in the United States. (This is the same company that considered a serious cash bid for Madison Square Garden, the Knicks and Rangers included.) Why was Asia a better choice? "Some of it clearly has to do with the cost of labor," Peters said. Then he brightened, remembering the South Koreans. "Nike owns no factories," he noted. "We contract with people," adding that the company demanded that workers be paid "at least the minimum wage mandated by law in the country we manufacture in." 16

"I would like to know how I, as a consumer, can feel good about buying shoes made under conditions that don't meet American human rights standards?" I said. "I would like to buy a home-grown product. Can you help me with that?" 17

"I might point out that there are 2,500 people who work for Nike right here." 18

"How many people work for Nike overseas?" I asked. Peters didn't know. Nike has only a few hundred actual employees in Asia, he said, many of them in quality control. But on the other side of the middlemen, about 75,000 people make Nike shoes and clothing. 19

So I called New Balance and talked to Catherine Shepard in the press relations department. She told me that 70 percent of their shoes are made in the United States, at four plants in Massachusetts and Maine; the rest are made in Europe and Asia. New Balance's plants aren't unionized, but all are 20 run on a modular manufacturing plan—meaning no assembly-line piecework. Employees are paid between $10 and $12 an hour, plus bonuses and benefits. "We're working toward being 100 percent U.S. made," she said. Then Shepard told me the bad news. The women's court shoe that would best meet my needs is one of the few made in China. But a man's court shoe might work, she added, since New Balance shoes come in several different widths.

Every time I turn on the television, I see Michael Jordan and Larry Bird, Nancy Kerrigan and Bo Jackson and Charles Barkley—ducking and jumping and running and skating for shoe companies. When I spoke with Keith Peters of Nike, I asked him how much money Nike spends on endorsement contracts. 21

"That number," he insisted, "is not divulged." It was widely reported that Nike signed Alonzo Mourning to a $16 million contract last year. 22

How much does it matter, I wondered, squeaking around the volleyball court in my frayed Reeboks? How easily do principles give way to the pressing need for ankle support? For brand loyalty? For fashion? 23

Manufacturing in the United States is not economically viable. Can't be done. But New Balance manages to survive, albeit on a scale smaller than Nike. How much would Nike, which had profits of $360 million in 1993, earn if it manufactured shoes here, or simply paid its overseas workers a living wage? Somewhat less. But the company would probably stay afloat. 24

Two weeks ago, I bought a pair of New Balance 665s with a little label inside reading "USA." The plain white shoe cost $59.95, and I like the fit. 25

It's comfortable in several different ways. 26

1994

Profile   Sallie Tisdale models yet another use of narrative, in this case, to present an exposé, a public disclosure of a practice that is—at the very least—controversial. Her first-person account tells how she set out to replace her worn athletic shoes, struggled to locate an American-made brand, and eventually found one. By the time she had done so, however, she had learned how an act as simple as buying shoes can involve us in other people's lives, involve us in ways we might not find comfortable. If eating is an agricultural act, as Wendell Berry argues ("The Pleasures of Eating"), than buying clothes can be a human rights issue.

Regardless of subject matter, the narrative technique has several advantages, beginning with organizational ones. The writer has simply to present information chronologically, in the order in which she gathered it, as Tisdale does by relating how she contacted shoe company after shoe company. But in Tisdale's case the first-person narrative is more than an organizational convenience. She could have presented the same information without telling her story, bypassing her adventures and simply reporting her findings. Such an account would have been briefer, more economical, but it would also have been more abstract and impersonal. We would have been treated to statistics, some quite shocking ($1.80 a day), but we would not have witnessed her investigations, not enjoyed the drama of watching the evidence accumulate, as in a detective story. Nor would we have heard the self-incriminating accounts of customer service representatives and public relations managers, their rationalizations and their bluster ("We're all management here"). The effect is to make the story more immediate, as immediate as the shoes on our feet. After all, most of her readers will own their own shoes manufactured "off-shore" and so have a stake in the story.

Beyond immediacy, though, the first-person narration has an even greater persuasive advantage. By tracing her investigations step by step, explaining her motives and relaying her findings, Tisdale can address a sensitive ethical issue in a nonaccusatory manner. Ostensibly, her purpose is simply informational, another consumer story about what happens when we set out to find an off brand or a discontinued or specialized product, an experience to which most readers can relate. But Tisdale is doing more than relating a personal anecdote. She is arguing a moral point, one that—presented less tactfully—might alienate her audience. After all, most of us don't want to hear that we are insensitive and exploitative simply because we found a bargain at the Shoe Barn. On the other hand, Tisdale probably trusts, many readers will want to learn if, unknowingly, they have been contributing to the misuse of other human beings.

Presenting Quotations   Quotation marks signal an instant change of voice. Occasionally, it is the writer reproducing her earlier words, as Tisdale does in several of her phone conversations with company representatives, but usually the voice is that of another person entirely. And when that voice is another speaker, the writer steps back, a Sallie Tisdale or a John McPhee, and that speaker steps forward, like a character in a play. And until the second set of quotation marks signals the end of the statement, the speaker has our ear, is speaking directly to us, without the intervention of the writer, especially when the *dialogue guide* appears afterward. But despite the promise of quotation marks—that the source is being quoted word for word—the writer can still filter the words of her source, can still shape our interpretation by the way she sets the stage and dramatizes the scene. Take the following:

> "Do you know if any of those factories are unionized?" *I asked.* There was a short silence.
> "I don't know if they *have* unions in Indonesia," *he finally said.*
> "Well, are Nike's domestic employees unionized?"
> But he'd grown impatient by then. "We're all management here," *he answered.* "We don't *need* unions."

"There was a short silence." This comment amounts to a stage direction: It invites the reader to visualize the perplexed service representative groping for an answer. Does he have something to hide? He tries to respond ("I don't know if they *have* unions in Indonesia"), but the dialogue guide adds to the impression that he is having trouble: "he finally said." Tisdale next asks if Nike's domestic employees are unionized, then interprets his response: "But he'd grown impatient by then." Without these details, and without italics to describe the tone of delivery, the conversation leaves a quite different impression:

"Do you know if any of those factories are unionized?" I asked.

"I don't know if they have unions in Indonesia," he said.

"Well, are Nike's domestic employees unionized?"

"We're all management here," he answered. "We don't need unions."

In this version the company representative sounds much more sure of himself, quick with an answer, afraid of nothing. Tisdale does not seem to have this speaker in the hot seat. But is it an accurate representation? Only Tisdale can say, and even she may be unconsciously influenced by her biases.

An honest writer will quote accurately, not misrepresenting the words or the spirit in which they were delivered. At the same time, she must decide whether and how to report the circumstances of the delivery, details that may bias the reader's response. She is faced with a dilemma. If she does present such details, she may be accused of partiality, of stacking the deck for or against the other party, as Tisdale might be accused of doing in the exchange quoted above. But if she does not, if she omits telling details that could help the reader interpret the scene, she knows that she is withholding essential information. One of her tasks, after all, is to record her observations accurately.

Consider the scene again as Tisdale presented it: " 'Do you know if any of those factories are unionized?' There was a short silence." The pause seems mildly incriminating; the company representative appears to be at a loss for words. But perhaps he is only taking care to give a measured answer. In making an official statement to an investigative journalist, a company spokesman had better weigh his responses, had better be careful not to make careless remarks for publication. "But he'd grown impatient by then." This is Tisdale's conclusion, one most of us might draw in her situation, perhaps based on the tone of his voice or other signals that he wants to end the conversation, but quotations like the following *tell* rather than *show* us: " 'We're all management here,' he answered. 'We don't *need* unions.' " The italicized *"need"* sounds almost belligerent—which it might have been—but the writer is stage-managing. She knows it, and so does the alert reader.

Direct and Indirect Quotations   As we have seen already, using quotations is more than a simple matter of recording someone else's words. By the way we introduce a quote or remark on its delivery, we influence the reader's interpretation. Still, the mere presence of another's words, especially another's speech, creates a sense of immediacy and drama and authenticity. Thus, quotations have an indispensable power to illustrate and convince. But in presenting the words of others, we have several options. We may quote a statement in its entirety, quote only a few words, quote indirectly, or summarize. To work the necessary material into her text and maintain a smooth narrative, Tisdale does all four. Thus, as in reporting her interview with Bill Krenn, the public relations manager for K-Swiss shoes, she frequently quotes entire sentences: " 'We do not talk about our manufacturing,' he said. 'All I can tell you is that we manufacture off-shore.' "

But at other times, when entire statements would be too cumbersome, or when a phrase or two will capture the spirit of a remark or publication, she uses only partial quotations. When she confronts a Nike representative, "he replied that the company was 'still manufacturing in Indonesia and a lot of other countries over in that area.' " And then she consults the Reebok Human Rights Standards brochure: "Artfully designed, done up in red, white and blue, it uses phrases like 'appropriate in light of national practices and conditions' to define acceptable wages and working schedules."

In some instances, perhaps to save time and speed her narrative and informational flow, Tisdale refrains from direct quotation entirely and summarizes what someone has told her:

> Jeff Ballinger, a labor lawyer specializing in Asian issues, told me that even Indonesia's minimum wage at 60 hours a week fails to meet the local poverty level. He pointed out that Bata, which makes a variety of cheap shoes largely for the Asian market, pays its workers $3.90 per day—quite a bit more than companies producing for the American market.

A paragraph later, when she interviews a union spokesman, she quotes only one phrase, summarizing most of his information:

> According to Jeff Fielder of the AFL-CIO, much of this kind of manufacturing is now done through third parties. American companies contract with Asian entrepreneurs, often South Korean, who buy and run the factories producing shoes for the American market. Fielder calls this "exploitation by proxy."

Between direct quotation and summary lies another choice: *indirect quotation*, presenting the content and the flavor of someone's remarks without reproducing the exact words. The advantage this method is that it allows the writer to maintain control of the material even while she suggests the sound of another voice. Thus, near the end of her interview with the Keith Peters of Nike, she quotes him indirectly:

> "How many people work for Nike overseas?" I asked. Peters didn't know. *Nike has only a few hundred actual employees in Asia,* he said, *many of them in quality control. But on the other side of the middlemen, about 75,000 people make Nike shoes and clothing.*

And in concluding her interview with the spokeswoman for New Balance (paragraph 20), she quotes one full statement, makes a summary remark, then quotes indirectly:

> "We're working toward being 100 percent U.S. made," she said. Then Shepard told me the bad news. *The women's court shoe that would best meet my needs is one of the few made in China. But a man's court shoe might work,* she added, *since New Balance shoes come in several different widths.*

Without such variation between summary and direct, indirect and partial quotation, Tisdale's article would have been cluttered with lengthy quotations. Instead of a lively narrative, we would have had a virtual transcript, and much more to read.

Showing and Telling   In telling a story, a writer must decide how much indeed to *tell* and how much to *show*. To tell is to maintain complete authority over the events, presenting material to the reader secondhand with all exhibits properly labeled and explained. It is, for example, to say, "He'd grown impatient by then." This statement produces no evidence of his impatience, only the writer's conclusion. Our role is to listen and believe. To show, on the other hand, is to present the physical particulars of an event and to invite readers to draw their own conclusions: "At this point he stopped answering my questions, tried several times to change the subject, and finally said that he had to hang up."

Telling has the advantage of economy and explicitness, enabling a writer to shape and summarize material so that the reader cannot mistake the meaning. And such writing does require the reader to *make* meaning, to supply details to fit the generalizations (to imagine how the company rep expressed impatience). But in telling, the writer stands between the reader and the material, interposing her personality and her assessment. It is her story, her *telling* of the story, that we are witnessing, not the events of the story themselves. The events come to us secondhand, prepackaged and predigested, and their credibility depends on our faith in the writer's judgment.

Showing has the advantages of concreteness and immediacy, of dramatizing events without the writer's intervention. Instead of commenting and interpreting, a writer focuses on re-creating events and scenes so that readers become not just listeners but witnesses. We hear a character's words and see his mannerisms, details that could be verified by other witnesses (as opposed to authorial interpretation, which is a matter of opinion). Without a critic to tell us what it means, we are watching a play or a movie and experiencing the challenge and satisfaction of finding meaning for ourselves. In fact, *experience* is the proper term. To show is to create an experience for the reader, an opportunity to live through and become personally involved.

In "Shoe and Tell?" Tisdale alternates between showing and telling (or should we say shoeing and telling?). Her principal mode is showing, with intermittent excursions into telling, as the following illustrates:

> I asked clerks about American-made shoes. *The ones who weren't bewildered by my request* told me there's no such thing as an American-made court shoe, unless you count Chuck Taylors. So I called Nike, and made my way through voice-mail until I reached a customer service representative. When I told him my problem, he replied that the company was "still manufacturing in Indonesia and a lot of other countries over in that area."

"The ones who weren't bewildered" conveys Tisdale's interpretation of the shoe clerks' responses, when she might have dramatized it: "You're kidding! Nobody's made court shoes in America in a zillion years." And "made my way through the voice-mail" may at first sound like one person's response, but not to anyone who has tried recently to phone a large business or institution. Except for the characterization of the clerks, then, the paragraph simply reports Tisdale's experience. The effect is to put us right there at her elbow, seeing for ourselves.

Tisdale alternates showing and telling because she has designs on our understanding. She wants our consent and she knows she is less likely to get it by launching into an angry denunciation of modern manufacturing practices, of greedy CEOs and boards of directors who are content to destroy jobs at home while exploiting virtual slave labor abroad. With the evidence she uncovered, she might have felt entitled to such a harangue, but not if she wanted to persuade a skeptical audience. Instead, she invites her readers to witness her investigations and, with a little nudging from stage directions, to draw their own conclusions. By limiting her own statements of opinion, by *showing* readers what she found instead of *telling* them what it means, she keeps the story foremost, the details of manufacture and the rationalizations of company representatives. Careful readers will not mistake Tisdale's response, but they will have grounds to draw their own.

Furthermore, by limiting expressions of personal opinion, or at least by understating it, she leaves a judgmental void that the reader is invited to fill. And finally, by being indirect, by being less openly accusatory, Tisdale is also being tactful. After all, most readers will not appreciate being called slave-drivers simply because they found a bargain at the Shoe Barn.

Revision Assignments   Select one of the following strategies and revise "Shoe and Tell?" Include a brief statement explaining your choice and its effect on the arrangement and presentation of material.

1. Write a purely expository essay on the low-wage, off-shore production of athletic shoes. Use all the information generated by Tisdale, including the quotations from company representatives, but do not embed it in a narration. In other words, omit the story of Tisdale's investigation. Simply write an informational piece such as might appear on the feature page of a Sunday newspaper.

2. Revise "Shoe and Tell?" into a question-and-answer format—that is, as an interview with Sallie Tisdale.

3. By and large, Tisdale restrains her expression of personal opinion, not indulging herself in harangues about the obscenity of paying 75,000 people $1.80 a day to make shoes while paying one person $15 million to advertise them. Instead, she leaves the reader to make connections. Write the first six paragraphs of the article as an explicit attack on overseas manufacturing, on the evils of exploiting foreign workers and the short-sightedness of sacrificing domestic jobs (how many jobs can we export before we destroy the customer base, sharply reducing the numbers who can afford Nikes?). In other words, begin Tisdale's article as it might have been written by Wendell Berry ("The Pleasures of Eating") or—perhaps more fun—Edward Abbey ("Even the Bad Guys Wear White Hats").

4. In reporting her interviews, Tisdale alternates between summary and direct, indirect, and partial quotation. To better appreciate the benefits of such variation, revise paragraphs 15–20 so that all the information is presented in the form of direct quotes (you will have to reconstruct some dialogue). Compare your results with the original.

Writing Assignments

1. Both Sallie Tisdale and Wendell Berry ("The Pleasures of Eating") address how we affect the lives of others by our style of consumption. Both would agree that ignorance is no excuse, that if we acknowledge our obligations to others we will try to understand the consequences of our

behavior, even when only buying a head of cabbage or a pair of shoes. Using Tisdale's investigative method, write about another area where we might injure others by careless consumption.

2. Following the example of Sallie Tisdale and Ann Hodgman ("No Wonder They Call Me a Bitch"), conduct your own investigation of a product or service, surveying, testing, and interviewing clerks and customer service representatives.

3. Tisdale and Berry seem to share many assumptions about economic connectedness, about how consumer decisions place us in one another's lives, yet their methods are quite different. Berry is quite open about his judgments and conclusions, whereas Tisdale either omits or understates hers. Compare and contrast their two methods, including an assessment of their relative effectiveness. Which writer, in other words, has been most effective in winning your consent?

Am I Blue?

ALICE WALKER

"Ain't these tears in these eyes tellin' you?"

For about three years my companion and I rented a small house in the coun-   1
try that stood on the edge of a large meadow that appeared to run from the
end of the deck straight into the mountains. The mountains, however, were
quite far away, and between us and them there was, in fact, a town. It was
one of the many pleasant aspects of the house that you never really were
aware of this.

It was a house of many windows, low, wide, nearly floor to ceiling in the   2
living room, which faced the meadow, and it was from one of these that I first
saw our closest neighbor, a large white horse, cropping grass, flipping its
mane, and ambling about—not over the entire meadow, which stretched well
out of sight of the house, but over the five or so fenced-in acres that were
next to the twenty-odd that we had rented. I soon learned that the horse,
whose name was Blue, belonged to a man who lived in another town, but was
boarded by our neighbors next door. Occasionally, one of the children, usually a stocky teen-ager, but sometimes a much younger girl or boy, could be
seen riding Blue. They would appear in the meadow, climb up on his back,
ride furiously for ten or fifteen minutes, then get off, slap Blue on the flanks,
and not be seen again for a month or more.

There were many apple trees in our yard, and one by the fence that Blue   3
could almost reach. We were soon in the habit of feeding him apples, which
he relished, especially because by the middle of summer the meadow
grasses—so green and succulent since January—had dried out from lack of
rain, and Blue stumbled about munching the dried stalks half-heartedly.
Sometimes he would stand very still just by the apple tree, and when one of
us came out he would whinny, snort loudly, or stamp the ground. This
meant, of course: I want an apple.

It was quite wonderful to pick a few apples, or collect those that had   4
fallen to the ground overnight, and patiently hold them, one by one, up to his
large, toothy mouth. I remained as thrilled as a child by his flexible dark lips,
huge, cubelike teeth that crunched the apples, core and all, with such final-
ity, and his high, broad-chested *enormity*; beside which, I felt small indeed.
When I was a child, I used to ride horses, and was especially friendly with
one named Nan until the day I was riding and my brother deliberately
spooked her and I was thrown, head first, against the trunk of a tree. When I
came to, I was in bed and my mother was bending worriedly over me; we silently agreed that perhaps horseback riding was not the safest sport for me.
Since then I have walked, and prefer walking to horseback riding—but I had
forgotten the depth of feeling one could see in horses' eyes.

I was therefore unprepared for the expression in Blue's. Blue was lonely.   5
Blue was horribly lonely and bored. I was not shocked that this should be the

case; five acres to tramp by yourself, endlessly, even in the most beautiful of meadows—and his was—cannot provide many interesting events, and once rainy season turned to dry that was about it. No, I was shocked that I had forgotten that human animals and nonhuman animals can communicate quite well; if we are brought up around animals as children we take this for granted. By the time we are adults we no longer remember. However, the animals have not changed. They are in fact *completed* creations (at least they seem to be, so much more than we) who are not likely *to* change; it is their nature to express themselves. What else are they going to express? And they do. And, generally speaking, they are ignored.

After giving Blue the apples, I would wander back to the house, aware that he was observing me. Were more apples not forthcoming then? Was that to be his sole entertainment for the day? My partner's small son had decided he wanted to learn how to piece a quilt; we worked in silence on our respective squares as I thought . . . 6

Well, about slavery: about white children, who were raised by black people, who knew their first all-accepting love from black women, and then, when they were twelve or so, were told they must "forget" the deep levels of communication between themselves and "mammy" that they knew. Later they would be able to relate quite calmly, "My old mammy was sold to another good family." "My old mammy was _____ _____." Fill in the blank. Many more years later a white woman would say: "I can't understand these Negroes, these blanks. What do they want? They're so different from us." 7

And about the Indians, considered to be "like animals" by the "settlers" (a very benign euphemism for what they actually were), who did not understand their description as a compliment. 8

And about the thousands of American men who marry Japanese, Korean, Filipina, and other non-English-speaking women and of how happy they report they are, "*blissfully*," until their brides learn to speak English, at which point the marriages tend to fall apart. What then did the men see, when they looked into the eyes of the women they married, before they could speak English? Apparently only their own reflections. 9

I thought of society's impatience with the young. "Why are they playing the music so loud?" Perhaps the children have listened to much of the music of oppressed people their parents danced to before they were born, with its passionate but soft cries for acceptance and love, and they have wondered why their parents failed to hear. 10

I do not know how long Blue had inhabited his five beautiful boring acres before we moved into our house; a year after we had arrived—and had also traveled to other valleys, other cities, other worlds—he was still there. 11

But then, in our second year at the house, something happened in Blue's life. One morning, looking out the window at the fog that lay like a ribbon over the meadow, I saw another horse, a brown one, at the other end of Blue's field. Blue appeared to be afraid of it, and for several days made no attempt to go near. We went away for a week. When we returned, Blue had decided to make friends and the two horses ambled or galloped along together, and Blue did not come nearly as often to the fence underneath the apple tree. 12

When he did, bringing his new friend with him, there was a different look 13
in his eyes. A look of independence, of self-possession, of inalienable *horse-ness*. His friend eventually became pregnant. For months and months there
was, it seemed to me, a mutual feeling between me and the horses of justice,
of peace. I fed apples to them both. The look in Blue's eyes was one of un-abashed "this is *it*ness."

It did not, however, last forever. One day, after a visit to the city, I went 14
out to give Blue some apples. He stood waiting, or so I thought, though not
beneath the tree. When I shook the tree and jumped back from the shower
of apples, he made no move. I carried some over to him. He managed to half-crunch one. The rest he let fall to the ground. I dreaded looking into his
eyes—because I had of course noticed that Brown, his partner, had gone—
but I did look. If I had been born into slavery, and my partner had been sold
or killed, my eyes would have looked like that. The children next door ex-plained that Blue's partner had been "put with him" (the same expression
that old people used, I had noticed, when speaking of an ancestor during
slavery who had been impregnated by her owner) so that they could mate
and she conceive. Since that was accomplished, she had been taken back by
her owner, who lived somewhere else.

Will she be back? I asked. 15

They didn't know. 16

Blue was like a crazed person. Blue *was*, to me, a crazed person. He gal- 17
loped furiously, as if he were being ridden, around and around his five beau-tiful acres. He whinnied until he couldn't. He tore at the ground with his
hooves. He butted himself against his single shade tree. He looked always
and always toward the road down which his partner had gone. And then, oc-casionally, when he came up for apples, or I took apples to him, he looked at
me. It was a look so piercing, so full of grief, a look so *human*, I almost
laughed (I felt too sad to cry) to think there are people who do not know that
animals suffer. People like me who have forgotten, and daily forget, all that
animals try to tell us. "Everything you do to us will happen to you; we are
your teachers, as you are ours. We are one lesson" is essentially it, I think.
There are those who never once have even considered animals' rights: those
who have been taught that animals actually want to be used and abused by
us, as small children "love" to be frightened, or women "love" to be muti-lated and raped. . . . They are the great-grandchildren of those who honestly
thought, because someone taught them this: "Women can't think," and "nig-gers can't faint." But most disturbing of all, in Blue's large brown eyes was a
new look, more painful than the look of despair: the look of disgust with hu-man beings, with life; the look of hatred. And it was odd what the look of ha-tred did. It gave him, for the first time, the look of a beast. And what that
meant was that he had put up a barrier within to protect himself from further
violence; all the apples in the world wouldn't change that fact.

And so Blue remained, a beautiful part of our landscape, very peaceful to 18
look at from the window, white against the grass. Once a friend came to visit
and said, looking out on the soothing view: "And it *would* have to be a *white*
horse; the very image of freedom." And I thought, yes, the animals are forced
to become for us merely "images" of what they once so beautifully ex-pressed. And we are used to drinking milk from containers showing

"contented" cows, whose real lives we want to hear nothing about, eating eggs and drumsticks from "happy" hens, and munching the hamburgers advertised by bulls of integrity who seem to commend their fate.

As we talked of freedom and justice one day for all, we sat down to steaks. I am eating misery, I thought, as I took the first bite. And spit it out.

19

1986

Profile   Like many personal essays "Am I Blue?" opens with an episode in the writer's life and then traces how it led to a major insight, an insight that the writer then explores. The form is infinitely flexible, as demonstrated by a comparison of Walker's essay with George Orwell's "Shooting an Elephant," and Frank Conroy's "Think About It."

Such essays usually begin with the writer in a state of puzzlement or unawareness, but also ripely receptive to some clarifying breakthrough. Thus, "Am I Blue?" opens with the writer positioned in a country house whose many large windows invite her to enjoy the view, to be a spectator of picturesque vistas (like a white horse grazing in a meadow against a backdrop of mountains). The setting does not yet suggest the problem, but it does prepare for its introduction, and it does invite attentiveness.

Walker's method is to take the reader through her experience, through the stages of her progressive involvement and then eventual identification with Blue (as suggested by the pun in the title). At first the horse is only a part of the scenery, then a source of entertainment as she feeds it apples ("It was quite wonderful to pick a few apples . . ."). Her, and the reader's, engagement is gradual. Not until the end of the fourth paragraph does she discover, or rediscover, "the depth of feeling one could see in horses' eyes," something she had known as a child.

Finally, in the fifth paragraph, having prepared the groundwork and disposed the reader to be receptive, Walker addresses her theme, the sensitivity of "nonhuman animals" and their claim on our attentions. This subject in turn leads her to think of slavery: As humans generally disregard animals, refusing to communicate with them, so whites disregarded their black slaves. And so the settlers disregarded the Indians. And so thousands of American men marry non-English-speaking women so they will not have to listen to them. And so parents look in puzzlement at the musical tastes of their children.

At this point some readers may guess that they have heard the last of Blue, suspecting the essayist of having exploited the horse as a convenient departure to "larger" issues. But Walker's point is one about connectedness, between races, between sexes, between "human animals and nonhuman animals." So in the eleventh paragraph, she returns to him for the climax of her discussion, the mournful episode of Blue and his temporary mate. Whatever she experienced before of the horse's feeling, principally boredom, has not prepared her for what she is about to witness (and share empathetically). First, there are the looks of independence and self-possession, of thoroughgoing satisfaction, even of justice and peace, shown by the two horses when they are together. Then, once he is isolated again, there is Blue's grief, his despair, his disgust, then his hatred—all feelings we would normally reserve for human beings. Even the apples have lost their appeal.

The essay concludes as it began, with Blue again just a part of the landscape, merely an object for human contemplation. And the writer is back inside her country house, but changed. She will no longer eat meat.

Pace (Slowing Down)   A nineteenth-century author proposed a simple formula for writing successful plays: "Make 'em laugh, make 'em cry, make 'em wait." In "Am I Blue?" Walker demonstrates the value of the latter, which, in any kind of writing, we might call pace but also suspense: deliberate preparation, setting the stage and gradually developing tension, making the reader wait. Pace creates *emphasis*. Consider the opening paragraph:

> For about three years my companion and I rented a small house in the country that stood on the edge of a large meadow that appeared to run from the end of our deck straight into the mountains. The mountains, however, were quite far away, and between us and them there was, in fact, a town. It was one of the many pleasant aspects of the house that you never really were aware of this.

Walker wants the reader to ponder her situation: her isolation in the country, the relative absence of human distractions, and the one overwhelming scenic fact—the meadow, like a great stage, stretching toward the mountains. The mountains themselves are quite far away and the town isn't visible, so we are to watch the meadow for action.

Then consider the second paragraph:

> It was a house of many windows, low, wide, nearly floor to ceiling in the living room, which faced the meadow, and it was from one of these that I first saw our closest neighbor, a large white horse, cropping grass, flipping its mane, and ambling about—not over the entire meadow, which stretched well out of sight of the house, but over the five or so fenced-in acres that were next to the twenty-odd that we had rented. I soon learned that the horse, whose name was Blue, belonged to a man who lived in another town, but was boarded by our neighbors next door. Occasionally, one of the children, usually a stocky teen-ager, but sometimes a much younger girl or boy, could be seen riding Blue. They would appear in the meadow, climb up on his back, ride furiously for ten or fifteen minutes, then get off, slap Blue on the flanks, and not be seen again for a month or more.

Even Walker's sentences are in no hurry. Instead of the more direct "The house had many windows, and from one of these I first saw . . . ," we get "It was a house of many windows, low, wide, nearly floor to ceiling in the living room . . ." (Stop, slow down, and *look*, her pace is saying.) And instead of "from one of these I first saw our closest neighbor," Walker uses a slower, more emphatic structure: "it was from one of these that I first saw our closest neighbor." But this seemingly climactic introduction still withholds the principal piece of information a moment longer, for "our closest neighbor" plays on the assumption that we will meet a human.

Then Walker introduces the horse, acting very much like a generic horse ("cropping grass, flipping its mane, and ambling about"). Its name is Blue, its owner lives in a small town, and the neighbor's kids ride it about once a month. So far so good, although the latter detail is a little unsettling. Walker may be suggesting something about neglect. But we still have no firm clue to why she wants us to be interested in the horse.

"There were many apple trees in our yard, and one by the fence" begins the third paragraph, and we watch the warmly innocent spectacle of feeding Blue, who grazes only half-heartedly on the dried summer grasses of his meadow, but who is intelligent enough to "whinny, snort loudly, or stamp the ground" when he wants to be fed apples ("Look, he is trying to tell us something!" we have all heard in the movies). The paragraph ends with Blue communicating.

The fourth paragraph has two parts: the first about the pleasures of feeding Blue ("his flexible dark lips, huge, cubelike teeth"), and the second about another horse Walker once befriended, but one that threw her against a tree. Will the essay be about the betrayal of humans by animals? But as the previous paragraph ended with Blue's message ("I want an apple"), this paragraph ends with Walker's awareness of the horse's sensitivity: "I had forgotten the depth of feeling one could see in horses' eyes."

And then the fifth paragraph finally reaches the heart of the matter, Walker's central concern: "I was therefore unprepared for the expression in Blue's. Blue was lonely."

Pace (Speeding Up)   We have seen how Walker slows down her presentation to fit her subject, a gradually dawning mental event. Thus, she rations out information deliberately, precisely, bringing her readers along carefully. She is not playing speed chess, but she could if she wanted to, as she demonstrates in paragraph 17. There, her subject becomes a physical event, the actions of the frenzied Blue. How does she capture his frenetic behavior? Look at sentences 3–7:

> [1]Blue was like a crazed person. [2]Blue *was*, to me, a crazed person. [3]He galloped furiously, as if he were being ridden, around and around his five beautiful acres. [4]He whinnied until he couldn't. [5]He tore at the ground with his hooves. [6]He butted himself against his single shade tree. [7]He looked always and always toward the road down which his partner had gone. [8]And then, occasionally, when he came up for apples, or I took apples to him, he looked at me. [9]It was a look so piercing, so full of grief, a look so *human* . . .

Five narrative sentences in a row begin not only with the subject, but with the same subject: *he*. And each subject is followed immediately by the verb: "He galloped/he whinnied/he tore at the ground/he butted himself/he looked." With no connectors or other transition terms to smooth the sequence of events or the flow of words from one sentence to the next, the effect is abrupt, staccato. (We get a more exaggerated display of this effect in the familiar advertisement for a kitchen utensil: "It slices. It dices. It shreds.")

Not until the eighth sentence, when the focus shifts to the transaction between horse and human, does the pattern change:

> And then, occasionally, when he came up for apples, or I took apples to him, he looked at me.

And what slows this sentence back down while also making it climactic? The previous five action sentences were *loose* sentences, sentences opening with their main clauses. This sentence is *periodic*, one that postpones the main statement until the end. First, there is transitional connector ("and then"), then a qualifying clause ("when he came up for apples, or . . ."), then the main clause ("he looked at me").

The *It* Pattern   Consider the following revision of Walker:

> *Never really being aware of this* [the town] **was one of the many pleasant aspects of the house.**

This version is a direct subject-predicate, topic-comment sentence. Such sentences do their work quickly and openly, identifying the topic and then immediately satisfying our curiosity about the nature of the comment. Now consider the original sentence:

> It was one of the many pleasant aspects of the house *that you never really were aware of this* [the town].

This sentence uses an inversion structure, opening with a dummy subject, the expletive *it* (like the *there* in "There were many apple trees in our yard"). Next follows the comment ("was one of the many pleasant aspects of the house"), and then, at the end of the sentence, in the climactic final position where we usually expect to find the news, appears the topic ("that you never really were aware of this"). The news of the typical sentence occurs in the predicate, in the comment on the subject; the news of the *it* pattern is the identity of the subject itself.

Why does Walker use the slower, wordier *it* version? For emphasis. To stay with her careful, deliberate pace, one that is meant to put the reader in a thoughtful frame of mind. She is not telling us an adventure story, trying to excite us, hurrying us to the next event. She wants less to disclose events than to share the thoughts they provoke.

Revision Assignments   Select one of the following strategies and revise "Am I Blue?" Include a brief statement explaining your choice of strategy and its effect on the arrangement and presentation of material.

1. Walker uses a casual but deliberate lead-in, carefully preparing the reader for her story. Compose an abrupt opening, cutting to the chase immediately. Then assess what the quick-fire opening both achieves and forfeits.

2. "Am I Blue?" models how an essay can use narrative to make a point, to argue a case. Revise the essay into a straight first-person account of what happens to Blue. Do not comment on the significance of the story; simply present the details. Try as much as you can to imply Walker's point, but do not state it explicitly.

Writing Assignments

1. Alice Walker uses a narrative episode to introduce her reflections on freedom and justice for all beings, for nonhuman as well as human animals, but something only possible when we respect their consciousness and sensitivity. Write a similarly structured account, tracing how an experience gave rise to a discovery (or rediscovery). Set the stage,

presenting the relevant circumstances, then introduce and develop the thought.

2. Alice Walker's "offense" or original sin is in taking Blue too lightly, in looking upon him condescendingly as, at first, a part of the landscape, then as a pet she can interact with at her convenience. Then she discovers that even horses have intelligence and feelings (Blue can ask for apples and look bored). Write about an occasion when you were guilty of selling someone else short (human or nonhuman animal), at first discounting the being's value, then being shocked into an awareness of his or her feelings. In other words, write about a time when you were insufficiently empathetic but then awakened to a greater sense of connectedness, of community.

3. Compare and contrast "Am I Blue?" with Orwell's "Shooting an Elephant" or Conroy's "Think About It." In particular, discuss their respective treatments of personal experience, the way they move from observation to understanding.

Once More to the Lake

E. B. WHITE

One summer, along about 1904, my father rented a camp on a lake in Maine   1
and took us all there for the month of August. We all got ringworm from
some kittens and had to rub Pond's Extract on our arms and legs night and
morning, and my father rolled over in a canoe with all his clothes on; but outside of that the vacation was a success and from then on none of us ever
thought there was any place in the world like that lake in Maine. We returned summer after summer—always on August 1st for one month. I have
since become a salt-water man, but sometimes in summer there are days
when the restlessness of the tides and the fearful cold of the sea water and
the incessant wind which blows across the afternoon and into the evening
make me wish for the placidity of a lake in the woods. A few weeks ago this
feeling got so strong I bought myself a couple of bass hooks and a spinner
and returned to the lake where we used to go, for a week's fishing and to re-
visit old haunts.

I took along my son, who had never had any fresh water up his nose and   2
who had seen lily pads only from train windows. On the journey over to the
lake I began to wonder what it would be like. I wondered how time would
have marred this unique, this holy spot—the coves and streams, the hills that
the sun set behind, the camps and the paths behind the camps. I was sure
the tarred road would have found it out and I wondered in what other ways it
would be desolated. It is strange how much you can remember about places
like that once you allow your mind to return into the grooves which lead
back. You remember one thing, and that suddenly reminds you of another
thing. I guess I remembered clearest of all the mornings, when the lake was
cool and motionless, remembered how the bedroom smelled of the lumber it
was made of and of the wet woods whose scent entered through the screen.
The partitions in the camp were thin and did not extend clear to the top of
the rooms, and as I was always the first up I would dress softly so as not to
wake the others, and sneak out into the sweet outdoors and start out in the
canoe, keeping close along the shore in the long shadows of the pines. I remembered being very careful never to rub my paddle against the gunwale for
fear of disturbing the stillness of the cathedral.

The lake had never been what you would call a wild lake. There were   3
cottages sprinkled around the shores, and it was in farming country although
the shores of the lake were quite heavily wooded. Some of the cottages were
owned by nearby farmers, and you would live at the shore and eat your meals
at the farmhouse. That's what our family did. But although it wasn't wild, it
was a fairly large and undisturbed lake and there were places in it which, to a
child at least, seemed infinitely remote and primeval.

I was right about the tar: it led to within half a mile of the shore. But   4
when I got back there, with my boy, and we settled into a camp near a farmhouse and into the kind of summertime I had known, I could tell that it was

going to be pretty much the same as it had been before—I knew it, lying in bed the first morning, smelling the bedroom, and hearing the boy sneak quietly out and go off along the shore in a boat. I began to sustain the illusion that he was I, and therefore by simple transposition, that I was my father. This sensation persisted, kept cropping up all the time we were there. It was not an entirely new feeling, but in this setting it grew much stronger. I seemed to be living a dual existence. I would be in the middle of some simple act, I would be picking up a bait box or laying down a table fork, or I would be saying something, and suddenly it would be not I but my father who was saying the words or making the gesture. It gave me a creepy sensation.

We went fishing the first morning. I felt the same damp moss covering 5 the worms in the bait can, and saw the dragonfly alight on the tip of my rod as it hovered a few inches from the surface of the water. It was the arrival of this fly that convinced me beyond any doubt that everything was as it always had been, that the years were a mirage and there had been no years. The small waves were the same, chucking the rowboat under the chin as we fished at anchor, and the boat was the same boat, the same color green and the ribs broken in the same places, and under the floor-boards the same fresh-water leavings and debris—the dead helgramite,[1] the wisps of moss, the rusty discarded fishhook, the dried blood from yesterday's catch. We stared silently at the tips of our rods, at the dragonflies that came and went. I lowered the tip of mine into the water, tentatively, pensively dislodging the fly, which darted two feet away, poised, darted two feet back, and came to rest again a little farther up the rod. There had been no years between the ducking of this dragonfly and the other—the one that was part of memory. I looked at the boy, who was silently watching his fly, and it was my hands that held his rod, my eyes watching. I felt dizzy and didn't know which rod I was at the end of.

We caught two bass, hauling them in briskly as though they were mack- 6 erel, pulling them over the side of the boat in a businesslike manner without any landing net, and stunning them with a blow on the back of the head. When we got back for a swim before lunch, the lake was exactly where we had left it, the same number of inches from the dock, and there was only the merest suggestion of a breeze. This seemed an utterly enchanted sea, this lake you could leave to its own devices for a few hours and come back to, and find that it had not stirred, this constant and trustworthy body of water. In the shallows, the dark, water-soaked sticks and twigs, smooth and old, were undulating in clusters on the bottom against the clean ribbed sand, and the track of the mussel was plain. A school of minnows swam by, each minnow with its small individual shadow, doubling the attendance, so clear and sharp in the sunlight. Some of the other campers were in swimming, along the shore, one of them with a cake of soap, and the water felt thin and clear and unsubstantial. Over the years there had been this person with the cake of soap, this cultist, and here he was. There had been no years.

Up to the farmhouse to dinner through the teeming, dusty field, the road 7 under our sneakers was only a two-track road. The middle track was missing,

---

[1]An insect used for bait.

the one with the marks of the hooves and the splotches of dried, flaky manure. There had always been three tracks to choose from in choosing which track to walk in; now the choice was narrowed down to two. For a moment I missed terribly the middle alternative. But the way led past the tennis court, and something about the way it lay there in the sun reassured me; the tape had loosened along the backline, the alleys were green with plantains and other weeds, and the net (installed in June and removed in September) sagged in the dry noon, and the whole place steamed with mid-day heat and hunger and emptiness. There was a choice of pie for dessert, and one was blueberry and one was apple, and the waitresses were the same country girls, there having been no passage of time, only the illusion of it as in a dropped curtain—the waitresses were still fifteen; their hair had been washed, that was the only difference—they had been to the movies and seen the pretty girls with the clean hair.

Summertime, oh summertime, pattern of life indelible, the fade-proof 8
lake, the woods unshatterable, the pasture with the sweet-fern and the juniper forever and ever, summer without end; this was the background, and the life along the shore was the design, the cottages with their innocent and tranquil design, their tiny docks with the flagpole and the American flag floating against the white clouds in the blue sky, the little paths over the roots of the trees leading from camp to camp and the paths leading back to the outhouses and the can of lime for sprinkling, and at the souvenir counters at the store the miniature birchbark canoes and the post cards that showed things looking a little better than they looked. This was the American family at play, escaping the city heat, wondering whether the newcomers in the camp at the head of the cove were "common" or "nice," wondering whether it was true that the people who drove up for Sunday dinner at the farmhouse were turned away because there hadn't been enough chicken.

It seemed to me, as I kept remembering all this, that those times and 9
those summers had been infinitely precious and worth saving. There had been jollity and peace and goodness. The arriving (at the beginning of August) had been so big a business in itself, at the railway station the farm wagon drawn up, the first smell of the pine-laden air, the first glimpse of the smiling farmer, and the great importance of the trunks and your father's enormous authority in such matters, and the feel of the wagon under you for a long ten-mile haul, and at the top of the last long hill catching the first view of the lake after eleven months of not seeing this cherished body of water. The shouts and cries of the other campers when they saw you, and the trunks to be unpacked, to give up their rich burden. (Arriving was less exciting nowadays, when you sneaked up in your car and parked it under a tree near the camp and took out the bags and in five minutes it was all over, no fuss, no loud wonderful fuss about trunks.)

Peace and goodness and jollity. The only thing that was wrong now, re- 10
ally, was the sound of the place, an unfamiliar nervous sound of the outboard motors. This was the note that jarred, the one thing that would sometimes break the illusion and set the years moving. In those other summertimes all motors were inboard; and when they were at a little distance, the noise they made was a sedative, an ingredient of summer sleep. They were one-cylinder and two-cylinder engines, and some were make-and-break and some were

jump-spark, but they all made a sleepy sound across the lake. The one-lungers throbbed and fluttered, and the twin-cylinder ones purred and purred, and that was a quiet sound too. But now the campers all had outboards. In the daytime, in the hot mornings, these motors made a petulant, irritable sound; at night, in the still evening when the afterglow lit the water, they whined about one's ears like mosquitoes. My boy loved our rented outboard, and his great desire was to achieve singlehanded mastery over it, and authority, and he soon learned the trick of choking it a little (but not too much), and the adjustment of the needle valve. Watching him I would remember the things you could do with the old one-cylinder engine with the heavy flywheel, how you could have it eating out of your hand if you got really close to it spiritually. Motor boats in those days didn't have clutches, and you would make a landing by shutting off the motor at the proper time and coasting in with a dead rudder. But there was a way of reversing them, if you learned the trick, by cutting the switch and putting it on again exactly on the final dying revolution of the flywheel, so that it would kick back against compression and begin reversing. Approaching a dock in a strong following breeze, it was difficult to slow up sufficiently by the ordinary coasting method, and if a boy felt he had complete mastery over his motor, he was tempted to keep it running beyond its time and then reverse it a few feet from the dock. It took a cool nerve, because if you threw the switch a twentieth of a second too soon you would catch the flywheel when it still had speed enough to go up past center, and the boat would leap ahead, charging bull-fashion at the dock.

We had a good week at the camp. The bass were biting well and the sun 11
shone endlessly, day after day. We would be tired at night and lie down in the accumulated heat of the little bedrooms after the long hot day and the breeze would stir almost imperceptibly outside and the smell of the swamp drift in through the rusty screens. Sleep would come easily and in the morning the red squirrel would be on the roof, tapping out his gay routine. I kept remembering everything, lying in bed in the mornings—the small steamboat that had a long rounded stern like the lip of a Ubangi, and how quietly she ran on the moonlight sails, when the older boys played their mandolins and the girls sang and we ate doughnuts dipped in sugar, and how sweet the music was on the water in the shining night, and what it had felt like to think about girls then. After breakfast we would go up to the store and the things were in the same place—the minnows in a bottle, the plugs and spinners disarranged and pawed over by the youngsters from the boys' camp, the fig newtons and the Beeman's gum. Outside, the road was tarred and cars stood in front of the store. Inside, all was just as it had always been, except there was more Coca-Cola and not so much Moxie and root beer and birch beer and sarsaparilla. We would walk out with a bottle of pop apiece and sometimes the pop would backfire up our noses and hurt. We explored the streams, quietly, where the turtles slid off the sunny logs and dug their way into the soft bottom; and we lay on the town wharf and fed worms to the tame bass. Everywhere we went I had trouble making out which was I, the one walking at my side, the one walking in my pants.

One afternoon while we were there at the lake a thunderstorm came up. 12
It was like the revival of an old melodrama that I had seen long ago with

childish awe. The second-act climax of the drama of the electrical disturbance over a lake in America had not changed in any important respect. This was the big scene, still the big scene. The whole thing was so familiar, the first feeling of oppression and heat and a general air around camp of not wanting to go very far away. In midafternoon (it was all the same) a curious darkening of the sky, and a lull in everything that had made life tick; and then the way boats suddenly swung the other way at their moorings with the coming of the breeze out of the new quarter, and the premonitory rumble. Then the kettle drum, then the snare, then the bass drum and cymbals, then crackling light against the dark, and the gods grinning and licking their chops in the hills. Afterward the calm, the rain steadily rustling in the calm lake, the return of light and hope and spirits, and the campers running out in joy and relief to go swimming in the rain, their bright cries perpetuating the death-less joke about how they were getting simply drenched, and the children screaming with delight at the new sensation of bathing in the rain, and the joke about getting drenched linking the generations in a strong indestructi-ble chain. And the comedian who waded in carrying an umbrella.

When the others went swimming my son said he was going in too. He 13 pulled his dripping trunks from the line where they had hung all through the shower, and wrung them out. Languidly, and with no thought of going in, I watched him, his hard little body, skinny and bare, saw him wince slightly as he pulled up around his vitals the small, soggy, icy garment. As he buckled the swollen belt suddenly my groin felt the chill of death.

1941

Profile   In "Once More to the Lake" one of America's great prose stylists reminisces about a "pattern of life indelible," the idyllic Augusts that his family used to spend at a lake in Maine. More particularly, though, the essay tells of his attempt to reenter the pattern, to re-create for himself and his son the serene, languid summers he had known as a boy. And for a while, by vis-iting some of the same sites and orchestrating the same experiences, he is able to convince himself that things are as they had always been: the dragon-fly is still on the end of the rod, the bather is still there with his bar of soap, the country store still has most of the same merchandise displayed on the same shelves. Nevertheless, there are clues that timelessness is an illusion, a wish: The three-track road now has only two tracks, automobiles have taken away the wonder of travel trunks, and the whine of outboard motors now buzz around one's ears like mosquitoes. And then there is—literally—the chilling conclusion. Just as White has reassured himself about "the genera-tions in a strong indestructible chain," his son pulls on his damp swimming suit. Watching the small boy pull on the icy garment, White feels the chill of death. Life is a one-time thing after all: Peace and goodness and jollity come to an end—at least for the individual—and, as Thomas Wolfe put it, you can't go home again.

Process Narration   Most narratives present one-time events: "One sum-mer, along about 1904, my father rented a camp on a lake in Maine and took us all there for the month of August." Even without the opening adverbial information, we would still have understood that the event occurred once and, until we are informed otherwise, we would expect to hear more about what happened on that occasion. It is its particularity that concerns us. Consider these alternatives, however:

> My father would rent a camp on a lake in Maine and take us all there for the month of August.

> My father rents a camp on a lake in Maine and takes us all there for the month of August.

These versions report recurrent events, the first recurrent events in the past (as signaled by "would"), and the second events recurring in the present (as signaled by the present tense). This kind of narration, what someone has described as an "abstract" narration, we call a *process*. It is abstract because it is an experience that has been thought about, classified. Concretely, we experience only narrative events—one thing, one at a time. I am physically present at *a ball game*; I remember going to *ball games*. If I want to talk about the spectacular play made in last night's game by our shortstop (if I want to discuss its unique features), I tell a narrative. If, on the other hand, I am interested in the way some double plays are executed (if I am interested in their common and predictable features), I report a process.

In "Once More to the Lake" there is a continual alternation (and tension) between narrative and process, between the unique details of the present and the patterns of the past (which White is trying to revive). He reports the concrete uniqueness of August 1941; he remembers the generic summers of his boyhood. The conflict is between his fleeting physical presence in the present and his memory, his mental existence, in the past (and in the eternal moment he is trying to re-create). By an act of will, White's mind attempts to impose permanence on the moment, but the illusion disappears when his son slides his body into the icy swimsuit. Where, after all, is White's father?

The Specific and Generic *The*   Individual nouns can suggest varying degrees of generality or specificity, depending on context and their preceding articles. The definite article (*the*) usually makes a noun concrete, unique ("Take *the* car" implies one particular car). The indefinite article (*a/an*) makes a noun more abstract and general ("Take *a* car" implies any car available). Thus, to create a sense of generality and timelessness, White uses the indefinite article in the following sentence:

> Approaching *a* dock in *a* strong following breeze, it was difficult to slow up sufficiently by the ordinary coasting method, and if *a* boy felt he had complete mastery over his motor, he was tempted to keep it running beyond its time and then reverse it *a* few feet from the dock.

Compare with: "Approaching the dock in the strong following breeze . . ." The repeated definite articles render this event unique, particular. Sometimes, though, repeated *the*'s, particularly before plural nouns, can identify details as being general, representative of their class:

They were one-cylinder and two-cylinder engines, and some were make-and-break and some were jump-spark, but they all made a sleepy sound across *the* lake. *The* one-lungers throbbed and fluttered, and *the* twin-cylinder ones purred and purred, and that was a quiet sound too. But now *the* campers all had outboards. In *the* daytime, in *the* hot mornings, these motors make a petulant, irritable sound; at night, in *the* still evening when *the* afterglow lit *the* water, they whined about one's ears like mosquitoes.

White's essay alternates between specific and general, the current August trip with his son and the past Augusts at the lake with his family. The essay represents his attempt to mediate the two.

There Patterns   Consider the following revision of a White sentence:

Cottages were sprinkled around the shores.

This is a typical sentence, consisting of two parts—a subject (a topic) and a predicate (a comment on the topic): "Cottages were sprinkled around the shores." The subject or topic is "cottages," and the principal "news" of the sentence, the focus, is on what we say about cottages—they "were sprinkled around the shores." Now consider the original version:

There were cottages sprinkled around the shores.

This sentence works differently. It also has two parts—"there" and the verb, and then the subject phrase. "There" is an *expletive*, a blank word having no literal meaning (if "there" were an adverb in this structure, it would be as unidiomatic to say, "There were cottages sprinkled there" as it would be to say, "Here are some cottages here"). The purpose of this structure, which has equivalents in other languages, is not to comment on the subject but to assert its very existence. Sometimes the news is that something actually exists. What were there? Cottages sprinkled around the shore. In the previous sentence—as in most sentences—the existence of the subject is a given, is taken for granted. The truth or falsity is in what we say about it.

White freely uses the *there* pattern, usually to "set" the details, to confirm their truth and solidity:

It was the arrival of this fly that convinced me beyond any doubt that everything was as it always had been, that the years were a mirage and *there had been* no years.

There had been no years between the ducking of this dragonfly and the other one . . .

Over the years *there had been* this person with the cake of soap, this cultist, and here he was.

There had always been three tracks to choose from in choosing which track to walk in; now the track was narrowed down to two.

There was a choice of pie for dessert, and one was blueberry and one was apple . . .

Revision Assignments   Select one of the following strategies and revise "Once More to the Lake." Include a brief statement explaining your choice and its effect on the arrangement and presentation of material.

1. In "Once More to the Lake" White recaptures a beloved family ritual, something that *would* happen every August. His concern is with the recurrent features, the dependable generic details, not the uniqueness of individual moments, which are, after all, fleeting and unrepeatable. Typical of his method is the following paragraph. Revise it so that it becomes a narrative of one specific moment, a one-time occurrence:

   > Summertime, oh summertime, pattern of life indelible, the fade-proof lake, the woods unshatterable, the pasture with the sweet-fern and the juniper forever and ever, summer without end; this was the background, and the life along the shore was the design, the cottages with their innocent and tranquil design, their tiny docks with the flagpole and the American flag floating against the white clouds in the blue sky, the little paths over the roots of the trees leading from camp to camp and the paths leading back to the outhouses and the can of lime for sprinkling, and at the souvenir counters at the store the miniature birchbark canoes and the post cards that showed things looking a little better than they looked. This was the American family at play, escaping the city heat, wondering whether the newcomers in the camp at the head of the cove were "common" or "nice," wondering whether it was true that the people who drove up for Sunday dinner at the farmhouse were turned away because there wasn't enough chicken.

2. "Once More to the Lake" is an essay, not a narrative. That is, it tells a story but its purpose is to present a meditation, an interpretation. Revise the essay as a narrative, either in the first or the third person. Restrict yourself to presenting the events. In other words, try to show instead of tell. Imply the nostalgia.

Writing Assignments

1. White's subject is a recurrent experience, not one August at the lake but his family ritual of spending every August there. It is the pattern of the experience that interests him, its predictability. Write about one such fondly remembered ritual from your own life, something "constant and trustworthy": celebrating a holiday, moving from one home or locale to another, visiting friends or a family member, being in a school play or on a sports team, taking music or dance lessons. Use the devices that White used to impart a sense of habit.

2. White's essay explores the connection between generations, the ways in which he is now performing his father's tasks (like taking his son out on the lake to fish), the ways in which his own son is doing what he used to do (like sneaking out in the early morning to use the boat). Yet the identification is imperfect: Presumably, White's father was not burdening the moment with attempts to recapture experiences from his own childhood, and White does not have the awesome but satisfying responsibility of managing travel trunks. As the saying goes, "That was then; this is now." Write about a similar experience from your own life, one in which parents or older relatives attempted to give you security and predictability by reproducing an experience from their own lives (urging you to work on a farm during the summer, take a certain trip, attend a certain college,

pursue a specific career). What did they encourage? What did they see in the experience for you? What was the result of the attempt?

3. Write about a that-was-then-this-is-now experience from your own life, something you used to enjoy but that has now lost its appeal (perhaps it is not what it used to be or perhaps you have changed, outgrown it, or simply moved on). Introduce the subject, portray its former attractions, then contrast it with its current disappointing condition.

Father Stories

Six years after his son was convicted of murder and sentenced to life imprisonment, a father addresses the paradox of time, the bars that separate and connect all fathers and sons.

JOHN EDGAR WIDEMAN

One day neither in the past nor in the future, and not at this moment, either, all the people gathered on a high ridge that overlooked the rolling plain of earth, its forests, deserts, rivers unscrolling below them like a painting on parchment. Then the people began speaking, one by one, telling the story of a life—everything seen, heard, and felt by each soul. As the voices dreamed, a vast, bluish mist enveloped the land and the seas below. Nothing was visible. It was as if the solid earth had evaporated. Now there was nothing but the voices and the stories and the mist; and the people were afraid to stop the storytelling and afraid not to stop, because no one knew where the earth had gone.

Finally, when only a few storytellers remained to take a turn, someone shouted: Stop! Enough, enough of this talk! Enough of us have spoken! We must find earth again!

Suddenly, the mist cleared. Below the people, the earth had changed. It had grown into the shape of the stories they'd told—a shape as wondrous and new and real as the words they'd spoken. But it was also a world unfinished, because not all the stories had been told.

Some say that death and evil entered the world because some of the people had no chance to speak. Some say that the world would be worse than it is if all the stories had been told. Some say that there are no more stories to tell. Some believe that untold stories are the only ones of value and we are lost when they are lost. Some are certain that the storytelling never stops; and this is one more story, and the earth always lies under its blanket of mist being born.

I begin again because I don't want it to end. I mean all these father stories that take us back, that bring us here, where you are, where I am, *needing to make sense*, to go on if we can and should.

Once, when you were five or six, all the keys to the camp vehicles disappeared. Keys for trucks, vans, rental cars, a school bus, a tractor, boats—the whole fleet necessary each summer to service the business of offering four hundred boys an eight-week escape in the Maine woods. In the innocence of the oasis that your grandfather had created—this gift of water, trees, a world apart—nobody bothered to lock things; keys were routinely left in the ignition for the next driver. Then, one day, the keys were gone. For hours, everybody searched high and low. I thought of you as I climbed into the cab of the dump truck to check for a key that might have fallen to the floor or slipped into some crevice or corner of the raw, gasoline-reeking interior. You because countless times I'd hoisted you into the cab, tucked you in the driver's seat. Nothing you enjoyed more than turning a steering wheel, roaring and vrooming engine noise while you whipped the wheel back and forth, negotiating some endless, dramatic highway only you could see. You were fascinated by that imaginary road and the wheels that rolled you there. Even before you could talk, you'd flip your toy trucks and cars on their sides or upside down so you could spin the wheels, growl engine noises.

You never admitted taking the keys, and nobody pressed you very hard 3 after they were found, in a heap in the sand under the boat dock. But, years later, Junie, the head caretaker, mentioned that he'd seen you making your usual early-morning rounds from vehicle to vehicle the day the keys were missing, and confided to me a suspicion he had felt then but had kept to himself till you were gone and were unlikely to return for a long time. Turns out your grandfather had been suspicious, too. He didn't miss much that happened in the camp, either, and had observed what Junie had observed. I recall being rather annoyed when your grandfather suggested that I ask you if you might have noticed keys anywhere the day they disappeared. Annoyed and amazed, because you were hardly more than a baby. No reason for you to bother the keys. I'd instructed you never to touch them, and that was one of the conditions you'd promised to honor in return for the privilege of installing yourself behind steering wheels. I trusted you. Questioning my trust insulted us both. Besides, the missing keys implied a plot, a prank, sabotage, some scheme premeditated and methodically perpetrated by older campers or adults, and you were just a kid. You were my son. His grandson. So he gently hinted I might casually check with you, not because you were a suspect but because you had access and had been noticed at the scene, and so perhaps might be able to assist the searchers with a clue.

I don't remember your grandfather's ever mentioning the keys again un- 4 til we'd lost you and all of us were searching once more for answers. And, since each of us had then begun to understand that answers were not around us, not in the air, and not exclusively in you, but inside us all, when your grandfather repeated ten years later his suspicions about the keys, it sounded almost like a confession, and we both understood that some searches never end.

A small army of adults, stymied, frustrated, turning the camp inside out. 5 A couple of hours of mass confusion, pockets, drawers, memories rifled, conspiracy theories floated, paranoia blossoming, numb searches and re-searches. Minor panic when duplicate keys weren't stashed where they should be; righteous indignation and scapegoating; the buzz, the edge for weeks afterward whenever keys were mentioned, picked up, or set down in the camp office. The morning of the lost keys became one of those incidents, significant or not in themselves, that lend a name, a tone to a whole camp season: the summer of the baby goats in the nature lodge, the hurricane summer, the summer a boy was lost for a night on Mt. Katahdin, the summer you-remember-who bit your grandfather's finger, the summer two counsellors from a boys' camp nearby were killed in a high-speed crash late at night, the summer the Israeli nurses swam topless, the summer you left and never returned.

If you'd ambled up on your short, chunky legs and handed me the lost 6 keys, it wouldn't have convinced me you'd taken them. Nor would a confession have convinced me. Nothing you might have said or done could have solved the mystery of the keys. No accident or coincidence would have implicated you. Without a reason, with no motive, no *why*, the idea of your re-moving the keys remained unthinkable.

You were blond then. Huge brown eyes. Hair on your head of many kinds, a storm, a multiculture of textures: kinky, dead straight, curly, frizzy, ringlets; hair thick in places, sparse in others. All your people, on both sides of the family, ecumenically represented in the golden crown atop your head.

7

You cried huge tears, too. Heartbreaking, slow, sliding tears that formed gradually in the corners of your dark eyes—gleaming, shapely tears before they collapsed and inched down your cheeks. Big tears, but you cried qui-etly, almost privately, even though the proof of your unhappiness was smear-ing your face. Then again, when you needed to, you could bellow and hoot—honking Coltrane explorations of anger, temper, outrage. Most of the time, however, you cried softly, your sobs pinched off by deep, heaving sighs, with a rare, high-pitched, keening wail escaping in spite of whatever was disciplin-ing you to wrap your sorrow so close to yourself.

8

I'm remembering things in no order, with no plan. These father stories. Because that's all they are.

9

Your mother said that the story she wishes she could write, but knows is so painful she hesitates to tell it herself, would be about her, of course, and you, yes, but also about her father, your grandfather: what he built, who he was, his long, special life, how many other lives he touched, the place he cre-ated out of nothing, in the woods, along the lake that I'm watching this morning, and that watches me as I write.

10

It is her father she has returned to all these summers in Maine. What he provided, no strings attached. His gift of water, trees, weather, a world apart, full of surprise, a world unchanging. Summers in Maine were the stable, rooted part of her.

11

One morning, as I sit on the dock staring at the lake, a man and a boy float past in a small boat. They have turned off the putt-putt outboard motor hanging over the stern and are drifting in closer to the rocky shoreline, cast-ing their fishing lines where the water is blackish green from shadows of tall pines lining the lake. A wake spreads languidly behind the boat, one wing plowing the dark water, its twin unfurling like a bright flag dragged across the surface. No sound except birdsong, the hiss of a fishing line arcing away from the boat, then its plopping like a coin in the bottom of a well. The weather has changed overnight. Wind from the west this morning—a cooling, drying wind lifting the mist before dawn, turning the sky unwaveringly blue at this early hour. A wind shunting away last week's mugginess and humid-ity, though it barely ruffles the skin of the water in this inlet. Gray bands of different shades and textures stripe the lake's center, panels of a fan lazily unfolding, closing, opening. Later, the west wind will perk up and bring chill gusts, stir a chop into the water. Smooth and quiet now for the man and the boy hunkered down in their boat. They wear baseball caps, layers of shirts and jackets, the same bulky shape twice; one form is larger than the other, and each is a slightly different color, but otherwise the two are identical, down to the way their wrists snap, their lines arc up and away from the boat.

12

The man's lure lands farther away than the boy's each time, in scale with the hunched figures drifting past in the boat.

I will see the boat again, about an hour later, when the water is louder, 13 when ripples driven from the west are forming scalloped waves. The boy, alone then, whips the boat full throttle in tight, spray-sluicing circles, around and around, gouging deep furrows. The nose of the boat high in the air, he hunches over the screaming engine, gunning it in short, sprinting bursts, then in sharp turns, around and around, as if he were trying to escape a swarm of hornets.

The wind is forgetting it's July. I wish for extra insulation under my 14 hooded sweatshirt and nylon windbreaker. Trees are a baffle for the wind and conjure its sound into colder, stronger, arctic messages shuttling through the upper atmosphere. In the same way, your mother's hair when it's long and loose, catching all the colors of light, falling down around her bare shoulders, carries within itself that wind rush of surf crashing far away, the muffled roar of a crowd in a vast, distant stadium.

You'd twist thick clumps of her chestnut hair in your fist, clutch it while 15 she held you and you sucked the thumb of your other hand. For hours. For hours if she'd let you.

Maybe all things happen, including ourselves, long before we see, hear, 16 know they are happening. Memory, then, isn't so much archival as it is a seeking of vitality, harmony, an evocation of a truer, more nearly complete present tense. All of this, of course, relates to personality—the construction of a continuous narrative of self. Our stories. Father stories.

Do you remember your fear of leaves? Of course you do. The teasers in 17 our family would never let you forget.

Once, in Laramie, Wyoming, after dinner, just as a full-moon night was 18 falling and the wide, straight-arrow streets were as empty and still as Long Lake at dawn, I was riding you on my shoulders—a rare moment, the two of us together, away from your mother and brother—when, suddenly, you cried out. The street we were on had a ceiling. Branches from trees planted in people's yards hung over fences lining the sidewalk, forming a canopy overhead. I panicked. Thought I'd knocked you against a low branch or you'd got your hair tangled—or, worse, been scratched in the eye or the face. Your fingers dug into my scalp. You didn't want to let go as I tried to unseat you from my shoulders, slide you down into the light from a street lamp to see what was the matter.

You'd given me a couple of good yanks, so I was both mad and scared 19 when I finally pulled you down, cradling you in my arms to get a clear look at your face.

No tears. No visible damage. Yet you were wild-eyed, trembling uncon- 20 trollably. The leaves had been after you. Probably not touching you but, worse, a blanket of quivering, rustling, mottled dread suddenly hovering about you. Surrounding you, rendering you speechless. Terrorized beyond words or tears, you'd gripped my hair and kicked my chest. I'd thought you were roughing me up because you wanted to play. Grabbed your wrists and squeezed them tight to hold you as I galloped down the quiet Laramie street, doing my best imitation of the bucking bronco on Wyoming license plates. You were rendered even more helpless with your hands clamped in mine, struggling to free yourself while I thought we were having fun. Your father snorting and braying, jiggedy-jig, jiggedy-jig, suddenly in league with your worst enemy, and nowhere to run, nowhere to hide—he was rushing you to your doom. No wonder your fingers tried to rip my hair out when I released your wrists. Holding on, reining me in, pounding on my skull, fighting back the only way you knew how, short of pitching yourself down from a dizzying height, down, down to the pavement, itself strewn with shadowy leaves.

When I was a kid, I harbored a morbid fear of feathers. Feathers. Not a [21] single feather or a few loose feathers, like the ones I'd stick in my naps to play Indian, but feathers in a bunch, attached to birds who could wriggle them, flutter them, transform them into loose flesh, rotting, molting, the unnatural sign of death-in-life and life-in-death, the zombie, mummy, decaying corpses of movies and my nightmares. Feathers of a kind of squirmy skin hanging off the bone, all the more horrible because feathers seemed both dry and sticky with blood.

My feathers, your leaves. One afternoon at the Belmar on Homewood [22] Avenue, in Pittsburgh, in one of those Bible-day epic movies, a man was tortured nearly to death, his bloody body flung off a fortress wall. He landed on a heap of corpses in a ditch. As the camera pans the mangled bodies, the sound of huge wings beating thumps through the Belmar's crackly speakers. After the Technicolor glare of carnage under a desert sun, the camera is blinded an instant by the black swoop of vultures. They land atop the corpses, feathers rippling, glinting as the birds begin their slow-motion, ponderously delicate lope toward the choicest morsels of meat—eyeballs, tongues, exposed guts—toward the not-quite-dead-yet man sprawled on a bed of other victims.

Then a closeup of the man's face. As he spots the vultures and screams, I [23] scream. I know I did. Even though I couldn't hear myself, because everybody in the Belmar joined in one shrieking whoop of fear and disgust. And I never forgot the scene. Never. Never forgot, never forgave. Hated pigeons. They became my scapegoats, or scapebirds. I'd hurt them any chance I got. Trapped one in a box and tormented it. Fully intended to incinerate the crippled one who wound up on the stone steps in the hallway of my dorm freshman year until my roommate shamed me out of it when I asked to borrow his lighter and some fluid and he demanded to know for what.

Pigeons were brown and dirty. They shat everywhere. Spoiled things. [24] Their cooing from the eaves of our roof on Finance Street could startle you awake. They sneaked around, hid in dark corners, carried disease, like rats. Far too many of the useless creatures. I focussed my fear and hate of feathers on them. Went out of my way to cause them difficulties.

Once, I was so angry at your mother's pain I thought I was angry at her. [25] She was sharing out loud for the first time how torn apart she'd felt that summer you never came back. How she feared her father's gift had been blighted forever. Woods, lake, sky a mirror reflecting absence of father, absence of son, the presence of her grief.

I couldn't deal with the pain in her voice, so I made up another story. [26] Presumed to tell her she was letting her pain exclude other ways of trying to make sense, with words, with stories, with the facts as given and the facts as felt, make sense of the enormity of what happens and doesn't happen, the glimmers of it we paste together trying to find peace. One different story would be the day she meets her father again in this place and what he might have to say to her and why he needed to see her and what he might remind her of and why it would need to be here, on a path through the thick pine woods where light can surprise you, penetrating in smoky shafts where it has no business being, where it sparkles, then shifts instantly, gone faster than the noises of creatures in the underbrush you never see. I make up her father, as I'm making up mine. Her father appearing to her in a suit of lights because that, too, could transpire, could redeem, could set us straight in a world where you never know what's going to happen next and often what happens is bad, is crushing, but it's never the worst thing, never the best, it's only the last thing, and not even exactly that, except once, and even then death is not exactly the last thing that happens, because you never know what's going to happen next. For better or worse, cursed and blessed by this ignorance, we invent, fill it, are born with the gift, the need, the weight of filling it with our imaginings. That are somehow as real as we are. Our mothers and fathers and children. Our stories.

I hope this is not a hard day for you. I hope you can muster peace within yourself and deal with the memories, the horrors of the past eight years. It must strike you as strange—as strange as it strikes me—that eight years have passed already. I remember a few days after hearing you were missing and a boy was found dead in the room the two of you had been sharing, I remember walking down toward the lake to be alone, because I felt myself coming apart: the mask I'd been wearing, as much for myself as for the benefit of other people, was beginning to splinter. I could hear ice cracking, great rents and seams breaking my face into pieces, carrying away chunks of numb flesh. I found myself on my knees, praying to a tree. In the middle of some absurdly compelling ritual that I'd forgotten I carried the memory of. Yet there I was on my knees, digging my fingers into the loose soil, grabbing up handfuls, sinking my face into the clawed earth as if it might heal me. Speaking to the roots of a pine tree as if its shaft might carry my message up to the sky, send it on its way to wherever I thought my anguish should be addressed.

I was praying to join you. Offering myself in exchange for you. Take me. Take me. Free my son from the terrible things happening to him. Take me in his place. Let them happen to me. I was afraid you were dying or already dead or suffering unspeakable tortures at the hands of a demon kidnapper. The tears I'd held back were flowing finally, a flood that brought none of the relief I must have believed that hoarding them would earn me when I let go at last. Just wetness burning, clouding my eyes. I couldn't will the spirit out of my body into the high branches of that tree. What felt familiar, felt like prayers beside my bed as a child, or church people moaning in the amen corner, or my mother weeping and whispering *hold on, hold on* to herself as she rocks side to side and mourns, or some naked priest chanting and climbing toward the light on a bloody ladder inside his chest—these memories of what might have been visions of holiness could not change the simple facts. I was a man who had most likely lost his son, and hugging trees and burying his face in dirt and crying for help till breath slunk out of his body wouldn't change a thing.

A desperate, private moment, one of thousands I could force myself to dredge up if I believed it might serve some purpose. I share that one example with you to say that the eight years have not passed quickly. The years are countless moments, many as intense as this one I'm describing to you, moments I conceal from myself as I've hidden them from other people. Other moments, also countless, when terrible things had to be shared, spoken aloud, in phone calls with lawyers, depositions, interviews, conferences, in the endless conversations with your mother. Literally endless, because often the other business of our lives would seem merely a digression from the dialogue with you, about you. A love story finally, love of you, your brother and sister, since no word except love makes sense of the ever-present narrative our days unfold. 29

Time can drag like a long string, studded and barbed, through a fresh wound, so it hasn't gone quickly. The moment-to-moment, day-to-day struggles imprint my flesh. But the eight years are also a miracle, a blink of the eye through which I watch myself wending my way from there to here. In this vast house of our fathers and mothers. 30

Your mother didn't need my words or images to work out her grief. She needed time. Took the time she needed to slowly, gradually, painstakingly unravel feelings knotted in what seemed for a while a hopeless tangle. No choice, really. She's who she is. Can give nothing less than her whole heart to you, to this place, inseparable from all our lives, that her father, your grandfather, provided. 31

For a while, I guess it must have felt impossible. And still can, I know. She may have doubted her strength, her capacity to give enough, give everything, because everything seemed to be tearing her apart, breaking her down. She needed time. Not healing time, exactly, since certain wounds never heal, but time to change and more time to learn to believe, to understand she could go on, was going on, for better or worse. She could be someone she'd never dreamed she could be. Her heart strong, whole, even as it cracks and each bit demands everything. 32

The fullness of time. The fullness of time. That phrase has haunted me since I first heard it and read it, though I don't know when or how the words entered my awareness, because they seem to have always been there, like certain melodies, for instance, or visual harmonies of line in your mother's body that I wondered how I'd ever lived without the first time I encountered them, although another recognition clicked in almost simultaneously, reminding me that I'd been waiting for those particular notes, those lines, a very long time. They'd been forming me before I formed my first impression of them. 33

The fullness of time. Neither forward nor backward. A space capacious enough to contain your coming into and going out of the world, your consciousness of these events, the wrap of oblivion bedding them. A life, the passage of a life: the truest understanding, measure, experience of time's fullness. So many lives, and each different, each unknowable, no matter how 34 similar to yours, your flesh and not your flesh, lives passing, like yours, into the fullness of time, where each of these lives and all of them together make no larger ripple than yours, all and each abiding in unruffled innocence of the fullness that is time. All the things that mattered so much to you or them sinking into a dreadful, unfeatured equality that is also rest and peace, time gone: but more, always more, the hands writing, the hands snatching, hands becoming bones, then dust, then whatever comes next, what time takes and fashions of you after the possibilities, permutations, and combinations—the fullness in you—are exhausted, played out for the particular shape the fullness has assumed for a time in you, for you. You are never it but what it could be, then is not: you not lost but ventured, gained, stretched, more, until the dust is particles and the particles play unhindered, unbound, returned to the fullness of time.

I know my father's name, Edgar, and some of his father's names, Hannibal, Tatum, Jordan, but I can't go back any further than a certain point, except that I also know the name of a place, Greenwood, South Carolina, and an even smaller community, Promised Land, nearly abutting Greenwood, where my grandfather, who, of course, is your great grandfather, was born, and where many of his brothers are buried, under sturdy tombstones bearing his name, our name, "Wideman," carved in stone in the place where the origins of the family name begin to dissolve into the loam of plantations owned by white men, where my grandfathers' identities dissolve, where they were boys, then men, and the men they were fade into a set of facts, sparse, ambiguous, impersonal, their intimate lives unretrievable, where what is known about a county, a region, a country and its practice of human bondage, its tradition of obscuring, stealing, or distorting black people's lives, begins to crowd out the possibility of seeing my ancestors as human beings. The powers and principalities that originally restricted our access to the life that free people naturally enjoy still rise like a shadow, a wall between my grandfathers and me, my father and me, between the two of us, father and son, son and father. 35

So we must speak these stories to one another. 36

Love
1994

Profile "I'm remembering things in no order, with no plan," confesses Wideman, as he tries to tell his father story to his son, as he tries to make sense out of his son's crime. The result is an intense and extremely personal meditation on kinship and on the impossibility of ever fully understanding another (another's story), even when that other is of our own flesh. But if Wideman's rememberings have no "plan," no premeditated scheme, a suggestive and even consoling order does begin to emerge. Previously unconnected episodes and images begin to coalesce, begin to comment on one another. As he tries to piece together a story, to put together seemingly random experiences, they begin to cohere—like the incident of the missing keys, which seems to anticipate the later unexplained episode in the cabin, or the leaf incident in Laramie, which has a counterpart in the father's dread of feathers ("My feathers, your leaves").

So the story progresses discontinuously, with bits and fragments that hold clues but no answers, challenging readers to find their own meaning, to construct their own interpretation. There are clues, for example, that suggest the boy's separation from the dreams of his elders. As they created a sanctuary, a "gift of water, trees, a world apart," the child finds a counterworld in the camp vehicles, in the trucks, vans, rental cars, school bus, tractor, and boats. While parents and grandparent dreamed of a quiet refuge (and as his paternal grandfather came from a community called Promised Land), the child was "roaring and vrooming engine noise," his imagination yearning for "some endless, dramatic highway only [he] could see."

The father can only try to tell his story, as the mother could try to tell hers, one involving her own father who out of nothing built a camp in Maine as a summer haven for boys, a story of perseverance and vision. But the vision came to tragedy, to a boy found dead in a cabin shared with the grandson. Did this tragedy write the final comment on "the innocence of the oasis that [the] grandfather had created," "the world apart" that was meant to touch other lives but that in the end could not protect his own grandson? Perhaps not, because, as Wideman observes, nothing is final:

> . . . but it's never the worst thing, never the best, it's only the last thing, and not even exactly that, except once, and even then death is not exactly the last thing that happens, because you never know what's going to happen next.

So "Father Stories" is an exploration, an attempted working-out, a perhaps futile attempt to find an all-encompassing story, except for one: "A love story, love of you, your brother and sister, since no word except love makes sense of the ever-present narrative our days unfold."

Coherence   *Coherence* comes from a word meaning "stick together." The alternative is disintegration. To break apart. To splinter. A piece of writing is coherent when its parts cooperate to make meaning, when each successive thought or image or detail both supplements and anticipates, commenting on what has preceded and preparing for what is to follow, either logically or by association or by any other principle of connection. A coherent piece of writing is never over until it is over, not achieving its full effect until the last remark. And, of course, from one work to the next, there are varying degrees of coherence.

Like most discussions of coherence, the preceding paragraph offers little assistance to a working writer. It is too vague and general. Coherence itself is an abstraction, a quality we find only in specific places, in specific pieces of writing. It exists nowhere else. We can list some coherence devices: transition terms, logical connections (implicit and explicit), parallel sentence structure, repetitions of various kinds, pronouns with their antecedents, demonstrative words like *this, these, such,* and so on, but these are not very helpful before the act of writing.

The most we can do to make coherence concrete is to look for its expression in individual texts. We can ask the question, "What does coherence mean here?" How did *this* writer working with *this* subject on *this* occasion for *this* audience achieve coherence? And the answer is always different. Talented writers are continually exploring and extending our idea of coherence, finding new ways to achieve it. As writers and as readers, then, we cannot approach a work with a prefabricated notion of what we should find. Like Joe Leaphorn, Tony Hillerman's Navajo detective, we must know better than to look for anything in particular or we won't find what we're *not* looking for. We will be denied the pleasure of discovering how the writer has found a new way to "stick something together."

As readers, then, as well as writers, we should keep open minds, have provisional, ever-widening notions of coherence. Our statements on the subject should always be specific to a given work: "Wideman achieves coherence here by . . ." And by developing a backlog of such recognitions, we will expand our own repertoires, our own flexible ideas as writers of how we might go about completing our own writing tasks. Our goal will not be to imitate a given writer in a given work, at least not precisely. Our goal will be to strike out on our own and to seek coherence on our own terms, in the spirit of any writer whose work inspires us.

And here is where reading and writing come together. We cannot create what we cannot recognize. In recognizing and relishing coherence in the work of another, we develop the criteria to evaluate and revise our own work. Having seen how coherence works in a variety of other writings, we can make informed assessments of our own work. We can weigh the aptness and effectiveness of our own coherence devices, then polish them. And we do this after the fact, after we have a draft. Then we go back to assess what coherence is there, weigh its adequacy relative to our own situation: subject, occasion, audience.

Exercise The following are brief passages and groups of sentences taken from different places in Wideman's "Father Stories" (the paragraph numbers appear in brackets). In what ways does each grouping achieve coherence?

1. [2] In the innocence of the oasis that your grandfather had created . . . [11] It is her father she has returned to all these summers in Maine. What he provided no strings attached. His gift of water, trees, weather, a world apart . . . [25] Once, I was so angry at your mother's pain I thought I was angry at her. She was sharing out loud for the first time how torn apart she'd felt that summer you never came back. How she feared her father's gift had been blighted forever.

2. [7] You were blond then. Huge brown eyes. Hair on your head of many kinds, a storm, a multiculture of textures . . . [15] You'd twist thick clumps of her chestnut hair in your fist, clutch it while she held you and you sucked the thumb of your other hand. For hours. For hours if she'd let you. . . . [20] No wonder your fingers tried to rip my hair out when I released your wrists.

3. [2] Nothing you enjoyed more than turning a steering wheel, roaring and vrooming engine noise while you whipped the wheel back and forth, negotiating some endless dramatic highway only you could see. [13] The boy, alone then, whips the boat full throttle in tight, spraying circles,

around and around, gouging deep furrows. The nose of the boat high in the air, he hunches over the screaming engine, gunning it in short, sprinting bursts . . .

4. [8] You cried huge tears, too. Heartbreaking, slow, sliding tears that formed gradually in the corners of your dark eyes . . . Most of the time, however, you cried softly, your sobs pinched off by deep, heaving sighs, with a rare, high-pitched keening wail escaping in spite of whatever was disciplining you to wrap your sorrow so close to yourself. . . . [20] No tears. No visible damage. Yet you were wild-eyed, trembling uncontrollably . . . terrorized beyond words or tears, you'd gripped my hair and kicked my chest.

Revision Assignments   Select one of the following strategies and revise a section of "Father Stories." Include a brief statement explaining your choice and its effect on the arrangement and presentation of material.

1. Wideman creates a voice by operating somewhere between a meditation and a letter, alternately and simultaneously speaking to himself and to his son. One result is clipped, abbreviated sentences—"fragments." Select a passage that is heavy with such incomplete sentences, then revise it so the sentences are complete (whether by punctuating them into other structures or by filling in the words that seem to be missing). Then compare the effects of the passages. What happens to Wideman's voice? To the portrayal of his emotional desolation, his confusion?

2. The essay records the father's attempt to make sense of the son's behavior, the son's thinking and motivation. The attempt is a record of mutual misunderstanding, of partial communications. Tell the story from the other side. Take the Laramie leaf episode (paragraphs 18–20), and narrate the story from the son's point of view (the adult son looking back on his childhood experience). Imagine that the son has read the father's account.

Writing Assignments

1. Discuss your understanding of the following passage. How does it help explain the rest of the essay?

   Maybe all things happen, including ourselves, long before we see, hear, know they are happening. Memory, then, isn't so much archival as it is a seeking of vitality, harmony, an evocation of a truer, more nearly complete present tense. All of this, of course, relates to personality—the construction of a continuous narrative of self. Our stories. Father stories.

2. The essay begins with a parable about the compulsion of humans to tell stories, and about the earth, which changes to fit the stories, "But it was also a world unfinished, because not all the stories had been told." Give your interpretation of the parable, explaining such things as the identity of the storytellers who had not yet had a turn. Then discuss how the parable relates to the "father story" that Wideman attempts to tell.

3. One could describe this essay as Wideman's "Once More to the Lake." Like E. B. White, Wideman is writing about summers at a Maine lake ("a world unchanging"), about fathers and sons who go fishing together, and about loss and mortality. Both address the attempt to unite the past and the present ("Memory, then, isn't so much archival as it is a seeking of vitality, harmony, an evocation of a truer, more nearly present tense" as Wideman observes and "Once More to the Lake" seems to confirm). Both essays even have scenes of boys operating outboard motorboats. Compare the two essays, looking first for significant similarities, then dwelling on the many more numerous differences.

4. The following passage is crucial to understanding "Father Stories." In the light of what Wideman reveals elsewhere in the essay, and perhaps drawing on your own observations and experiences, discuss what you understand it to mean.

> I make up her father, as I'm making up mine. Her father appearing to her in a suit of lights that, too, could transpire, could redeem, could set us straight in a world where you never know what's going to happen next and often what happens is bad, is crushing, but it's never the worst thing, never the best, it's only the last thing, and not even exactly that, except once, and even then death is not exactly the last thing that happens, because you never know what's going to happen next. For better or worse, cursed and blessed by this ignorance, we invent, fill it, are born with the gift, the need, the weight of filling it with our imaginings. That are somehow as real as we are. Our mothers and fathers and children. Our stories.

5. Tell your own story (a son, daughter, sister, or brother if not a father or mother story). "Make up" your father (or mother).

The Death of the Moth

VIRGINIA WOOLF

Moths that fly by day are not properly to be called moths; they do not excite   1
that pleasant sense of dark autumn nights and ivy-blossom which the commonest yellow-underwing asleep in the shadow of the curtain never fails to
rouse in us. They are hybrid creatures, neither gay like butterflies nor somber like their own species. Nevertheless the present specimen, with his narrow hay-colored wings, fringed with a tassel of the same color, seemed to be
content with life. It was a pleasant morning, mid-September, mild, benignant, yet with a keener breath than that of the summer months. The plough
was already scoring the field opposite the window, and where the share had
been, the earth was pressed flat and gleamed with moisture. Such vigor came
rolling in from the fields and the down[1] beyond that it was difficult to keep
the eyes strictly turned upon the book. The rooks[2] too were keeping one of
their annual festivities; soaring round the tree tops until it looked as if a vast
net with thousands of black knots in it had been cast up into the air; which,
after a few moments sank slowly down upon the trees until every twig
seemed to have a knot at the end of it. Then, suddenly, the net would be
thrown into the air again in a wider circle this time, with the utmost clamor
and vociferation, as though to be thrown into the air and settle slowly down
upon the tree tops were a tremendously exciting experience.

The same energy which inspired the rooks, the ploughman, the horses,   2
and even, it seemed, the lean bare-backed downs, sent the moth fluttering
from side to side of his square of the windowpane. One could not help
watching him. One was, indeed, conscious of a queer feeling of pity for him.
The possibilities of pleasure seemed that morning so enormous and so various that to have only a moth's part in life, and a day moth's at that, appeared
a hard fate, and his zest in enjoying his meager opportunities to the full, pathetic. He flew vigorously to one corner of his compartment, and, after waiting there a second, flew across to the other. What remained for him but to fly
to a third corner and then to a fourth? That was all he could do, in spite of the
size of the downs, the width of the sky, the far-off smoke of houses, and the
romantic voice, now and then, of a steamer out at sea. What he could do he
did. Watching him, it seemed as if a fiber, very thin but pure, of the enormous energy of the world had been thrust into his frail and diminutive body.
As often as he crossed the pane, I could fancy that a thread of vital light was
visible. He was little or nothing but life.

Yet, because he was so small, and so simple a form of the energy that was   3
rolling in at the open window and driving its way through so many narrow
and intricate corridors in my own brain and in those of other human beings,

[1]Rolling, grassy, treeless land used for grazing.

[2]A crow-like Old World bird.

there was something marvelous as well as pathetic about him. It was as if someone had taken a tiny bead of pure life and decking it as lightly as possible with down and feathers, had set it dancing and zigzagging to show us the true nature of life. Thus displayed one could not get over the strangeness of it. One is apt to forget all about life, seeing it humped and bossed and garnished and cumbered[3] so that it has to move with the greatest circumspection and dignity. Again, the thought of all that life might have been had he been born in any other shape caused one to view his simple activities with a kind of pity.

After a time, tired by his dancing apparently, he settled on the window ledge in the sun, and, the queer spectacle being at an end, I forgot about him. Then, looking up, my eye was caught by him. He was trying to resume his dancing, but seemed either so stiff or so awkward that he could only flutter to the bottom of the windowpane; and when he tried to fly across it he failed. Being intent on other matters I watched these futile attempts for a time without thinking, unconsciously waiting for him to resume his flight, as one waits for a machine, that has stopped momentarily, to start again without considering the reason of its failure. After perhaps a seventh attempt he slipped from the wooden ledge and fell, fluttering his wings, on to his back on the windowsill. The helplessness of his attitude roused me. It flashed upon me that he was in difficulties; he could no longer raise himself; his legs struggled vainly. But, as I stretched out a pencil, meaning to help him to right himself, it came over me that the failure and awkwardness were the approach of death. I laid the pencil down again.

The legs agitated themselves once more. I looked as if for the enemy against which he struggled. I looked out of doors. What had happened there? Presumably it was midday, and work in the fields had stopped. Stillness and quiet had replaced the previous animation. The birds had taken themselves off to feed in the brooks. The horses stood still. Yet the power was there all the same, massed outside, indifferent, impersonal, not attending to anything in particular. Somehow it was opposed to the little hay-colored moth. It was useless to try to do anything. One could only watch the extraordinary efforts made by those tiny legs against an oncoming doom which could, had it chosen, have submerged an entire city, not merely a city, but masses of human beings; nothing, I knew, had any chance against death. Nevertheless after a pause of exhaustion the legs fluttered again. It was superb this last protest, and so frantic that he succeeded at last in righting himself. One's sympathies, of course, were all on the side of life. Also, when there was nobody to care or know, this gigantic effort on the part of an insignificant little moth, against a power of such magnitude, to retain what no one else valued or desired to keep, moved one strangely. Again, somehow, one saw life, a pure bead. I lifted the pencil again, useless though I knew it to be. But even as I did so, the unmistakable tokens of death showed themselves. The body relaxed, and instantly grew stiff. The struggle was over. The insignificant little creature now knew death. As I looked at the dead moth, this minute wayside triumph of so great a force over so mean an antagonist filled me with wonder.

[3] *humped*—bent over (as from weight); *bossed*—bullied; *garnished*—taxed; *cumbered*—encumbered.

Just as life had been strange a few minutes before, so death was now as strange. The moth having righted itself now lay most decently and uncomplainingly composed. Oh yes, he seemed to say, death is stronger than I am.

1942

Profile   "The Death of the Moth" is a classic example of the personal essay, an individual meditation on the value and meaning of life arising from a seemingly insignificant event. Where do such ideas come from? How does one incident stimulate such an acute response, such intense thoughtfulness? Such an essay might originate, of course, with the writer in a particularly receptive mood, with the writer thinking something like this:

> Here it is a mild September morning and I am sitting at my window trying to read. Outside, the day is full of autumn activity: ploughmen are turning under the fallow from this year's crop to fertilize next year's; a huge flock of rooks is flying from tree to tree, rising and falling. The rooks, the horses, the ploughmen, even the downs seem inspired by the same energy, even the lowly yellow-underwing moth fluttering from side to side of my windowpane. And, of course, here I am, doing what I do while others do what they do; while they plough or fly, one plunging and one soaring, here I read and watch. I feel sorry for the moth, stuck inside here with me, so frail next to those plough horses and those restless rooks. It is so small but somehow so alive . . .

Essays like this begin with the germ of an idea, in this case perhaps Woolf's curiosity about her own interest in something as seemingly insignificant as the death of an insect ("Why do I keep thinking about this?"). Sometimes it is the very lack of an understanding that prompts one to write. To give herself a push, perhaps she wrote something down, a few tentative notions that she might hope to develop later. But the very act of writing, even of the jotting of a few words, engages the mind more deeply, the act of phrasing being a stimulus to yet more thought. And once she started, maybe she could not stop playing with it, exploring it, working it up. Or perhaps she put her notes aside and let her subconscious work on the subject a while (Robert Louis Stevenson compared this to leaving something to simmer on a back burner: We return later to find more in the pot).

Perhaps she began to look for an answer in some of the details. Moths are of the same order as butterflies but generally defined by their nocturnal activities. By contrast, butterflies are colorful, decorative daytime creatures. In other words, the moth is a pale, humble reminder of its more glamorous cousin, but it is still contains the life spirit. Who can say that moths do not live as fully as butterflies? Aren't all butterflies and moths gray in the dark?

And then there are the contrasts: indoors—Woolf and the one lonely moth fluttering around a window pane; outdoors—the downs, the ploughmen with their horses, a great flock of rooks soaring from tree to tree. So much dispersal of life outside, so much more size and energy than the single drop of life distilled in the one insignificant moth. Any connection? All seem to be exploiting their opportunities for living, whatever those might be.

And then perhaps Woolf began to think, at whatever level of consciousness, about subdividing her topic, about finding parts. To find them, she looks both without and within. The behavior of the moth falls into stages: its seeming efforts to move outwards, to expand its frontiers from a window pane to the wide world of the downs, to join in the possibilities for pleasure offered by such a day; its gradual weakening and loss of vitality; finally, its death. And Woolf notices the progression of her own attentions, from casual observation to rapt involvement, and her stages of increasing sympathy, from pity for the moth's limited mobility, to pity for all that the moth has missed by being born a moth, to sorrow for its death but also admiration for the determination of "the little hay-colored moth" in the face of death, the power that can level cities.

There are no easy formulas, no paint-by-numbers approaches that will ensure our best effort, whether as writers we are butterflies or moths. But by careful immersion in the idea and patient persistence, and by attention to the details—comparisons, contrasts, tensions, parts or stages—and by appreciation of the dynamics of one's own engagement, one's own connection, we begin to find something to write about, something to arrange and present.

Audience   Virginia Woolf came from a wealthy and cultured English family, and her primary audience consisted almost certainly of genteel, well-educated readers of her own nationality. Thus, we see the British spelling of "plough" and "ploughman," and the reference to "downs" (grassy rolling hills used for grazing) and "rooks" (crowlike birds native to Europe). Reflecting her class's education in Greek and Latin, she also wields terms like "benignant" (beneficial, kind), "vociferation" (loud, violent outcries), "animation" (full of life, vitality, from a word meaning "soul"), and "circumspection" (prudence, from a word meaning "look around"). Furthermore, reflecting the greater emphasis that British education places on biology and botany, Woolf also speaks familiarly of "the commonest yellow underwing" (perhaps the equivalent of the American miller) and "hybrid creatures."

Like Orwell, then, in "Shooting an Elephant," Virginia Woolf was not thinking of readers living fifty years later in another country, even an English-speaking one. To situate ourselves comfortably in her audience, then, we must familiarize ourselves with unfamiliar spellings and strange terms. In addition, we must appreciate the connotations of certain words that, by late twentieth-century American standards, seem unnecessarily polysyllabic, even pretentious, like "vociferation." Why didn't Woolf simply say "outcry"? For the same reason that Charlotte the spider in *Charlotte's Web* first greets Wilbur the pig with "salutations." "Vociferation" is a more energetic and ceremonial way of saying "outcry," a term communicating as much about the mood of the user as about the idea conveyed. The best writing summons us to a higher level of attention, of appreciation and receptivity. In the case of Woolf, we must make some adjustments for time and place, and we must occasionally use our dictionaries.

The best writing is both localized and universal (nobody addresses a general, universal audience—it doesn't exist; each of us is one of a kind, rooted in a very specific time and place, possessing our own unique backlog of experience). Virginia Woolf was of a specific nationality and class, the product of an unusual background, including exposure from early childhood to extremely well-educated and cultured people, so her writing reflects this privileged background. At the same time, her insights are not restricted to members of her class. Writing out of a highly particularized environment, coming from her unique direction, she reached understandings useful to anyone who will read her sympathetically.

To reach our audiences, then, we do not have to strip ourselves of our distinguishing traits, the very traits which give each of us a unique and privileged perspective. Even while respecting and preserving our uniqueness, we can remember what we share with the rest of humanity, such as the tides of energy that ebb and flow in all of us, ultimately to ebb.

Using *One*   American essay writers freely use both the first person *I* and the indefinite *you*, even when writing more formal essays. By contemporary standards *one* often seems formal, stuffy (except for one American writer who uses *one* to refer to himself). A British writer working before the Second World War, out of the range of American informality, Virginia Woolf uses the first person throughout "The Death of the Moth," as is fitting for a personal essay. Nevertheless, when she wishes to generalize her subject, to elevate it above the musings of one sensitive and perhaps eccentric individual, she uses *one*. To have used *I* exclusively would have been to maintain her own personal possession of the experience, and perhaps to stress the exquisite sensibilities of the writer, to have overparticularized the significance of the experience. At several junctures in her essay, though, Woolf wishes to rise above her individual musings, to identify what many other attentive and sensitive people would have seen and thought. Consider what the first-person pronoun does to narrow the impact of the following:

> The same energy which inspired the rooks, the ploughmen, the horses, and even, it seemed, the lean bare-backed downs, sent the moth fluttering from side to side of his square of the windowpane. *One* could not help watching him. *One* was, indeed, conscious of a queer feeling of pity for him.

> **The same energy which inspired the rooks, the ploughmen, the horses, and even, it seemed, the lean bare-backed downs, sent the moth fluttering from side to side of his square of the windowpane. *I* could not help watching him. *I* was, indeed, conscious of a queer feeling of pity for him.**

The second version focuses much more on the writer than on the moth. In the next pairing, though, notice how the indefinite *you* makes a better substitute for *one*:

> Thus displayed *one* could not get over the strangeness of it. *One* is apt to forget all about life, seeing it humped and bossed and garnished and cumbered so that it has to move with the greatest circumspection and dignity. Again, the thought of all that life might have been had he been born in any other shape caused *one* to view his simple activities with a kind of pity.

> **Thus displayed *you* could not get over the strangeness of it. *You* are apt to forget all about life, seeing it humped and bossed and garnished and cumbered so that it has to move with the greatest circumspection and dignity. Again, the thought of all that life might have been had he**

been born in any other shape caused *you* to view his simple activities with a kind of pity.

The difference is one of idiom. Many contemporary American readers will still feel more comfortable with *one*, but *you* is becoming commonplace for writers wishing to generalize their experiences and observations.

Exercise   The following are some sentences from "The Death of the Moth," each followed by a revision. Compare the effect of the revision to the original, considering how the former would work in the place of the latter:

1.   He flew vigorously to one corner of his compartment, and, after waiting there a second, flew across to the other.

     He flew vigorously to one corner of his compartment, waited there for a second, then flew across to the other.

2.   Yet, because he was so small, and so simple a form of energy that was rolling in at the open window and driving its way through so many narrow and intricate corridors in my own brain and in those of other human beings, there was something marvelous as well as pathetic about him.

     Yet, there was something marvelous as well as pathetic about him because he was so small, and so simple a form of energy that was rolling in at the open window and driving its way through so many narrow and intricate corridors in my own brain and in those of other human beings.

3.   After a time, tired of his dancing apparently, he settled on the window ledge in the sun, and, the queer spectacle being at an end, I forgot about him.

     After a time he settled on the window ledge in the sun, apparently tired of his dancing, and I forgot about him, the queer spectacle being at an end.

4.   But, as I stretched out a pencil, meaning to help him to right himself, it came over me that the failure and awkwardness were the approach of death.

     But, as I stretched out a pencil to help him right himself, I realized that the failure and awkwardness signaled the approach of death.

5.   Also, when there was nobody to care or to know, this gigantic effort on the part of an insignificant little moth, against a power of such magnitude, to retain what no one else valued or desired to keep, moved one strangely.

     Also, when there was nobody to care or to know, this gigantic effort—on the part of an insignificant little moth against a power of such magnitude to retain what no one else valued or desired to keep—moved one strangely.

Revision Assignments   Select one of the following strategies and revise "The Death of the Moth." Include a brief statement explaining your choice and its effect on the arrangement and presentation of material.

1. Revise "The Death of the Moth" as if it were written by a contemporary American, someone seated by her windowpane but perhaps in an ordinary urban or suburban setting. There should still be the sense of keenness, of vigor and energy, outside, and there should still be the insect flapping away its last moments (perhaps a common housefly). Firmly localize the event in your time and place, but address the same theme. In updating Woolf's essay, make whatever changes are necessary: additions, subtractions, rearrangements, and substitutions.

2. Woolf begins thoughtfully and indirectly, eventually working her (and the reader's) way into her subject and her thesis. In other words, her opening works a variation on the specifics-to-general pattern of development, beginning with a narrative episode, then exploring its significance. Revise the opening of the essay so that it begins with a generalization (not about moths but about the meaning of life and death), then introduce the moth episode.

Writing Assignments

1. Woolf expresses a sense of connectedness, between herself, the ploughmen, the horses, the rooks, the downs themselves, and the moth—a mere insect. Explore this theme of connectedness further, either by drawing on your own experiences and observations or by comparing Woolf's treatment of the theme with that of other writers in this collection, such as Annie Dillard, Leslie Marmon Silko, Lewis Thomas, or Alice Walker.

2. Read Tristram Wyatt's "Submarine Beetles," then—after the fashion of Virginia Woolf—write a meditation on the life of the beetles, the significance of their behavior, its reflection on the nature of life, all life.

Submarine Beetles

TRISTRAM WYATT

One summer evening, I watched the tide as it flowed gently up the creek   1
like a river in reverse, creeping slowly over the salt-marsh shore in Norfolk,
England. Out of the corner of my eye I saw a flash of red. A small, shiny
black-and-red beetle had run in and out of its burrow; then, moments later, it
disappeared under the rising water. I had not expected to see a land beetle
here, but remembered reading about a species that lives in intertidal zones.
Was this the salt-marsh beetle? Yes, it was *Bledius spectabilis*, a staphylinid
beetle about half an inch long. During the next low tide, I discovered hundreds of burrows among the *Salicornia*—stubby little plants with water-swol-
len stems—that follow a contour around the salt-marsh creeks. Each burrow
had a characteristic little heap of tailings above its entrance. The beetle I saw
had emerged to scrape algae from around the burrow's entrance; then it carried the morsels down below, to be stored and later eaten in safety.

The intertidal zone is a difficult habitat that few animals can exploit. It is   2
between land and sea, and a creature adapted to one is often poorly adapted
to the other. Most intertidal animals are essentially marine species, such as
crabs, that colonize the land. Their major risk is drying out on a sandy beach
or rocky shore. By contrast, muddy salt-marsh shores in northern Europe,
with their wetland acres of mud and quiet creeks, can support such land animals as spiders and mites that have moved into intertidal zones. Some have
evolved great tolerance for seawater and can pump excess salt from their
bodies; others simply develop behaviors to avoid getting drenched. Insects'
cuticles are already impermeable to prevent water loss on land, but their
main challenge has been to adjust to the tides. Those that have adapted to
life in this difficult environment can exploit a rich habitat. The only serious
competitor of *Bledius* is the gray mullet, a fish that comes in at high tide and
also feeds on shoreline algae, leaving its tooth marks in the mud.

Colonies of salt-marsh beetles may occupy hundreds of square yards in   3
the intertidal zone, with densities of a thousand adults per square yard. Colony perimeters are abrupt; no beetles dig burrows outside its boundaries.
Sometimes the muddy beach is covered with beetles; on a given shore, they
can number in the millions.

How does this land beetle survive the twice daily tides without any spe-   4
cial bodily adaptations? It lacks, for example, snorkel tubes that might allow
it to breathe under water. The answer lies in its behavior: the salt-marsh beetle builds and maintains a snug, watertight burrow. And the females are good
parents, protecting their eggs and larvae from predators as well as from the
tides.

When I first dug up some burrows, I could see that they were made with   5
care and were perhaps the key to understanding the beetles' adaptation. The
mud is firm and will hold any shape into which it is sculpted; a pencil hole
made in the surface will last for weeks. To study the burrows' shapes and

preserve the eggs in place, I filled a few burrows with clear silicone resin. When the clear, hardened resin cast was removed from the mud, the egg chambers, each containing an egg, resembled miniature table-tennis balls stuck to the burrow's characteristic "wine bottle" shape. The burrow is about two and one-half inches long, with a living chamber one-quarter of an inch in diameter; a narrow neck three-quarters of an inch long opens out to the surface. The individual egg chambers extend from the living space.

I saw no evidence that burrows ever become flooded, even at high tide. To find out why, I sculpted an artificial burrow in clear agar (the kind of gel used for bacterial plates) and then submerged it. At first the narrow neck seemed effective in keeping the water out, while artificial burrows with wider openings quickly became flooded. Eventually, however, even narrow-necked burrows took on water. Since this didn't happen in the field, I introduced a female beetle into one of my transparent burrows to observe her during my artificial "high tide." A few minutes after the "tide" began, the beetle suddenly ran up to the burrow neck and sealed the entrance with a neat plug of agar "mud" taken in mouthfuls from the walls. When I tested for the same behavior in salt marshes, burrows from which I removed the female did indeed flood, while those with a female inside remained dry. Rather than anticipate the tide and block their burrows in advance, females can continue to feed until the very last moment, when the water reaches their doorstep.

A dry, sealed burrow poses other dangers, however. Salt-marsh beetles usually burrow into "blue" mud, which is so tightly compacted that it allows no oxygen into the burrows. (This mud is unlike the surrounding, looser, aerobic "brown" mud, which is tinged by iron oxides.) During low tide, when the burrows must be reopened to allow oxygen replenishment, each beetle pushes up a new heap of tailings as it clears the entrance of washed-in debris. Only by plugging and unplugging her home in sync with the tides can a female salt-marsh beetle rear eggs and larvae in the airless mud—a life style very much like that of fiddler crabs.

For most of the year, male *Bledius* dig burrows very similar to those of females, but without the egg chambers. During the spring, they walk the marsh surfaces in search of mates, pausing at burrow entrances. If caught by the tide during their search, males grip the mud and flip their abdomens over their heads to create an air bubble. After the tide subsides, those that remain continue their search, but many have been washed away. When he finds a female that allows him access, the male stays with her for some hours underground, where copulation takes place. Right after mating, the male leaves and goes in search of another female.

After fertilization, the female lays an egg every other day in an individual chamber off the main burrow. After about twenty-seven days, the first-instar larva hatches, crawls into the main living chamber and begins to feed on its mother's algae collection. Eight days later, it leaves to dig its own burrow. After six more days, it molts into a second instar; then into a third, thirteen days later. It remains in its third and final instar stage for twenty-eight days. Finally, it spends about fifteen days as a pupa. A beetle's development from egg to adult takes about a hundred days during a British summer.

Since older larvae were found alone in their own burrows, I wondered at what stage they venture above ground. William Foster, of Cambridge

University, and I went to the salt marsh about midnight with red flashlights to observe the tiny first instars. They come out only at night and walk over the beach exploring every crevice and dimple in the mud. (They were very interested in a hole I made with a pencil point.) If a larva ventures into an occupied burrow, the owner chases off the intruder, which continues to search for a home. Within dense colonies, the young larvae roam in tight circles during their search, but run quickly in straight lines through areas without burrow entrances. These movement patterns (also used by parasitoid wasps hunting for hosts) tend to keep the larvae within the colony.

For the dispersing larvae, survival is a race against two clocks. They have 11 to find or dig a burrow before the next tide washes them away or before the sun rises, whichever comes first. At night most predatory shorebirds are asleep. The mud is cool and damp, making burrowing easy. The air is relatively humid, so the larvae (accustomed to high humidity below ground) do not risk drying out. On a summer day, the salt-marsh surface is a baking desert covered with salt crystals.

By emerging at night, the instar larvae are protected from some hazards, 12 but are exposed to others. During our nocturnal prowls, we noticed hundreds of carabid beetles, whose numbers on the muddy beach peak about midnight. Before long, we saw one bump into a first-instar salt-marsh beetle and eat it. Soon we realized that all over the marsh, *Bledius* larvae were being gobbled up. As though in a game of "blindman's bluff," the predators lunged in the direction of the larvae as soon as their antennae touched one. Sometimes larvae escaped by suddenly running backward or forward (they can move just as fast in either direction) or by jerking their heads. With such tactics, they were able to escape about half the encounters with the carabids. But when we plucked newly hatched first instars from maternal burrows and placed them on the beach, they were always caught. And when we removed females, we found that the burrows were soon invaded by carabid adults that fed on newly hatched larvae.

Once a larva has successfully emerged, run the midnight gauntlet on the 13 beach, and dug itself a home, it may be safe. Most predators are too large to descend into a larva's burrow, which is very similar to that of an adult. For the rest of its life, the larva does not travel again, coming up to the burrow's entrance only to collect algae as adults do, and enlargening its burrow as it grows. Unlike adults, the larvae leave their feces neatly at the side of the burrow, instead of at the bottom.

One summer, we were fascinated to see a female parasitoid wasp walking 14 along the flat mud, stopping at each heap of beetle tailings. We marked each one she visited with a little numbered flag. Within ninety-nine minutes she had visited sixty-two heaps, walking a total of fifty-nine feet, but there was more to the story. After investigating some heaps with her antennae, she quickly moved on. At others she patted the little mound with her antennae and then vigorously probed with her ovipositor to find the hole hidden below. If successful, she lifted up her wings and, ovipositor first, disappeared down the burrow for up to six minutes. Underground, we learned later, the wasp had attempted to paralyze the resident larva with its sting in order to lay a pearly white egg inside its body. Why did she behave so differently on different heaps? To find out, we dug up the burrows beneath each heap she had touched. When a burrow contained a lone larva, the wasp had usually entered, but if an adult female was present, in thirteen out of fourteen cases the wasp did not enter.

When the female beetle is with her young, she defends them vigorously. 15 Her good-sized jaws can nip, and she also lifts her poison-tipped abdomen over her head to jab at an intruder. Glands in the tip emit noxious chemicals, some of which smell strong even to humans. Perhaps the pungent odor of adult females alert the wasps to stay away from guarded burrows.

A parasitoid wasp that hatches out of a beetle larva must emerge from its 16 pupa, mate, and find salt-marsh beetle larvae to parasitize, all between tides. Once inside the unfortunate beetle larva, the wasp's egg is protected from saltwater and predators. After depositing her eggs, a female wasp is swept up in the next tide and ends as lifeless flotsam. When mature, the wasp larva bursts out of its living larder and spins a cocoon. It will overwinter in the chamber its host dug as its last act, emerging as an adult wasp the next summer.

Parental care appears to have evolved independently in several groups of 17 beetles in similar environments. Ecologist Ellinor Larsen, working in Danish salt marshes in the 1930s, found two other species in which the mother digs narrow-necked burrows and remains with her eggs. (The three species belong to unrelated beetle families: the Staphylinidae, Carabidae, and Heteroceridae.)

When she compared close relatives of the salt-marsh beetles, Larson 18 found one species that lives a few yards below them on the shore and also cares for its eggs and larvae. However, other closely related species that inhabit the high marsh or sand dunes, rarely covered by tides, do not show any parental care at all. Apparently, species that burrow in fast-draining, aerated, sandy beaches can also safely leave their eggs. So parental care seems to be an adaptation to the combined dangers of tidal flooding and airtight burrows. Additional advantages, such as foiling predators and reducing larval parasitism, were secondary gains.

After some years, beetle burrows honeycomb the muddy shore, increas- 19 ing aeration and drainage. Now the soil is just right for bushy salt-marsh plants that move in and proliferate, shading and killing the algae on which the beetles feed. Soon, only abandoned burrows remain under these bushes, and beetles must find a new young marsh to colonize. Neither time nor tide waits for these beetles.

1993

Profile   In his lively article on salt-marsh or submarine beetles, Tristram Wyatt illustrates one approach to organizing and presenting specialized information. To deliver his findings, he overlaps two narratives, integrating a general one about the behavioral patterns of the strange insect into a specific one about his own investigations. Thus, he alternates between specific and general, between "One summer evening I watched the tide" and "For most of the year, the male *Bledius* dig burrows very similar to those of females." Many writers, especially those in textbooks and encyclopedias, rely on generalized explanation alone. The result: concise, informative, impersonal, and often dry deliveries that presuppose an existing interest in the subject (if not a captive audience). Wyatt, however, engages the reader with the problem-solving approach common to detective stories. As scientific investigator he walks us through his research, from his first notice of the red-and-black insects on the evening beach to his successive inquiries into their behavior, until he has solved the mystery of their life cycle. The article could have delivered inert information; instead, it tells a story. The article is as much about the workings of an inquisitive mind as about the adaptations of a resourceful insect.

Narrative Openers   Imagine that Wyatt had opened his essay like this:

> **The salt-marsh beetle (*Bledius spectabilis*), a staphylinid beetle found in the intertidal zones of eastern England, has developed a unique adaptive strategy to survive in an environment usually hostile to land creatures.**

With such a *thesis* statement, he would have followed the classic general-to-specifics strategy, a no-nonsense beginning that immediately informs the reader of the writer's intentions. To inform and to interest, though, are two different things, so Wyatt tries something else. He begins with a story, probably the world's oldest technique for organizing experience and one primed by the eternal question, "What happened next?":

> One summer evening, I watched the tide as it flowed gently up the creek like a river in reverse, creeping slowly over the salt-marsh shore of Norfolk, England. Out of the corner of my eye I saw a flash of red.

It turns out to be an unexpected sight on tidal flats—a land beetle. By now, most readers (or at least those interested in nature) will feel a stirring of curiosity. Wyatt has disclosed how he became interested in the subject, created a significant context for his information, and whetted his audience's appetite for what he has to reveal. Whatever he may have lost by not immediately identifying his subject, he has more than regained with suspense and the gradual, progressive disclosure of information, dealing out one piece of information after another, asking questions, giving answers that raise more questions, until he has covered his subject.

Good openers do everybody a favor: They make it easier for the reader to keep reading and for the writer to keep writing. Wyatt succeeds on both counts, as the easy unfolding of his essay indicates. Narrative offers more than a catchy way to open, though. Narratives put facts in context, a dynamic context. They energize material, placing it in an environment that grows and shifts and progressively reveals. At the same time, they make an important point: The process of collecting information is often as interesting as the information itself (as any reader of detective stories will confirm). Without a narrative we might present the same material more economically, but with less reader involvement, less incentive and opportunity to remember. Narrative, then, is also a device of *emphasis*.

Knowing the Audience   To reach the targeted readers, a writer must know what they know, must know what to explain (see the section next on appositives). As an entomologist, a specialist in insects, Wyatt's prime audience consists of other entomologists. He does make a few concessions for a more general audience by defining terms like *Bledius spectabilis* and *salicornia*, but he still assumes knowledge of staphylinid beetles (beetles with segmented bodies), instar larva, carabid beetles, parasitoid wasps, and intertidal (between the tides) zones. Even scientifically illiterate readers will know from the context that instar larva are a growth stage and that carabid beetles are predators. In spite of a few technical terms (which the general reader need not understand precisely), the article appeals to a wider audience than just entomologists. Aside from these terms, Wyatt's language—like that of Lewis Thomas—is direct, familiar, free of jargon, easy to read. His article affirms that we can write engagingly about specialized subjects for a general audience. Salt-marsh beetles (and many other specialized subjects) are of potential interest to more than specialists.

Defining With Appositives   Science and other technical writers rely heavily on *appositives*, structures (like this one) that describe or define by renaming. In most cases they can substitute for the term or terms they rename ("Behold my son, *the weightlifter*" —"Behold the weightlifter"). As the name suggests (*appositive* means "placed next to"), the appositive offers a quick and painless way to explain terms, a convenience when dealing with a technical vocabulary that may be unfamiliar to some of the audience. Wyatt uses appositives freely, especially at the beginning when he is orienting his readers:

> It was *Bledius spectabilis, a styphylinid beetle about half an inch long.*

> I discovered hundred of burrows among the *Salicornia—stubby little plants with water-swollen stems . . .*

> The only serious competitor of *Bledius* is the gray mullet, *a fish that comes in at high tide and also feeds on the shoreline algae . . .*

As in Wyatt's article, definitional appositives are usually set apart with commas. They may also be punctuated with dashes, colons, or parentheses:

> Only by plugging and unplugging her home in sync with the tides can a female salt-marsh beetle rear eggs and larvae in the airless mud—*a life style very much like that of fiddler crabs.*

> (The three species belong to unrelated beetle families: *the Staphylinidae, Carabidae, and Heteroceridae.*)

> . . . I sculpted an artificial burrow in clear agar (*the kind of gel used for bacterial plates*) . . .

Revision Assignments   Select one of the following strategies and revise "Submarine Beetles." Include a brief statement explaining your choice and its effect on the arrangement and presentation of material.

1. Less to find a workable alternative than to appreciate what Wyatt has done, do your best to arrange and present the material on the submarine beetle—but without any narrative of the researcher's investigations (no

first person, no *I* or *me*). One possibility: Revise the article as an entry in an encyclopedia or a section in a textbook.

2. As an extreme exercise in identifying with someone quite unlike yourself, present the life cycle of the submarine beetle in the first person, that is, imagine that you are a salt-marsh beetle, giving a tour of your wine-bottle home and explaining your habits. Perhaps you are talking to a reporter or social worker and trying to express what it is like to live in a tough neighborhood. Or you might consider a question-and-answer format (imagine you are appearing on a television talk show dealing with the subject "Unwed Mothers Whose Children Are Eaten by Parasitoid Wasps").

Writing Assignments

1. Wyatt focuses on submarine beetles because of their unique adaptive abilities. By whatever process, they have learned to prosper where most land creatures cannot. Drawing upon submarine beetles for an analogy, write about some instance of human adaptability and resourcefulness with which you are familiar. Stress the good news, the ability to salvage value in unpromising circumstances.

2. Use a narrative framework to inform the reader how you mastered some skill or body of knowledge, beginning with how it first came to your attention and tracing the steps whereby you became informed.

3. Write about a process familiar to you (the way Wyatt writes about the beetle's life cycle), focusing on a series of repeated, predictable steps. Remember that a process is a generalized narrative, about a recurrent pattern of events (as opposed to the average narrative, which is about a one-time event).

4. Reread Virginia Woolf's "The Death of the Moth," and then—after the fashion of Tristram Wyatt—write an essay on the common moth. That is, introduce the subject (the nocturnal spectacle of moths bouncing off of screens, circling light bulbs), then narrate your investigations as you inform yourself about them, beginning with some library research and perhaps concluding with field work.

The Bell

GUY DE MAUPASSANT

He had known better days, in spite of his misery and infirmity. At the age of fifteen, he had had both legs cut off by a carriage on the highway near Varville. Since that time he had begged, dragging himself along the roads, across the farmyards, balanced upon his crutches which brought his shoulders to the height of his ears. His head seemed sunk between two mountains.

Found as an infant in a ditch by the curate of Billettes, on the morning of All Souls' Day, he was, for this reason, baptized Nicholas Toussaint (All Saints); brought up by charity, he was a stranger to all instruction; crippled from having drunk several glasses of brandy offered him by the village baker, for the sake of a laughable story, and since then a vagabond, knowing how to do nothing but hold out his hand.

Formerly, Baroness d'Avary gave him a kind of kennel full of straw beside her poultry-house, to sleep in, on the farm adjoining her castle; and he was sure, in days of great hunger, of always finding a piece of bread and a glass of cider in the kitchen. He often received a few sous, also, thrown by the old lady from her steps or her chamber window. Now she was dead.

In the villages, they gave him scarcely anything. They knew him too well. They were tired of him, having seen his little, deformed body on the two wooden legs going from house to house for the last forty years. And he went there because it was the only corner of the country that he knew on the face of the earth—these three or four hamlets where he dragged out his miserable life. He had tried the frontier for his begging, but had never passed the boundaries, for he was not accustomed to anything new.

He did not even know whether the world extended beyond the trees which had always limited his vision. He had never asked. And when the peasants, tired of meeting him in their fields or along their ditches, cried out to him, "Why do you not go to some other villages, in place of always stumping about here?" he did not answer, but took himself off, seized by a vague and unknown fear, that fear of the poor who dread a thousand things, confusedly—new faces, injuries, suspicious looks from people whom they do not know, the police, who patrol the roads in twos, and make a plunge at them, by instinct, in the bushes or behind a heap of stones.

When he saw them from afar shining in the sun, he suddenly developed a singular agility, the agility of a wild animal to reach his lair. He tumbled along on his crutches, letting himself fall like a bundle of rags and rolling along like a ball, becoming so small as to be almost invisible, keeping close as a hare running for cover, mingling his brown tatters with the earth. He had, however, never had any trouble with them. But this fear and this slyness were in his blood, as if he had received them from his parents whom he had never seen.

He had no refuge, no roof, no hut, no shelter. He slept anywhere in summer, and in winter he slipped under the barns or into the stables with a remarkable adroitness. He always got out before anyone was aware of his presence. He knew all the holes in the buildings that could be penetrated; and, manipulating his crutches with a surprising vigor, using them as arms, he would sometimes crawl, by the sole strength of his wrists, into the hay-barns, where he would remain four or five days without budging, when he had gathered together sufficient provisions for his needs.

He lived like the animals in the woods, in the midst of men without knowing anyone, without loving anyone, and exciting in the peasants only a kind of indifferent scorn and resigned hostility. They nicknamed him "Bell," because he balanced himself between his two wooden pegs like a bell between its two standards. 8

For two days he had had nothing to eat. No one would give him anything. They would, now, have nothing more to do with him. The peasants in their doors, seeing him coming, would cry out to him from afar: "You want to get away from here, now. 'Twas only three days ago that I gave you a piece of bread!" 9

And he would turn about on his props and go on to a neighboring house, where he would be received in the same fashion. 10

The women declared, from one door to another: "One cannot feed that vagabond the year round." 11

Nevertheless, the vagabond had need of food every day. He had been through Saint-Hilaire, Varville, and Billettes without receiving a centime or a crust of bread. Tournolles remained as his only hope; but to reach it he must walk two leagues upon the highway, and he felt too weary to drag himself along, his stomach being as empty as his pocket. 12

He set out on the way, nevertheless. 13

It was December, and a cold wind blew over the fields, whistling among the bare branches. The clouds galloped across the low, somber sky, hastening one knew not where. The cripple went slowly, placing one support before the other with wearisome effort, balancing himself upon the part of a leg thatremained to him, which terminated in a wooden foot bound about with rags. 14

From time to time he sat down by a ditch and rested for some minutes. Hunger gave him a distress of soul, confused and heavy. He had but one idea: "to eat." But he knew not by what means. 15

For three hours he toiled along the road; then, when he perceived the trees of the village, he hastened his movements. 16

The first peasant he met, of whom he asked alms, responded to him: "You here yet, you old customer? I wonder if we are ever going to get rid of you!" 17

And Bell took himself away. From door to door he was treated harshly, and sent away without receiving anything. He continued his journey, however, patient and obstinate. He received not one sou. 18

Then he visited the farms, picking his way across ground made moist by the rains, so spent that he could scarcely raise his crutches. They chased him away, everywhere. It was one of those cold, sad days when the heart shrivels, the mind is irritated, the soul is somber, and the hand does not open to give or to aid. 19

When he had finished the rounds of all the houses he knew, he went and threw himself down by a ditch which ran along by M. Chiquet's yard. He unhooked himself, as one might say to express how he let himself fall from between his two high crutches, letting them slip along his arms. And he 20 remained motionless for a long time, tortured by hunger, but too stupid to well understand his unfathomable misery.

He awaited he knew not what, with that vague expectation which ever dwells in us. He awaited, in the corner of that yard, under a freezing wind for that mysterious aid which one always hopes will come from heaven or mankind, without asking how, or why, or through whom it can arrive. 21

A flock of black hens passed him, seeking their living from the earth which nourishes all beings. Every moment they picked up a grain or an invisible insect, then continued their search slowly, but surely. 22

Bell looked at them without thinking of anything; then there came to him—to his stomach rather than to his mind—the idea, or rather the sensation, that these animals were good to eat when roasted over a fire of dry wood. 23

The suspicion that he would be committing a robbery only touched him slightly. He took a stone which lay at his hand and, as he had skill in this way, killed neatly the one nearest him that was approaching. The bird fell on its side, moving its wings. The others fled, half balanced upon their thin legs, and Bell, climbing again upon his crutches, began to run after them, his movements much like that of the hens. 24

When he came to the little black body, touched with red on the head, he received a terrible push from the back, which threw him loose from his supports and sent him rolling ten steps ahead of them. And M. Chiquet, exasperated, threw himself upon the marauder, rained blows upon him, striking him like a madman, as a robbed peasant strikes with his fist and his knee, upon all the infirm body which could not defend itself. 25

The people of the farm soon arrived and began to help their master beat the beggar. Then when they were tired of beating, they picked him up, carried him and shut him up in the woodhouse while they went to get a policeman. 26

Bell, half dead, bloody and dying of hunger, lay still upon the ground. The evening came, then the night, and then the dawn. He had had nothing to eat. 27

Toward noon, the policemen appeared, opening the door with precaution as if expecting resistance, for M. Chiquet pretended that he had been attacked by robbers against whom he had defended himself with great difficulty. 28

The policeman cried out: "Come there, now! Stand up!" 29

But Bell could no longer move, although he did try to hoist himself upon his sticks. They believed this a feint, a sly ruse for the purpose of doing some mischief, and the two men handled him roughly, standing him up and planting him by force upon his crutches. 30

And fear had seized him, that native fear of the yellow longbelt,[1] that fear of the Newgate-bird[2] before the detective, of the mouse before the cat. And, by superhuman effort, he succeeded in standing. 31

"March!" said the policeman. And he marched. All the employees of the farm watched him as he went. The women shook their fists at him; the men sneered at and threatened him. They had got him, finally! Good riddance. 32

---

[1] An item of clothing used to identify French convicts.

[2] Newgate was an English prison. A "Newgate bird" would be a convict, especially an habitual one.

He went away between the two guardians of the peace. He found energy enough in his desperation to enable him to drag himself along until evening, when he was completely stupified, no longer knowing what had happened, too bewildered to comprehend anything. 33

The people that he met stopped to look at him in passing, and the peasants murmured: "So that is the 'robber'!" 34

They came toward nightfall to the chief town in the district. He had never been seen there. He did not exactly understand what was taking place, nor what was likely to take place. All these frightful, unheard-of things, these faces and these new houses, filled him with consternation. 35

He did not say a word, having nothing to say, because he comprehended nothing. Besides, he had not talked to anybody for so many years that he had almost lost the use of his tongue; and his thoughts were always too confused to formulate into words. 36

They shut him up in the town prison. The policemen did not think he needed anything to eat, and they left him until the next day. 37

When they went to question him, in the early morning, they found him dead upon the ground. Surprise seized them! 38

1884

Profile "The Bell," the story which so engaged young William Saroyan, tells a tale of neglect, insensitivity, and abuse. An entire community shares guilt in creating the legless beggar, and an entire community participates in his destruction. In search of a laugh, a baker gets an illiterate simpleton drunk, and in this condition the boy falls under the wheels of a carriage and is disabled for life. There is no mention that the baker accepts any responsibility for the life he has ruined, no mention that his fellow villagers encourage him to accept responsibility. Nor is there a sign that any villagers or farmers ever try to sympathize with the beggar, ever try to put themselves in his place. They see him only as a burden, an unpleasant presence in their field of vision (like the Irish poor as described by Swift's modest proposer). Even his religious name (Toussaint—"All Saints") invokes no Christian charity, not even from the Church itself. One wealthy old woman does take a qualified pity on him, giving him a "kennel" of straw by her chicken coop, and some bread and cider, but she still signals her contempt by the way she gives him a few small coins, throwing them from her steps or chamber window. And these are the people who traditionally think of themselves as being honest, hard-working, respectable, "the salt of the earth."

Alone, without a single friend or relative, burdened with a depersonalizing nickname ("Bell"), he knows no more of the world than what he sees in the small circuit of his travels. The entire human race is represented only by those he meets in the countryside and four hamlets, and who is to say the sampling is inadequate? For him there is no enlightenment or kindness to be found anywhere. At best, someone will give him a morsel to eat; at worst, someone will stone him. Furthermore, illiterate, barely able to speak, capable of only the most scrambled thoughts, he is as deprived mentally as he is physically and emotionally. Even the chickens with whom he is compared ("half balanced on their thin legs") are better off. They can find their living from "the earth which nourishes all beings"—but not legless beggars.

But within the terms of his wretched existence, Bell achieves a kind of triumph, becoming a testimonial to human persistence and adaptability. Forced to live "like animals in the woods," sustained only by "that vague expectation which ever dwells in us," and plagued by nameless fears, he nevertheless endures beyond his injury for four decades. In the face of "indifferent scorn" and "resigned hostility," ever surrounded by suspicion and resentment, he continues his rounds. And in the process he displays "a remarkable adroitness" and "a surprising agility." He learns to roll and tumble, to make himself invisible behind stones and hedges, to slip into barns and stables, to move "like a hare running for cover," and, of course, to throw with great accuracy. Alone, in spite of all his limitations and all that he must endure, he becomes something of a wonder, but that is not enough. One individual, regardless of how resourceful and resolute, cannot stand indefinitely against an entire community.

Beginning a Story   Consider for a moment how "The Bell" does *not* begin.

> **Once upon a time there was a legless man who was forced to beg for a living.**

> **One day in the middle of the nineteenth century a legless beggar was dragging himself along a road outside the village of Varville in France.**

The first version suggests the classic fairy tale, a story that will have a happy ending (the beggar will meet a genie or a fairy godmother and eventually be restored to wholeness, after he passes some test). The second is a favorite of romantic and realistic writers alike (the beggar will either be a supporting player whose function is to contribute to the happiness of the hero and heroine, or a witness or a victim of some kind). Both versions, despite the different expectations they create, presuppose no knowledge of the setting or events, treating readers like strangers or outsiders. Both openers, in other words, keep readers at a distance, if only temporarily.

But look at how de Maupassant opens his story:

> He had known better days, in spite of his misery and his infirmity.

The story begins with a personal pronoun (*he*), a word normally taking its meaning from an *antecedent* or preceding term. But in this case, the first sentence of a story, there is no antecedent. The narrator is behaving as if his readers are already in the know, as if he is in midconversation with a group of insiders. The pronoun arouses our curiosity, of course, making us wonder who this person is, but the polite fiction is that we already know. We are inside the loop, confidants of the storyteller.

Like other kinds of writing, stories operate somewhere on a scale between distance and intimacy. Storytellers must decide how close they want their listeners to be, both to themselves and to the events and characters in their stories. In this case de Maupassant takes the role of the *omniscient* (all-knowing) narrator (see the next section), summarizing and condensing and explaining. Such a perspective distances us from the events and characters, appealing more to our understanding than to our sympathy. De Maupassant wants us to understand the plight of Bell, to see it in a larger social perspective, but not to become so immersed in the character himself that we can feel only pity (he gives us credit for being able to see that Bell deserves compassion). But while he distances us from the characters and events, he draws us to the narrator, the person with whom we share all this existing knowledge, say, of "M. Chiquet's yard," not of "the yard of a farmer named Chiquet." And being drawn (and limited) to the narrator's perspective, we are more likely to share his judgment, open or implied.

Point of View   In telling a story, one of a writer's most crucial decisions is the selection of point of view, the angle from which to present the events. When this angle is that of a character in the story, whether a central or a peripheral one, we have a first-person narrator. This point of view may be the most convincing or "realistic" one, the one that sounds least "made up," because it is also the form of autobiography (see "Shooting an Elephant"). We are getting the story straight from a participant or witness. But what first-person narration gains in verisimilitude it loses in scope. An "I" narrator can tell us only what he or she knows, what he or she did, thought, or experienced. As for what passes beyond the narrator's sight and hearing, we can know only by report. And as for what passes in the minds of other characters, the "I" can only guess.

First-person narration is especially effective when the writer's interest is psychological, when the central concern is for the narrator's character and outlook rather than the events he or she relates. In an "I"-narrated story, after all, every word and detail issues from the mind of the story teller, so the tale is also an act of self-dramatization, even of self-revelation, intentional or unintentional.

With "thoughts [that] were always too confused to formulate into words," Bell could not have told a coherent story, and a local villager or farmer would have lacked sufficient information. De Maupassant's only choice, then, was to try a third-person storyteller (*he, she, it,* or *they*): a *third-person objective, third-person subjective,* or *omniscient narrator.* A third-person objective narrator remains neutral, presenting details, recording dialogue, but refraining from comment. The objective narrator simply *shows,* leaving interpretations and conclusions to the reader. A few details in "The Bell" could have been presented by an objective narrator ("Found as an infant in a ditch by the curate of Billettes, on the morning of All Souls' Day, he was, for this reason, baptized Nicholas Toussaint [All Saints]").

A third-person subjective (or *limited omniscient*) narrator focuses on one character and presents only what that person does, sees, or thinks. Descriptive details may be subjective (clouds may be "heavy and threatening" rather than simply "dark"), but they usually reflect the sensibility of the central figure, the one who is always on stage. As for other characters, we experience them only as they appear to the focus character, their thoughts but a matter of conjecture. Some details in "The Bell" could have been presented by a third-person subjective narrator ("He had but one idea: 'to eat'"). Most of the time, however, de Maupassant uses an omniscient narrator.

An omniscient narrator knows all, controls all. This narrator overviews all the characters and events, even when choosing to focus on only one person. He knows all the background detail ("crippled from having drunk several glasses of brandy offered him by the village baker, for the sake of a laughable story"). He records dialogue, summarizes, interprets, and can report what anyone is thinking, even the supporting characters ("In the villages, they gave him scarcely anything. They knew him too well."). In sum, an omniscient narrator holds a license to *tell* the reader anything necessary to advance the story, even to painting dramatic scenery ("The clouds galloped across the low, somber sky, hastening one knew not where"), and philosophizing ("He awaited, in the corner of that yard, under a freezing rain for that mysterious aid which one always hopes will come from heaven or mankind, without asking how, or why, or through whom it can arrive").

Omniscient narration works best for taking the long view, for presenting the big picture. But if it is more of a telling than a showing method, it still demands strenuous reader participation. Where a writer *shows* ("He often received a few sous, also, thrown by the old lady from her steps or her chamber window"), the reader must infer the significance (in this case, the implied scorn). Where a writer *tells* ("But this fear and this slyness were in his blood, as if he had received them from his parents whom he had never seen"), the reader must imagine particulars, must supply incidents and actions to fit the conclusions.

Revision/Writing Assignments

1. De Maupassant tells the story as an all-knowing narrator, commenting and interpreting, setting moods and assigning responsibilities. Sometimes he gives picturesque details, like clouds galloping across skies; other times he lays out events with circumstantial precision ("He would turn about on his props and go on to a neighboring house, where he would be received in the same fashion"). Tell the story differently, using a first-person narrator, a villager or farm wife typical of the country population depicted by de Maupassant, or perhaps a village priest. Remember, such a person would probably think of him- or herself as a good Christian and an honest citizen.

2. Tell the story using a subjective third-person narrator, that is, one who knows in detail what Bell is thinking and feeling. Begin your story at the district jail. Bell has been dragged there, he is slowly dying of starvation, there is much he does not understand, and he is trying to make sense of his situation. Remember, he has had no education, no training, no family or friends. He does not have to remember all the details in the order given by de Maupassant.

3. You are William Saroyan sitting in a high school library in Fresno and reading "The Bell" with the fullest possible involvement and appreciation. (To give yourself a chance to reach his level of absorption, read the story four or five times.) Now, read the introduction (paragraphs 1-8), which set up the final episode in Bell's life. How well does this section prepare for the rest of the story? How many details in the introduction anticipate the details of Bell's disastrous end? How do the details of setting, characterization, and action set the stage? What is the significance of his nickname, "Bell" (think of church bells and their role in summoning believers to some kind of religious observance). In other words, how do the first eight paragraphs help us understand Bell and what happens to him? What is apt and inevitable about de Maupassant's storytelling?

He went away between the two guardians of the peace. He found energy $\quad$ 33
enough in his desperation to enable him to drag himself along until evening,
when he was completely stupified, no longer knowing what had happened,
too bewildered to comprehend anything.

The people that he met stopped to look at him in passing, and the peas- $\quad$ 34
ants murmured: "So that is the 'robber'!"

They came toward nightfall to the chief town in the district. He had $\quad$ 35
never been seen there. He did not exactly understand what was taking place,
nor what was likely to take place. All these frightful, unheard-of things, these
faces and these new houses, filled him with consternation.

He did not say a word, having nothing to say, because he comprehended $\quad$ 36
nothing. Besides, he had not talked to anybody for so many years that he had
almost lost the use of his tongue; and his thoughts were always too confused
to formulate into words.

They shut him up in the town prison. The policemen did not think he $\quad$ 37
needed anything to eat, and they left him until the next day.

When they went to question him, in the early morning, they found him $\quad$ 38
dead upon the ground. Surprise seized them!

1884

Profile $\quad$ "The Bell," the story which so engaged young William Saroyan,
tells a tale of neglect, insensitivity, and abuse. An entire community shares
guilt in creating the legless beggar, and an entire community participates in
his destruction. In search of a laugh, a baker gets an illiterate simpleton
drunk, and in this condition the boy falls under the wheels of a carriage and
is disabled for life. There is no mention that the baker accepts any responsibility for the life he has ruined, no mention that his fellow villagers encourage him to accept responsibility. Nor is there a sign that any villagers or farmers ever try to sympathize with the beggar, ever try to put themselves in his
place. They see him only as a burden, an unpleasant presence in their field
of vision (like the Irish poor as described by Swift's modest proposer). Even
his religious name (Toussaint—"All Saints") invokes no Christian charity,
not even from the Church itself. One wealthy old woman does take a qualified pity on him, giving him a "kennel" of straw by her chicken coop, and
some bread and cider, but she still signals her contempt by the way she gives
him a few small coins, throwing them from her steps or chamber window.
And these are the people who traditionally think of themselves as being honest, hard-working, respectable, "the salt of the earth."

Alone, without a single friend or relative, burdened with a depersonalizing nickname ("Bell"), he knows no more of the world than what he sees in
the small circuit of his travels. The entire human race is represented only by
those he meets in the countryside and four hamlets, and who is to say the
sampling is inadequate? For him there is no enlightenment or kindness to
be found anywhere. At best, someone will give him a morsel to eat; at worst,
someone will stone him. Furthermore, illiterate, barely able to speak, capable of only the most scrambled thoughts, he is as deprived mentally as he is
physically and emotionally. Even the chickens with whom he is compared
("half balanced on their thin legs") are better off. They can find their living
from "the earth which nourishes all beings"—but not legless beggars.

But within the terms of his wretched existence, Bell achieves a kind of triumph, becoming a testimonial to human persistence and adaptability. Forced to live "like animals in the woods," sustained only by "that vague expectation which ever dwells in us," and plagued by nameless fears, he nevertheless endures beyond his injury for four decades. In the face of "indifferent scorn" and "resigned hostility," ever surrounded by suspicion and resentment, he continues his rounds. And in the process he displays "a remarkable adroitness" and "a surprising agility." He learns to roll and tumble, to make himself invisible behind stones and hedges, to slip into barns and stables, to move "like a hare running for cover," and, of course, to throw with great accuracy. Alone, in spite of all his limitations and all that he must endure, he becomes something of a wonder, but that is not enough. One individual, regardless of how resourceful and resolute, cannot stand indefinitely against an entire community.

Beginning a Story   Consider for a moment how "The Bell" does *not* begin.

> **Once upon a time there was a legless man who was forced to beg for a living.**

> **One day in the middle of the nineteenth century a legless beggar was dragging himself along a road outside the village of Varville in France.**

The first version suggests the classic fairy tale, a story that will have a happy ending (the beggar will meet a genie or a fairy godmother and eventually be restored to wholeness, after he passes some test). The second is a favorite of romantic and realistic writers alike (the beggar will either be a supporting player whose function is to contribute to the happiness of the hero and heroine, or a witness or a victim of some kind). Both versions, despite the different expectations they create, presuppose no knowledge of the setting or events, treating readers like strangers or outsiders. Both openers, in other words, keep readers at a distance, if only temporarily.

But look at how de Maupassant opens his story:

> He had known better days, in spite of his misery and his infirmity.

The story begins with a personal pronoun (*he*), a word normally taking its meaning from an *antecedent* or preceding term. But in this case, the first sentence of a story, there is no antecedent. The narrator is behaving as if his readers are already in the know, as if he is in midconversation with a group of insiders. The pronoun arouses our curiosity, of course, making us wonder who this person is, but the polite fiction is that we already know. We are inside the loop, confidants of the storyteller.

Like other kinds of writing, stories operate somewhere on a scale between distance and intimacy. Storytellers must decide how close they want their listeners to be, both to themselves and to the events and characters in their stories. In this case de Maupassant takes the role of the *omniscient* (all-knowing) narrator (see the next section), summarizing and condensing and explaining. Such a perspective distances us from the events and characters, appealing more to our understanding than to our sympathy. De Maupassant wants us to understand the plight of Bell, to see it in a larger social perspective, but not to become so immersed in the character himself that we